# CIVILIAN OVERSIGHT OF POLICING

# Civilian Oversight of Policing

## *Governance, Democracy and Human Rights*

Edited by

ANDREW J GOLDSMITH

and

COLLEEN LEWIS

·HART·
PUBLISHING
OXFORD – PORTLAND OREGON
2000

Hart Publishing
Oxford and Portland, Oregon

Published in North America (US and Canada) by
Hart Publishing c/o
International Specialized Book Services
5804 NE Hassalo Street
Portland, Oregon
97213-3644
USA

Distributed in the Netherlands, Belgium and Luxembourg by
Intersentia, Churchillaan 108
B2900 Schoten
Antwerpen
Belgium



Hart Publishing Ltd is a specialist legal publisher based in Oxford, England.
To order further copies of this book or to request a list of other publications please write to:

Hart Publishing Ltd, Salter's Boatyard,
Folly Bridge, Abingdon Road, Oxford OX1 4LB
Telephone: +44 (0)1865 245533 or Fax: +44 (0)1865 794882
e-mail: mail@hartpub.co.uk
www.hartpub.co.uk

British Library Cataloguing in Publication Data
Data Available
ISBN 1 84113–030–3 (cloth)

Typeset by Hope Services (Abingdon) Ltd.

To Jane, for whom I shall always be accountable

AG

To my sister Yvonne

CL

# *Acknowledgments*

As editors we are indebted to the authors of these chapters for their contributions and professionalism. We have also been fortunate in having the support of several colleagues who kindly agreed to read drafts of the introduction and our respective chapters. In particular we would like to thank Ken Coghill, Brian Costar, Denis Woodward, Mark Israel and Jane Turner Goldsmith for their time and for their insightful comments. Angela Bott cheerfully typed many editorial changes and reformatted chapters. We thank her for her dedication and constant good humour. Thanks also to Richard Hart of Hart Publications. It has been a pleasure to work with him and his team.

The editing of a book requires more than professional and collegial assistance. Throughout this project we have had the support and encouragement of our families. Colleen would like to thank John for his endless patience and understanding. Andrew would like to thank Jane, Christophe, Sebastien, and Jack for their moral support and patient forbearance.

# Contents

# *Contributors*

**Cheryl-Anne Beattie** received her PhD in 1997 in Sociology at George Washington University in Washington, DC. Her doctoral dissertation compared the development of civilian review boards in Washington, DC and New York City. She is currently participating in research on police-community relations in Washington, DC.

**David Brereton** is the Director of the Research and Prevention Division of the Queensland Criminal Justice Commission (CJC). He has published extensively in reputable academic journals including the *British Journal of Criminology*, *Law and Society Review*, and the *Australian and New Zealand Journal of Criminology*. He previously taught Legal Studies at La Trobe University, and was a Principal Consultant to the Law Reform Commission of Victoria. Dr Brereton holds a PhD in Political Science from Stanford University.

**Andrew Goldsmith** was appointed Foundation Professor of Legal Studies at Flinders University, Adelaide, in 1997. In addition to degrees in law, he has an MA in Criminology and Doctorate of Juridical Science from the University of Toronto, Canada. He has a longstanding research and teaching interest in policing, and has published extensively on police culture, police violence, and police accountability issues. He edited, and contributed to, *Complaints Against the Police: The Trend to External Review* (Oxford: Clarendon Press, 1991). He is on the editorial boards of *Policing and Society*, *Current Issues in Criminal Justice*, and *International Criminal Justice Review*.

**Sergio Herzog** PhD, is an associate professor at the Department of Sociology, University of Haifa, Israel. His research interests lie in the areas of police deviance, investigations against the police, police organisation, motor vehicle theft, unemployment and crime, and the criminal justice system.

**Tammy C Landau** received her PhD from the Centre of Criminology, University of Toronto. She has published on a variety of topics, including first nations policing, mandatory charging for wife assault and public complaints against the police. Dr Landau has been a consultant to federal, provincial and municipal authorities in a wide range of criminal justice issues. Dr Landau is currently an Assistant Professor in the Department of Psychology and School of Justice Studies at Ryerson Polytechnic University in Toronto, Canada.

**Colleen Lewis** is a senior lecturer in Criminal Justice and Criminology, School of Political and Social Inquiry, Monash University, Victoria, Australia. Her research interests include public sector accountability and ethics. Dr Lewis is co-editor and contributor to the books *Corporate Management in Australian Government* (Macmillan, 1989) and *Un-peeling Tradition: Contemporary Policing* (Macmillan, 1994). She recently authored the book *Complaints Against Police: The Politics of Reform* (Hawkins, 1999) and has published journal articles and chapters in books on the subject of civilian oversight of complaints against police.

**Eileen Luna** is an Assistant Professor of American Indian Studies/Law and Policy at the University of Arizona, Tucson. She is Choctaw and Cherokee. She holds a JD, and an MPA from Harvard University. She directed a number of law enforcement oversight agencies in California and is a consultant on civilian oversight procedures and police discipline. She is a member of the Advisory Board for the US evaluation of Victim of Crime Act (VOCA), and is Principal Investigator for the US National Institute of Evaluation of the STOP Violence Against Indian Women programmes funded through the Violence Against Women Act (VAWA). Professor Luna is the author of a number of law and criminal justice articles, focusing on community oversight, American Indian tribal police, and tribal governments.

**Bronwen Manby** is a London-based researcher in the Africa Division of Human Rights Watch, where she is responsible for the work of the organisation on South Africa and Nigeria, as well as advocacy work on other African countries. She has written on a range of human rights issues in both South Africa and Nigeria, including articles in academic journals as well as reports published by Human Rights Watch. During 1994 and 1995 she worked mainly for the Pretoria office of the South African organisation Lawyers for Human Rights, while continuing to work for Human Rights Watch. She trained as a solicitor, and has a BA in Modern History from Oxford University (1985), and a Masters in International Affairs from Columbia University (1992).

**Beverley Milton-Edwards** is currently a Visiting Fellow at the Centre for Islamic Studies, Oxford University. She is also a Reader and Assistant Director of the Centre for the Study of Ethnic Conflict, in the School of Politics at The Queen's University of Belfast. She has published books on Islamic politics in Palestine, contemporary politics in the Middle East as well as co-authored books on Jordan; the politics of deeply divided territories; and conflicts in the Middle East. She has published extensively on the subject of policing in relation to societies in conflict, transition and peace-building.

**Linda Moore** has recently been appointed as the first investigations worker of the new Northern Ireland Human Rights Commission. Prior to this appointment Dr Moore was research officer in the youth justice unit of the Northern Ireland Association for the Care and Resettlement of Offenders. Dr Moore also previously lectured in criminology at Edge Hill College, Lancashire and is the author of several publications on policing, including *Human Rights on Duty* which she co-authored with Mary O'Rawe. Dr Moore is convenor of the policing subgroup of the Committee on the Administration of Justice.

**Rachel Neild** is Public Security Program Director at the Washington Office on Latin America (WOLA) and author of numerous publications on police reform in Haiti and on the role of civil society in promoting public security reform. Recent publications include "Themes and Debates in Police Reform; A Manual for Civil Society"; a technical note for the Inter-American Development Bank on police and crime prevention and a paper entitled "From National Security to Citizen Security; Civil Society and the Evolution of Public Order Debates" published by the International Center for Human Rights and Democratic Development, Montreal, Canada. Neild holds a Masters in International Relations from the Columbia University, New York, and a Bachelor's from the University of Manchester, UK.

**Mary O'Rawe** graduated with a first class honours degree in English and French Law from the University of Kent at Canterbury in 1990. She holds an LLM in Human Rights, Emergency Law and Discrimination from Queens University, Belfast, and has practised as a barrister in Northern Ireland since 1991. She presently lectures in law and is part of the Human Rights and Equality Centre of the University of Ulster. Publications to date are in the areas of human rights, criminal justice and policing. She is currently chairperson of the Belfast-based Committee on the Administration of Justice.

**Philip Stenning** is an Associate Professor at the Centre of Criminology, University of Toronto, Canada. His research has focused primarily on public and private policing, the prosecution process, criminal law and procedure, accountability in the criminal justice system, firearms abuse and gun control, and Aboriginal policing and justice. He has acted as a consultant to several federal and provincial governments and commissions of inquiry, as well as to the United Nations and the Council of Europe. Among his publications is *Accountability for Criminal Justice: Selected Essays* (University of Toronto Press, 1995).

**Samuel Walker** is Isaacson Professor of Criminal Justice at the University of Nebraska at Omaha. He is the author of many books and articles in the area of criminal justice. His primary research interests in recent years involve police accountability, and he is the author of the forthcoming book, *Police Accountability: The Role of Citizen Oversight* (Wadsworth, 2000). He recently completed a national study of early warning systems for problem police officers.

**Ronald Weitzer** is a Professor of Sociology at George Washington University in Washington, DC. He received his PhD from the University of California at

Berkeley in 1985. He has published extensively on policing in Northern Ireland and South Africa, and he is currently writing a book on police-community relations in Washington.

# *Introduction*

ANDREW GOLDSMITH and COLLEEN LEWIS

Holding the police to account has become a growth industry. This book deals with just one area of this growth—civilian oversight of public complaints about policing.[1] Since the 1960s procedures for handling complaints against police have emerged as the pre-eminent means for dealing with problems of police conduct and accountability. Well-publicised instances of police brutality and racial discrimination, often in the context of social and political protest, lent weight to proposals for changes to the way in which citizens could complain about police actions and, in some cases, omissions. The procedures proposed reflected a rights-based, individualistic view of the relationship between the police and citizens, in which individual redress for specific wrongdoings by particular police officers was the primary and, indeed often, only objective. In many jurisdictions this "first wave" phenomenon saw civilian involvement in complaint handling curtail the police monopoly of the process. If not actually involved in investigating complaints made against police officers, civilian-staffed agencies began at least to monitor and review complaint investigations, and to make recommendations on the appropriateness of police conduct raised by complainants. Police no longer monopolised policing the police.

What remained implicit and barely acknowledged for the most part during this phase was the importance of looking at complaints not simply as grounds for legal or disciplinary redress, but also as a mechanism for providing feedback to police management on the activities and policies of their departments. A number of public administration scholars recognised the value of citizens' complaints data for public sector organisational learning, but this was not readily appreciated by the police. The deep conservatism of most police departments and their entrenched reluctance to engage in public self-examination ensured that the transition to outsider involvement in the complaints process was frequently difficult, grudging, and indeed minimalist.[2]

[1] Other areas of police accountability include civil liability in tort, criminal prosecution, new disciplinary and employee management procedures, internal auditing practices, and financial accountability. While public complaints can lead to taking action through legal channels, or pose questions of performance relevant to auditing and financial objectives, these other dimensions of accountability are beyond the scope of this collection.

[2] See for example, Walter Gellhorn, *When Americans Complain: Governmental Grievance Procedures* (Cambridge, MA, Harvard University Press, 1966).

Police resistance to the implementation of shared authority arrangements for citizens' complaints is part of the "second wave" of developments in this area.[3] Coping with police obstructionism to the introduction of new complaints procedures is a familiar tale in the history of police accountability reform. Nor is it now a thing of the past. It is one that continues to challenge those seeking to implement forms of civilian oversight today, as recent experience in Ontario, Canada, demonstrates (Landau, this volume). In several instances the practical difficulties of operation faced by civilian bodies in their early days led to requests for further powers, especially in the area of independent investigation, and for the relaxation of applicable evidential standards, from the criminal to lesser civil standards of proof (on the Australian position, see Lewis, this volume). Needless to say, many police have favoured fewer, rather than more, powers of this type. The dimension of struggle for authority over policing, between police management and external accountability bodies, has therefore lost little of its pertinence in the recent history of civilian oversight.

Another facet of the evolution of police complaint procedures has been the attempt to systematically collect and analyse complaints data as a tool for organisational learning. While there is still some way to go, the annual reports of police oversight bodies contain a variety of information concerning types and patterns of complaints which was far less visible when complaint handling was solely in the hands of the police. Increasingly these reports also contain the policy recommendations of oversight bodies based on patterns of complaints or serious issues raised through individual grievances. In part, these changes indicate a partial withdrawal from a strongly punitive, legalistic approach to police conduct and, at the same time, suggest a movement towards a more systematic approach to reforming police behaviour and improving organisational effectiveness.

However, while attention was increasingly focused upon systemic issues, some early critics of "first wave" developments began to express scepticism about the claim that civilian involvement in complaint handling necessarily delivered a more effective system for resolving citizen complaints and improving police conduct. Symbolically, it might be argued, the reasons for rejecting police-dominated accountability mechanisms had been strong and persuasive. The incidence of police scandals of one kind or another pointed overwhelmingly to the police's inability to deal decisively with problems of corruption and excessive force. Harassment of particular groups and incivility towards citizens also appeared to be beyond police control. In concrete terms however, the reality of more effective accountability delivered through these new complaint procedures was, and remains, difficult to substantiate. As several contributors to this

[3] The experience of the Victorian Police Complaints Authority is just one example among many possible examples that might be chosen. On this see Ian Freckelton, "Shooting the Messenger: The Trial and Execution of the Victorian Police Complaints Authority" in Andrew Goldsmith (ed), *Complaints Against the Police: The Trend to External Review* (Oxford, Clarendon Press, 1991). The chapters by Beattie and Weitzer, and Lewis (this volume), are also pertinent.

volume argue, more experimentation with, as well as evaluation of, civilian oversight is needed.

The third, emergent, phase (or "third wave") of civilian oversight presents a complex picture. Simply put, in established democracies where civilian oversight has been present in some form for a decade or more, there are signs of consolidation and improvement (e.g. Queensland), as well as change, retreat and even rejection (Ontario—see Landau, this volume). Outside the so-called developed countries, we are witnessing the extension of the principles and practices of oversight into countries and regions with very different social, political and cultural traditions. In many instances these places have been also marked by pronounced socio-economic inequalities, an absence of political stability, and little experience with, or understanding of, democratic practices. These different traditions and circumstances, not surprisingly, have also affected the functions and uses of state police forces. They have also influenced the reception given to civilian oversight, as several contributors outline and analyse in their chapters.

One interesting dimension to recent changes in the practice of police accountability in established democracies is the attempt by police to reassert ownership over complaints and the complaints process. In many ways, the move by police to reclaim responsibility for complaints is predictable, understandable and, under certain circumstances, even laudable. Many scholars have long expressed the view that the police should not be excluded from the complaints area, on the basis that police management must exercise operational control over their members, whether in the field of discipline or organisational performance.[4] More recently, commissions of inquiry,[5] civilian complaint bodies, and police managers have argued the importance of approaching citizens' complaints as a management tool, indeed as a "customer service" matter to be used for tactful resolution and organisational learning and adaptation. Complaints, or at least certain categories of them, are being reconceptualised in some jurisdictions as "service issues" or indeed as "incidents", before being channelled into more informal, and often police-dominated, processes.

The reasons for these changes are complex, and not yet widely understood.[6] While not the focus of any particular contribution to this book, they are worth noting here in passing in relation to understanding the complexities of the field of police accountability reform. The "recolonisation" of complaints by police

[4] David Bayley has made this point on several occasions. See for example Bayley "Preface" to Goldsmith, *ibid*; also Douglas Perez, *Common Sense About Police Review* (Philadelphia, Temple University Press, 1994).

[5] In New South Wales, the Wood Royal Commission recommendations in its Final Report, Volume II, strongly endorsed the Employee Management System idea as a way of linking citizen complaints with the internal organisational needs of the NSW Police. See New South Wales, *Royal Commission into the New South Wales Police Service, Final Report* (Sydney, NSW Government, 1997).

[6] But see Goldsmith, "Informal Resolution of Police Complaints in Australia: Better Understanding or Mere Bureaucratic Convenience?" (2000) 17 *Law in Context* (forthcoming).

departments, it should be noted, fits philosophically with a corporate management approach to policing, in which private sector management concepts and practices are being applied to the organisation and management of policing.[7] One clear implication from this shift is the gradual withdrawal in an apparently expanding variety of citizen complaints from the rights-focused procedures which typified "first-wave" reforms. These reforms are increasingly being replaced by more expeditious, cheaper methods for dealing with the grievances of ordinary citizens under the rubric of informal resolution. While it is perhaps too early to evaluate thoroughly the significance of informal resolution for civilian oversight or police accountability,[8] experience to date serves to underline the constant state of flux operating in the area of reforms affecting the exercise of police authority, and to some different ways in which police are reclaiming authority over citizen complaints.

Needless to say, the very recent introduction of the concept of civilian oversight in countries in transition to democracy, or in countries where democracy has never been firmly or effectively established, has led to a rather different set of issues, which also form part of this "third wave.". In these countries, institutional changes in government have included attempts to establish independent judiciaries, more effective, efficient and fair procedures for the administration of justice, as well as attempts to strengthen and re-educate police and other security forces. Reform efforts have often had to explicitly juggle Western-driven initiatives for justice institutions based upon liberal democratic principles (the Rule of Law, individual rights etc.) with profoundly different contextual considerations. In some of the reform settings considered in this collection (e.g. Colombia), state power and authority face internal political conflict, powerful non-state actors engaged in illegal activities including the lucrative drug market, high levels of ordinary crime, and mass poverty. Regime insecurity, therefore, is an important defining element of the reform setting.

Finding a place for police accountability reforms in countries where internal security is widely seen as the fundamental problem is one of the greatest challenges facing Western countries and international organisations committed to strengthening and improving governance mechanisms (e.g. World Bank),[9] or to protecting human rights in other parts of the globe (e.g. Amnesty International, Human Rights Watch). Perhaps the greatest obstacle for police accountability reform in transitional states and emerging democracies lies in convincing those vulnerable groups who have been most victimised by state police forces in the past, either through abuse or neglect, that they should now trust the police. Because of previous negative experiences with police these groups suffer deeply from insecurity, yet they are the very people who most need better police

[7] See Cindy Davids and Linda Hancock, "Policing, Accountability and Citizenship in the Market State", 31 *Australian and New Zealand Journal of Criminology* 38 (1997).

[8] But see Goldsmith, supra n. 7.

[9] World Bank, *World Development Report 1997: The State in a Changing World* (New York, Oxford University Press, 1997).

protection as well as more accountable police. Currently in many emerging democracies, there is an abyss separating the vulnerable from their police forces, a breached relationship which civilian oversight could help to restore.

## THE THEMES OF THE COLLECTION

In this collection of commissioned essays, we attempt to look at the state of civilian oversight of policing in a wide variety of contexts. States and societies examined range from Australia, Canada, the United States of America, and Northern Ireland, to South Africa, Israel, Palestine, Haiti, Brazil and Colombia. While it is possible to chart the influence and impact of the concept of civilian oversight in each of these places, the circumstances are often markedly different and the degree of influence has varied. Consequently, the issues examined by the contributors sometimes differ considerably. Underlying the discussion in each instance however is the exploration of a particular approach to police accountability that has spread significantly across the globe since its origins both in the concept of the ombudsman and in developments in North American city management several decades ago.[10] Indeed one of the key concerns of several essays (e.g. Goldsmith, Milton-Edwards, Neild) is to examine the ability to successfully transplant legal-political ideas, strongly grounded in liberal democratic principles within established Western countries, to regions and countries with very different political traditions and experiences.

Like no other period in human history the last decade or so has signalled the likely future diffusion of key political ideas and philosophies (as well as particular social and economic ideologies, e.g. consumerism) from a small number of dominant countries and transnational institutions to other regions, countries and institutions around the world.[11] Western human rights discourse, for example, is now being used more generally and effectively than ever before to evaluate the record of individual nation-states, and as a basis for influencing future conduct by states. Institutional capacity-building in so-called underdeveloped countries is often a condition, or an explicit objective, of foreign aid. Political corruption and abuses by state officials increasingly draw together concerns about good governance, human rights and democratisation. These themes, we suggest, increasingly suffuse and influence the debates about, and applications of, police accountability.

[10] On the origins of civilian oversight, see Goldsmith, "External Review v Self-Regulation: The Dialectic of Police Accountability Procedures" in Goldsmith, *supra* n. 3.

[11] The spread of "Western" ideas has been the subject of comment by a number of scholars, most conspicuously perhaps Samuel Huntington. See in particular, Huntington, *The Clash of Civilizations and the Remaking of World Order* (New York, Touchstone, 1996). While there is obviously still a range of competing ideologies on the world stage in the areas of politics and economics, the spread of English-language media, especially in recent times through the Internet, and the influence of international economic and political institutions has arguably done much to advance "Western" thought in comparison with other systems of thought over the past fifty years.

While the most obvious trajectory for these movements of ideas and practices has been from the Western "centre" to the non-Western or non-First World "periphery", the "centre" remains vulnerable in terms of these standards. Amnesty International's recent report on brutality in the New York City Police Department,[12] and the Patten Commission's adoption of "human rights" as the organising principle for restructuring policing in Northern Ireland,[13] are just two examples of how these ideas and practices are having significant and surprising consequences for those societies which have historically been at the forefront in the promotion of democratic values in other countries. In other words, it is not just "the periphery" that is being held to account in subst -tive terms to these universalising norms.

We have broadly organised the essays in this collection into three substantive sections. The first looks at how successfully civilian oversight has been *entrenched* in police governance arrangements and the reasons for greater or lesser degrees of success in implementing the idea. Inevitably, the contributions in this section examine influences on some of the changing forms of civilian oversight over time. Adaptation, revision and compromise characterise the experiences with the implementation of oversight in many jurisdictions. Often this has been forced upon reformers by the substantial resistance to new ideas and organisational change by police. At other times, the cumulative lessons of experience, and changing budgetary and reform priorities, have played their part. Landau's analysis of recent changes to the oversight scheme in Ontario, Canada, points to the attempt to return greater responsibility for complaints handling to the police chiefs, while reducing the procedural entitlements of complainants, for example, to know about progress in the investigation of their complaints. Her argument is that while the former scheme attracted much international attention, it itself was flawed in certain ways; yet, in the final analysis, the recent changes have weakened the symbolic value of civilian oversight that previously existed, signalling a reduction, rather than enhancement, of accountability of the police in Ontario to the public.

One lesson posed in particular by Beattie and Weitzer for understanding police reform in this area is the conceptual ambiguity introduced by the idea of civilian oversight. Is the citizen's complaint simply a claim for legal redress, and therefore best dealt with by legal or quasi-legal investigations and determinations, or is it primarily a signal of administrative malfunction, warranting a change of police department practice or policy? Viewed conceptually, the term "complaint" can signify a variety of meanings, and be seen to warrant a range of possible responses. These will often vary from one cultural context to another (see e.g. Goldsmith, this volume), as well as between different participants in particular police systems (the complainant, the subject officer, the police depart-

[12] Amnesty International, *Police Brutality and Excessive Force in the New York City Police Department* (1996) http://www.voyagerco.com/amnesty/ai.

[13] *A New Beginning for Northern Ireland: The Report of the Independent Commission on Policing for Northern Ireland* (1999).

ment etc). Remedial and disciplinary goals typically coexist uneasily within complaints systems, rendering selection of the appropriate procedural response problematic (Stenning, this volume). Lack of political will is also a factor in entrenching the civilian oversight concept. As Lewis argues, governments' initial enthusiasm for the concept is frequently overtaken by pragmatic politics. It seems that in the formulation stage of the policy process it is often easier for governments to acquiesce to the demands of the powerful police lobby group than to refuse them outright. Once established, structural tensions also arise between oversight bodies and the governments who were forced through democratic political imperatives to create them. When this happens government support for the civilian oversight body can wane to the point where the actions and inaction of governments threaten to undermine the legitimacy of the process.

In Section Two, the essays focus on a theme little considered to date in the police complaints literature—the *evaluation* of civilian oversight mechanisms. The importance of civilian oversight as a public-confidence building mechanism as well as a device for providing feedback on police organisational performance has been argued by a number of commentators in support of its adoption and implementation.[14] Yet our knowledge base for making such judgments and recommendations remains limited. This is why evaluation is such a crucial issue to the future of civilian oversight. At present we know more about the politics of failure in specific cases of civilian oversight schemes than we do about the bases for assessing their effectiveness, efficiency, or legitimacy in practice. Civilian oversight continues to be a key principle of police accountability reforms (e.g. the recent changes in Northern Ireland—see O'Rawe and Moore, this volume). Therefore it is imperative that more attention be devoted to establishing criteria and methods for assessing the kinds of positive contributions which have been offered and that remain possible through oversight arrangements.

How well civilian oversight performs may be viewed through legal, economic, administrative, and political lenses. For the individual complainant, the effectiveness of legal redress will often, but not always, be a consideration. A complainant will also quite frequently be moved to complain by concerns about administrative ineffectiveness, or, though less often, by a perceived problem between police and a particular group within the community. For the police department and those involved directly in police governance, in addition to the costs of dealing with citizen complaints, concerns might reasonably be anticipated in terms of legal liability, administrative effectiveness and political legitimacy, though historically, it has not been clear that police departments have been particularly responsive to some of these implications.[15] Of paramount

[14] See for example Goldsmith, "External Review and Self-Regulation: Police Accountability and the Dialectic of Complaints Procedures" in Goldsmith, *supra* n. 3.

[15] Chevigny has expressed the view that US police departments have been particularly unmoved to change their practices even by quite large legal liabilities arising out of civil suits brought by complainants. See for example Chevigny, *Edge of the Knife: Police Violence in the Americas* (New York, New Press, 1995), p. 266.

importance to the general public however is the political lens, linking the issue of agency effectiveness to broader questions of public trust in police governance and policing. This preoccupation raises issues of democracy and legitimacy, in terms of focusing upon respect for individual rights and the responsiveness of governments, the oversight agencies, and the police to matters raised through citizens' grievances.

Stenning's essay takes a legal perspective on evaluation, proposing a series of criteria for determining the adequacy of the legislative framework used to establish civilian oversight schemes. Based on work initially conducted in British Columbia, Canada, Stenning's approach is essentially normative. He proposes a number of features of complaints legislation that lay the foundations for a strong oversight system. In so doing, however, he is mindful of the need for attention to specific cultural contexts and the importance of finding appropriate personnel when transferring and implementing schemes from one setting to another. He stresses the importance of striking the right balance between competing or at least parallel considerations: discipline and remedy, police management and external oversight, formality and informality, the individual complainant and the public interest, and so on. Accessibility and transparency are key process values suggested by Stenning.

While acknowledging the symbolic importance of civilian oversight bodies, Brereton points out that assessments as to their effectiveness require a more solid empirical basis than has been evident to date. His chapter raises important and timely questions about whether civilian oversight has delivered the promised improvements to investigation outcomes and standards of police conduct made by reformers and policy makers during the first and second waves of civilian oversight. Evaluating effectiveness is also taken up by Herzog. He uses questionnaires, surveys and interviews to ascertain the effectiveness of civilian oversight in dealing with use of force complaints in the divided society of Israel where there is often a blurring between military and community policing. Herzog questions whether the "individual-judicial model" used by internal and external complaints bodies is too limiting in dealing with this most common form of complaint. He suggests that if they are to be effective, external civilian oversight bodies need to expand their range of activities beyond the traditional individual-legal approach and adopt a more proactive strategy designed also to target organisational problems.

Finally, in Section Three, the contributors consider the theme of *extension*—the extent to which civilian oversight of policing has had, or in the future may plausibly have, any impact on police governance arrangements in countries where state police forces have been linked to human rights abuses. Does it offer a means of at least reducing the incidence of human rights violations by police officers? How might civilian oversight best be implemented in these settings so as to have most likelihood of success? What exactly does "success" mean? Or, perhaps, is the whole exercise pointless, given insuperable cultural and political differences between Western and underdeveloped, often unstable countries?

These are profoundly difficult, but important, questions that the contributors address in this section of the book.

Pervasive violence and insecurity, linked to longstanding political conflicts, have characterised daily life for many residents in the underdeveloped world.[16] In many such circumstances, the states involved are weak, and the role of the police, or those engaged in policing tasks,[17] is coloured by their involvement in internal conflicts, rather than by their commitments to the security and safety needs of ordinary citizens. But how can civilian oversight function if respect for the Rule of Law is modest or non-existent? In countries where the security needs of ordinary citizens have taken a back seat in the political priorities of states and their police forces, we see what Neild calls *regime*, rather than *democratic*, policing practised. Instead of prosecuting or attempting to prevent crime, these police forces have spent their energies harassing or attacking the opponents of their political masters.

However, as Goldsmith argues in his chapter on Colombia, it is sometimes too easy to see state police forces as unilaterally engaged in repression on behalf of a dominant state, when in fact these regimes can be beleaguered by various armed opponents well-versed in deploying violence against the state and its security apparatus, including the police. In such varied but difficult environments, the applicability of Western policing ideas, particularly sensitive ideas about police accountability, has to be problematised on practical grounds as well as on grounds of principle, since quite different political traditions and immediate security needs distinguish many developing countries from countries in North America or Western Europe.

The difficulty of transplanting concepts and practices from one cultural context to another is addressed in the Northern Ireland context by O'Rawe and Moore and by Milton-Edwards' essay which examines developments in Palestine. Western agendas for democratisation present many practical difficulties where democratic traditions are largely absent and political power is organised strongly along sectarian lines. However Milton-Edwards points to an irony in the case of Palestine that is also to be found in other developing regions—that is, a certain ambivalence within the foreign policy of major sponsoring countries towards democratic development. The ambivalence is to be found in an apparent clash between the pursuit of *security* versus *democratic* and *human rights* agendas. Establishing a strong central political authority that is able to largely contain dissident elements within its territorial responsibility is widely seen as a precondition to other aspects of state-building and economic advancement.

[16] The examples here are too numerous to instance. However, many African states (e.g. Liberia, Rwanda), as well as Central American (e.g. El Salvador, Guatemala) and Latin American states (Brazil, Colombia) could be mentioned.

[17] In some situations, the lines between the state and other interest groups, and between different kinds of militias and armed groups involved in security, are so blurred that it is difficult to point to "the state" or to "the police" as distinct bodies. Rather, it can be said that certain groups, typically armed and prepared to use force if necessary, are engaged in security functions or in governance.

Typically this policy priority has major consequences for the recognition as well as implementation of police accountability reforms.

The pre-eminence of internal security agendas, frequently supported by foreign governments, has influenced the police reform agendas in a number of other countries examined in this collection: South Africa (Manby), Israel (Herzog), Northern Ireland (O'Rawe and Moore), Colombia (Goldsmith), and other Latin American countries (Neild). Ways of keeping police accountability on the development agenda of countries racked by internal conflict is a central question for several of the essays, but particularly those of Neild, Goldsmith, and Milton-Edwards. Extending the concept of civilian oversight can be impeded paradoxically by donor countries who are otherwise engaged in police development in recipient countries. This is particularly evident in countries which have deeply divided societies, where political order cannot be guaranteed. Strengthened repressive and criminal intelligence capabilities are often favoured forms of police assistance in these settings.[18] As Milton-Edwards explains, the foreign policy concerns of donor countries can take precedence over the developing countries' needs for improved police accountability.

Despite inherent problems in introducing the concept into emerging democracies, Neild believes civilian oversight has the potential to address a number of problems in Latin American countries. While acknowledging that it is not a "magic bullet", she is optimistic that it can help to improve the internal police discipline process, provide information about police conduct not previously on the public record and make recommendations for reform of police practices and policies which are based on hard data. However, Neild does express concerns. While noting that governments are no longer committing human rights abuses as a matter of policy, she notes that they are still tolerating them in the more marginalised sectors of society.

O'Rawe and Moore's historical account of attempts to reform police accountability in Northern Ireland demonstrates a common problem for police reform in emerging and established democracies: the intertwining of politics and police accountability. Their chapter documents how governments, for political reasons, often favour incremental change over the need to introduce the type of radical reforms necessary to prevent human rights abuses from continuing in a divided society. Indeed successive governments in Northern Ireland have tended to extol the virtues of reports calling for increased police accountability while ignoring those recommendations which they consider politically unpalatable. Despite two recent extensive and high profile investigations into policing, the legislation to establish a new civilian oversight body in Northern Ireland "fails spectacularly", in their view, to come to terms with the needs of the civilian oversight body and to sever some of the unnecessary political ties. The police culture, O'Rawe and Moore maintain, will not be changed by a

[18] On the forms of police assistance to developing countries, particularly from the United States of America, see Ethan Nadelmann, *Cops Across Borders* (Pennsylvania State University Press, 1993), and David Bayley, "A Foreign Policy for Democratic Policing" (1995) 5 *Policing and Society* 79 (1995).

continued incremental approach to serious police accountability problems. Governments' failure to "get tough" is to deny Northern Ireland the commitment needed to stop human rights abuses by and against police.

High crime rates and the exposure of police involvement in criminal and human rights abuses has resulted in low public confidence in the South African police. Immediately after being elected, the African National Congress (ANC) led Government of National Unity began a programme of police reform which emphasised the need to move toward a community policing model and to establish mechanisms for a more democratic control of policing,[19] which includes civilian involvement in the complaints process. However, as noted earlier in relation to many countries in the transitional stage of democratic nation building, an escalating crime problem and other internal security issues often take precedence over ensuring that suspects' due process rights are respected. Indeed public dissatisfaction in South Africa has recently been directed toward the still-young oversight body, the Independent Complaints Directorate (ICD), which is seen by many as "tying the hands" of police officers when dealing with criminals. Arguments by human rights organisations and the ICD that effective police accountability and investigation of crime go hand in hand appear to be misunderstood or ignored in the quest for sweeping solutions to the rising crime problem. In such scenarios, police accountability and respect for human rights tend to be given a low priority. As Lewis points out in her chapter, this misunderstanding is being fuelled by the public pronouncements of the Minister for Safety and Security.

Manby, like many other contributors to this book identifies flaws in the model introduced to oversee complaints against police. The ICD, like the newly created Police Ombudsman in Northern Ireland, is tied to the political authority of the minister responsible for police. The ICD also suffers from the common problem afflicting most civilian oversight bodies: a lack of resources. Manby takes the position that even though the ICD is a step forward in terms of raising police accountability standards in South Africa, it is not being allowed to fulfil its full potential. Whether it ever will depends as much on government and community support as it does on the internal workings of the oversight body. At present, it seems, vital external supports for civilian oversight remain shaky or indeed elusive.

Finally, in addition to describing and analysing a wide range of experiences with civilian oversight in practice, the essays in this volume pose a set of questions and challenges for the future of police accountability. One of the key lessons to be drawn from the collection as a whole is the legacy established incrementally through experimentation with civilian oversight in an expanding array of countries and cultural contexts. Even when specific examples might be said to have "failed" in a particular setting, or to have not yet been implemented

[19] For an account of this evolution in thinking about the South African police, see M Brogden and C Shearing, *Policing For A New South Africa* (London, Routledge, 1992).

despite clear attempts to do so, we should not too readily dismiss the significance of what has occurred. As several contributors (e.g. Neild, Goldsmith, Herzog, Manby and Milton-Edwards) have shown, a number of specific engagements with the principles, if not always the practices, of police accountability and in particular, civilian oversight, have occurred in political settings far removed from those of Western liberal-democratic states. These settings have not, at least until recently, been exposed in any depth to the ideas and practices of ombudsmen, civil liberties, and universal human rights which have emerged over the past five or so decades as checks and balances on the exercise of state power.

As ideologies of power and governance increasingly converge globally, to trial or even discuss such ideas as civilian oversight in new surroundings is to contribute to the process of advancing state accountability. At the very least, such attempts at debate and implementation assist in consciousness-raising about police accountability and the entitlements of citizens in other systems. They thus help to shape future agendas on law, order and police governance. Like children in underdeveloped countries gaining access through television to the world of McDonalds, Nike and MTV, states and civil societies once exposed to these powerful institutional and philosophical ideas will find it increasingly difficult to ignore them in the future.

Another implication of the collection as a whole is that the "missionary influence" of such ideas will be reinforced if international NGOs and other transnational agencies such as development banks begin to argue for the relevance of particular institutional reforms at the state or even local level in countries in which they have programmes. Just as international and regional development banks are starting to look more broadly at the political and social contexts in which economic "re-adjustments" are taking place, NGOs such as Amnesty International and Human Rights Watch are starting to look in greater depth at the settings in which human rights abuses occur. As Neild's chapter shows, through organisations such as the Washington Office on Latin America, we are beginning to see not just documentation and denunciation of such abuses, but also specific practical suggestions and encouragement at the local level for institutional reform of the police and other security forces, designed to lead to fewer abuses in future. Increasingly, these institutional reforms encompass the establishment of civilian oversight mechanisms.

In this diffusion process, there is a specific role for a body such as the International Association for Civilian Oversight of Law Enforcement (IACOLE) in facilitating debate and information-exchanges on police accountability with a wide range of policing and political systems. This association has members from countries around the world, many of whom are directly involved in, and hence experienced in, the running of oversight bodies. IACOLE has begun to move in the direction of technical assistance to fledgling oversight agencies and in developing manuals for those contemplating such moves, but might readily do much more to promote these ideas and practices internationally.

In sum, we believe there is considerable potential, and some cause, for optimism in what is being described in this book. Within the current, and in our view likely future, trajectories outlined, there remains an important place for civilian oversight and other forms of police accountability, albeit only as part of the wider set of commitments needed and opportunities available for the improvement of policing and citizen safety. There is a momentum gathering world-wide for ideas and practices such as civilian oversight of policing that future governments of all descriptions will find increasingly difficult to ignore.[20] While different countries and states will continue to pursue different practices, they will be less likely in the future to have been devised in ignorance of civilian oversight and similar police accountability reforms.

The work undertaken to date, and described here, remains unfinished. More will need to be done to find the best ways of implementing such ideas in different settings. Scholars and practitioners will have to do more work in the areas of entrenchment and evaluation of oversight mechanisms. There are attendant risks and dangers in such work. Along the way, misunderstanding, fear and active resistance to change will not be uncommon. Determining the worth of such reforms however should not be too closely bound to standards of absolute efficiency or infallible accountability as might be interpreted and applied in developed Western nations. Realism as well as contextual sensitivity are crucial to defining progress. Aiming high in terms of the improvement sought, but remaining realistic given constraints applicable in the local setting, is one way to move forward. If ultimately an improvement is achieved which is less than might ideally have been realised, but is nonetheless a significant positive step forward towards reducing police abuses, this ought to be an acceptable performance indicator when assessing progress in these areas. Civilian oversight could do worse than meet the standard of the cross-eyed javelin thrower competing in the Olympic Games—while this athlete might not win the particular event, he or she is guaranteed to always keep the crowd on the edge of its' seats![21]

## DEFINITIONAL ISSUES

We have chosen the term "civilian oversight" as the key concept linking the various contributions to this book. There is undoubtedly a variety of terms used to describe developments in the "civilianisation" of police accountability, through

[20] Canada's foreign aid agency, CIDA, has recently promoted a collaborative project between the University of Ottawa's Human Rights Education and Research Centre and policing and academic institutions in Brazil, as part of its attempt to tackle police violence in Brazil. Civilian oversight has been expressly promoted within this dialogue and set of institutional exchanges. See E Mendes, J Zuckerberg, S Lecorre, A Gabriel and J Clark (eds), *Democratic Policing and Accountability: Global Perspectives* (Aldershot, Ashgate, 1999).

[21] We have taken this allusion from a book by D McBarnet and C Whelan, entitled *Creative Accounting and the Cross-eyed Javelin Thrower* (London, Wiley, 1999). It is attributed to Sir David Tweedie, Chairman of the UK Accounting Standards Board, in describing his Board's role in tackling creative accounting by professional accountants.

the insertion of civilian staff in some or other aspect of handling complaints lodged by members of the public (and in some systems, by the police) against police behaviour. These matters of definition, and the range of mechanisms that have fallen one way or another under this rubric, have been addressed previously by both editors separately,[22] as well as by others. However, for present purposes, it should be made clear that "citizen" and "civilian" are both terms employed to describe the mechanisms of handling citizen complaints at the core of this book. We have chosen the term "oversight" in preference to "review" to suggest a wider range of functions than simply post-hoc, "second guessing" reviews, often conducted simply on the basis of investigation reports and witness statements. Most significantly, by "oversight" we explicitly countenance investigations by civilian staff of complaints and civilian supervision of police-staffed investigations as aspects of the mechanisms established outside police departments to process individual complaints. It is also worth noting that our focus in this collection is upon generalist bodies for receiving and processing citizen complaints against police, and not specialist bodies that focus on particular kinds of serious misconduct (most commonly, corruption) at the expense of other types of citizen grievances.[23]

## References

Amnesty International, *Police Brutality and Excessive Force in the New York City Police Department*, (1996) http://www.voyagerco.com/amnesty/ai.

D Bayley ,"Preface" to A Goldsmith, (ed), *Complaints Against the Police: The Trend to External Review* (Oxford: Clarendon Press, 1991).

D Bayley, "A Foreign Policy for Democratic Policing" 5 *Policing and Society* 79 (1995).

M Brogden and C Shearing, *Policing For A New South Africa* (London: Routledge, 1992).

P Chevigny, *Edge of the Knife: Police Violence in the Americas* (New York: New Press, 1995).

C Davids and L Hancock, "Policing, Accountability and Citizenship in the Market State" 31 *Australian and New Zealand Journal of Criminology* 38 (1997).

I Freckelton, "Shooting the Messenger: The Trial and Execution of the Victorian Police Complaints Authority" in A Goldsmith, 1991.

W Gellhorn, *When Americans Complain: Governmental Grievance Procedures* (Cambridge, MA: Harvard University Press, 1966).

[22] Andrew Goldsmith, *supra* n. 3; Colleen Lewis, *Complaints Against Police: The Politics of Reform* (Sydney: Hawkins Press, 1999). Others who have addressed these issues include Paul West, "Investigation of complaints against the police: Summary report of a national survey", *American Journal of Police*, vol VII, no. 2, pp. 101–21.

[23] Here, the example of the Independent Commission Against Corruption model, found in Hong Kong as well as New South Wales, springs to mind. These bodies, as their titles convey, do not deal with all grievances against police, nor are the forms of corruption considered limited to police matters. Also see Landau, this volume, who deals briefly with the Ontario Special Investigations Unit (SIU), a civilian body that focuses on serious criminal allegations made against police.

A Goldsmith, "External Review and Self-Regulation: Police Accountability and the Dialectic of Complaints Procedures" in A Goldsmith (ed), *Complaints Against the Police: The Trend to External Review* (Oxford: Clarendon Press, 1991).
A Goldsmith, "Informal Resolution of Police Complaints in Australia", 17 *Law in Context* (forthcoming).
S Huntington, *The Clash of Civilizations and the Remaking of World Order* (New York: Touchstone, 1996).
C Lewis, *Complaints Against Police: The Politics of Reform* (Sydney: Hawkins Press, 1999).
D McBarnet and C Whelan, *Creative Accounting and the Cross-eyed Javelin Thrower* (London: Wiley, 1999).
E Mendes, J Zuckerberg, S Lecorre, A Gabriel and J Clark (eds), *Democratic Policing and Accountability: Global Perspectives* (Aldershot:Ashgate, 1999).
E Nadelmann, *Cops Across Borders* (Pennsylvania State University Press, 1993).
New South Wales, *Royal Commission into the New South Wales Police Service, Final Report* (Sydney: NSW Government, 1997).
Northern Ireland, *A New Beginning for Northern Ireland: The Report of the Independent Commission on Policing for Northern Ireland* (1999).
D Perez, *Common Sense About Police Review* (Philadelphia: Temple University Press, 1994).
P West, "Investigation of complaints against the police: Summary report of a national survey" *American Journal of Police*, vol VII, no. 2, 101–21.
World Bank, *World Development Report 1997: The State in a Changing World* (New York: Oxford University Press, 1997).

SECTION ONE

# ENTRENCHING CIVILIAN OVERSIGHT

# 1

# *The Politics of Civilian Oversight: Serious Commitment or Lip Service?*

COLLEEN LEWIS

*Power held by our officials is not matched by adequate institutional arrangements and practices which can reassure the community that our service is, and is honoured as, their first obligation. Adequacy, I should say immediately, is not a matter of what is tolerable to our governors; is not a matter of what they believe can be conceded to us. Rather, it should be the expression of our entitlement; should be a consequence of our sovereignty.*[1]

## INTRODUCTION

Over the past two decades many despotic and totalitarian regimes have been replaced by states which are in the transitional stage of democratic nation-building. Having embraced democratic principles, such as representative government; the right to free speech, association and assembly; a free media; independent judiciary and adherence to the Rule of Law, emerging democracies are now struggling with the task of restructuring their institutions to reflect those ideals. The way in which their police services are reformed will play a pivotal role in determining their success, for as Bayley points out, it is the police that "regulate the freedoms which are essential to democracy".[2]

Bayley goes on to outline ways in which established democracies could assist emerging democracies with police reform. He suggests eleven principles which should guide the exporting of "a foreign policy for democratic policing".[3] However, Bayley's foreign policy does not address one of the issues that goes to the heart of democracy: how complaints against police should be handled. Democratic societies are held together by an accountability chain and the way in which the internal, coercive arm of the state, the police, are held accountable

[1] P Finn, "The Abuse of Public Power in Australia: Making our Governors our Servants", 77 *Canberra Bulletin of Public Administration* 18.

[2] D Bayley, "A Foreign Policy for Democratic Policing", 5 *Policing and Society* 97.

[3] *Ibid.*, 90–2.

for their actions provides one of the vital links. This point was emphasised by Dr Budimir Babovic at the International Association for Civilian Oversight of Law Enforcement's Fourteenth World Conference, where he argued convincingly that "Fundamentally and in principle, without police accountability, one can hardly speak of democracy . . .".[4]

But, even if this important aspect of police accountability did form part of a foreign policy, it is highly probable that the emphasis in any export package would be on the theory, as the practice often reveals a reality which is far removed from what citizens have a right to expect from their elected and appointed representatives.

It was the abusive and illegal behaviour of many police, and the failure of governments to deal with the problem by introducing transparent and potentially more effective police accountability processes, which eventually led to the establishment of external, independent, civilian bodies to oversight complaints against police. However, there is a wide gap between civilian oversight the principle, and civilian oversight the practice. Factors which determine the breadth and depth of the gap are not confined to internal matters under the control of the oversight body. Many are external and can be linked to the vested interests of police, the special relationship between police and governments and the tensions which sometimes arise between independent oversight bodies and governments.[5]

Police have had a disproportionate and negative influence on the powers granted to many of the external civilian bodies established to oversight them. This influence has impeded the oversight agency's ability to deliver effective accountability. But police influence alone does not adequately explain the gap between principle and practice. Actions and lack of action by democratic governments (independent of pressure from the police), has been also instrumental in hindering effective police accountability. Many governments' initial enthusiasm for establishing an independent civilian police complaints body wanes once the body is operational and begins to make politically embarrassing findings.

Two themes, police influence and government action, are used to support the central thesis of this chapter: that governments often pay only lip service to the democratic principle of effective police accountability. Evidence will be presented to show that in relation to civilian oversight, they do this in a number of ways. For example, while extolling the virtues of their response to citizens' demands for improved accountability standards, some governments simultaneously acquiesce to police demands which limit the oversight body's capacity to deliver effective accountability. Governments also starve oversight bodies of resources and attempt to undermine their credibility. Tactics used to achieve the latter include ignoring their reports; subjecting them to biased inquiries and

[4] B Babovic, "Some problems of establishing oversight in countries in transition", paper presented at the Fourteenth Annual World Conference of the International Association for Civilian Oversight of Law Enforcement, Seattle, 1998.

[5] Colleen Lewis, *Complaints Against Police: The Politics of Reform* (Sydney, Hawkins, 1999).

questioning the oversight body's message that police must respect the rule of law and due process when dealing with all people, including criminals. Another important consideration when determining whether a civilian oversight policy translates into symbolic politics is the reporting, monitoring and review processes laid down for the oversight body itself. This issue is addressed in the latter part of the chapter.

## DEMOCRATIC SAFEGUARDS

O'Rawe and Moore explain that a fundamental objective of policing in democratic societies is:

> to protect and defend the rights of all, to ensure equality before the law, and to do this by having as a primary goal the maintenance of the rule of law.[6]

This constitutional principle is the ideal. In practice, police often choose to ignore the rule of law and behave in a manner which suggests that it does not and should not apply to them. Their non-compliance is considered by some to be a type of "perk" that goes with the job. However, the reality is that when police ignore laws which are designed to protect citizens' human rights they become criminals masquerading as law enforcement officials. As Crawshaw points out, their actions do not reduce criminality, rather they add to it.[7]

Police in democratic societies often defend their illegal behaviour by asserting that adherence to principles such as due process and the rule of law hinders rather than enhances their effectiveness as law enforcers. However, they have not presented any persuasive evidence to support this claim, and until they do, police cannot expect citizens to trade hard won civil rights for a supposed, but not proven, reduction in crime. It is interesting and telling to note that police arrested and charged with a criminal offence are not prepared to relinquish their right to due process and the rule of law. It seems that when circumstances affect an officer's freedoms, police understand and appreciate only too well the importance of having democratic safeguards.

Many people, including the former Chief Justice for New South Wales (now Chief Justice of the High Court of Australia), Murray Gleeson, are sympathetic to the difficulties police can experience in having to comply with the law while enforcing the law. But despite these difficulties he believes that, the community "must insist as a minimum condition upon the application of the rule of law" to all aspects police work.[8] In democracies it is expected that governments will introduce the necessary mechanisms to try to ensure that they do. Yet the

[6] M O'Rawe and L Moore, *Human Rights on Duty: Principles for Better Policing—International Lessons for Northern Ireland* (Belfast, Committee on the Administration of Justice, 1997) 82.

[7] *Ibid.*, 112.

[8] A M Gleeson, "Police Accountability and Oversight: An Overview" in D Moore and R Wettenhall (eds.), *Keeping the Peace: Police Accountability and Oversight* (Canberra, UC and RIPAA, 1994) 26.

evidence suggests that many governments have not done enough to encourage police to abide by democratic safeguards, or introduced policies which can hold them to account when they do not.

For years many governments ignored repeated complaints by citizens that the internal, police controlled complaints systems allowed police to engage in corrupt activities, abuse citizens' rights and treat the rule of law and due process with contempt. Governments often justified their position by claiming that evidence of police misconduct reflected the actions of the occasional rogue officer in an otherwise ethical organisation (the much cited "rotten apple" theory), and as such police were best able to deal with the problem internally. This approach, which merely reiterated the police position, had the effect of shielding police misconduct from proper scrutiny. It also helped to create a feeling among some officers that they were immune from accountability. Over time, as this feeling became more pervasive, police misconduct became more brazen.

## LOSS OF CONTROL OVER COMPLAINTS

Detailed accounts of why police lost their monopoly over the complaints process have been addressed by several writers.[9] While there are differences in emphasis between countries/jurisdictions, there appears to be consensus over the major events which led to civilian involvement. These factors range from a general demand for more "open government" to police-specific issues.

Matters relating directly to police include the continued exposure of police misconduct by public inquiries; the undeniable failure of the police controlled complaints system to deliver effective accountability; police actions during the civil unrest of the 1960s and 1970s; and television.

The anti-war and pro civil liberties demonstrations served to broaden the "class" of persons directly experiencing police behaviour. The "middle class", who previously had little contact with police, now found themselves the subject of police attention. The televising of police actions at these demonstrations also meant that, for the first time, police conduct was beamed into the homes of law-abiding, "respectable" citizens. Though not directly involved in any protest

[9] J Hudson, "Police Review Boards and Police Accountability", 36 *Law and Contemporary Problems*, 515–38; M Goode, "Administrative systems for the resolution of complaints against police: A proposed reform", 5 *Adelaide Law Review*, 55–78; H Goldstein, *Policing a Free Society* (Cambridge MA, Ballinger, 1977); M McMahon and R Ericson, *Policing Reform: A Study of the Reform Process and Police Institution in Toronto* (Toronto, Centre of Criminology, 1984); D Brown, "Civilian review of complaints against police: A survey of United States literature", in K Heal, R Tarling and J Burrows (eds.), *Policing Today* (London, HMSO, 1985); Clare Lewis, Sidney Linden and Judith Keene, "Public complaints against police in metropolitan Toronto: The history and operation of the office of the Public Complaints Commissioner", 29 *Criminal Law Quarterly*, 115–44; M Maguire, "Complaints against the police: The British experience" in A Goldsmith (ed.), *Complaints Against the Police: The Trend to External Review* (Oxford, Clarendon, 1991); S Watt, "The future of civilian oversight policing", 33 *Canadian Journal of Criminology*; Colleen Lewis, *Complaints Against Police: The Politics of Reform*, *supra* n. 5.

movement, these people became gravely concerned about the undemocratic tactics used by police to quell community dissent.[10] They joined the previously ignored voices of civil rights and minority groups in demanding more transparent and effective police accountability mechanisms.

In many jurisdictions, governments responded to the demands by establishing independent commissions of inquiry which revealed systematic monetary and process corruption and physical abuse by police. The public outcry which followed these revelations meant that governments, for political reasons, could no longer afford to ignore the reality: internal, police controlled complaints systems were a gross failure.

Police strongly resisted their loss of control over police complaints and had limited success in bringing about the temporary demise of some civilian oversight bodies. But they quickly realised that closure was an unrealistic long-term goal. Accordingly, police decided to use their influence with governments to try to shape the legislation governing civilian oversight bodies.

## INFLUENCE ON LEGISLATIVE FRAMEWORKS

By appointing commissions of inquiry to examine allegations of police misconduct, and to explore how best to deal with complaints against police, many governments were able to put a buffer between themselves and policies which would, in effect, remove the police monopoly over the complaints process. In other words, they could claim to be one step removed from the decision. It also allowed governments time to negotiate the parameters of the civilian oversight policy with the police hierarchy and police unions. This may have been beneficial for the respective governments, in that it avoided the naked display of police power experienced in New York, but it came at a cost for effective civilian oversight.[11] That cost was the omission of certain reactive powers needed by oversight bodies to fulfil their charter.

In several Australian states police unions exercised their considerable power and influence to shape the legislative frameworks of many oversight bodies. This happened in South Australia in the early 1980s, where repeated threats of

[10] P Hain, "Introduction", in P Hain, D Humphry and B Rose-Smith (eds.), *Policing the Police, Volume 1, The Complaints System: Police Powers and Terrorism Legislation* (London, John Calder, 1979); D Bayley, "Preface", in A Goldsmith (ed.), *Complaints Against the Police: The Trend to External Review, ibid*; W Petterson, "Police accountability and civilian oversight of policing: An American perspective", in A Goldsmith (ed.), *Complaints Against the Police: The Trend to External Review, ibid*; M Goode, "Complaints Against the Police in Australia: Where are we now, and what we might learn about the process of law reform, with some comments about the process of legal change" in A Goldsmith (ed.), *Complaints Against the Police: The Trend to External Review, ibid.*

[11] In the mid 1960s a Civilian Complaints Review Board was established in New York City. Opposition to the Board by the Patrolmen's Benevolent Association was so fierce that within four months the Board was closed down. D Brown, "Civilian review of complaints against the police: A survey of United States literature" in K Heal, R Tarling and J Burrows (eds.), *Policing Today, supra* n. 9.

a police strike were used as a bargaining tool to reduce the powers of the proposed civilian oversight body, the Police Complaints Authority (PCA) and to advantage police. During the policy formulation phase of the oversight process, police successfully negotiated, among other things, for an increase in the penalties which could be imposed for bribing a police officer.[12] At the same time as police were campaigning to increase the penalties for bribing an officer, they were also campaigning to lessen the powers of the body which would oversight investigations of police allegedly taking bribes. Throughout the negotiation phase, the powers of the South Australian police were also increased to allow them to stop and search people without a warrant. However, the Police Complaints Authority's legislation required it to obtain a search warrant before it could conduct a search.

As a result of police-government negotiations, the PCA was also denied the power to examine people on oath, anonymous complaints could only be investigated in particular circumstances, and police officers and their close relatives had privilege against self-incrimination. The Internal Investigation Branch was defined in legislation as the agency charged with the primary investigation of complaints, subject to oversight by the PCA, and the onus of proof for disciplinary matters was set at the criminal standard, beyond reasonable doubt.[13] Once the police had negotiated these concessions, the police association agreed to the Bill which established the Police Complaints Authority.[14]

In Western Australia in 1984 a concerned government did act to try to improve police accountability by introducing a Complaints Against Police Bill. However, the Bill was strongly opposed by the police union and their tactics, like those of their South Australian counterparts, included the threat of strike action.[15] The negotiation process between police and government went on for some twenty months. During that time the Labour Government agreed to several changes but they did not go far enough to satisfy the union. It passed a vote of no confidence in the premier, the police minister and the government. After much heated debate, the Bill was passed through the legislative assembly. However, the police successfully lobbied the majority opposition members in the upper house and consequently the Complaints Against Police Bill failed to make it through the legislative council. The compromise was an amendment to the Parliamentary Commissioner for Administrative Investigation's legislation. The amendment allowed for the investigation of complaints against police

[12] M Goode, "Controlling Police Misconduct, Complaints Against the Police and the Process of Law Reform: As it Happens—An Academic War Story" in P Grabosky and I Le Lievre, *Government Illegality* (Canberra, Australian Institute of Criminology, 1987) 65.

[13] In 1997 the standard of proof for disciplinary matters was changed to the balance of probabilities.

[14] *Ibid.*

[15] I Freckleton, "Shooting the Messenger: The Trial and Execution of the Victorian Police Complaints Authority", in A Goldsmith (ed.), *Complaints Against the Police: The Trend to External Review*, *supra* n. 9.

officers and civilian members of the police department, but only after the police commissioner had first been given a reasonable opportunity to carry out his or her own investigation.[16]

In the United Kingdom, the establishment of the Police Complaints Board (PCB) in the mid 1970s saw an end to the police monopoly over the complaints process. However, in the bargaining process between police and government prior to the establishment of the PCB, considerable concessions were made to the police. For example, the investigative stage of the complaints process remained with the police.[17] Police also fought successfully to maintain the right to silence and criminal standard of proof in disciplinary hearings.[18] Even though non-police were now involved in dealing with complaints against police, their involvement was limited, and the extent of the limitation can be directly linked to police bargaining power.

In the mid 1980s the PCB was replaced by a more powerful oversight body, the Police Complaints Authority (PCA). But, it has also been a constrained watchdog. For many years police maintained virtual control of the investigative stage of the complaint process and the criminal standard of proof and right to silence remained for disciplinary matters. It took the PCA more than ten years to convince government that the standard of proof for disciplinary issues should be changed from beyond reasonable doubt to the balance of probabilities and that the right to silence in disciplinary inquiries should be modified.[19] These recent changes can hardly be described as radical or draconian policy, they only serve to bring police into line with their civilian colleagues and other professions.

For over twenty years the effectiveness of the civilian oversight process in Britain has been impeded by external factors beyond the oversight body's control. But the struggle is not over. The PCA is currently trying to persuade government that it should be allowed to use non-police as investigators,[20] a power which I have argued elsewhere is fundamental to effective oversight.[21]

In Toronto, Canada, it took the recommendations of six independent inquiries and reports into police conduct, within a period of five years, before a

16 I Freckleton and H Selby, "Piercing the Blue Veil: An Assessment of External Review of Police" in D Chappell and P Wilson (eds.), *Australian Policing: Contemporary Issues* (Sydney, Butterworths, 1989).

17 S Robbilliard and J McEwan, *Police Powers and the Individual* (Oxford, Blackwell, 1986).

18 D Humphry, "The Complaints System" in P Hain, D Humphry and B Rose-Smith (eds.), *Policing the Police Volume 1, The Complaints System: Police Powers and Terrorism Legislation*, *supra* n. 10.

19 Police Complaints Authority, Press Release, "Police Complaints Authority Welcomes Change to Police Disciplinary System", 23 March 1998. In disciplinary hearings, the modified version of the caution applies. In effect, it does not deny a person the right to remain silent but does allow an adverse inference to be drawn from silence in certain circumstances.

20 *Ibid.*

21 See Colleen Lewis, *Complaints Against Police: The Politics of Reform*, *supra* n. 5.

non-police element was introduced into the complaints process [22] and then it was initially only for a three-year trial period.[23]

Aspects of the legislation establishing the Office of Public Complaints Commissioner (OPCC) received widespread criticism. The ability of police to conduct the initial investigation was seen as a major and fundamental weakness in the new system, as was the application of the criminal standard of proof for disciplinary hearings. Regardless of how minor the alleged misconduct, it had to be proved beyond reasonable doubt.[24]

These few examples from different democratic societies reflect the outcome of police-government negotiations in many jurisdictions. They demonstrate that, faced with the inevitability of some form of civilian oversight, police can usually influence governments to limit the powers and functions of the oversight body. While the concessions won by police at the policy formation stage have varied from jurisdiction to jurisdiction, two have been particularly common. They are:

- that police maintain control of the crucially important initial investigative stage of the complaints process; and
- that the very high criminal standard of proof apply for all disciplinary matters including public complaints.

Police are trained investigators. Consequently, they are well aware of how important the initial stage of the investigative process is to a successful outcome. Through their work they also understand how difficult it is to secure a conviction on the criminal standard of proof. If police secure only these two concessions from government a civilian oversight body will initially and for some time thereafter operate at a grave disadvantage. It is difficult to believe that democratic governments are ignorant of this fact, yet many have, and in some instances

[22] In 1975 Arthur Maloney QC was appointed to conduct an inquiry into the police complaints system. He recommended that an independent civilian commissioner of complaints be appointed. Recommendations for an independent element were also made in three subsequent inquiries: the Morand Royal Commission into Metropolitan Toronto Police Practices (1976); the Pitman Inquiry into Race Relations (1977) and a study by Sidney Linden QC, commissioned to examine possible ways of introducing a civilian component into the handling of complaints against police. In 1979 a study on police-minority relations was conducted by a Catholic cardinal at the request of the Metropolitan Toronto Council. Again, civilian involvement in the complaints process was recommended. Clare Lewis, Sidney Linden and Judith Keene, "Public complaints against police in metropolitan Toronto: The history and operation of the office of the Public Complaints Commissioner", *supra* n. 9, 117–21.

[23] In 1984 the OPCC's temporary status became permanent and in 1990 its jurisdiction was extended to all of Ontario. T Landau, *Public Complaints Against the Police: A View from Complainants* (Toronto, Centre of Criminology, 1994). In 1996, the police complaints system was reviewed by the government and as a result, the complaints against police process was virtually returned to the police and the OPCC was closed down. Colleen Lewis, *Complaints Against Police: The Politics of Reform*, *supra* n. 5, 46–7.

[24] Clare Lewis, "Complaints in metropolitan Toronto: Perspectives of the Public Complaints Commissioner" in A Goldsmith (ed), *Complaints Against the Police: The Trend to External Review*, *supra* n. 9.

still are, establishing police accountability agencies which because of these restrictions are forced to operate with one hand tied behind their backs.

Clare Lewis a former Public Complaints Commissioner in Toronto agrees that "... initial police involvement can have considerable impact in shaping the ultimate result" of a complaint investigation.[25] He goes on to point out that "no other employee or professional group has the protection of the criminal burden of proof in employment or professional disciplinary hearings".[26] Nevertheless, Lewis argues that critics need to consider the "considerable turmoil" which surrounds the establishment and maintenance of a "non-traditional complaints structure".[27] Police organisations, he explains:

> ... are very hostile to efforts to increase their public accountability through civilian incursion into their disciplined service. While police in democratic societies are subject to the rule of law and state allegiances both to legal constraints on their authority and to their obligations to account to civilian masters, they also operate organisationally by much more informal rules understood within the institutions as more reflective and supportive of police attitudes and values.[28]

What democratically elected governments have to decide is whose opinions should influence the powers granted to civilian oversight bodies, the community or the police. It seems that in terms of the complaints against police process, the police have had an undue and negative influence on attempts to raise standards of police accountability beyond those acceptable to the police.

## BOUNDARIES OF PRESSURE GROUP POLITICS

It can be argued that the tactics used by police to gain concessions in the civilian oversight process are no different from those employed by many other pressure groups in democratic societies, particularly when the parameters of a policy are being established. Indeed, police behaviour, it could be said, is nothing more than democracy at work.

McLeay, referring specifically to the British police, argues that:

> All groups and governmental agencies behave similarly in that they attempt to define the policy areas which "belong" to them; they enclose new areas, attempt to impose limits on some and expand others. Groups which regard themselves as policy specialists are particularly adept at these sorts of tactical manoeuvres in the battle for issue territory.[29]

[25] *Ibid.*
[26] *Ibid.*, 160.
[27] *Ibid.*, 161.
[28] *Ibid.*, 161.
[29] E M McLeay, "Defining Policing Policies and the Political Agenda" 38 (4) *Political Studies*, 624.

Moreover,

> A cursory examination of the contemporary British police suggests that this occupational sector has joined the upper reaches of pluralist politicking and behaves rather like other state employees—teachers, nurses or prison officers.[30]

McLeay's observations need not be confined to British police, they are applicable to police in many other democratic societies. However, there is one important difference when comparing the pressure group tactics applied by police in terms of civilian oversight policies and those used by other government departments. The difference is not one of tactics but rather the issue which is the subject of negotiation and compromise.

Police union campaigns in relation to civilian oversight are not about industrial matters such as pay and conditions, downsizing or departmental restructuring, which usually concerns other powerful public sector unions and organisations when they engage in "pluralist politicking". As said before, the police campaign is about limiting police accountability. Governments are negotiating and compromising on a principle which is fundamental to democratic societies: establishing accountability mechanisms which can, when necessary, protect citizens' civil and human rights against the coercive arm of the state and/or expose the abusive behaviour of some police and hold them to account. Hence, another consideration for democratic governments is whether such an important and fundamental matter should form part of the bargaining process between the elected and appointed representatives of the people, or whether it should be exempt from pressure group politics?

Perhaps, Duncan Kerr's comments when he was Minister for Justice in the Australian Commonwealth Government go some way to addressing the question. As Kerr points out, when the community's expectations of police behaviour and actual police conduct do not coincide it is the government's duty to respond "in the interest of the community".[31]

Governments could claim they acted to give expression to the will of the people by removing the police monopoly over complaints. However, acquiescing to police demands by limiting the power and functions of an external (sometimes) independent civilian oversight body is not acting in the interests of the community, or good police governance, it is responding to the vested interests of the politically powerful police.

I am not arguing that police should have no input into police accountability policies, but rather to borrow the persuasive words of O'Rawe and Moore:

> Police knowledge and opinions must be accorded their place. However, this is not the criterion upon which a democratic society should base legislative decisions.[32]

[30] E M McLeay, "Defining Policing Policies and the Political Agenda" 38 (4) *Political Studies*, 624.

[31] D Kerr, "Government and the Police", in D Moore and R Wettenhall (eds.), *Keeping the Peace: Police Accountability and Oversight*, *supra* n. 8.

[32] M O'Rawe and L Moore, *Human Rights on Duty: Principles for Better Policing—International Lessons for Northern Ireland*, *supra* n. 6, 113.

This is particularly so when those legislative decisions are fundamental to democracy.

## ACCOMMODATION OF POLICE PERSPECTIVE

Government policy in relation to civilian oversight bodies appears to run counter to important principles which help to distinguish totalitarian and democratic regimes: the standards set by citizens for police behaviour and the accountability mechanisms then introduced by governments to encourage or coerce police into complying with those standards. But why do democratic governments accommodate the police perspective at the expense of effective accountability?

The answer lies in the special position police occupy in liberal democratic societies. Factors which contribute to that position have been debated at length. They include police discretion, police independence, the diversity of the policing function and the reciprocal nature of police-government relations, which as Bayley points out, leads to an intertwining of police and political life.[33] Combined, these factors give police a "privileged position"[34] in bureaucratic politics and as a pressure group.[35]

The "privileged position" of police is further strengthened when governments use them to prop up their strong law and order policies. This happened in Queensland, Australia, during the Bjelke-Petersen government's nineteen year term in office (1968–87). The government, with the willing cooperation of many police, tried to prevent citizens from exercising their right to peaceful protest. On several occasions police action more closely resembled that of a totalitarian force than a democratic service. Premier Bjelke-Petersen's disregard for the often violent actions used by police, and his refusal to hold them accountable for their actions, was made clear to all Queenslanders on several occasions.[36]

It seems that in the Queensland situation the *quid pro quo* for the police force's blind loyalty to government was deliberate blindness on the part of government to police behaviour. When such a relationship exists, the already "privileged position" of police is further enhanced and they become an even more powerful pressure group.

[33] D Bayley, *Patterns of Policing: A Comparative International Analysis* (New Brunswick, Rutgers, 1985) 189–211.

[34] When Lindblom discussed "privileged" positions he was referring to the economic power of business. C Lindblom, *Politics and Markets: The World's Political-Economic Systems* (New York, Basic Books, 1977) 170–88. The privileged position of police is not the same as business because business is able to make economic decisions independent of government and contrary to their wishes. But there are other types of privileged positions in terms of policy. As the enforcement arm of the state police enjoy a different but nevertheless privileged position.

[35] Colleen Lewis, *Complaints Against Police: The Politics of Reform*, *supra* n. 5, 51–2.

[36] *Courier-Mail*, 5 October 1976; Colleen Lewis, *Police Accountability Queensland Style*, Unpublished Honours Dissertation (Brisbane, Griffith University, 1988).

McLeay's examination of police as an interest group in the British state highlights a number of advantages police have when lobbying government about particular policy issues, including their "direct, uncomplicated access to government decision-making processes, deriving from institutional relationships".[37] Police are the internal keepers of the peace, maintainers of law and order and as McLeay points out:

> they seem to be regarded by governmental decision-makers as the key owners of specialised information on all sorts of issues relating to policing practices . . . Their expert knowledge is part of the regular policy process.[38]

Police have used their specialist knowledge on law and order issues, their easy access to governments and the other factors which help to make them privileged, to advance their position in the civilian oversight debate. Also because, as stated earlier, police power is usually exercised at the formulation stage of the policy process, their ability to influence in enhanced. At this point the oversight body is not yet an entity, consequently, it is largely left to civil liberties and minority groups and a few academics to oppose the police perspective on the powers and functions an external non-police body needs.

This accommodation of the police perspective results in oversight bodies continually having to play catch-ups in order to simply do the job they were (theoretically) established to do. Playing catch-ups is time-consuming, resource intensive and not always successful. Despite being in existence for many years, some oversight bodies are still asking for basic reactive powers, such as the right to conduct the initial investigation, to have "own motion" powers, for disciplinary matters to be decided on the civil standard of proof and to be able to appeal a disciplinary penalty imposed by a police commissioner/chief of police. Until civilian oversight bodies receive these basic reactive powers, citizens in some jurisdictions will continue to believe there is effective external scrutiny of police conduct, when the reality is quite different.

But, the power of the police to influence government policy is not the only problem confronting civilian oversight bodies. Once they are established, government attitudes and actions toward them can have serious consequences.

## UNDERMINING BY GOVERNMENTS

Governments can undermine an oversight body's ability to deliver effective police accountability in a number of ways.[39] As already discussed, they can deny the accountability institutions the powers they need to fulfil their citizens' watchdog role. They can also undermine an oversight body's credibility in the eyes of honest police and the community by making inappropriate appoint-

[37] E McLeay, "Defining Policing Policies and the Political Agenda", *supra* n. 29, 626.
[38] *Ibid.*, 628.
[39] Colleen Lewis, *Complaints Against Police: The Politics of Reform*, *supra* n. 5, 87–99.

ments to the civilian body. Appointments may be inappropriate in relation to a particular person but also in terms of the permanent occupation of those appointed as part-time members. For example, the head of a police union, or a union official would be placed in an obvious conflict of interest situation if they were also invited to serve as a member of an external oversight body; a fact which seems to have been overlooked or ignored by some governments.

Government can also undermine an oversight body's effectiveness by ignoring it. They do this when they decide not to comment on or debate issues raised in an agency's report. It is more difficult for them to ignore a police oversight body when it raises matters which capture the media's attention. When this happens, governments often choose to shoot the messenger rather than heed the message. This, it can be argued, is what happened to Victoria's Police Complaints Authority (PCA) when the government viewed it as a political liability.[40]

The Victorian government commissioned a report into the internal investigation department (IID) which involved looking at the relationship between the PCA and IID. The relationship was found to be poor and the recommendation made, that if the situation did not improve, the oversight of police complaints should be returned to the Ombudsman's office. The report's findings gave the government the reserve ammunition it needed to close the PCA at a time of its choosing, without being accused of putting party political concerns higher than effective police accountability. In this instance, shooting the messenger proved fatal for the controversial civilian oversight body.

Questioning the democratic requirement that police must respect the rule of law and abide by due process when dealing with all citizens not only undermines the credibility of an oversight body, it also questions the very reason it exists. This is particularly so when the minister responsible for police is the one doing the questioning.

In a recent address to fifteen hundred police officers, South Africa's Safety and Security Minister Steve Tshwete was reported as having "made promises that will send shivers down many spines".[41] One of those spines no doubt belongs to the Independent Complaints Directorate (ICD), the organisation established to oversight police conduct and raise accountability standards in South Africa. Tshwete recently announced that in future police would be dealing with criminals in the way "a bulldog deals with a bull" and if human rights bodies interfered he would "reason with them". He explained that he had already conducted discussions with the Independent Complaints Directorate and informed it that "We are not going to treat them [criminals] with kid gloves. We are going to make them feel like cowboys should not cry".[42] The minister

[40] I Freckleton, "Shooting the Messenger: The Trial and Execution of the Victorian Police Complaints Authority", in A Goldsmith (ed.), *Complaints Against the Police: The Trend to External Review*, *supra* n. 15.

[41] *Business Day South Africa*, 13 July 1999.

[42] *The Star*, 13 July 1999.

further commented, "Those who raise dust must not complain that they cannot see. We will unleash the police force on them".[43]

Tshwete also announced that if police were unhappy with sections of the Criminal Procedures Act which restricts police use of lethal force to situations where human life is at risk, he would look at it. If it was an impediment to police, he would approach parliament to have it amended. The minister went on to assure police that he did not want a situation where they felt timid.[44]

The message Tshwete's words sends to South Africa's police is a dangerous one. He runs the risk of at worst encouraging, and at best not discouraging, the type of human rights abuses perpetrated by police during the Apartheid era. He should also refrain from using the word "we" when addressing police. The minister is not a police officer, he is a member of a democratically elected government. His appointment as Minister of Safety and Security includes the democratic responsibility to ensure police actions are in accordance with due process and the rule of law.

Also, if the ICD is truly independent in terms of how it deals with complaints against police, it is out of order for the minister to be implying that this accountability institution should re-examine its standards and tolerate certain human rights abuses by police in the unproven belief that it may reduce South Africa's crime problem. Tshwete should be supporting the ICD's attempts to raise standards of police conduct by making police account for any abuse of human rights and due process, not the reverse. If the minister does not support and respect the job of the citizens' watchdog body, he should not be surprised if police behaviour slips back to pre-democracy standards where the police were often brutal instruments of state power.

Tshwete's unwise and unfortunate words have created a situation which has the potential to undermine the role of the ICD. It forced its then head, Advocate Neville Melville, to issue a statement saying that he hoped police did not interpret the minister's words as a licence to use excessive force where such force was not necessary.[45]

While many oversight bodies suffer to a greater or lesser extent from the various types of undermining mentioned above, lack of adequate resources is the common problem facing most agencies. It single-handedly can prevent them from performing to their full potential. The effectiveness of an independent police watchdog body is severely curtailed if public knowledge of its role or indeed its very existence is limited because the government failed to give it sufficient funds to operate, let alone conduct a public awareness campaign. Indeed some oversight bodies have questioned why they were established if they are unable to actively promote their role and functions.[46]

[43] *Business Day South Africa*, 13 July 1999.

[44] *Business Day South Africa*, 13 July 1999.

[45] *Sowetan*, 16 July 1999.

[46] New South Wales Ombudsman, *Special Report to Parliament Pursuant to Section 31 of the Ombudaman Act: The Effective Functioning of the Office of the Ombudsman* (Sydney, NSW Ombudsman, 1991).

Another resource related issue is staffing. A police oversight body has virtually no chance of success if it is under-staffed. This problem, which has beset many oversight bodies, manifests itself in a number of ways including not having sufficient people to conduct an investigation, despite having the power to do so.

Lack of expertise and corporate memory can also be a problem when levels of funding force oversight bodies to hire temporary staff just to keep functioning. In 1995, the Police Complaints Authority for South Australia, Peter Boyce, pointed out how the PCA had been the recipient for at least five years of "reactive piecemeal and bandaid responses to its urgent and continual requests for more funding and resourçes".[47] Because of the government's highly unsatisfactory response to the PCA's needs the Authority was forced to hire staff on short-term contracts. Not surprisingly, this resulted in a high staff turnover, which in turn created an extra burden on the already over-burdened few permanent staff.

Former Australian Commonwealth Ombudsman, Phillipa Smith, reported that her "greatest disappointment" while in office was the failure of government to provide adequate resources. Insufficient funds, she explained, meant that her office was unable to properly cater to the needs of those who complained and as a result was not fulfilling its statutory obligation. In the longer term this single factor, according to Smith, would undermine the credibility of the Commonwealth Ombudsman.[48]

Governments' attitudes to resourcing citizen watchdog bodies, including police oversight agencies, is taken up by Finn who points out that:

> governments herald the emergence of each new accountability institution as evidence of their commitment to democratic principles. However, they do not herald the reduction in resources to these bodies.[49]

To herald reductions would highlight the purely symbolic nature of many civilian oversight bodies. Poorly resourced accountability institutions can only create illusions of action. In effect, they are often maintaining the status quo which, over time, promotes cynicism about governments.

While lack of resources can have a devastating effect on the ability of civilian bodies to deliver effective police accountability, so too can establishing a biased inquiry to examine their role, functions and future direction.

In 1996 the Borbidge National-Liberal Party coalition government established an inquiry (commonly referred to as the Connolly-Ryan Inquiry) into the future role, structures, powers and operations of Queensland's (Australia) Criminal Justice Commission.[50] This was despite the fact that the all-party

[47] South Australia Police Complaints Authority, Annual Report 1992–4 (Adelaide, Government Printing Service, 1995).

[48] Commonwealth Ombudsman, *Twenty Years of the Commonwealth Ombudsman* 1977–97 (Canberra, AGPS, 1998).

[49] P Finn, "The Abuse of Public Power in Australia: Making our Governors our Servants", *supra* n. 1, 20.

[50] The Commission of Inquiry Pursuant to Orders in Council dated 7 October 1996 (Connolly-Ryan Inquiry).

Parliamentary Criminal Justice Committee has the statutory obligation to monitor and review the Criminal Justice Commission (CJC) every three years and to report its findings to parliament. Each parliamentary committee has diligently undertaken that task.

The Fitzgerald Report which was the catalyst for the establishment of the CJC deliberately recommended that "A standing parliamentary committee, not charged with any other responsibility" should oversee the Commission's operations and that the executive's relationship with the CJC should be confined to:

> what is necessary to finance it, provide administrative and resource needs, and that necessary for public financial and other accounting purposes.[51]

These recommendations were designed to try to exclude, or at least significantly reduce party political interference in the administration of criminal justice. The government's attempt to overturn this safeguard raises questions about its motives for establishing the inquiry. But the concerns do not stop there.

Once the inquiry into the Criminal Justice Commission was announced it was strongly suggested that, because of his close connection to the then police minister, it should not be chaired by former Queensland Supreme Court Judge, Peter Connolly QC.[52] Ignoring what subsequently proved to be wise advice, the government appointed Connolly as a commissioner.

The inquiry sat for ten months but never brought down a report. The reason is that approximately nine months after it commenced hearings, the Criminal Justice Commission, and others, instigated action in the Supreme Court alleging political bias on the part of the inquiry. On 5 August 1997, the Court made legal history by ruling that the Connolly-Ryan Inquiry be closed down. In his judgment Mr Justice Thomas stated, among other things, that:

> In view of the political controversy surrounding the creation of the Connolly-Ryan Inquiry and the issues which it examined, it was particularly important that the Commissioners be seen to be impartial and as not minded to serve the interests of one side or other of politics. There was a strong case of ostensible bias on the part of Mr Connolly such as would give rise in the mind of a fair-minded and informed member of the public to a reasonable apprehension of a lack of impartiality on his part with respect to the subject matter of the Inquiry. A similar fear would also reasonably arise in the minds of the plaintiffs.[53]

Justice Thomas disqualified Connolly and Ryan from proceeding any further and ordered that their inquiry be closed down.

Before its demise the inquiry cost the Queensland taxpayer eleven million dollars. The dollar cost to the CJC (which further increases the cost to tax-payers)

[51] Commission of Inquiry into Possible Illegal Activities and Associated Police Misconduct, *Report* (Brisbane, Queensland Government Printer, 1989) 309 (The Fitzgerald Report).

[52] *Courier-Mail*, 19 September 1996, 16; Colleen Lewis, "The Criminal Justice Commission: A Political Football?", 2 *Queensland Review*, 1–12.

[53] Criminal Justice Commission Annual Report 1997–8 (Brisbane, CJC, 1998) 96–9.

was approximately one and a half million dollars. It also absorbed in excess of seventeen thousand hours of CJC staff time, excluding that of the then Chairperson, Mr Frank Clair. The effect of this was outlined in the Criminal Justice Commission's 1997 Annual Report:

> This additional impost on the resources and energy of the organisation, over and above its normal demanding work, posed a significant threat of destabilisition—particularly against the background of budget cuts and resultant redundancies.[54]

Throughout its term in office much of the Borbidge government's energies appeared to be directed toward controlling the independent civilian oversight body which has a history of exposing issues politically embarrassing to the National-Liberal Party coalition. The government's strategy had negative spin-off effects on police accountability.[55] However, this did not seem to concern the government—or perhaps they were not interested in anything beyond destabilising the Criminal Justice Commission.

The Borbidge government's decision to establish the Connolly-Ryan Inquiry also raises the important question of who should monitor and review independent civilian oversight bodies; to whom should they account? This somewhat neglected issue needs to be addressed when trying to determine whether a civilian oversight policy is more than symbolic politics. This chapter concludes by evaluating three possible reporting options.

Before proceeding, the arguments raised below need to be put into the appropriate context. Liberal democratic societies do not necessarily share the same political systems. Australia, for example, has adapted the British Westminster system of responsible government while the United States of America operates according to a presidential system. While the issues raised here are framed in the context of the Westminister system, they are applicable to other political systems in liberal democratic societies. In other words, institutions may vary but the principle remains constant.

## SCRUTINISING CIVILIAN OVERSIGHT BODIES

Many commissions of inquiry and royal commissions in liberal democratic societies have confirmed that non-transparent, often secretive processes cannot deliver effective police accountability.[56] Nor can such processes ensure that civilian oversight bodies are held to account for the way they exercise their powers, or that these citizens' watchdog bodies are able to issue public reports on matters which are concerning them and/or impeding their effectiveness.

If for only these reasons, civilian oversight bodies should not be directly accountable to the executive, to governments or government bodies and if they

[54] Criminal Justice Commission Annual Report 1996–7 (Brisbane, CJC, 1997) 5.
[55] See Criminal Justice Commission, *The Impact of the Connolly-Ryan Inquiry on the Criminal Justice Commission* (Brisbane, CJC, 1998).
[56] Colleen Lewis, *Complaints Against Police: The Politics of Reform, supra* n. 5, 19.

are, they should not be called independent. In countries which adhere to the Westminster system of responsible government, accountability to the executive allows government to decide if and when a matter is made public. This results in politically controversial issues being swept under the non-transparent "Westminster carpet", which in turn means a deterioration in the quality of governance. At the very least, civilian oversight bodies should be accountable to the parliament, but preferably to all party parliamentary committees rather than to the "Committee of the Whole"—to the parliament as a whole.

## Reporting to Parliament

Even though in theory parliament is sovereign, many people, including former Speakers lament about the widening gap between theory and practice, and the implications it has for the relevancy of parliament. Strict adherence to a party political agenda means that it is increasingly difficult for parliament to perform its supervisory role.[57] In practice, it is dominated by the government, more precisely by the executive. As Emy and Hughes explain, tight party discipline has served to diminish "the significance and reality of debates in the parliament".[58]

Also the sheer size of the plenary "Committee of the Whole", which can range from sixty nine to six hundred and twenty nine members depending on the jurisdiction, precludes detailed discussion about many issues, as does the procedures and processes of the parliament.[59] Yet a detailed understanding of matters which come before the parliament is crucial if there is to be meaningful analysis of administrative practices and an informed discussion on policy matters.

## Advantages of Parliamentary Committees

Specialist parliamentary committees can go a long way to overcoming some of the problems experienced by the parliament.[60] Because committees are made up of back-bench MPs from all political parties, they provide an opportunity for issues to be considered in a bipartisan way. The adversarial nature of the parliament need not apply. The role of the chairperson is crucial in this regard. If he or she works toward fostering and developing a bipartisan committee that explores fundamental issues, the monitoring and review of the civilian oversight body and decision-making process of the parliamentary committee is enhanced.

[57] Electoral and Administrative Review Commission, *Report on Review of Parliamentary Committees, Volumes one and two* (Brisbane, EARC, 1992) 11.

[58] H Emy and O Hughes, *Australian Politics: Realities and Conflict* (Melbourne, Macmillan, 1988) 307.

[59] S Prasser quoted in Electoral and Administrative Review Commission, *Report on Review of Parliamentary Committees*, Volumes one and two, *supra* n. 57, 48.

[60] P Baines, "History and Rationale of the 1979 Reforms", in G Drewry (ed.), *The New Select Committees* (2nd ed.) (Oxford, Clarendon, 1989) 15.

Committees promote dialogue between political parties and allow back-benchers to contribute to policy formulation in a way which would otherwise be denied them. This can have a positive flow-on effect when issues to do with civilian oversight and police accountability are debated in the House.

Committees are able to gather the type of information that the "Committee as a Whole" cannot. They can hold public hearings, call witnesses, sift evidence, discuss a matter in detail and as a result, draw reasoned conclusions.[61] Their recommendations are tabled in the parliament and as such become public documents.

Wisdom does not reside solely within the bureaucracy and parliament.[62] A parliamentary committee's ability to call for public submissions on controversial or topical issues, such as the powers, functions or conduct of a civilian oversight body, promotes discussion and communication from interested groups ranging from trained experts to lay people (police, lawyers, civil liberty groups and concerned citizens). It also fosters discussion across disciplines (law, politics, social justice, human rights and public administration) and professions (lawyers, police and community workers).

A parliamentary committee can help give effect to an oversight body's recommendations. Many requests by oversight bodies for increased powers and more adequate resources are, after due consideration and analysis, supported by the parliamentary committee which monitors and reviews it.

Even if governments berate or ignore a committee's recommendations, the issues they raise can be resurrected at any time. While it is true that most committee reports lie on library shelves gathering dust, sometimes researchers brush off the dust and make politically embarrassing findings. These findings often draw attention to the fact that, had the suggestions of a particular parliamentary committee been implemented, the current problems could have been averted.

Parliamentary committees can be a cost effective means of obtaining information. Other forms of accountability, such as ad hoc commissions of inquiry, are very expensive as evidenced by the Connolly-Ryan Inquiry referred to earlier. Over the past two years, the Parliamentary Criminal Justice Committee has cost Queensland taxpayers approximately five hundred and thirty thousand dollars. This is at least nine million dollars less that the ten month Connolly-Ryan Inquiry.[63]

[61] Electoral and Administrative Review Commission, *Report on Review of Parliamentary Committees*, Volumes one and two, *supra* n. 57, 46–8.

[62] *Ibid.*, 48.

[63] Parliamentary Criminal Justice Committee Annual Reports 1996–7 and 1997–8 (Brisbane, Parliamentary Criminal Justice Committee).

## Necessary Powers and Functions

Parliamentary committees have the potential to provide a more effective form of scrutiny than the parliament as a whole. But like the civilian oversight bodies they monitor and review, they can be "hobbled" if their powers are limited.

In 1992 Queensland's Electoral and Administrative Review Commission conducted an extensive inquiry into the parliamentary committee system and found that parliamentary committees need to be able to:

- conduct public hearings, unless such hearings are deemed contrary to the public interest;
- have the power to examine witnesses;
- be able to obtain information and documents;
- investigate particular matters;
- form sub-committees;
- have their powers and functions upgraded to reflect changing circumstances;
- prepare reports and table them in the parliament; and
- have their reports debated by the parliament.[64]

These findings apply to committees which monitor and review oversight bodies.

## Impediments to Effectiveness

Being accountable to a parliamentary committee rather than parliament does not automatically ensure effective scrutiny of the civilian oversight process. A parliamentary committee's monitoring and review role can become politicised. Even a normally bipartisan committee can split along party lines if an issue is seen to be politically embarrassing or advantageous to one side of politics. When this happens the ability to objectively appraise an issue on its merits is abandoned, and the gap between theory and practice widens.

The gap also widens when back benchers abuse their position on controversial and powerful committees to try and enhance their public profile. Their tactics can include being as obnoxious and unhelpful as possible to some people called before the committee. This is done in the hope of attracting maximum media attention. These back benchers, whom I hasten to add constitute only a small minority of elected representatives, appear to suffer from the "any publicity is good publicity" syndrome.

Structural tensions between a parliamentary committee and the civilian oversight body it monitors and reviews, can also impede effective scrutiny. The Davies Parliamentary Criminal Justice Committee's conduct toward the Criminal Justice Commission on many occasions suggests it was intent on

[64] *Supra* n. 62, 41–4.

ensuring that the independent oversight body understood that ultimate power lay with the committee. It mistakenly interpreted its role as controlling the Criminal Justice Commission, rather than scrutinising the oversight body's functions, powers and actions. This kind of interpretation can be damaging to the civilian oversight process as parliamentary committees which scrutinise oversight bodies, are also obliged to review, monitor and make recommendations to the parliament on the oversight body's future role, functions and powers. The Davies Parliamentary Committee's behaviour often called into question its ability to conduct its legislatively required review of the Criminal Justice Commission in an objective fashion.[65]

As mentioned previously, lack of resources can impede an oversight body's ability to be effective. The same applies to parliamentary committees. Insufficient financial support, too few staff and not enough time to properly scrutinise the activities of a civilian oversight body,[66] prevent a committee from being effective. So too can spending limited resources on overseas "study tours" rather than on probing the activities of the civilian oversight body. Besides visiting several Australian States, Queensland's former Parliamentary Criminal Justice Committee, chaired by Vince Lester, also visited Wellington, Auckland, Washington DC, New York, London and Amsterdam.[67]

No system is perfect and parliamentary committees are no exception. But despite the problems highlighted above, a reporting line to government is not a credible alternative, if for no other reason than it contradicts the very reason oversight bodies exist: to foster transparent processes. While reporting to parliament as a whole is always the preferable alternative, its limitations in terms of effective scrutiny are considerable. Even though parliamentary committees are an imperfect solution to a vexed problem they at least offer the opportunity for maximum public input from all interested parties, which in theory at least, is a basic tenet of democracy.

## CONCLUSION

When governments in democratic societies establish external, independent, civilian oversight bodies it is assumed that they do so to improve rather than hinder police accountability. It is also assumed that they want these accountability bodies to be effective. Accordingly, citizens should be able to expect that civilian oversight bodies will receive the necessary powers, resources and support to allow them to adequately fulfil their charter and that these citizens'

[65] Colleen Lewis, "In support of the Criminal Justice Commission", 1 *Queensland Review*, 53–7.

[66] Commission of Inquiry into Possible Illegal Activities and Associated Police Misconduct, *Report* (Brisbane, AGPS, 1989) 124–5.

[67] Parliamentary Criminal Justice Committee, *Report on the visit to Washington DC, New York, London and Amsterdam*, Report no. 41, November 1997 (Brisbane, Parliamentary Criminal Justice Committee).

watchdogs will be monitored, reviewed and be able to report via the most transparent method possible.

But what if these assumptions do not hold? Does this mean that many democratic governments are not serious in their attempts to protect citizens' rights from abuse by the coercive agents of the state? If governments fail to give independent, external, civilian oversight bodies the necessary powers and resources to effectively oversight complaints against police, and/or if they deliberately try to undermine the credibility of the oversight body for perceived party political or personal advantage, are democratic governments merely hoodwinking citizens into believing they have introduced effective police accountability, when in reality they have not?

If, as this chapter suggests, many governments are not seriously committed to introducing and maintaining effective civilian oversight policies, further questions arise. For example, is it in a democratic government's best interest to introduce a policy which can seriously deal with police misconduct and improve police accountability, or given the power of the police and the symbiotic relationship between police and government, is it more logical for them to play "lip service" to principles of effective accountability? If the latter proves to be the case, what implications does this have for police accountability in emerging democracies?

There is no denying that civilian oversight comes at a price, but financially and in terms of creating and maintaining respect for individual rights and the rule of law it is a price worth paying. It is understood and accepted that governments have to prioritise competing demands on the public purse, but human rights and good governance should be given high priority when deciding what level of investment to commit to improving and maintaining effective police accountability. To do otherwise is to put at risk citizens' fundamental democratic entitlements.

# 2

# *Race, Democracy and Law: Civilian Review of Police in Washington, DC*

CHERYL BEATTIE and RONALD WEITZER

## INTRODUCTION

In 1995, Washington, DC's Civilian Complaint Review Board (CCRB) was abolished after thirteen years of operation. Years earlier, the CCRB's Executive Director described it as having been "designed to fail".[1] Given the history of strong police opposition to civilian review in the United States, one might presume that the board had, at its inception, been fatally compromised by concessions to the police, that it was an inherently "weak" board that finally gave way under police resistance. Ironically, the opposite is true.

When the CCRB was created in 1980 it was one of a handful of strong, "independent" review boards in the United States.[2] Other cities were incorporating civilians into the oversight of complaints, but often these mechanisms relied on police investigators, or civil servants to review cases, or had limited jurisdiction or powers. Civilians, representative of the community and appointed for limited terms, controlled Washington's CCRB. It had sole jurisdiction to conduct investigations into complaints of excessive force, harassment, and demeaning language; it could subpoena documents and witnesses; and it held hearings to decide cases and recommend punishment for officers.[3]

What accounts for the demise of the CCRB and what general lessons can be drawn from the operation of a board that once seemed so promising?

Case histories of civilian review boards often focus on group conflict: racial or ethnic minorities and civil rights advocates versus police unions and

[1] City Paper, 28 June 1991, p. 24.

[2] S Walker and V Bumphus, Civilian Review of the Police: A National Survey of the Fifty Largest Cities, 1991 (Omaha, NE, Department of Criminal Justice, University of Nebraska at Omaha, April 1991); D Perez, Police Accountability: A Question of Balance (PhD dissertation, University of California, Berkeley, 1978), p. 267.

[3] Except for boards of police commissioners, who function as police administrators, no civilian oversight mechanism in the United States supersedes the authority of the police executive to discipline officers. S Walker and V Bumphus, "The Effectiveness of Civilian Review: Observations on Recent Trends and New Issues Regarding the Civilian Review of the Police", 11 *American Journal of Police* 4.

administrators.[4] At times intense and dramatic, these conflicts are important in understanding the development and functioning of civilian review. Police resistance may be responsible for compromises in the design or powers of a board, may persuade government to limit resources or obstruct board operations. An exclusive focus on this and other kinds of social conflict, however, can overlook the deeper structural problems inherent in civilian review. We argue that civilian review is shaped not only by conflicts among groups, but also by fundamental tensions between democracy and law.

Analysts argue that police are caught in a structural dilemma, where equally legitimate but conflicting sets of principles and rules guide behaviour. Officers undertake a difficult balancing act in maintaining order within the constraints of the law.[5] We extend this insight to the operation of a particular form of civilian oversight of police: civilian review boards. That is, the agents of civilian review are similarly caught between the contradictory demands of law and democracy. Civilian review, especially the type of independent board that existed in Washington, is a forum for both legalistic adjudication of specific complaints and for the representation of diverse community interests. Members of review boards must be objective, impartial judges *and* represent, if not advocate for, their civilian constituencies. As one Washington resident put it: "I hope the review board is made up of people . . . who are able to look at the situation in an unbiased fashion. . . . Civilians view the situations differently than [the police] do, and we need someone to represent the opinion of civilians".[6]

The structural tension between law and democracy does not necessarily lead to review board failure. The "failure" and "success" of review boards depends on a great many factors, such as the extent of police opposition, funding, political support, and citizens' perceptions of the board. Structural problems reflect deeper, inherent dilemmas that shape the context in which actors succeed or fail.[7] The case of Washington is useful for exploring the effects of structural problems because group conflicts have been more subdued there than in other cities and Washington has a long history of experimenting with civilian review dating back to 1948. This long history reveals structural problems that underlie the vagaries of group conflicts.

[4] For example, D Abbott, L Gold, and E Rogowsky, Police, Politics and Race: The New York City Referendum on Civilian Review (New York, American Jewish Committee and The Joint Center for Urban Studies, 1969); I Freckelton, "Shooting the Messenger: The Trial and Execution of the Victorian Complaints Authority" in A Goldsmith (ed.), *Complaints Against the Police: The Trend Toward External Review* (Oxford, Clarendon Press, 1991); S Halpern, "Police Employee Organisations and Accountability Procedures in Three Cities: Some Reflections on Policy-Making", 8 *Law and Society Review*, 561.

[5] C Dandeker, *Surveillance, Power and Modernity* (New York, St. Martin's Press, 1990); L Lustgarten, *The Governance of the Police* (London, Sweet and Maxwell, 1986); H Packer, *The Limits of the Criminal Sanction* (Stanford, Cal., Stanford University Press, 1968); J Skolnick, *Justice Without Trial* (New York, John Wiley & Sons, 1966).

[6] Interview with a resident of Washington, DC, 1997.

[7] W Chambliss and R Seidman, *Law, Order and Power* (2nd ed.) (Reading, Mass., Addison-Wesley Publishing, 1982), pp. 144–9.

This is not to say that group conflict is not important in Washington. Racial conflict was the driving impetus behind the creation of Washington's first civilian review board in 1948 and the reforms to that board in 1965. But racial factors receded in importance with the advent of a predominantly black police department and city government. During the period of the CCRB's operation, 1982–95, the mayor's office, the city council, and the population of the city was predominantly African-American, politically liberal, and favourably disposed toward civilian review. Also the police department was majority black. The familiar conflict between black civilians and white police cannot readily account for the demise of this board.

In the following section, we review the history of civilian review in Washington, drawing on secondary sources, newspapers and archival documents. We then turn to the 1982–95 period. Our sources for this period are official reports, observations of CCRB hearings, and interviews with the board members, investigators, and police representatives.

### THE CRB: 1948–73

Washington in the 1940s was racially segregated and white-dominated. A three-man Board of Commissioners led the city government. The Board of Commissioners, the Superintendent of Police, and other city leaders were white, while Washington's black population was, proportionately, the largest of any major US city (twenty eight per cent). Many blacks were middle-class and employed by the federal government. Although the absence of an elected local government made participation in electoral politics moot for all city residents, African-Americans in Washington did engage in local protest politics.[8]

Alerted by a national concern with racism and police brutality,[9] Washington chapters of the Urban League and the National Conference of Christians and Jews "watched police methods with growing apprehension".[10] By December 1947, following a number of cases where police use of force was questioned, Washington residents became similarly apprehensive. A *Washington Post* poll showed that two thirds of residents could recall reading criticisms of the police in the press, nearly half recalled allegations of brutality. When asked if they thought the criticisms were justified, sixty-three per cent of all respondents said they believed they were. Black respondents were especially inclined to believe

[8] For example, L Wittner, "The National Negro Congress: A Reassessment", Winter 1970 *American Quarterly* 888, M. Pacifico, " 'Don't Buy Where You can't Work': The New Negro Alliance of Washington", 6 *Washington History* 67.

[9] United States, President's Committee on Civil Rights, *To Secure These Rights: The Report of the President's Committee on Civil Rights* (Washington DC, Government Printing Office, 1947)

[10] C Green, *The Secret City: A History of Race Relations in the Nation's Capital* (Princeton, N.J., Princeton University Press, 1967), p. 288.

criticism of the police: eighty-one per cent of those who could recall specific criticisms believed they were justified.[11]

One such publicised event prior to the *Washington Post* poll was the 1947 arrest of Julius Clegg. Clegg was an African-American war veteran and an employee of the *Washington Post* who was arrested for harassing a white woman on a city street. Clegg denied the charges and alleged that police detectives had struck him during an interrogation. The inquiry that followed revealed flaws in the department's disciplinary procedures and underscored the particular threat that civilian complaints presented to the department's reputation. In addition, Clegg's attorney, the *Washington Post*, and others demanded that civilians, not the police, consider whether or not the officers involved should be disciplined for misconduct.[12]

In October 1948, regulations regarding civilian complaints were revised, establishing the Complaint Review Board (CRB), which would function as a sort of grand jury—that is, the board would decide whether or not an accused officer should appear before a department tribunal. The new regulations also created the Special Police Trial Board (SPTB), a police department tribunal specifically called into action for civilian complaints against police officers. The CRB was composed of three residents of the city, excluding municipal employees or officials, appointed by the District Commissioners.[13] Upon the request of the Superintendent of Police, the CRB would determine if a civilian complaint merited consideration by a SPTB. The SPTB, which was composed of two police officials and a civilian attorney drawn from names supplied by the local Bar associations, would decide if a complaint should be sustained.[14]

Officials expected that the CRB would help to deflect claims that police were using disciplinary procedures to cover-up abuses, but it made few concessions to the interests of black residents. The Board of Commissioners appointed three white men active in business and community affairs to the CRB. For the civilian slot on the SPTB names were accepted from the predominantly black Washington Bar Association as well as the whites-only District of Columbia Bar Association. In practice neither the CRB nor the SPTB was very active. The CRB reviewed only fifty-four cases in its first seventeen years of operation (1948–64).[15] The vast majority of civilian complaints were handled as they had been prior to the formation of the board, by precinct sergeants and other supervisory officers.

The CRB had little power or status (see Table 1, below at p. 48). It had no staff, offices, stationery, or independent power to receive or investigate complaints; instead, the Superintendent of Police referred complaints to the board.

[11] *Washington Post*, 1 December 1947, p. A1.

[12] *Washington Post*, 12 February 1948, p. B1.

[13] *Times-Herald*, 2 October 1948, p. 7.

[14] The decisions of all trial boards were subject to the approval of the Superintendent and the District Commissioners.

[15] President's Commission of Crime in the District of Columbia, *Report* (Washington, DC, Government Printing Office, 1966), p. 218.

Regulations did not specify any criteria for selection. A review of the surviving records suggests that department officials referred cases they believed needed the imprimatur of an external and ostensibly objective body.[16] Of sixty-eight known cases considered by the CRB from 1948 to 1965, the board recommended that officers be brought before a trial board in at least sixteen (twenty-four per cent).[17] The SPTB should have handled all sixteen cases, but the department sometimes overlooked it and placed cases before the regular Police Trial Boards, manned only by police officials.[18]

In general, both activists and city officials ignored the CRB, even though African-American organisations in Washington sporadically protested alleged incidents of police brutality through the 1950s. By 1964, however, both the national and local Washington context changed dramatically. The issue of police brutality was becoming increasingly important to the civil rights movement, both because activists were themselves the targets of police violence and because it was an issue that might win support from inner-city blacks as the movement expanded.[19] The "first wave" of the civilian review movement had also swept the country. Following the successful creation of a citizen review board in Philadelphia in 1958, the American Civil Liberties Union, often in cooperation with local African-American civil rights groups, led a campaign in cities across the nation to establish civilian review boards in 1960 and 1961.[20]

In this context, the CRB came under critical scrutiny. A review of complaints procedures published in 1964 observed that, "the utility of the District of Columbia Complaint Review Board is questionable" as "its limited jurisdiction and authority . . . cannot provide more than a mere illusion of civilian control".[21] That same year the National Capital Area Civil Liberties Union (NCACLU) reported that the police department was discouraging complaints by charging civilians with filing a false police report if their complaints were not sustained.[22] NCACLU demanded reforms in the complaint process and to the CRB.

In the US the "first wave" of civilian oversight combined democracy and law by advocating the creation of panels of citizens representative of a city's majority and minority groups that would have the authority to adjudicate

16 C Beattie Repetti, "The Politics of Civilian Review: Police Accountability in Washington DC and New York City, 1948–1974" (PhD dissertation, George Washington University, 1997), pp. 169–70.

17 President's Commission of Crime in the District of Columbia, *Report.* (Washington, DC: Government Printing Office, 1966), p. 218.

18 C Beattie Repetti, *supra* n. 16, pp. 169–70.

19 D McAdam, *Political Process and the Development of Black Insurgency* (Chicago, University of Chicago Press, 1982), pp. 153, 187; A Meier and E Rudwick, *CORE: A Study in the Civil Rights Movement 1942–1968* (New York, Oxford University Press, 1973) pp. 194–5.

20 L Brown, "Police Review Boards: An Historical and Critical Analysis", 10 *Police* 21; H Beral and M Sisk, "The Administration of Complaints by Civilians Against the Police", 77 *Harvard Law Review* 511.

21 H Beral and M Sisk, *supra* n. 20, p. 510.

22 *Evening Star*, 14 June 1964, p. B1.

civilian complaints against the police. To increase the Washington board's representation of diverse groups, NCACLU proposed that the CRB be expanded from three to nine members. They also proposed that the powers of the board should be expanded to include receipt and investigation of complaints and recommendations for discipline. Envisioning a more adversarial forum for the hearing of evidence, NCACLU also recommended that board members should include a number of practising attorneys.[23]

These proposals, made in 1964, were seriously entertained by the city government, which was worried about urban unrest. The summer of 1964 marked the beginning of four years of urban riots in the US, which were due in part to hostility between ghetto residents and the police.[24] Perhaps unrealistically, many advocates believed that civilian review could help prevent unrest by providing "some agency outside the police department where the Negro can feel he will get an even break with the white man".[25] Civilian review would function as an alternative to violence for resolving grievances against the police, particularly if the board had representatives from minority communities and independence from the police. Washington was also undergoing a significant demographic shift: in 1960 it became the nation's first major city with a majority-black population (about fifty-five per cent of the city's residents). The city government and the police department, however, were still dominated by whites: about eighty per cent of the officers were white in 1966.

A biracial committee appointed by the Police Chief considered NCACLU's proposed reforms. The committee included a number of well-known civil rights leaders who had criticised the police in the past. Following the committee's recommendations, the membership of the CRB was expanded in 1965 from three to five (see Table 1, below at p. 48). In contrast to 1948, the citizens appointed were active in civil rights organisations and included African-Americans. At CRB hearings accused officers now had the right to legal counsel and cross-examination of witnesses. Two of the new members were attorneys who were expected to make evidentiary and procedural rulings at the hearings. The CRB would then vote to recommend to the Chief and the Board of Commissioners[26] (who had final authority) whether a complaint should be dismissed or if disciplinary action should be taken (the CRB could also recommend dismissal or disciplinary action without first holding a hearing). The police department would continue to investigate complaints and to handle internally complaints brought to a local police station.

Though improved over the old CRB, the new board lacked the more radical reforms proposed by NCACLU. This was largely a consequence of police resistance and broader racial conflicts. The Police Association publicly opposed

[23] *Evening Star*, 14 June 1964, p. B1.

[24] National Advisory Commission on Civil Disorders, *Report of the National Advisory Commission on Civil Disorders* (New York, Bantam Books, 1968), p. 299.

[25] Seattle NAACP Chapter President June Smith quoted in *Evening Star*, 22 August 1965, p. A19. See also, *New York Times*, 31 October 1966, pp. 1, 39.

[26] The Board of Commissioners functioned as the chief executive officers of the city government.

NCACLU's proposals, especially its recommendation that a civilian investigator be hired. But the Chief's committee was swayed less by these objections than by its concern to avoid Congressional intervention. Hiring an investigator, for example, would have been subject to the approval of the Congressional committees that oversee the District of Columbia, which, at this time, included some rather outspoken racists.[27] The Police Chief did not oppose his committee's recommendations, but he took steps to ensure that most of the complaints brought to the local precincts would continue to be handled as in the past. Thus the CRB operated only as an alternative forum for difficult cases and savvy complainants.

Police resistance and the racial and political turmoil during the 1960s similarly contributed to undermining the operations of the reformed CRB. Police opposition was not publicly visible, but it was evident in their control of investigations. Concerned that citizens were dissuaded from filing complaints because police controlled complaint investigations, local activists and CRB members requested that civilians conduct investigations. The city government took no action, but the Police Chief did assign responsibility for complaint investigations to the Internal Affairs Unit. Ostensibly, this was done to improve the impartiality of investigation, but in practice it only resulted in lengthy delays.[28]

Public criticisms of the CRB came, not from the police, but from Washington's growing African-American activist and community groups. Dissatisfied with the CRB's weaknesses or interested in more radical alternatives such as community control of police, activists and community leaders did not refer complainants to the board. Some, such as future mayor Marion Barry, created their own ad hoc forums to address grievances against the mostly white police force. CRB board members joined activists in requesting reforms and greater resources from the city government but their requests were generally ignored. With increasing crime and concern about urban unrest (dramatised by riots in Washington in 1968), the government was reluctant to interfere too much with the police.[29] The CRB was also hampered by the structural tension between law and democracy inherent in this form of civilian review. The reforms had both expanded the democratic representativeness of the board and enhanced the legal formality of the review proceedings. To an extent, the expansion of due process rights was a means of assuring officers that the process would be fair, but it could also be justified as an end in its own right. That is, civilian review advocates, police, and others saw due process rights as being good in principle. But they are also costly, in terms of attorneys' fees and time.

[27] Letter from F Joseph Donohue and George E C Hayes to Walter L Trobriner, 18 November 1964, Records of the Government of the District of Columbia, Record Group 351, File 4–294a, National Archives, Washington, DC.

[28] *Evening Star*, 20 May, 1966, p. B1. 18 July 1967, p. B1. See also *Washington Post*, 2 March 1973, p. C1.

[29] C Beattie Repetti, *supra* n. 16, pp. 260–75, 278–80, 287–91.

**Table 1** Civilian Review Boards in Washington, D.C.

| Review Board | Created by Legislation? | Members | Complaint Investigators | Powers |
|---|---|---|---|---|
| Complaint Review Board (CRB), 1948–1964 | No | 3 civilians | Local police officers | Received complaints referred by police department; recommended if complaint should be heard by department tribunal. |
| Complaint Review Board (CRB), 1965–1973 | No | 5 civilians (2 attorneys) | Internal Affairs Unit | Received complaints referred by police department and from civilians; recommended if complaint should be heard by department tribunal. |
| Civilian Complaint Review Board (CCRB), 1980–1992 | Yes | 5 civilians (2 attorneys) 2 police officers | Civilian CCRB staff | Jurisdiction over complaints of excessive force, demeaning language, and harassment; adjudicated via hearing only; recommended disciplinary action. |
| Civilian Complaint Review Board (CCRB), 1992–1995 | Yes | 3 7-member panels of civilians and police | Civilian CCRB staff | urisdiction over complaints of excessive force, demeaning language, and harassment; adjudicated via hearing, summary review, or conciliation; recommended disciplinary action. |
| Office of Citizen Complaint Review (OCCR), 1998– | Yes | 4 civilians 1 police officer | Civilian OCCR staff | urisdiction over complaints of excessive force, demeaning language, harassment, discrimination, and retaliation for filing a complaint; adjudicates via hearing, summary review, conciliation or mediation. |

Because of these constraints, shortly after it began to operate, the CRB announced that citizens could opt to appear before the board informally to tell their stories.[30] Community activists had criticised the board for being inaccessible and removed from troubled communities. More informal procedures were a means by which the board might reach out to complainants and assure them that, as the CRB Chairman said, "there is an agency in the government whose task is to lend an ear to any citizen who complains of abusive conduct by a policeman".[31] But less formal proceedings left the CRB vulnerable to charges of denying officers due process. For example, when the board recommended that three officers be disciplined after a summary review of a complaint (based on medical reports and the police investigation report), the attorney for the accused officers objected because no hearing had been held. The Board of Commissioners agreed and the CRB was compelled to schedule a hearing.[32]

The CRB was thus caught, as one board member said, between "establishing confidence on the part of citizens that the police are not overreaching themselves and, on the other hand, giving the Police Department assurance it will not be handicapped by complaints"[33]—a dilemma faced by all review boards. The city government was caught in the same problem and thus found the CRB, as one city official said, "awkward to keep and awkward to get rid of".[34] Frustrated with the board's ineffectiveness, members resigned in 1973, ending Washington's first attempt at civilian oversight. A decade later, however, the idea of a civilian review board was revived.

## THE CCRB: 1982–95

### The Revival of Civilian Review

The racial conflicts that drove the development of the "first wave" of civilian review boards in the United States also led to a backlash against them. Urban riots alienated whites and justified the expansion of police activity in the name of restoring "law and order."[35] Civilian review appeared to be a dead issue.[36] But during the 1970s and 1980s, "governments quietly created mechanisms external to the police for receiving and investigating complaints".[37] One likely reason for this "quiet" expansion of civilian oversight is the rapid increase in the number of African-American elected officials during this period. Another reason is a

[30] *Evening Star*, 31 October 1965, p. K1.

[31] *Ibid.*

[32] *Evening Star*, 19 May 1966, p. A1; 22 May, p. B2; 26 May, p. B1.

[33] *Evening Star*, 27 April 1966, p. D1.

[34] *Washington Post*, 18 September 1972, p. C1.

[35] J Button, *Black Violence: Political Impact of the 1960s Riots* (Princeton NJ, Princeton University Press, 1978), pp. 108–55.

[36] R Fogelson, *Big City Police* (Cambridge Mass., Harvard University Press, 1977), p. 286.

[37] D Bayley, "Preface" in A Goldsmith (ed.), *Complaints Against the Police: The Trend to External Review* (Oxford, Clarendon Press, 1991), p. vi.

change in police perception of civilian oversight, at least among police administrators.[38] Both factors are evident in the creation of the Civilian Complaint Review Board (CCRB) in Washington.

Home rule was established in Washington in 1974, allowing residents to elect a city council and mayor. The city council considered proposals for re-establishing some form of civilian review during the 1970s but no legislation passed until 1980, after the election of Mayor Marion Barry. Like many of the members of the city council, Barry made his reputation in Washington as a civil rights activist and critic of the police department.[39] The police force he presided over as mayor, however, was different from the department Barry had confronted as an activist. White officers were still in the majority in 1980, but black officers made up nearly half the force. Burtell Jefferson became the department's first African-American Chief of Police in 1977, and the police union endorsed Barry's 1978 election bid.

In the summer of 1979 a number of stories criticising the department's handling of civilian complaints appeared in the press. A department study showed that it received, on average, nearly one complaint per day and sustained eight per cent of the complaints it investigated. Chief Jefferson told reporters that he discussed the possible revival of the civilian review board with Mayor Barry and would "welcome" its return.[40] Before the year was over, two Bills proposing the creation of civilian oversight mechanisms were being discussed by the city council.[41]

In contrast to the justifications advanced for civilian review in the mid-1960s, city officials did not anticipate that the board was needed to function as a "safety valve" to prevent civil unrest. Indeed, the Barry administration projected that most complaints received by the board would not be serious.[42] City officials favoured the creation of the board because they believed the police handled complaints poorly resulting in a small number of sustained complaints and contributing to an increase in the number of successful civil suits brought against the city for police brutality. They also believed in the principle of external civilian review.[43]

[38] D Bayley, *ibid*, pp. vii–xi; R Browning, D Marshall and D Tabb, *Protest is Not Enough: The Struggle of Blacks and Hispanics for Equality in Urban Politics* (Berkeley, University of California Press, 1984), p. 155.

[39] C Harris and A Thornton, *Perspectives of Political Power in the District of Columbia* (Washington DC, National Institute of Public Management, 1981), pp. 101–10.

[40] *Washington Post*, 26 July 1979, p. B7.

[41] These were Bills 3–214, "Human Rights Act of 1977 Amendments of 1979/1980", and 3–247, "Complaint Review Board Act of 1980".

[42] Testimony of Elizabeth Reveal, Executive Director of the Office of Criminal Justice Plans and Analysis, at Joint Hearing by Committee on the Judiciary and Committee on Public Services and Consumer Affairs, Council of the District of Columbia, on Bill 3–247, "Civilian Complaint Review Board Act of 1980" and Bill 3–214, "Human Rights Act of 1977 Amendments of 1980", 26 March 1980, Audio Tape, District of Columbia Legislative Services Division, Washington, DC.

[43] Memorandum from Ivanhoe Donaldson, General Assistant to the Mayor to Mayor Marion Barry, re. Civilian Complaint Review Board, 13 November 1979; Memorandum from Wilhelmina Rolark, Chairperson, Committee Public Services and Consumer Affairs to Council of the District of Columbia re. Bill 3–247, "Civilian Complaint Review Board Act of 1980", 22 July 1980;

Despite the Chief's endorsement, most members of the police force objected to the proposed board, but opposition was milder than in other cities. The police union staged no public demonstrations against the proposed CCRB, nor did they, as New York City police officers had, organise a referendum to stop the board. By this time in Washington there was no constituency that might be rallied by such appeals, such as a population of working-class whites, nor was there much support for the police union among local politicians. As a union official explained: "people . . . running for council . . . all say the board is a fact of life".[44]

The Civilian Complaint Review Board Act was passed in 1980. Like the reformed CRB of 1965, the new Civilian Complaint Review Board (CCRB) empowered a panel of citizens representative of the community to adjudicate complaints (see Table 1, above at p. 48). The CCRB was required to adjudicate all non-frivolous cases by means of a full evidentiary hearing with rights to representation and cross-examination. In her endorsement of the CCRB legislation, Councilwoman Rolark wrote that the CCRB "protects the civil rights of the public with a fair system that respects the rights of the accused". As important as the due process rights, the hearings were expected to provide a public forum for the airing of complaints, a feature city officials contrasted with the "secretive" handling of complaints within the police department. To this end, the legislation required that hearings be open to the public. Rolark said she expected that the board would "receive considerable public scrutiny and evaluation".[45]

City officials also believed that "public involvement in the review of citizen complaints" was "a key feature" of the CCRB.[46] A panel of seven voting members, the majority of whom were civilians, would review complaints. The mayor would appoint three members and the city council would appoint two. Two of the five civilian members would be attorneys who would function as Chair and Vice-Chair of the board and make rulings on evidence and procedures. As a concession to police interests, two officers would also sit on the review panel and cast votes to decide cases: one appointed by the police chief and one by the police union.

Unlike the CRB, the new board was given sole jurisdiction over complaints of excessive force, harassment, and demeaning language. The police department could not, as it had with the old CRB, operate an alternative system and thus marginalise the board. Moreover, this exclusive jurisdiction extended to the

Memorandum from David Clarke, Chairperson, Committee on the Judiciary to Members of the Council of the District of Columbia, re. Bill 3–247, the "Civilian Complaint Review Board Act of 1980", 10 September 1980, Legislative History of Bill 3–247, District of Columbia Legislative Services Division, Washington, DC; Statements by Council members David Clarke and Wilhelmina Rolark, and testimony of Elizabeth Reveal, n. 42 *supra*.

[44] Interview with police union representative, 24 November 1991, Washington, DC.

[45] Council of the City of the District of Columbia, Committee on Public Services and Consumer Affairs, W Rolark Chair, Comments Concerning Bill 3–247, 22 July 1980.

[46] Council of the District of Columbia, Committee on the Judiciary, D Clarke, Chair, "Civilian Complaint Review Board's Legislative History", 10 September 1980.

investigation of complaints, which would be conducted by CCRB staff. In addition, board members were immunised against libel and slander suits to prevent police groups "intimidating and silencing those who cry out for police accountability".[47] Barry's administration was optimistic about the new board. As one administration official declared to the mayor, "We are the beneficiaries of prior mistakes. . . . The legislation . . . will avoid the pitfalls of the past".[48]

## Operating Dilemmas

Fiscal problems in 1980 delayed funding of the board until June 1982. Once the board was operational, it operated quietly until the *Washington Post* published a story in 1987 about a backlog of nearly one thousand cases and noted that, as a result, errant officers were not being disciplined and continued to patrol city streets.[49] CCRB staff responded by proposing amendments to the CCRB legislation so that some cases might be resolved by conciliation and the processing of others be expedited by the operation of a number of smaller review panels working in parallel. Despite repeated requests from the CCRB, the city council took no action.[50] In 1991, a succession of incidents of alleged police abuse, including the shooting of a Latino man that sparked a riot, prompted the mayor and city council into passing emergency legislation (in 1992) to deal with the backlog. The review panel was expanded to twenty-one members and given new powers to decide cases summarily without a hearing and to conciliate less serious cases (see Table 1, above). These changes improved the rate at which complaints were processed but did not dramatically reduce the backlog. In April 1995, facing a very serious fiscal crisis, the city council voted to abolish the CCRB, explaining that "it just doesn't make sense to fund an agency that is ineffective".[51] When the board closed its doors a month later, some seven hundred and seventy pending cases, most more than two years old, were turned over to the police department.[52]

The primary cause of the board's backlog—at least until 1992—was the requirement that complaints be resolved through a formal hearing.[53] Hearings

[47] Council of the City of the District of Columbia, Committee on Public Services and Consumer Affairs, W Rolark Chair, Comments Concerning Bill 3–247, 22 July 1980.

[48] Memorandum from Ivanhoe Donaldson, General Assistant to the Mayor to Mayor Marion Barry, re. Civilian Complaint Review Board, 13 November 1979, Legislative History of Bill 3–247, District of Columbia Legislative Services Division, Washington, DC.

[49] District of Columbia, Civilian Complaint Review Board, Statistical Reports, 1985, 1986, 1987; *Washington Post*, 30 November 1987.

[50] *City Paper*, 27 March 1992, pp. 19–21; *Washington Post*, 18 December 1987; 11 July 1989, p. B3; 27 September 1991, A28; 9 July 1992, B5.

[51] *Washington Post*, 16 April 1995, p. B1; Field notes on Council of the District of Columbia Budget Hearings, 18 April 1995.

[52] *Washington Post*, 25 June 1995, B3.

[53] Piper and Marbury, *Analysis of the District of Columbia's Civilian Complaint Review Board and Recommendations for its Replacement: A Report Prepared for the American Civil Liberties Union of the* National Capital Area (Washington, DC., National Capital Area Civil Liberties Union, 1995), p. 3.

are inherently cumbersome and costly, but the CCRB's hearing process was further limited by the "democratic" nature of the panel. The board's members were chosen to reflect the interests of Washington's diverse communities. But as volunteers, who had full-time jobs and interests apart from the CCRB, there was a limit to the time they could offer the board.[54] Consequently hearings were generally held once or twice a week on weekday evenings. Furthermore, one or two of the civilian panelists were often absent. Since four panelists constituted a quorum, this did not interfere with holding a hearing, but it did undermine the influence of the civilian majority on the panel because the police officers appeared regularly as part of their assigned duties.

From 1982 to 1991, the seven-member panel held fifty-five hearings a year, on average, against an annual average of three hundred and fifty four complaints received.[55] At this rate the mountain of back-logged cases could only grow higher every year as the number of frustrated complainants multiplied.

Had the city government taken action to expand the board and permit conciliation and summary adjudication prior to 1992, it is possible that the board might have reduced its backlog and avoided abolition. The council remained committed to civilian review, but the board requests for new powers and resources were stymied by political struggles inside and outside the board. That is, council members' interests influenced some board members and affected the operation of the board. The following episode further illustrates tensions between the operation of the board as a mechanism for the adjudication of complaints and democracy.

Shortly after the CCRB presented its proposed changes to the city council, attorney Kimi Morten was appointed to the position of chair of the review panel. She became the centre of conflict among the panelists, between the CCRB and certain key council members, and between the board and the police union. Morten described herself as "an advocate for the rights of citizens who have been victims of police brutality" and said she "quickly pushed for improvements to correct what I perceived to be a board bias against citizens/complainants".[56] She also pushed to have the board relocated to an area of the city represented by a powerful council member, believed to be responsible for her appointment.[57] Morten's chairmanship generated what one board member described as a "conservative/liberal conflict" within the CCRB.[58] Her colleagues on the board eventually removed her because of her "inability to hold fair and impartial

[54] Interview with CCRB staff member, April 1992, Washington, DC.

[55] This average reflects the "normal" operations of the board. It might be lower if data from the years the board was preoccupied with an internal dispute were included, but reports from these years are not available. District of Columbia, Civilian Complaint Review Board, Statistical Report for 1985, 1986, 1987, 1990, 1991.

[56] Letter to the Editor from Kimi Morten, *Washington Post*, 23 August 1989, A26.

[57] Interview with CCRB panel members, 20 May and 6 July 1992, Washington, DC.

[58] Interview with CCRB panel member, 20 May, 1992, Washington, DC.

hearings",[59] but Mayor Barry reinstated her.[60] When the case backlog remained unchanged despite efforts to increase the number of hearings held and the internal conflict persisted, Barry reversed himself and fired Morten.[61] Subsequently, the CCRB's requests for reforms went unheeded until relations between the CCRB and Morten's powerful patron on the city council were repaired a number of years later.[62]

The democratic structure of independent review boards makes it possible for them to become fora for various political conflicts. Conflicts over the creation of civilian review may also be recapitulated once it is operational. For example, Morten blamed the police union for the CCRB's failings and for the internal conflict regarding her chairmanship. Similarly New York City's all civilian complaint board has been troubled by alleged "pro-police" appointments of former prosecutors to replace departing members who had backgrounds in community activism.[63] Such conflicts are typical of democratic processes, but the significant "politicisation" of a review board undermines its claims to impartial judgment. As an experienced civilian member of the CCRB commented:

> when you've been there for awhile . . . you can see the politics actually playing there. [Politics] should not be there because they're supposed to be objective, and make sure you're a representative of the constituency of the people who appoint you, but theoretically, you're not supposed to be representing that, you're supposed to have a fair mind when you go in there.[64]

This comment nicely captures the tension between objective legal process and democratic political interests.

To what extent was Morten correct in blaming the police union for the CCRB's difficulties? The union disliked the board and was criticised for refusing to "cooperate" with it. When the CCRB first began to operate, the union openly resisted and encouraged its members to boycott the board by failing to appear when summoned to hearings. The CCRB succeeded in breaking the boycott by holding hearings in absentia. As a CCRB staff member explained: "After a year or so the officers decided to come back. They'd rather fight then lose in abstention".[65] A union representative confirmed this, explaining that one of the lessons he had learned from his experiences with the board was not to boycott it: "Don't do that; if you don't play the game you can't get any points at all".[66]

"Playing the game" is precisely what the union did: much of what has been interpreted as "lack of cooperation" might alternatively be interpreted as

[59] The International Association for Civilian Oversight of Law Enforcement, Proceedings of the Sixth Annual Conference (Washington, DC, 4–7 September 1990), p. 254; Letter to the Editor from Kimi Morten, *Washington Post*, 23 August 1989, A26.

[60] *Washington Post*, 11 July 1989, B3.

[61] *Washington Post*, 10 August 1989, D3.

[62] *City Paper*, 27 March 1992, pp. 19–21.

[63] *New York Times*, 20 November 1995, B3.

[64] Interview with civilian CCRB panel member, 6 July 1992, Washington, DC.

[65] Interview with CCRB staff member, April 1992, Washington, DC.

[66] Interview with police union representative, November 1991, Washington, DC.

"staunch advocacy". Like good defence attorneys, the union exploited every opportunity presented in the rules governing the CCRB, exercised every right officers had, and objected to and appealed any actions that may have violated procedure. This impeded the progress of hearings and contributed to the backlog. And, in encouraging accused officers to exercise their appellate rights, the union also contributed to undermining the CCRB's impact on police discipline, since the Police Trial Board and the Office of Employee Appeals often overturned or mitigated CCRB decisions.[67] Indeed, the union was so effective at "playing the game" that it had little cause to engage in direct opposition to the board and assumed what one CCRB staff member described as "more of a benign position" toward the CCRB.[68]

Not surprisingly, relations between the CCRB and the union were "lousy".[69] This was a consequence of the union's antipathy toward the CCRB as well as the adversarial structure of the review process and the civilian ethos of the board. Union representatives frequently complained that the civilian members of the review panel failed to appreciate the demands and stress of police work, especially the perceived need to use force or forceful language to control certain citizens on the street. Panel members were not easily swayed by such arguments. As one member recalled:

> I'll never forget the position taken by Police Officer T__, [at] one of our first hearings. He says if you don't curse those people out in the same way that they curse you . . . you're not gonna get the respect. . . . And I say, "No, I don't buy that, I don't buy that at all".[70]

> We generally agree that we need to use whatever force is necessary to keep an officer from getting hurt, without going overboard. You've got a guy who's harassing and pawing, you gotta use a little bit of force. But that doesn't mean pull out your club and club him across the head.[71]

The CCRB sustained complaints at a fairly high rate; among the few cases that made it to a hearing, the board sustained about one third. Though most panelists did not share the definitions and assumptions of the police culture, they were not, contrary to union assertions, biased against officers. Civilian panelists were very conscious of their obligation to judge cases on the merits of the evidence presented.[72] What they were perhaps less conscious of was how their civilian ethos compromised their appearance of impartiality.

[67] United States Commission on Civil Rights, Racial and Ethnic Tensions in American Communities: Poverty, Inequality, and Discrimination. Volume I: The Mount Pleasant Report. (Washington DC: Government Printing Office, 1993); interview with CCRB staff member, April 1992, Washington, DC.

[68] Interview with CCRB staff member, April 1992, Washington, DC.

[69] Interview with civilian CCRB panel member, 20 May 1992, Washington, DC.

[70] Interview with civilian CCRB panel member, 20 May 1992, Washington DC.

[71] Interview with civilian CCRB panel member, 1 July 1992, Washington, DC.

[72] Interviews with civilian CCRB panel members, 20 May, 1 July and 6 July 1992, Washington, DC.

The CCRB also had to cope with the fact that formal procedures of a hearing guaranteed an equality of rights, but not a substantive equality.[73] At the hearings both parties had the right to be represented by counsel. The union, provided accused officers with counsellors who were union officials trained to represent fellow officers before the CCRB. As "repeat players" they knew the rules of the CCRB "game" well. Complainants, on the other hand, had to provide themselves with representation. The vast majority chose not to, probably because they could not afford to, especially since the board could offer no monetary award to make a lawyer's services worthwhile. (The few complainants who appeared with an attorney were pursuing a civil suit against the city in addition to the CCRB complaint.) Thus, most complainants presented their own case before the panel: this included conducting examinations of witnesses, summary statements, the right to make objections, and so forth. Complainants were, obviously, not skilled at this, so the CCRB panelists, who also interrogated witnesses, compensated for it: "We as a board have to in a way overstep to draw out information from the complainants".[74] According to panelists and union representatives alike, this tended to prolong hearings. The union regarded some of the panelists' efforts in this vein as excessive and as impairing their objectivity. In particular, the union objected when the panel allowed unrepresented complainants to "get away" with violation of CCRB decorum or rules, such as deadlines for introducing evidence.[75] Other review boards struggle with this problem. In San Diego, review board Vice Chair Arthur Ellis explains that: "if we don't, in fact, become partial in the sense that we take on the civilian perspective, then the civilian is the only one in this whole ball game that is left without representation."[76]

CCRB staff were also involved in "correcting" the inequalities created by a complainant's lack of representation. Investigative reports, distributed to all parties prior to a hearing, were deliberately attenuated in order to limit the effectiveness of the union's defence of a subject officer—a defence that was often based on attacking the credibility of the complainant and his or her witnesses. As a staff member explained:

> We had all this information on the complainant's side and then you'd get to the subject officer's side you'd have nothing. . . . So we thought, to make it a little bit more even, since the officers aren't giving us anything, we're going to give up as little of the complainant's information as we can.

Otherwise, the union representative, drawing on the complainant information provided could often find discrepancies:

[73] I Balbus, "Commodity Form and Legal Form: An Essay on the 'Relative Autonomy' of the Law", 2 *Law and Society Review* 571.

[74] The International Association for Civilian Oversight of Law Enforcement, Proceedings of the Sixth Annual Conference (Washington, DC, 4–7 September 1990), p. 125.

[75] Interviews with police union representatives, 24 November 1991 and 25 June 1992, Washington, DC.

[76] The International Association for Civilian Oversight of Law Enforcement, n. 58 above, p. 123.

> And then he'd pummel the complainant with questions about the differences and get the complainant all flustered and mad and say, "See how he's acting? That's how he acted with the police that day!" It was just a mess. . . . So when we took all that information out it did take away the opportunity for the [union] rep to just completely destroy the complainant's credibility, or at least give the appearance of destroying it.[77]

CCRB panelists, however, were also encumbered by the abbreviated reports. As membership on the panel changed and emphasis was placed on more efficient hearing to address the backlog, panelists demanded more detailed investigative reports. Still concerned about the lack of representation of complainants at hearings, the new board sought in vain for volunteers from the legal community. The operation of the CCRB was crippled by the requirement that complaints be resolved through formal hearings. This flaw is best understood in the context of structural tensions between those formal legal proceedings the democratic aspects of the board. The operating dilemmas we describe, including relying on volunteers, politicisation, and problems with legal representation, all contributed to the CCRB's insurmountable backlog and its eventual demise.

## STRUCTURAL TENSIONS AND THE EVALUATION OF CIVILIAN REVIEW

The history of civilian review in Washington presents an interesting puzzle, reflective of the history of civilian review in the United States more generally. The history of the first review board, the CRB, is clearly driven by forces of group conflict: the larger struggles over racial equality and local ones between the African-American community and a mostly white police force. But racial conflict is less evident in the history of the CCRB, and in the history of "second-wave" boards in the United States. The CCRB was founded by a largely African-American government to watch over a police force that was nearly majority black in composition and that offered little opposition to the creation of the board. The police union certainly disliked the CCRB and did nothing to assist it. But, apart from the early boycott, it put up little resistance to the board, apart from staunch advocacy for its members. The CCRB's failure was not the result of crippling compromises won by the police.

The CCRB was designed with the intention of creating a forum that would be just, fair, and representative of the local community. We argue that an unintended consequence of this design was to place CCRB actors in a position where they had to struggle with inherent tensions between formal law and democracy.

Within the context of this structural problem, the CCRB failed because it was chronically unable to handle a large and growing caseload and because city officials came to see the overworked board as cost-ineffective in the context of the city's dire financial straits in the mid-1990s.

[77] Interview with CCRB staff member, 19 May 1992, Washington, DC.

Tensions between democracy and law also affect how we evaluate civilian review and its goals. Andrew Goldsmith, for example, contends that investigations of complaints are "too legalistic in their approach."[78] Maeve McMahon's analysis of the Police Complaints Commission in Toronto similarly emphasises that the independent board's adoption of "an official objectified account" of complaints tends to eliminate the complainant's perspectives and rationalises police conduct.[79] To what extent should civilian review be a means to decide, impartially and objectively, the merits of specific complaints and to what extent should it represent the interests of community groups? At present there are review boards that try to be all these things and when measured against all these standards come up short in one or more areas. Other forms of civilian oversight, such as the ombudsman or auditor models,[80] which are not directly involved in adjudicating complaints or which make no claims to represent the community, may avoid some of the structural dilemmas we describe here, at least in terms of their internal operations. But less "democratic" forms of civilian oversight may not satisfy community groups wary of the police and perhaps also of the government. That is, the democratic aspects of civilian review often have a significant symbolic value.[81] Research on public attitudes regarding police accountability in Washington shows widespread support for a civilian review board of some kind either because it will help to control police misconduct or because of its symbolic value in "sending a message" to officers that they are not entirely free of outside scrutiny.[82] As one member of the CCRB observed, civilian review is important, "for no other reason than that the people know it's there watching over the department."[83]

Recently a consulting firm, hired to assist the city in reforming the police department, proposed that a civilian review board composed of judges be established. Community groups, including local police-liaison committees and the National Association for the Advancement of Colored People (NAACP), counter-proposed that the board should be made up of representatives drawn from the community, not the ranks of law enforcement institutions. The city council sided with the citizen groups and, in 1998, passed legislation creating yet another civilian review board in Washington (see Table 1, above at p. 48).[84] Like the old CCRB, the new Office of Citizen Complaint Review will be composed

[78] A Goldsmith, "What's Wrong with Complaint Investigations? Dealing with Difference Differently in Complaints Against the Police", 15 *Criminal Justice Ethics* 36.

[79] M McMahon, "Police Accountability: The Situation of Complaints in Toronto", 12 *Contemporary Crises* 301.

[80] S Walker, "New Directions in Citizen Oversight: The Auditor Approach to Handling Citizen Complaints", in T Shelley and A Grant (eds.), *Problem-Oriented Policing* (Washington, Police Executive Research Forum, 1998).

[81] J Skolnick and J Fyfe, *Above the Law* (New York, Free Press, 1993), p. 230.

[82] Ronald Weitzer, "Citizen Perceptions of Police Misconduct and Accountability: Race and Neighborhood Context", paper presented at the annual meeting of the American Society of Criminology, Toronto, November 1999.

[83] Washington City Paper, 28 June 1991, p. 33.

[84] Office of Citizen Complaint Review Establishment Act of 1998, DC Act 12–495, 16 October 1998.

of volunteer citizens, but they will review complaints as a panel only if the police department chooses to question a sustained complaint. The new board is intended to facilitate a more efficient processing of complaints through hearings before a single member of the panel, summary adjudication, conciliation, and mandatory mediation.[85] Whether the addition of these informal methods of complaint resolution will overcome the structural problems we describe here and aid the new board to operate more effectively than its predecessor remains to be seen (as of mid-2000 the board was not in operation).

## References

### *Books and Articles*


D Abbott, L Gold, and E Rogowsky, *Police, Politics and Race: The New York City Referendum on Civilian Review* (New York, American Jewish Committee and The Joint Center for Urban Studies, 1969).

I Balbus, "Commodity Form and Legal Form: An Essay on the 'Relative Autonomy 'of the Law", 2 *Law and Society Review* 571.

D Bayley, "Preface" in A Goldsmith (ed.), *Complaints Against the Police: The Trend to External Review* (Oxford, Clarendon Press, 1991).

C Beattie Repetti, "The Politics of Civilian Review: Police Accountability in Washington D.C. and New York City, 1948–1974" (PhD dissertation, George Washington University, 1997).

H Beral and M Sisk, "The Administration of Complaints by Civilians Against the Police", 77 *Harvard Law Review* 510.

L Brown, "Police Review Boards: An Historical and Critical Analysis", 10 *Police* 21.

R Browning, D Marshall and D Tabb, *Protest is Not Enough: The Struggle of Blacks and Hispanics for Equality in Urban Politics* (Berkeley, University of California Press, 1984).

J Button, *Black Violence: Political Impact of the 1960s Riots* (Princeton NJ, Princeton University Press, 1978).

W Chambliss and R Seidman, *Law, Order and Power*, Second Edition (Reading, Mass., Addison-Wesley Publishing, 1982).

M C Dandeker, *Surveillance, Power and Modernity* (New York: St. Martin's Press, 1990).

I Freckelton, "Shooting the Messenger: The Trial and Execution of the Victorian Complaints Authority" in A Goldsmith (ed.), *Complaints Against the Police: The Trend Toward External Review* (Oxford, Clarendon Press, 1991).

R Fogelson, *Big City Police* (Cambridge Mass., Harvard University Press, 1977).

A Goldsmith, "What's Wrong with Complaint Investigations? Dealing with Difference Differently in Complaints Against the Police", 15 *Criminal Justice Ethics* 36.

C Green, *The Secret City: A History of Race Relations in the Nation's Capital.* (Princeton, N.J., Princeton University Press, 1967).


[85] Previously, many officers refused to agree to conciliation. The new legislation requires the police chief to punish any officer who refuses mediation.

S Halpern, "Police Employee Organisations and Accountability Procedures in Three Cities: Some reflections on Policy-Making", 8 *Law and Society Review*, 561.

C Harris and A Thornton, *Perspectives of Political Power in the District of Columbia.* (Washington D.C.: National Institute of Public Management, 1981).

The International Association for Civilian Oversight of Law Enforcement, *Proceedings of the Sixth Annual Conference* (Washington, D.C., September 4–7, 1990).

L Lustgarten, *The Governance of the Police* (London, Sweet and Maxwell, 1986).

D McAdam, *Political Process and the Development of Black Insurgency* (Chicago: University of Chicago Press, 1982).

M McMahon, "Police Accountability: The Situation of Complaints in Toronto", 12 *Contemporary Crises* 301.

A Meier and E Rudwick, *CORE: A Study in the Civil Rights Movement 1942–1968* (New York: Oxford University Press, 1973).

M. Pacifico, " 'Don't Buy Where You can't Work': The New Negro Alliance of Washington", 6 *Washington History* 67.

H Packer, *The Limits of the Criminal Sanction* (Stanford, Cal., Stanford University Press, 1968).

D Perez, Police Accountability: A Question of Balance (Ph.D. dissertation, University of California, Berkeley, 1978).

Piper and Marbury, *Analysis of the District of Columbia's Civilian Complaint Review Board and Recommendations for its Replacement: A Report Prepared for the American Civil Liberties Union of the National Capital Area* (Washington, D.C., National Capital Area Civil Liberties Union, 1995).

J Skolnick, *Justice Without Trial* (New York, John Wiley & Sons, 1966).

J Skolnick and J Fyfe, *Above the Law* (New York, Free Press, 1993).

S Walker, "New Directions in Citizen Oversight: The Auditor Approach to Handling Citizen Complaints", in T Shelley and A Grant (eds.), *Problem-Oriented Policing* (Washington, Police Executive Research Forum, 1998).

S Walker and V Bumphus, Civilian Review of the Police: A National Survey of the 50 Largest Cities, 1991 (Omaha, NE, Department of Criminal Justice, University of Nebraska at Omaha, April 1991).

S Walker and V Bumphus, "The Effectiveness of Civilian Review: Observations on Recent Trends and New Issues Regarding the Civilian Review of the Police", 11 *American Journal of Police* 4.

Ronald Weitzer, "Citizen Perceptions of Police Misconduct and Accountability: Race and Neighborhood Context," paper presented at the annual meeting of the American Society of Criminology, Toronto, November 1999.

L Wittner, "The National Negro Congress: A Reassessment", Winter 1970 *American Quarterly* 888.

## *Government Documents*

### *District of Columbia Legislative Services Division*

Bill 3–214, "Human Rights Act of 1977 Amendments of 1979/1980."

Bill 3–247, "Complaint Review Board Act of 1980."

Council of the District of Columbia, Committee on the Judiciary, D Clarke, Chair, "Civilian Complaint Review Board's Legislative History", September 10, 1980.

Council of the City of the District of Columbia, Committee on Public Services and Consumer Affairs, W Rolark Chair, Comments Concerning Bill 3–247, July 22, 1980.
Memorandum from Ivanhoe Donaldson, General Assistant to the Mayor to Mayor Marion Barry, re. Civilian Complaint Review Board, November 13, 1979.
Office of Citizen Complaint Review Establishment Act of 1998, D.C. Act 12–495, October 16, 1998.
Testimony of Elizabeth Reveal, Executive Director of the Office of Criminal Justice Plans and Analysis, at Joint Hearing by Committee on the Judiciary and Committee on Public Services and Consumer Affairs, Council of the District of Columbia, on Bill 3–247, "Civilian Complaint Review Board Act of 1980" and Bill 3–214, "Human Rights Act of 1977 Amendments of 1980", March 26, 1980, Audio Tape.

### *National Archives*

Letter from F. Joseph Donohue and George E. C. Hayes to Walter L. Trobriner, November 18, 1964, Records of the Government of the District of Columbia, Record Group 351, File 4–294a, National Archives, Washington, D.C.

### *Reports*

District of Columbia, Civilian Complaint Review Board, Statistical Reports, 1985, 1986, 1987, 1990, 1991.
United States, Commission on Civil Rights, *Racial and Ethnic Tensions in American Communities: Poverty, Inequality, and Discrimination.* Volume I: The Mount Pleasant Report. (Washington D.C.: Government Printing Office, 1993).
United States, National Advisory Commission on Civil Disorders, *Report of the National Advisory Commission on Civil Disorders.* (New York: Bantam Books, 1968)
United States, President's Committee on Civil Rights, *To Secure These Rights: The Report of the President's Committee on Civil Rights* (Washington D.C., Government Printing Office, 1947).
United States, President's Commission of Crime in the District of Columbia, *Report.* (Washington, DC: Government Printing Office, 1966).

## *Newspapers*

*City Paper* (Washington)
*Evening Star* (Washington)
*New York Times*
*Times-Herald* (Washington)
*Washington Post*

# 3

# Back to the Future: The Death of Civilian Review of Public Complaints Against the Police in Ontario, Canada[1]

TAMMY LANDAU

## INTRODUCTION

Meaningful civilian involvement in the handling of public complaints against the police has been a central focus of police scholars,[2] police reformers,[3] and commissions of inquiry[4] for over two decades. Indeed,

> there is no longer much question as to whether the public should be subject to some

1 Tammy C Landau, Assistant Professor, Department of Psychology and School of Justice Studies, Ryerson Polytechnic University, 350 Victoria Street, Toronto, Ontario, Canada, M5B 2K3. The author would like to thank Inspector Gary Ellis, Toronto Police Service, for his expertise on the complaints system in Toronto, and Stephanie Long, for her assistance in the preparation of this manuscript.

2 D Brown, *The Police Complaints Procedure: A Survey of Complainants Views* (London, Home Office Research and Planning Unit Report, 1987); M Maguire and C Corbett, "Patterns and Profiles of Complaints Against the Police" in R Morgan and D Smith (eds.), *Coming to Terms With Policing: Perspectives in Policing* (New York, Routledge, 1989); A Goldsmith (ed.), *Complaints Against the Police: The Trend to External Review* (Oxford, Clarendon Press, 1991); T Landau, *Public Complaints Against the Police: A View From Complainants* (Toronto, Centre of Criminology, University of Toronto, 1994).

3 M McMahon and R V Ericson, *Policing Reform: A Study of the Reform Process and Police Institution in Toronto* (Toronto, Centre of Criminology, University of Toronto, 1984); Community Coalition Concerned About Civilian Oversight of Police, *In Search of Police Accountability* (Toronto, Community Coalition, 1997).

4 W Pitman, *Now Is Not Too Late: Report of the Metropolitan Toronto Task Force on Human Relations* (Toronto, The Task Force, 1977); Mr Justice D C McDonald, *Commission of Inquiry Concerning Certain Activities of the Royal Canadian Mounted Police* (Ottawa, Supply and Services Canada, 1981); A Maloney, *The Metropolitan Toronto Review of Citizen-Police Complaint Procedures* (Toronto, Metropolitan Toronto Board of Commissioners of Police, 1975); R Marin, *Report of the Commission of Inquiry Relating to Public Complaints, Internal Discipline and Grievance Procedures Within the Royal Canadian Mounted Police* (Ottawa, Information Canada, 1976); D R Morand, *The Royal Commission into the Metropolitan Toronto Police* (Toronto, The Commission, 1976); Mr Justice W Oppal, *Report of the Commission of Inquiry into Policing in British Columbia: Final Report* (Victoria, The Commission, 1994); Independent Commission on Policing for Northern Ireland, *A New Beginning: Policing in Northern Ireland* (Belfast, The Commission, 1999).

sort of external review in their handling of public complaints against the police. Instead, current discussion centres on what form that review should take.[5]

Even senior police managers in the late 1990s have abandoned their wholesale resistance to external scrutiny by civilian authorities and, at least publicly, support the view that "[c]ivilian oversight is an essential mechanism of accountability".[6] On the eve of the new millennium familiar echoes ring out. "In a democratic society based on the rule of law, the police, who are often the guardians of our civil liberties, must be responsible to the public they serve".[7]

Nor has the nature of discussions on civilian oversight of public complaints against the police changed during that same period. Two themes persist: the steady quest for police accountability in its various forms and the essential features of civilian oversight to best achieve them.[8]

While there are numerous mechanisms both inside and outside police organisations to achieve "accountability", the precise arrangements for handling public complaints against the police have emerged as a flashpoint for assessing both police accountability to the public and "progress" in reform of policing.[9] While Goldsmith[10] rightly notes that the emphasis on complaints procedures has deflected analysis from other significant forms of police accountability, they nevertheless embody many of the essential features of police accountability, control and legitimacy of democratic policing.

The Province of Ontario, Canada, has long been considered a pioneer in the development and implementation of civilian review of public complaints against the police.[11] The journey was a long and arduous one to arrive at an arrangement where civilians had both legal and moral jurisdiction to oversee the handling of complaints.[12] After a period of relatively peaceful co-existence between police services across Ontario and the civilian Public Complaints Commissioner,[13] recent amendments to the Police Services Act 1990 eliminated

[5] Landau, *supra* n. 2 at 1.

[6] Ontario Association of Chief of Police, *Brief to Police Summit* (Toronto, Ontario Association of Chiefs of Police, 1996).

[7] Oppal, *supra* n. 4 at 2.

[8] Landau, *supra* n. 2; Goldsmith, *supra* n. 2; Oppal, *supra* n. 4; Independent Commission on Policing for Northern Ireland, *supra* n. 4; also see S Walker and B Wright Kreisel, "Varieties of Citizen Review: The Implications of Organizational Features of Complaint Review Procedures for Accountability to the Community", 1(4) *International Journal of Police Science and Management*, 390.

[9] Landau, *supra* n. 2.

[10] A Goldsmith, "Necessary But Not Sufficient: The Role of Public Complaint Procedures in Police Accountability" in P Stenning (ed.), *Accountability for Criminal Justice: Selected Essays* (Toronto, University of Toronto Press, 1995).

[11] C Lewis, "Public Complaints in Metropolitan Toronto: Perspectives of a Public Complaints Commissioner" in A Goldsmith (ed.), *Complaints Against the Police: The Trend to External Review* (Oxford, Clarendon Press, 1991).

[12] See Landau, *supra* n. 2, for a detailed review of the establishment of the Office of the Public Complaints Commissioner in Ontario. Also see The Honourable G Lapkin and S James, "The Rise and Fall of the Police Complaints Commission of Ontario" (Toronto, unpublished, 1999).

[13] The *Metropolitan Toronto Public Complaints Project, 1981* originally established the Office of the Public Complaints Commissioner, which became the Office of the Police Complaints

both the Commissioner and any effective civilian role in the handling of complaints by the public against the police. Goldsmith has referred to this as "the single-most retrograde step for Canada's leadership role in civilian oversight".[14]

Ironically, however, Ontarians can expect little to change in the way in which complaints from the public against the police are handled, as the now-defunct Office of the Public Complaints Commissioner was an extremely limited tool of civilian oversight[15] falling into what Mr Justice Oppal described as "[t]he weakest form of oversight".[16] Nevertheless, there were significant symbolic, if not material, dimensions under the former scheme which distinguished the 1990s from earlier eras during which there was a virtual "hands-off" approach to policing the police.

This chapter will review the development of civilian oversight of public complaints against the police in Ontario, Canada, and the effectiveness of the reforms of the 1980s and 1990s. The main changes to the legislation for handling of complaints will also be reviewed. It is suggested that, while "[o]ther provinces and countries are moving toward stronger forms of oversight for citizen complaints"[17] in Ontario we find our future in our past, with police forces increasingly immune from political, legal and moral accountability. While a different model for policing the police in Ontario, in particular the provincial Special Investigations Unit, may provide a better example of significant external oversight and police accountability, it too, is threatened in the current political climate.

## THE DEVELOPMENT OF CIVILIAN OVERSIGHT OF POLICE IN ONTARIO: THE WONDER YEARS

The most significant round of reforms to the civilianisation of the handling of public complaints against the police in Ontario occurred during the 1980s, after at least a decade of hostile, even volatile, police-community relations.[18] These were compounded by findings of procedural irregularities and criminal wrongdoing within a number of Canadian police forces, including the Royal Canadian Mounted Police[19] and the Metropolitan Toronto Police Force.[20] In each instance, the completely internal handling of complaints against the police, and

Commissioner under the Police Services Act 1990. To add to the confusion, the name was changed back to the Office of the Public Complaints Commissioner in the mid-1990s. For the sake of clarity, the Office of the Public Complaints Commissioner will be used throughout this chapter.

14 A Goldsmith, Plenary Paper Presented at the Canadian Association of Civilian Oversight of Law Enforcement Second Annual Conference, Ottawa, September, 1997.

15 Landau, *supra* n. 2.

16 Oppal, *supra* n. 4 at 4.

17 Oppal, *supra* n. 4 at 4.

18 McMahon and Ericson, *supra* n. 3; Landau, *supra* n. 2.

19 MacDonald, *supra* n. 4; Marin, *supra* n. 4.

20 Pitman, *supra* n. 4; Maloney, *supra* n. 2; Morand, *supra* n. 4.

the lack of transparency in the process, were identified as significant barriers to police accountability and legitimacy to the public.

The political landscape of the time demanded a significant civilian role in police accountability, although the battle over the precise nature of that involvement was a bitter one. Predictably, police managers sought to limit the role of civilians in policing the police (as "[h]e who controls discipline does, in fact, control the organization")[21] while community groups active in police reform felt independence at the investigative, adjudicative and disciplinary stages was crucial to a credible and accountable system.

The "hands-off" approach to policing the police ended in Toronto with the passage of the Metropolitan Toronto Police Force Complaints Project Act 1981. The model on which the project was ultimately based was one in which the responsibility for management and discipline within the force rested with the police, but which established a civilian authority—the Public Complaints Commissioner—who could intervene when that responsibility was breached. The Toronto scheme:

> [w]as intended as a means of giving the police a stake in the system, thereby encouraging their acceptance of it and preserving an important management role. The monitoring and review power of the public complaints commissioner, together with the commissioner's extraordinary right of initial investigation, was intended to ensure that initial investigation and adjudication by police would be thorough and impartial.[22]

Clearly, police managers were more successful in limiting reform than community reformers were at achieving it. The rank and file, however, never accepted the legitimacy of a civilian authority. In the view of the President of the Metropolitan Toronto Police Association, "[t]he only good external complaints system is a dead system".[23]

Still, an independent civilian agency with even minimal powers over investigation, adjudication, discipline and appeal was unprecedented in Canada and seen as a watershed in police accountability. Both the establishment of the Office of the Public Complaints Commissioner and the legislative framework under which it was to operate were explicitly and implicitly seen as providing a successful and effective means of civilian oversight of public complaints against the police. The pilot project was made permanent under the Metropolitan Toronto Police Force Complaints Act 1984, and expanded to cover all police services in Ontario under the Police Services Act 1990.[24]

[21] W Kolender, "Police Executive Perspectives of Civilian Oversight", paper presented at the Third Annual Meeting of the International Association of Civilian Oversight of Law Enforcement, Evanston, Illinois, 1987.

[22] Lewis, *supra* n. 11 at 159.

[23] P Walter, cited in Lewis, *supra* n. 11.

[24] While there were numerous, high-profile clashes between police and various communities in Toronto, few directly involved the complaints system. One notable exception is an incident in 1985 in which the Commissioner ordered a hearing before a board of inquiry after the chief had dismissed a complaint against an officer which alleged excessive use of force. The board found misconduct on

Part VI of the Police Services Act 1990, set out the structure, function and powers of the Public Complaints Commissioner and the procedures for handling public complaints against the police. While these developments must be seen as significant in the context of police accountability in Toronto in the 1980s, both the legislation and the way in which the Commission carried out its mandate reveal significant limitations which undermine the very goals they set out to achieve.

The legal powers of the Commissioner are a case in point. All public complaints against the police were presumptively investigated in the first instance by the police force whose officer was subject to the complaint. The Commissioner had limited powers to initiate a complaint[25] or an investigation.[26] While the Commissioner had powers to monitor the investigation, this was achieved largely through the receipt of regular reports from the police investigators.

In addition, the adjudicative decision with respect to the outcome of a complaint rested with the chief of police,[27] even in the few cases where the Commissioner may have conducted the investigation. Despite the powers of the Commissioner to review the decision of the chief at the request of the complainant or the subject officer,[28] or initiate the review if it was in the public interest to do so,[29] the alternatives available to the Commissioner at this point were extremely limited: she or he could have decided to take no further action in the complaint or order a hearing before a board of inquiry but only if the Commissioner decided it was in the public interest to do so.[30]

An analysis of complainants' views of the Toronto scheme clearly indicated that the arrangement whereby the police investigated themselves had a devastating impact on the legitimacy of the system.[31] Sixty per cent of complainants who had experienced the whole complaints process and whose complaint had been resolved did not think that Toronto had a fair system for handling complaints against the police: over two-thirds stated that they were either unsatisfied or very unsatisfied with their experience making a complaint and over half said that, knowing what they knew at the time of the interview, they would not use the same system again.

Perhaps a more critical analysis of the effectiveness of the Public Complaints Commissioner could be directed at the extent to which those powers which the

the part of the officer, and ordered him dismissed. To protest the "interference" with a disciplinary decision of the chief by civilians, the Metropolitan Toronto Police Association launched an illegal job action: officers donned baseball caps instead of their regular-issue hats, and refused to issue traffic tickets. While unprecedented, it was ultimately an unsuccessful attempt to undermine, even abolish, the Public Complaints Commissioner.

[25] Police Service Act, R.S.O. 1990, c.P.15. at s. 78.

[26] *Ibid.* at s. 88.

[27] *Supra* n. 25, at s. 90.

[28] *Supra* n. 25, at s. 90.

[29] *Supra* n. 25, at s. 91.

[30] *Supra* n. 25, at s. 91.

[31] T Landau, "When Police Investigate Police: A View From Complainants", 38(3) *Canadian Journal of Criminology* 291.

Commissioner did have were exercised. Again, however, the Public Complaints Commissioner was a disappointment:

> The ongoing monitoring of police investigations into complaints is tied in almost exclusively with the receipt of interim reports produced by the Public Complaints Investigation Bureau of the police. Reviews of the initial decisions by the chief of police occur almost exclusively as a result of requests from complainants, but rarely involve more than a review of the existing file created by the police investigators, although the Commissioner has powers to re-investigate. After review, the Commissioner is unlikely to be able to justify ordering a hearing before a Board of Inquiry in the public interest, and must, therefore, find that no further action is warranted . . .[32]

In spite of the significant limitations on the powers of the Complaints Commissioner, there were important procedural stipulations which were intended to grant additional legitimacy to the process as a whole. For example, complainants could lodge their complaint verbally or in writing at any police station/detachment, with the Public Complaints Investigation Bureau of the local force or directly with the Office of the Public Complaints Commissioner,[33] although in every case the complaint was nevertheless sent directly to the police. All complaints had to be recorded,[34] and copies sent to the chief of police, the Complaints Commissioner, the Public Complaint Investigation Bureau of the force, the complainant, and the subject officer.[35] In addition, complainants had to be given information on the complaints process,[36] including the rights of the complainant. An initial report on the investigation had to be sent to the Public Complaints Commissioner, the complainant, and the subject officer,[37] with the first interim report sent within thirty days of the receipt of the complaint.[38] Regular interim reports would be sent thereafter.

The same study of complainants' experiences with the Toronto system suggests that these procedures, too, had a limited impact on the legitimacy of the Ontario scheme.[39] Most complainants could not state clearly whether they had lodged their complaint with the police or with the Office of Public Complaints Commissioner and most had a poor understanding of the nature of the process, or the role of the police and the independent Commissioner. Indeed, two-thirds of complainants did not know about the Public Complaints Commissioner. Few who did know about it had an accurate understanding of its role in monitoring (vs investigating) complaints. Receipt of regular interim reports from police investigators often created cynicism among complainants, since the reports

[32] Landau, *supra* n. 2 at 76.
[33] *Supra* n. 25 at s. 71(1).
[34] *Ibid*, at s. 77(2).
[35] *Supra* n. 25 at s. 77(5).
[36] *Supra* n. 25 at s. 77(3).
[37] *Supra* n. 25 at s. 87(2).
[38] *Supra* n. 25 at s. 87(3).
[39] Landau, *supra* n. 2.

generally outlined the subject officers' version of events or stated that "there are no new matters to report".

Still, there remained a modicum of legitimacy to the process: over three-quarters of complainants were advised by friends, family members and community agencies to lodge a formal complaint. In addition, almost seventy per cent of complainants who registered their complaint directly with the Office of the Public Complaints Commissioner were either satisfied or very satisfied with their experience making a complaint, compared with only fifty-six per cent of complainants who registered their complaint with a public station and forty per cent of complainants who registered their complaint with the Public Complaints Investigation Bureau of the local police force. At the end of the day, the impact of the Office of the Public Complaints Commissioner was, from the perspective of complainants, equivocal: twenty-eight per cent of complainants whose complaints had gone through the entire process stated that they thought the Public Complaints Commissioner played an important role in the handling of complaints, almost twenty-four per cent stated that the Public Complaints Commissioner did not play an important role in the handling of complaints, and forty-seven per cent were uncertain if the Public Complaints Commissioner played an important role in the handling of complaints.

In spite of these limitations, the Public Complaints Commissioner had a political legitimacy which, while arguably unwarranted, achieved international status. One visitor on a "fact-finding mission" from Northern ireland commented: "We came to Toronto to learn . . . and we learned that all roads lead to Toronto".[40] Even criticism from the community eventually subsided:

> While the record of the Public Complaints Commission is not as effective as many would wish, it apparently had some positive results. And, even more important, the fact that a Public Complaints Commissioner exists has an important symbolic effect.[41]

It is in this context that the most recent changes must be understood.

## RECENT CHANGES TO CIVILIAN REVIEW IN ONTARIO

The most recent wave of police reform differs from earlier ones in that it emerged in the absence of community concerns over the handling of public complaints against the police.[42] Indeed, reform occurred during an era where the myth of an effective, efficient and accountable public complaints mechanism was virtually complete and supported by evidence of a decline in the number of

[40] M Hayes, cited in *Civilian Oversight of Police Conduct: A Position Paper*.Toronto: Police Complaints Commissioner, 1996.

[41] Urban Alliance on Race Relations, cited in Lewis, *supra* n. 1..

[42] This is not to suggest that volatile police-community relations have subsided. Indeed, the *Report of the Commission on Systemic Racism in the Ontario Justice System*, released in 1996, concluded that there is empirical evidence to support community concerns of persistent and repeated allegations of anti-black racism on the part of the Toronto police.

official complaints lodged against the police.[43] However, when the governing provincial Conservatives came to power in 1995, they embarked on an agenda of downsizing, devolution and dismantling of most public services within provincial jurisdiction. Restructuring and reform of various aspects of policing services were included in this larger plan. These reforms thus combined a law and order, pro-police agenda with massive restructuring and, in the case of policing the police, disturbing results.

The Conservatives seized the opportunity to address a variety of structural and financial anomalies in policing to implement significant reforms to civilian oversight of the police.[44] They embarked on a limited and superficial consultative process which structurally excluded representation from the community. Indeed, the Community Coalition Concerned About Civilian Oversight of Police, which represents twenty-five community organisations, was formed "in response to the systematic exclusion of Ontario citizens from the review of the current system of civilian oversight of police".[45] In contrast, the Ontario Association of Chiefs of Police noted that their position "is being accepted by Government and other stakeholders".[46] It is not surprising, then, that issues which would be of most concern to the community or which would have the greatest effect on legitimacy with the public were neglected.

For example, in June, 1996, the government hosted a two-day "Police Summit" which included "key police and municipal stakeholders", and held additional consultations after the summit with, by its own admission, representatives from those same groups. On 6 October 1996, the government commissioned Rod McLeod, a lawyer with considerable Tory connections, to "consider and advise on how the current system of civilian oversight of police in the province can be improved" and to report back five weeks later.[47] By McLeod's own admission, many community groups boycotted the process as a direct result of untenable time constraints imposed on them by the process. Consequently, input from community stakeholders, most notably those involved in the earlier rounds of policing reform, were virtually absent before specific amendments were proposed.

In January, 1997 An Act to Review the Partnership Between the Province, Municipalities and the Police and to Enhance Community Safety (Bill 105) was released. While most of McLeod's specific recommendations were not adopted,

[43] "Complaints Against Police Drop Again", *Toronto Star*, 20 May 1998.

[44] For example, a small number of police forces in Ontario had been receiving free policing services while most others had to pay for services from municipal taxes. In addition, the Police Services Act required the majority of members to local Police Services Boards, which establishes the police budget, be appointed by the provincial government, and the minority be appointed by the municipality. However, the municipal government was responsible for funding those services.

[45] Community Coalition Concerned About Civilian Oversight of Police, *In Search of Police Accountability: Report* (Toronto, The Coalition, 1997) at 1.

[46] Ontario Association of Chiefs of Police, cited in Community Coalition Concerned About Civilian Oversight, *ibid.*

[47] R McLeod, *A Report and Recommendations on Amendments to the* Police Services Act *Respecting Civilian Oversight of Police* (Toronto, Queen's Printer, 1996).

two of his main principles constituted major themes in the Bill 105. Firstly, in the absence of input from the community, McLeod clearly attempted to tip the balance toward favouring police perspectives on external control and discipline:

> Complaints/discipline systems must recognize the complex and dangerous nature of a police officer's work. Police officers are called upon to make split second decisions in life and death situations. These decisions will be analyzed in minute detail over successive months or years through a large number of mechanisms for accountability . . . Complaints/discipline systems must treat both complainants and police officers in the fairest manner possible.[48]

He further concluded that "[t]he current laws are highly technical, confusing and amount to over-regulation".[49] McLeod's report was literally void of any empirical or theoretical analysis of the essential issues at stake. Indeed, in listing the various internal and external bodies with responsibility for oversight of policing (e.g. the internal Professional Standards Review Board, the external civilian Office of the Public Complaints Commissioner), McLeod included the "local collective bargaining unit" as having an essential role in the civilian oversight system,[50] thus revealing an incredible lack of sophistication in grasping the true essence of the role of civilian authorities in police accountability.

Addressing the problem of "over-regulation" led to the second significant principle on which McLeod based his recommendations: that the system should "devolve responsibility and authority down from the Province to the local authorities"[51] and rely instead on a "minimal legislative foundation". The precise procedures would be left to regulations, and the main responsibilities for handling complaints would be left to the local force.

These principles foreshadowed the most significant reforms under Bill 105: a complete internal handling of complaints against the police along with elimination of meaningful civilian review. This was to be achieved by abolishing the Public Complaints Commissioner and removing the power from any civilian authority to investigate, adjudicate or even review complaints.

Once Bill 105 was announced there remained one opportunity of any significance for community response, through formal hearings before the Legislative Committee. In their submission before the Committee, the Ontario Association of Chiefs of Police made no reference to civilian oversight, an implicit endorsement of the proposed bill. Of those presentations which directly addressed the proposed amendments to the handling of public complaints against the police, virtually all condemned them. The Canadian Civil Liberties Association submitted that:

> Under Bill 105 the successor commission will be virtually bereft of investigative powers, so it will be a system of complete police self-investigation . . . Bill 105 will threaten

[48] McLeod, *ibid* n. 47 at 37.
[49] McLeod, *supra* n. 47 at 37.
[50] McLeod, *supra* n. 47 at 37.
[51] McLeod, *supra* n. 47 at 3.

> to exacerbate the very tensions—racial, ethnic, class—that brought about the changes that so many have worked so hard to create.[52]

The Black Action Defence Committee objected that "Bill 105 totally destroys the principles of police accountability, accessibility, fairness and impartiality".[53] Even the President of the Metropolitan Toronto Police Association, the same man who had, in 1987, tried to abolish civilian oversight over complaints against the police, himself expressed concern that a totally internal process would remove any management accountability on how investigations are conducted.[54]

The Ombudsman of Ontario noted how the "new" system echoes from the past. She stated that the proposed changes were "cause for very serious concern . . . Bill 105, as currently drafted, represents a step backward".[55] Not surprisingly, this reversion back to an earlier era received support from the Ontario Provincial Police Association, which supported handing the investigation and adjudication of complaints back to the chief or commissioner of police: "It is quite refreshing to see the pendulum swing back from general mistrust of the police to a system which we believe the public has great faith in and will support".[56]

Nevertheless, there were few, if any, significant changes to the amendments to the complaints procedures proposed in Bill 105 before it was passed into law on 27 November 1997. The Solicitor-General of the time announced that:

> The new oversight system will be fair, objective, and accountable for the police and the communities they serve. At the end of the day we will have a modernized, streamlined and simplified oversight system that is more responsive and accountable to the complainant.[57]

As alluded to earlier, the two most dramatic aspects of the amendments for independent review of public complaints against the police are that they abolished the Office of the Public Complaints Commissioner and reduced even further the possibility of meaningful review of the investigation and adjudication of complaints carried out by the chief or commissioner of police.[58] The Ontario

[52] Canadian Civil Liberties Association, Brief to the Legislative Committee, *Hansard*, 17 March 1997.

[53] Black Action Defence Committee, Brief to the Legislative Committee, *Hansard*, 17 March 1997.

[54] Paul Walter, President, Metropolitan Toronto Police Association, Brief to the Legislative Committee, *Hansard*, 17 March 1997.

[55] Roberta Jamieson, Ombudsman of Ontario, Brief to the Legislative Committee, *Hansard*, 17 March 1997.

[56] Brian Adkin, President, Ontario Provincial Police Association, Brief to the Legislative Committee, *Hansard*, 17 March 1997.

[57] The Honourable Robert Runciman, Solicitor-General and Minister of Correctional Services, *Press Release*, 14 January 1997.

[58] For the sake of simplicity, the use of "chief of police" will include the Commissioner of Ontario Provincial Police, although the Act refers to both.

Civilian Commission on Police Services[59] (OCCOPS) already existed as an independent agency with general responsibilities to ensure compliance of municipal forces with province-wide standards,[60] or to "investigate, inquire into and report on" the conduct or performance of officers, including the chief, the administration of a municipal police force, the provision of police services to a municipality and the police needs of a municipality.[61] The new amendments added to those responsibilities token powers of review involving public complaints against the police, described below. After a closer examination of the main provisions of the "new" system, we might be in a better position to evaluate the assertion of the then Solicitor-General for Ontario, of a system which is "credible, fair, objective, transparent and open with levels of accountability that are understandable and which have the confidence of both the police and the general public".[62]

As under the previous scheme, the chief is largely responsible for deciding how, or whether a complaint will be dealt with, as well as the outcome of a complaint. For example, the chief must decide if the complaint is about the policies or services provided by the force.[63] The chief may decide not to deal with the complaint because it is frivolous, vexatious or made in bad faith,[64] because the complaint was made more than six months after the incident,[65] or if the chief deems the complaint to be a third-party complaint.[66] Under all of these circumstances, the chief must, within thirty days after the complaint was made, notify the complainant and subject officer (if any) of such decisions, and the right to request that the decision be reviewed.[67]

With respect to those complaints which are not excluded under the provisions outlined above, the Act directs the chief to ensure that a "review" is begun if the complaint is about the policies or services provided by the force, and an investigation is begun into complaints involving allegations of the conduct of an officer.[68]

The chief will adjudicate the complaint, based on a written report presumptively prepared from within the chief's own service, although the chief can request an investigation be carried out by another service.[69] The complainant

[59] While the legislation uses the term "Commission" to refer to the Ontario Civilian Commission on Police, "OCCOPS" will be used here in order to avoid any confusion with previous references to the now-defunct Office of the Public Complaints Commissioner.

[60] *Supra* n. 25 at s. 22.

[61] *Supra* n. 25 at s. 29. The Ontario Civilian Commission on Police also has additional significant powers under s. 23, including powers to suspend a chief of police, or to remove one or more members of a Police Services Board, or to disband a municipal police service.

[62] *Supra* n. 57.

[63] *Supra* n. 25 at s. 59(1).

[64] *Supra* n. 25 at s. 59(3).

[65] *Supra* n. 25 at s. 59(4).

[66] *Supra* n. 25 at s. 59(5).

[67] *Supra* n. 25 at s. 59(6).

[68] *Supra* n. 25 at s. 59(8).

[69] *Supra* n. 25 at s. 64(2).

must be informed of the chief's decision within sixty days, including any decision not to deal with the complaint[70] and of the right to request a review by OCCOPS.[71]

The provisions described thus far are not dramatically different from those under the previous complaints system. However, there are significant changes to the options available to the chief at the dispositional stage. Under the previous scheme, the chief decided not only whether to deal with a complaint, but whether it was substantiated or unsubstantiated. If the chief found it was substantiated, the chief also decided on the penalty, an arrangement which instilled little confidence to either subject officers or complainants about the independence of the process.

The new scheme appears to inject an arm's length process into the disciplinary stage, which is, at the same time, clearly geared toward keeping the responsibility for administering discipline out of the hands of civilian authorities and within the jurisdiction of the chief. For example, if the chief is of the view that the complaint is unsubstantiated, the chief shall take no action;[72] however, if the chief is of the opinion that the police officer's conduct may constitute misconduct or unsatisfactory work performance, the chief must inform both the complainant and the officer, and hold a hearing into the matter.[73] While this new arrangement may give the pretence of an arm's length adjudicative process for the benefit of both the complainant and the subject officer, the "prosecutor" is appointed by the chief and may be an officer of equal or superior rank to the subject officer from within the same force.[74]

At the same time, if the chief is of the opinion that the misconduct or unsatisfactory work performance was not of a serious nature (a decision which is itself reviewable at the request of the complainant), the chief "may resolve the matter informally without holding a hearing" with the consent of the officer and the complainant.[75]

Complainants have not, on the face of it, lost any significant rights to have their complaint reviewed. They retained the right to request a review of the chief's initial decision with respect to a complaint, i.e. that the complaint will not be dealt with under the Act;[76] the complaint is unsubstantiated; or that any misconduct which may have occurred is not serious.[77] Under these sections, OCCOPS is directed to "review" the decision, "taking into account any material provided by the complainant or the chief of police" and is further directed to complete its review within thirty days.[78] However, in conducting reviews under

[70] *Supra* n. 25 at s. 61(3).
[71] *Supra* n. 25 at s. 59(6).
[72] *Supra* n. 25 at s. 64(6).
[73] *Supra* n. 25 at s. 64(7).
[74] *Supra* n. 25 at s. 64(8).
[75] *Supra* n. 25 at s. 64(11).
[76] *Supra* n. 25 at s. 72(2) to s. 72(4).
[77] S. 72(5).
[78] *Supra* n. 25 at s. 72(7).

this section, OCCOPS "shall not hold a hearing into the matter." After completion of the review, OCCOPS may "confirm the decision or may direct the chief of police . . . to process the complaint as it specifies", an unclear mandate to say the least. Finally, OCCOPS may also assign the review or investigation of the complaint to another police force.[79] The decision of OCCOPS at the end of this process "is final and binding and there is no appeal therefrom".[80]

The outcome of a hearing into possible misconduct on the part of an officer is also subject to review.[81] If the request is from the officer, OCCOPS must hold hearing;[82] OCCOPS shall also hold a hearing if the request is from the complainant and the appeal is from the finding that misconduct or unsatisfactory work performance was not proved on clear and convincing evidence,[83] presumably excluding complainants' appeals of penalties imposed at hearings.

There have been some notable, albeit weak, improvements to the complaints scheme. For example, it is now possible to lodge a complaint about "the policies or services provided by a police force" although the Act is silent on how such complaints might be dealt with differently from complaints about the conduct of a police officer. In addition, there are various attempts to deal with the length of time it took to resolve a complaint under the previous scheme: the chief must inform complainants within thirty days of a decision not to deal with the complaint under the Act, and must inform the complainant and subject officer (if any) of his/her decision within sixty days of receiving a report of an investigation. OCCOPS "shall endeavour to complete its review within thirty days",[84] although no time constraints are apparently placed on the length of time it may take to conduct the investigation.

There are new problematic dimensions under the new scheme. While the legislation requires all complaints to be made in writing only, there is no longer any requirement to give the complainant a copy of the complaint, or information about the process or the rights of complainants. Requirements under the previous scheme to send regular reports (i.e. every thirty days) to complainants about the progress of the investigation have been eliminated. While the Public Complaints Commissioner was sent a copy of all complaints received by a police service, the regular interim reports, and a report of the final decision by the chief, there is no requirement under the new scheme to inform OCCOPS of complaints which are lodged, to send them copies of any reports, or to inform them about the resolution of complaints.

The principle of "simplification" has had additional significance in the final legislation, particularly in terms of what is not in the Act. Indeed, as recommended by McLeod, many critical procedures are left to the regulations, to be

[79] *Supra* n. 25 at s. 72(8).
[80] *Supra* n. 25 at s. 72(12).
[81] *Supra* n. 25 at s. 70(1).
[82] *Supra* n. 25 at s. 70(2).
[83] *Supra* n. 25 at s. 70(3).
[84] *Supra* n. 25 at s. 72(7).

developed by individual police services. For example, unlike the previous scheme, the Act does not direct the chief to establish an internal investigatory body (such as the Public Complaints Investigations Bureau mandated under the previous legislation). It is not clear, therefore, who will be conducting the investigations in any given police force. Under the interim procedures developed by the Toronto Police Service, investigations are generally carried out by the unit commander of the division where the complaint occurred, who is also likely to be the supervisor of the subject officer.

The use of informal resolutions are another case in point. While informal resolutions to complaints were possible under the old scheme, they were rare, likely due to the fact that they were far from informal at all. Indeed, officers contemplating entering into an informal resolution were warned that such a resolution did not preclude the chief from commencing or continuing disciplinary action against the officer.

The new procedures also allow for the use of informal resolutions with respect to "conduct that is not of a serious nature".[85] Again, however, the Act is similarly silent on what constitutes an informal resolution or the procedures to be followed both before and after a complaint is resolved in this manner. The interim procedures developed in Toronto have taken the lack of legislative guidelines to a disturbing extreme: no record is kept on complaints which are resolved informally, including the name of the complainant, the subject officer, the nature of the complaint, the division of the complaint or the nature of the resolution. Consequently, no review, appeal or audit of informal resolutions will be possible. While this scenario may or may not have been anticipated by the legislation, it is a clear example of the consequences of legislation designed to permit the unaccountable operation of police forces.

## CONCLUSIONS

At the conclusion of this overview of the recent changes to the role of civilians in handling public complaints against the police, do we have cause to be concerned about police accountability in Ontario? At the end of the day, the answer to this question must be "yes", we surely do.

It is true that the role of the Public Complaints Commissioner which was abolished by the amendments was extremely limited in its ability to achieve effective review of complaints. In fact, under the old scheme the chief of police could, in effect, carry on with the business of administering complaints with little meaningful interference from civilian authority. The statistics on the resolution of complaints confirm this: between 1993 and 1996, roughly ninety-seven per cent of all decisions by the chief resulted in the dismissal of the complaint.[86]

[85] *Supra* n. 25 at s. 58(1) and s. 64(11).
[86] Toronto Police Service *Annual Statistical Report* (Toronto, Toronto Police Service, 1998).

Given the narrow mandate of the Public Complaints Commissioner to interfere with this decision, it is not surprising that these outcomes were rarely overturned. In spite of the fact that the Ontario Civilian Commission on Police has, under the new scheme, even more limited jurisdiction over complaints, this is not the most serious source of concern.

What is far more disturbing are the symbolic dimensions of removing any pretence to civilian review of police. In the face of routine, rather shallow proselytising about the inherent accountability of community-based policing and the "win-win" partnerships it creates, other significant forms of accountability have been overshadowed. In the current political climate, government sponsored pro-police, law-and-order legislation is coupled with an increasingly militant police association and sends out warning signals for meaningful accountability of the public police. The pre-reform era of the 1960s and 1970s foreshadows our present, if not our future and a policing culture entrenched in political, legal and moral untouchability.

We might perhaps look to other arenas in which civilian review of police is perhaps more "successful", if equally volatile. The history and operation of the Special Investigations Unit (SIU) in Ontario has been stormier than that of the handling of public complaints against the police. First established under the Police Services Act 1990, to investigate police actions resulting in serious injury or death of a citizen,[87] the SIU has all of the significant powers identified for effective impartial investigation: it can initiate and conduct investigations,[88] investigators are not current police officers, nor can they be part of an investigation if they were a former member of the same force as the officer(s) under investigation.[89] In addition, the Director of the Special Investigations Unit is a civilian appointed by the Lieutenant Governor in Council on the recommendation of the Solicitor General,[90] decisions with respect to laying criminal charges are made independently by the director[91] and cases in which criminal charges are laid are heard in criminal court. Indeed, the Police Services Act directs that "members of police forces shall co-operate fully with the members of the unit in the conduct of investigations".[92] Clearly, its powers, mandate and jurisdiction by far exceed those of any complaints mechanisms which Ontario has ever had. Ironically, no changes were made to the powers or the mandate of the SIU under the most recent amendments to the Police Services Act. Indeed, the Government has even increased its resource base to permit it to operate more effectively and efficiently.[93]

Nevertheless, there are many storms brewing on this front, too. Short of an outright abolition of the SIU, police services continue to attempt to disrupt its

[87] *Supra* n. 25 at s. 113(5).
[88] *Supra* n. 25 at s. 113(5).
[89] *Supra* n. 25 at s. 113(6).
[90] *Supra* n. 25 at s. 113(2).
[91] *Supra* n. 25 at s. 113(7).
[92] *Supra* n. 25 at s. 113(9).
[93] "SIU Deserves a Fair Chance", *Toronto Star*, 12 July 1999.

operation, by, for example, refusing to cooperate with investigators or in delaying notification of the SIU when an incident clearly under their mandate has occurred. The threat to police forces has as much to do with the symbolic significance of the powers invested in the Special Investigations Unit as it does the material impact that it has on police business: of seventeen investigations carried out by the SIU in 1998, only one resulted in the laying of criminal charges.[94]

The complaints system in Ontario may never have been the powerhouse it was hoped to be, or held out to be. What was perhaps nonetheless significant was the political commitment to strike a meaningful balance between competing interests and political ideologies about police independence and accountability. The recent reforms take us further and further away from that goal.

## References

G Adams, Consultation Report of the Honorable George W Adams QC to the Attorney-General and Solicitor-General Concerning Police Cooperation with the Special Investigations Unit, May 14, 1998, http://siu.on.ca/adams.htm.

D Brown, The Police Complaints Procedure: A Survey of Complainants Views (London: Home Office Research and Planning Unit Report, 1987).

Community Coalition Concerned About Civilian Oversight of Police In Search of Police Accountability (Toronto: Community Coalition, 1997).

A Goldsmith (ed.), Complaints Against the Police: The Trend to External Review (Oxford: Clarendon Press, 1991).

A Goldsmith, "Necessary But Not Sufficient: The Role of Public Complaint Procedures in Police Accountability" in P Stenning (ed.), Accountability for Criminal Justice: Selected Essays (Toronto, University of Toronto Press, 1995).

A Goldsmith, Plenary Paper Presented at the Canadian Association of Civilian Oversight of Law Enforcement Second Annual Conference, Ottawa, September, 1997.

Independent Commission on Policing for Northern Ireland, A New Beginning: Policing in Northern Ireland (Belfast: The Commission, 1999).

W Kolender, "Police Executive Perspectives of Civilian Oversight". Paper presented at the Third Annual Meeting of the International Association of Civilian Oversight of Law Enforcement, Evanston, Illinois, 1987.

T Landau, Public Complaints Against the Police: A View From Complainants (Toronto: Centre of Criminology, University of Toronto, 1994).

T Landau, "When Police Investigate Police: A View From Complainants" 38(3) Canadian Journal of Criminology 291.

The Honourable G Lapkin and S James, "The Rise and Fall of the Police Complaints Commission of Ontario" (Toronto, unpublished, 1999).

C Lewis, "Public Complaints in Metropolitan Toronto: Perspectives of a Public Complaints Commissioner" in A Goldsmith (ed.), Complaints Against the Police: The Trend to External Review (Oxford, Clarendon Press, 1991).

[94] "Police Complaints Lowest in 15 Years", *Toronto Star*, 17 June 1999. On the nature and impact of police lack of cooperation with the SIU, see G Adams, *Consultation Report of the Honorable George W Adams QC to the Attorney-General and Solicitor-General Concerning Police Cooperation with the Special Investigations Unit, 14 May 1998.*

B Loveday, "Improving Police Integrity and Accountability to the Community" 1(4) International Journal of Police Science and Management 390.

Mr Justice D C McDonald, Commission of Inquiry Concerning Certain Activities of the Royal Canadian Mounted Police (Ottawa: Supply and Services Canada, 1981).

R McLeod, A Report and Recommendations on Amendments to the *Police Services Act* Respecting Civilian Oversight of Police (Toronto: Queen's Printer, 1996).

M McMahon and R V Ericson, Policing Reform: A Study of the Reform Process and Police Institution in Toronto (Toronto: Centre of Criminology, University of Toronto, 1984).

M Maguire and C Corbett, "Patterns and Profiles of Complaints Against the Police" in R Morgan and D Smith (eds.), Coming to Terms With Policing: Perspectives in Policing (New York, Routledge, 1989).

A Maloney, The Metropolitan Toronto Review of Citizen-Police Complaint Procedures (Toronto: Metropolitan Toronto Board of Commissioners of Police, 1975).

R Marin, Report of the Commission of Inquiry Relating to Public Complaints, Internal Discipline and Grievance Procedures Within the Royal Canadian Mounted Police (Ottawa: Information Canada, 1976).

D R Morand, The Royal Commission into the Metropolitan Toronto Police (Toronto, The Commission, 1976).

Ontario Association of Chief of Police, Brief to Police Summit (Toronto, Ontario Association of Chiefs of Police, 1996).

Mr Justice W Oppal, Report of the Commission of Inquiry into Policing in British Columbia: Final Report (Victoria: The Commission, 1994).

Report of the Commission on Systemic Racism in the Ontario Justice System (Toronto, 1996).

Toronto Police Service Annual Statistical Report (Toronto: Toronto Police Service, 1998).

W Pitman, Now Is Not Too Late: Report of the Metropolitan Toronto Task Force on Human Relations (Toronto: The Task Force, 1977).

S Walker and B Wright Kreisel, "Varieties of Citizen Review: The Implications of Organizational Features of Complaint Review Procedures for Accountability of the Police" 16(3) American Journal of Police 65.

SECTION TWO

# EVALUATING CRITICAL OVERSIGHT

# 4

# *Institutional Structure v Political Will: Albuquerque as a Case Study in the Effectiveness of Civilian Oversight of Police*

EILEEN LUNA and SAMUEL WALKER

## INTRODUCTION

From the early 1980s through the mid-1990s the city of Albuquerque, New Mexico had two citizen oversight agencies for its police department: the Independent Counsel (IC) and the Public Safety Advisory Board (PSAB).[1] Yet, by 1996 there was bitter controversy over a high number of fatal shootings by Albuquerque police officers and the effectiveness of the two oversight agencies. Thirty citizens had been fatally shot and killed in the previous ten years, an average of three per year. This represented an extremely high fatal shooting rate compared with other cities.[2]

In response to continuing community protests, the Albuquerque City Council contracted with the authors of this chapter for an evaluation of the two oversight agencies and the Internal Affairs (IA) unit of the police department. This chapter reports on the findings of that evaluation.[3]

This study of the Albuquerque oversight mechanisms explores the structure versus process in citizen oversight of the police. The political debate in the US has largely focused on the issue of the formal structure and powers of oversight agencies, particularly on the question of whether an oversight agency should have original jurisdiction to independently investigate citizen complaints. Relatively little attention has been given to issues of process and implementation. These include questions about whether powers granted by law are actually used and, if so, whether use of those powers achieve their intended goals. This article argues, that oversight officials in Albuquerque failed to use many of the

[1] These mechanisms were replaced by a new ordinance enacted in the fall of 1998. Albuquerque City Council, Enactment No 31–1998 (19 October 1998).
[2] S Walker and E Luna, *A Report on the Oversight Mechanisms of the Albuquerque Police Department* (Albuquerque: City Council, 1997), pp. 7–14.
[3] *Ibid.*

powers expressly granted to them by law. The reasons for this failure are discussed at the end of this chapter.[4]

## ALBUQUERQUE IN CONTEXT

### The Albuquerque Police Crisis

Fatal shootings by police have been a major controversy in the United States since the early 1960s. In this respect, the political crisis surrounding the police in Albuquerque was fairly typical of police-related crises in other American cities over the last thirty-five years.[5] Other aspects of the crisis and the subsequent evaluation, however, are somewhat different than the norm. These differences include trends in fatal shootings, the role of race and ethnicity in the crisis, and the role of citizen oversight mechanisms in responding to the crisis.

Generally, most crises involving police violations of human rights in the United States have involved issues of discrimination on the basis of race and ethnicity.[6] Many of the riots of the 1960s, for example, were precipitated by fatal shootings of African Americans.[7] Beginning in the 1970s, however, the number of citizens shot and killed by the police declined significantly.[8] The principal cause of this decline was the development of restrictive deadly force policies by police departments, that represented a "defence of life" standard as opposed to the old, permissive "fleeing felon" standard. The restrictive policies included accountability measures requiring officers to complete a formal report on each weapons discharge, with all reports being subject to an automatic review by supervisors.[9] In short, the continued high rate of shootings in Albuquerque occurred in the context of significant reductions in most major American cities, and thus was a legitimate cause for public concern.

Despite the salience of race in American police crises, the pattern of shootings in Albuquerque did not represent a prima facie case of racial or ethnic discrimination. Many of the victims were white, non-Hispanics, and many of the most questionable shootings involved persons who were apparently suffering from psychological disorders. Contributing to this problem was the fact that the

[4] A comprehensive study of citizen oversight of the police is in S Walker, *Police Accountability* (forthcoming, 2000).

[5] The best introduction to the police crises of the 1960s is National Advisory Commission on Civil Disorders, Report (New York: Bantam Books, 1968). For events of the 1970s see US Commission on Civil Rights, *Who is Guarding the Guardians?* (Washington: Government Printing Office, 1981); for the 1990s, see Human Rights Watch, *Shielded From Justice: Police Brutality and Accountability in the United States* (New York: Human Rights Watch, 1998).

[6] *Ibid.*

[7] National Commission on Civil Disorders [Kerner Commission], Report (New York, Bantam Books, 1968).

[8] W A Geller and M S Scott, Deadly Force: *What We Know* (Washington: Police Executive Research Forum, 1992).

[9] J J Fyfe, "Administrative Intervention on Police Shooting Discretion: An Empirical Examination", 7 *Journal of Criminal Justice* 309 (Winter 1979). S Walker, *Taming the System* (New York, Oxford University Press, 1994), Ch. 4.

county suffered from a severe lack of adequate facilities for persons suffering from short-term mental health crises.[10]

The lack of a racial or ethnic dimension to the shootings in Albuquerque was particularly surprising given the fact that the population of the city is forty per cent Hispanic according to official US census data.[11] Moreover, given its location in the southwestern region of the United States, the city experienced a significant population of recent immigrants from Mexico, with which the state shares a border. It is also likely that the city has a significant population of undocumented persons not counted by the official census. Additionally, although the official resident population of Albuquerque is only three per cent Native American, a number of Native American communities are located nearby. This means that the city has a significant transient Native American population.

The unique ethnic history of Albuquerque contributed to the absence of ethnic conflict within the police department. Hispanic people have been residents of the city for many generations, and today comprise much of its political establishment. At the time of the evaluation, both the mayor and the president of city council were Hispanic. Additionally, about forty per cent of the officers in the Albuquerque Police Department are Hispanic. The fact that the percentage of Hispanic officers roughly matches the population of the community means that the Albuquerque Police Department conforms to generally recognised standards for minority employment.[12] Interviews with police officers and community representatives during the course of the evaluation determined that, unlike many other police departments in the United States at this time, the department did not suffer from strong internal divisions along racial or ethnic lines.[13]

Interviews suggested that the problem of a high rate of fatal shootings in the Albuquerque Police Department (APD) was due not to racial or ethnic discrimination per se, but to a general organisational culture that emphasised aggressive law enforcement and to a specific organisational culture within the Special Weapons and Tactics unit (SWAT) that was involved in many of the controversial shootings. (Several observers of the police have expressed concern about the growing militarisation of the American police, as indicated by the increase in both the number of SWAT teams and the level of weaponry available to officers assigned to these units.)[14] Many interviewees stated that the SWAT unit

[10] S Walker and E Luna, *supra* n. 2.

[11] US Bureau of the Census, Statistical Abstract of the United States, 1998 (Washington, Government Printing Office, 1998), p. 47.

[12] Bureau of Justice Statistics, Law Enforcement Management and Administrative Statistics—1993 (Washington: Government Printing Office, 1995). On the recommended standards, see *Commission on Accreditation for Law Enforcement Agencies, Standards for Law Enforcement Agencies* (3rd ed.) (Fairfax, VA: CALEA, 1994), Ch. 31.

[13] Many interviewees did state that they believed that a system of favouritism existed within the department, but that the divisions did not fall along clear ethnic lines.

[14] P B Kraska and L J Cubellis, "Militarizing Mayberry and Beyond: Making Sense of American Paramilitary Policing", 14 *Justice Quarterly* 607 (December 1997). For a less critical view of trends related to SWAT teams, see the forthcoming study of SWAT teams by Professor David Klinger, University of Missouri—St. Louis.

appeared to escalate rather than de-escalate confrontations with armed and psychologically disturbed citizens, with the result that citizens at some point took some action that justified police use of deadly force. The police department, in fact, cited reviews of shooting incidents by outside experts that concluded that the department's deadly force policy conformed to established professional standards and that particular shootings were within those policy guidelines. Nonetheless, as the evaluation was in process the APD was implementing a Crisis Intervention Team (CIT) programme, borrowed from the Memphis, Tennessee Police Department which is designed to train officers to de-escalate situations involving the mentally ill.

In short, the specific police problem in Albuquerque was more subtle and complex than is normally the case in most American cities. The problem was not directly related to racial or ethnic bias, or the lack of adequate guidelines on use of deadly force, but instead to a more elusive and difficult to document organisational culture—one that valued confrontation and de-valued conciliation.

The impact of organisational culture on police practices is a phenomenon that has not been adequately studied, even though many experts believe it is extremely important. Studies of police corruption, for example, have argued that corruption is reduced in departments where the chief conveys the message, by word and deed, that it will not be tolerated.[15] Similarly, studies of police use of excessive force suggest that misconduct is reduced in departments where the chief "set[s] a tone" of high standards of professionalism.[16] The concept of organisational culture is a variation on the concept of a police subculture. Originally developed by Westley and Skolnick, the concept of a police subculture holds that certain norms of conduct are common to all police officers.[17] The concept of organisational culture suggests that the attitudes and behaviour of police officers varies considerably from department to department.

The Los Angles Police Department (LAPD) represents one well-known example of the apparent impact of organisational culture on police conduct. The 1991 beating of Rodney King and the subsequent Christopher Commission investigation highlighted the existence of a long-standing problem of racism within the LAPD.[18] Nonetheless, with respect to the employment of African American officers, the LAPD has, at least superficially, an exemplary record. That is to say, the percentage of African American officers on the force perfectly matches the percentage of African Americans in the city of Los Angeles.[19] Thus, the problem

[15] L W Sherman, *Scandal and Reform: Controlling Police Corruption* (Berkeley: University of California Press, 1978). See especially, "Changing the Organization", pp. 120–34.

[16] Human Rights Watch, *Shielded From Justice*, p. 62.

[17] W A Westley, *Violence and the Police* (Cambridge, MIT Press, 1970). J H Skolnick, *Justice Without Trial* (3rd ed.) (New York, Macmillan, 1994).

[18] Christopher Commission, *Report of the Independent Commission on the Los Angeles Police Department* (Los Angeles, Christopher Commission, 1991).

[19] S Walker and K B Turner, *A Decade of Modest Progress* (Omaha: University of Nebraska at Omaha, 1992).

of racism within the LAPD goes beyond the question of the number of African American officers and involves issues of the place of those officers within the organisation, the culture of the organisation, and how that culture affects on-the-street policing.

### THE ALBUQUERQUE OVERSIGHT MECHANISMS

The context of the police crisis in Albuquerque also involved the role of citizen oversight. Unlike the typical police crisis in the United States where there is no citizen oversight, Albuquerque maintained two separate external oversight mechanisms together with the traditional police internal affairs (IA) unit. Thus, the crisis raises important questions about the role of these mechanisms in responding to the high rate of fatal shootings by Albuquerque police officers.

#### The Independent Counsel

The office of the Independent Counsel (IC) was created in 1987. The ordinance gave the IC extraordinary power, including full authority to "direct the overall manner" of the complaints process in the Albuquerque Police Department (APD). The purpose of the IC was "to ensure a fair, objective and impartial investigation" of citizen complaints by the internal affairs unit of the APD. Its independence was designed to "enhance the credibility of this process" and to ensure "public confidence" that there was a proper review of "the conduct of members" of the police department. The ordinance specifically directed the IC to review all IA investigations, to make recommendations for discipline, and to make recommendations on any and all matters of police policy where it deemed appropriate.[20]

The IC was an attorney in private practice, working under a fixed-term contract with the city. Two individuals had served as IC by the time of the evaluation. The initial IC established, and the subsequent IC continued, a procedure whereby individual citizen complaints would be investigated by IA and then forwarded to the IC for review. The IC could disagree with IA and order additional investigation of a complaint. If the IC and IA disagreed over the final disposition of a complaint, the case would be submitted to the Chief Administrative Officer (CAO) of the city for resolution.

In the context of existing citizen review procedures in the US, the structure of the Albuquerque IC was somewhat unique. In many respects it had extraordinary power compared with other procedures.[21] The language of the legislative authority to "direct" the complaints process contained no clear limits. One of

[20] S Walker and E Luna, *supra* n. 2, Ch. 9.

[21] See *Ibid.*, Ch. 9. See also the comparative analysis in S Walker and B W Kreisel, "Varieties of Civilian Review" XV *American Journal of Police* 65 (1996).

the major problems with oversight agencies in most other US jurisdictions is that their powers are extremely limited. Many have neither independent investigatory power nor access to police internal investigation files.[22] The two ICs chose to leave primary responsibility for investigating complaints with the police department and to confine the IC's role to the review of the department's work. On the one hand, this decision limited the IC's role and precluded opposition from the police department that the IC was completely usurping its functions in this sensitive area. At the same time, the more limited role kept the actual work load of the IC to a minimum.

In certain respects, the Albuquerque IC represented a version of the auditor model of citizen oversight of the police, insofar as it regularly reviewed the work of internal affairs. At the same time, however, it was stronger, or at least potentially stronger than other auditor systems by virtue of its statutory power to "direct" the complaints process.[23] Whether the IC could have interpreted its legislative mandate more broadly, and assumed full authority to investigate complaints, is a matter of conjecture at this point. As is so often the case in American law, statutory authority is framed in general terms and actual implementation involves a series of discretionary decisions reflecting political and/or administrative considerations.

There is no clear explanation for the structure and power of the Albuquerque IC. The history of citizen oversight in the US, however, indicates that most agencies have developed locally, with no guidance from any standard model. Agencies in other cities and counties have developed in an ad hoc experimental fashion, reflecting the vagaries of local leadership and political compromise. The result is considerable variety across the country in terms of structure and power. The auditor systems in San Jose, California, Portland, Oregon, Seattle, Washington, and Los Angeles County, California have somewhat different structures and powers.[24]

## The Public Safety Advisory Board

The Public Safety Advisory Board (PSAB) was a board of citizens, appointed by the mayor and city council, with the authority "to conduct studies, receive information, and make recommendations" related to the "policies, practices, and procedures" of the police department, fire department, corrections department, and detention facility of the city of Albuquerque. The PSAB had no direct involvement in the complaints process of the APD, but its mandate clearly

[22] S Walker and B W Kreisel, *ibid.*

[23] S Walker, "New Directions in Citizen Oversight: The Auditor Approach to Handling Citizen Complaints" in T O Shelley and A C Grant (eds.), *Problem Oriented Policing* (Washington, Police Executive Research Forum, 1998), pp. 161–78.

[24] The history of the oversight movement is described in detail in S Walker, *supra* n. 4, Ch. 2.

authorised it to investigate and report on any problems that it deemed important.[25]

Compared with other oversight mechanisms, the PSAB was very weak. It had no power or responsibility directly related to citizen complaints or the complaints process. It more closely resembled various citizen advisory committees that have existed over the years in the US, agencies that are authorised to conduct studies and prepare reports but which have no power specifically related to the complaints process.[26]

### Internal Affairs Unit

The Internal Affairs (IA) unit of the Albuquerque Police Department closely resembles the standard form of IA units in contemporary police departments.[27] Its function is to receive citizen complaints (and handle internally generated allegations of misconduct), investigate such complaints, and forward recommendations for discipline to the chief of police. As a matter of policy, disciplinary actions were decentralised. Captains in the various units made the operative decisions on the level of discipline to be imposed. The IA unit was commanded by a lieutenant, with a staff of sworn officer investigators and clerical staff. The unit was housed in a municipal building separate from the main police headquarters. A number of other police departments in the US now follow this practice, in an effort to create the appearance of independence.[28] As indicated above, all IA investigations were subject to review by the IC.

### The Albuquerque Oversight Mechanisms in Context

The two external mechanisms in Albuquerque need to be specified within the range of oversight agencies that exist in the US. External oversight is a relatively new phenomenon in the United States. At the time of the evaluation, only about sixty-five law enforcement agencies (out of a national total of over fifteen thousand agencies) had any form of external oversight. About seventy-five per cent of the fifty largest cities in the country, representing Albuquerque's peer group, did have some form of oversight.

[25] S Walker and E Luna, *supra* n. 2, Ch. 6.

[26] The President's Crime Commission, among other groups, recommended the creation of such advisory boards in the 1960s, in response to police-community relations crisis. President's Commission on Law Enforcement and Administration of Justice, *The Challenge of Crime in a Free Society* (Washington, Government Printing Office, 1967), p. 101.

[27] P West, "Investigation of Complaints Against the Police: Summary Report of a National Survey" 7 *American Journal of Police* 101 (1988). Commission on Accreditation for Law Enforcement Agencies, Standards for Law Enforcement Agencies (Fairfax, CALEA, 1994).

[28] While a separate location helps relieve the fears of citizen complainants, it is also intended to lessen the embarrassment of police officers who are called for interviews. Separate locations exist in New Orleans and San Jose, among other cities.

The evaluation quickly determined that the Public Safety Advisory Board (PSAB) was not a true form of external oversight as that concept has developed in the United States and other Western democracies. The crucial factor was the fact that the PSAB had no direct involvement in the process for handling citizen complaints.[29] The Independent Counsel (IC), meanwhile, represented the auditor model of external oversight. Unlike the more commonly found citizen review boards, auditor forms of oversight do not themselves investigate citizen complaints. Instead, they audit internal affairs units and are empowered to comment on specific problems and/or the level of professionalism.[30] At the time of the evaluation, there were only four auditor models of oversight in the United States, representing less than ten per cent of all external oversight agencies.[31] (As noted above, the ordinance creating the IC was somewhat vague. By one interpretation the IC had power to investigate individual complaints. The persons who held the position of IC, however, chose not to assert that power.) Thus, the existing external oversight agencies in Albuquerque at the time of the evaluation were not typical of the most common forms of oversight in the United States.

## EVALUATING THE EFFECTIVENESS OF CITIZEN OVERSIGHT

The experience of evaluating the Albuquerque oversight mechanisms provides an opportunity to discuss the proper criteria and performance measures for evaluating citizen oversight agencies. Despite the fact that citizen oversight has grown significantly in the United States and other countries over the past twenty years,[32] the question of its effectiveness remains a matter of controversy. There have been relatively few evaluations that rise to the level of scientific standards.

Previous evaluations suffer from a number of serious limitations. First, the issue of effectiveness is generally framed in dichotomous either/or terms of external oversight versus internal review.[33] This approach fails to take into account the substantial variation in oversight agencies. There are at least four different models of oversight, along with significant variations within each category.[34] In one model, external review boards have independent authority to

[29] The various models are discussed in Ch. 5 of S Walker and E Luna, *supra* n. 2.

[30] S Walker, *supra* n. 23.

[31] S Walker and B Wright, *supra* n. 21.

[32] A Goldsmith (ed.), *Complaints Against the Police: The Trend to External Review* (Oxford: Clarendon Press, 1991). S Walker, *Citizen Review of the Police—1998 Update* (Omaha, University of Nebraska at Omaha, 1998).

[33] See for example, D Perez, *Common Sense About Police Review* (Philadelphia, Temple University Press, 1994).

[34] S Walker and B W Kreisel, "Varieties of Citizen Review". The literature on police internal affairs units very limited. See P West, "Investigation of Complaints Against the Police: Summary Report of a National Survey" and the data in A M Pate and L A Fridell, *Police Use of Force*, 2 Vols. (Washington, The Police Foundation, 1993).

investigate citizen complaints. In two other models, that reflect political compromise, review boards examine investigative files compiled by police internal affairs units. The fourth model is the auditor approach. At the same time, there are substantial variations among police internal affairs units.[35]

Second, evaluations to date, with a few exceptions, have failed to take into account the multiple goals of citizen oversight. These goals include (1) providing thorough and fair investigation of complaints; (2) sustaining a proper percentage of complaints (although it should be noted that there is no generally agreed upon standard for what that percentage should be);[36] (3) deterring police misconduct (4) providing satisfaction to individual complainants, and improving public opinion about the police; and (5) helping to improve the overall quality of the police department, including the complaints process.[37] Advocates of oversight argue that external citizen oversight will achieve these goals more effectively than traditional police internal complaint review procedures.

Third, many of these goals have been separately evaluated. Moreover, there has been little discussion of what indicators should be used as performance measures for each of these goals. There is, for example, little discussion of how one would determine the thoroughness and fairness of a complaint investigation.[38] Nor has there been any serious attempt to evaluate how one would measure the deterrent effect of oversight.[39]

Fourth, many discussions of effectiveness have focused narrowly on the sustain rate: the percentage of complaints resolved in favour of the complainant. These discussions, however, fail to take into account the problems with official complaint data. These data are affected by extremely low rates of complaining,[40] extreme variations in official complaint rates,[41] the failure of police in many instances to record complaints that are brought to them,[42] the absence of

[35] P West, *ibid.*

[36] This issue is discussed in detail in S Walker, *supra* n. 4.

[37] The notable exception to this rule, which investigates several goals of oversight is S Herzog, "Police Violence in Israel: The Police Complaints System on Use of Force Complaints", Ph.D. Dissertation, Hebrew University of Jerusalem, 1988 (in Hebrew). See the chapter in this volume.

[38] There is almost nothing in the scholarly literature on this subject. The most important contributions are in the professional literature, where the oversight agencies in Portland, Oregon, San Jose, California, and Los Angeles County regularly audit complaint investigations.

[39] Any such effort encounters two serious problems. First, the data on official citizen complaints is highly problematic and is not a reliable indicator of police performance. Some analysts argue that significant improvements in a police complaints system is likely to produce an increase in complaints, because citizens feel more confident about receiving a fair hearing. Second, assuming there were reliable indicators of police misconduct, it would be difficult to specify the impact of the complaint procedure as opposed to other factors, such as higher recruitment standards, improved training, better supervision, and so on. A full discussion of these issues is in S Walker, *Citizen Complaints and Police Accountability*, *supra* n. 4, Chs. 5 and 6.

[40] S Walker and N Graham, "Citizen Complaints in Response to Police Misconduct: The Results of a Victimization Survey", I *Police Quarterly* 65 (1998).

[41] A M Pate and L A Fridell, *Police Use of Force*, *supra* n. 34.

[42] Los Angeles Inspector General, Sixth Month Report (Los Angeles, The Police Commission, 1997), p. 15.

standardised categories for complaint data,[43] and variations in the processing of complaints.[44]

## EVALUATION METHODOLOGY

The evaluation of the Albuquerque oversight mechanisms sought to determine the effectiveness of the IC and the PSAB based on (1) official documents and data, and (2) the perceptions of relevant stakeholders. This evidence was assessed in terms of the three criteria defined by Perez: integrity, legitimacy, and learning.[45] Integrity involves the question of whether an agency conducts thorough and fair investigations, and otherwise fulfils its official mandate. Legitimacy involves the question of whether the agency is perceived as being legitimate in the eyes of the relevant stakeholders (e.g., complainants, police officers, elected officials, the general public). Learning involves the question of whether the complaints process is part of a process to provide feedback that leads to improvements in the organisation.

The evaluation used a wide range of data sources. First, it examined all relevant official documents related to the IC, the PSAB, and IA. These documents include ordinances, official reports issued by all three agencies, and city council documents related to the police department.

Second, interviews were conducted with relevant stakeholders to obtain perceptions of the effectiveness of the IC and the PSAB. The research strategy was to cast as wide a net as possible and interview individuals from all possible perspectives. The persons interviewed included past and present ICs, past and present members of the PSAB, police officials, including the chief and the commanders of the IA unit and leaders of the police union, members of city council and the council's legislative staff, the mayor, the city attorney, leaders of community groups critical of the police, leaders of community groups believed to be neutral toward the police, attorneys in public and private practice with substantial contact or interest in the police, and friends and family members of persons shot and killed by the police. It should be noted that several people, upon learning that the evaluation was in progress, contacted the evaluators and requested to be interviewed. The director of the city risk management office was contacted but declined to be interviewed.

Third, a survey was administered to over three hundred rank and file APD police officers to obtain their perceptions of the IC, PSAB, and IA unit.[46] In the

[43] Most important, some police departments report citizen complaints while others report all allegations. A single complaint may include several allegations (e.g., use of force and racial slur). The result is that the data from these agencies are not comparable.

[44] A full discussion of these problems is in S Walker, *Citizen Complaints and Police Accountability*, *supra* n. 4.

[45] D Perez, *supra* n. 33.

[46] These surveys provide the basis of B W Kreisel, "An Evaluation of Police Officers's Perceptions of Internal and External Systems of Citizen Complaint Procedures of Police Misconduct", PhD Dissertation, University of Nebraska at Omaha, 1998.

course of administering these surveys, members of the evaluation team had the opportunity to talk informally with many rank and file APD officers.

Fourth, the operations of the IA unit were evaluated through an audit of all IA complaint files for the years 1994, 1995, and 1996 (complaint files are purged after three years). An in-depth audit was conducted of every tenth file. The in-depth audit involved a total of twenty-three complaint files for the three-year period. (The APD received a very low number of complaints per year. The reasons for this are discussed below). The audit was designed to assess the thoroughness and fairness of complaint investigations. The Quarterly Reports submitted by IA were reviewed, and the captain and lieutenant in charge of IA were interviewed.

Fifth, a mail survey was sent to a sample of one-tenth of all citizen complainants for the years 1994–6 to obtain their assessment of the complaints process. Sixth, unannounced visits were made to APD district stations to determine if citizen complaint forms were available.

Table 1 indicates the data sources used for each criterion relating to the two external oversight agencies and the IA unit of the Albuquerque Police Department.

**Table 1** Evaluation Methodology

| | Data Sources for Each Agency for Each Criterion | | |
|---|---|---|---|
| | Independent Counsel | Public Safety Advisory Board | Internal Affairs |
| Integrity | Review of Official Documents<br>Interviews with Key Stakeholders | Review of Official Documents<br>Interviews with Key Stakeholders | Audit of Complaint Files<br>Interviews with Key Stakeholders<br>Unannounced Visits to Precinct Stations |
| Legitimacy | Interviews with Key Stakeholders<br>Survey of rank and file officers | Interviews with Key Stakeholders<br>Survey of rank and file officers | Interviews with Key Stakeholders<br>Survey of rank and file officers<br>Mail survey of Complainants |
| Learning | Interviews with Key Stakeholders | Interviews with Key Stakeholders | Interviews with Key Stakeholders |

FINDINGS

The evaluation team found a high degree of polarisation in the community over the police department as a consequence of the series of fatal shootings by police officers. Additional controversy involved allegations of police use of excessive force, the failure of the police department to respond to citizen protests, and the perceived failure of the existing oversight mechanisms to function effectively. Additional bitterness and distrust of the police department reflected controversies that extended back over fifteen years.

The evaluation concluded that neither the IC, the PSAB, or the IA unit were functioning effectively with respect to the criteria of integrity, legitimacy, and learning. Neither the IC nor the PSAB had completely fulfilled their legislative mandates. There was mixed evidence with respect to the effectiveness of the IC, but virtually all of the evidence indicated that the PSAB was ineffective. The evaluation found that the IA unit was not responsive to the public, and failed to conduct thorough and fair investigations in all cases.

## The Independent Counsel

Both interviews and review of official documents revealed that the IC took an active role in the complaints process as authorised by statute, reviewing complaint investigation files and on occasion requesting that more investigation be done. In that respect, the IC did provide an independent perspective on the investigation of complaints. Documents related to individual complaints indicated that the IC rejected a certain number of cases and ordered further investigation by IA. IA unit officers stated that the IC helped them to "see things from a citizen's point of view". An interview with the current IC indicated that he was sincere and took his responsibilities seriously. Interviews indicated a professional working relationship between the IC and IA that was free of overt conflict and where disagreements were resolved amicably. In terms of integrity, then, the IC was at least partially effective.

Interviews and documents also revealed, however, that the current IC was not making full use of the powers granted the office by statute. The IC took an extremely narrow interpretation of his role, defining it in terms of a lawyer-client relationship, which under the standards of legal ethics in the United States means that information gathered by the IC is confidential and cannot be disclosed publicly. The lawyer-client definition of the IC's role was then used to justify the fact that the IC played virtually no public role in the community. The current IC, for example, did not appear at public meetings related to police issues and rarely, if ever, spoke to the news media about his role. The current IC saw this role not only as a virtue—keeping the office independent of political controversy—but legally required by the lawyer-client relationship.

As a consequence of the IC's very limited public role, community representatives who were interviewed knew little about the activities of the IC with respect to oversight of the APD. Some could not identify the current IC by name. Others who knew him professionally were not aware that he served as the IC. The lack of detailed information about the role of the IC led some community leaders to question the IC's independence, and to assume that he was closely tied to the police department. The survey of police officers also found a low level of awareness of the actual role and activities of the IC. Surprisingly, however, a significant percentage of officers accepted the role of the IC as an external oversight mechanism.[47] The only individuals to speak favourably of the activities of the IC were the current IC himself and the mayor (who, of course, appointed the IC).

Because community representatives lacked both awareness of and credibility in the IC, the evaluation concluded that it was ineffective in terms of the criterion of legitimacy. The IC had failed to achieve its legislatively mandated goal of enhancing the credibility of the complaints process and ensuring "public confidence" that there was proper review of police officers' conduct.

Documents and interviews indicated that the IC did provide some feedback to the APD regarding policies and procedures that needed to be corrected. These activities were fairly minimal, however, and not as extensive as the policy review activities of other oversight agencies in the US.[48] Oversight agencies in San Francisco, San Jose, Los Angeles County, and San Diego County, for example, routinely make anywhere from five to ten policy recommendations annually to their respective law enforcement agencies. Most, although not all of those recommendations are accepted (the acceptance rate is particularly high in San Jose and low in San Diego County). The cumulative impact of such recommendations over time is unknown now because of an absence of empirical research. One may reasonably speculate, however, that the process has some long-term impact on the operations and culture of the agencies receiving and being forced to respond to them.[49] The Albuquerque IC's activities in this regard, by contrast, were limited to only occasional policy recommendations. As a result, the evaluation found that the IC was only partially successful with respect to the criterion of learning.

## The Public Safety Advisory Board

The PSAB was found to be ineffective with respect to all three criteria. Interviews found a near-unanimous consensus of opinion that the PSAB was ineffective. Many expressed the opinion that it was even counter-productive, by promising to be an avenue of accountability and then not fulfilling those

[47] Phd Dissertation, University of Nebraska at Omaha, 1998.
[48] S Walker, *supra* n. 23.
[49] The data on this point is discussed in detail in S Walker, *supra* n. 4.

promises. Interviews with a number of citizens indicated that they had considerable expectations of the PSAB, and were bitter over its failure to act effectively. These citizens had far higher expectations of the PSAB than they did of the IC in large part because the PSAB played a more public role. The PSAB held monthly meetings that included time for citizen input on the agenda. PSAB meetings were, for a time, broadcast over the local public access cable television channel. For some of the more militant community activists, the monthly PSAB meetings were a convenient rallying point for their criticisms of the APD. Citizens concerned about police problems took literally the language of the statute creating the PSAB and expected it to conduct studies and make reports. They were understandably frustrated and angry when they saw it failing to engage in such activities. Significantly, both the police chief and the police department's harshest critics were equally critical of the PSAB, and independently of each other stated that it was dysfunctional. Even the current Chairperson of the PSAB was highly defensive, and admitted that it had not been effective in the past. The survey of rank and file officers found that they were not well-informed about the role of the PSAB.[50]

A review of official documents found that the PSAB had not fully used its authorised power to conduct studies and issue reports. It did conduct a study of police use of force in 1991, and issued a lengthy report with forty recommendations.[51] This report was the exception rather than the rule, however, and there was little evidence that it had made a sustained effort to pursue implementation of the recommendations in this report or that any of the recommendations had been adopted.

Direct observation of one PSAB meeting (January 1997) confirmed the perceptions of persons interviewed. The meeting was conducted in an atmosphere of extreme tension and polarisation. The agenda placed reports from the police chief and other agency heads at the beginning of the meeting, relegating community input to the end. The police chief and his aides left after giving his report and did not stay for the citizen input portion of the meeting. Interviews with many individuals indicated that this particular meeting was not atypical of PSAB meetings in recent years, and that some previous meetings had been marked by even greater overt conflict.

On the basis of this evidence, the evaluation concluded that the PSAB was ineffective with respect to all three criteria: integrity, legitimacy, and learning. With respect to legitimacy, in fact, the PSAB was not merely ineffective, but counterproductive.

[50] B W Kreisel, *supra* n. 46.

[51] Public Safety Advisory Board, Report to Mayor Louis E Saaverda on Police Use of Deadly Force (4 September 1991).

**Internal Affairs Unit**

Interviews with community representatives found a high level of distrust and often hostility to IA. Much of this hostility and distrust reflected perceptions of the APD as a whole and not IA in particular. The police officials directly responsible for IA felt they were doing a good job, although were willing to concede that they needed to make some improvements. The mayor and the police chief expressed strong support for IA. Members of city council were not well informed about the operations of IA. The survey of rank and file officers yielded some surprising findings. Contrary to the literature on policing, officers were not completely hostile to IA.[52] A significant number of officers, in fact, indicated that they wanted the department to impose more rather than less discipline.

The audit of IA complaint files for the years 1994–6 (including an in-depth audit of every tenth file [n = 23]) found that seventeen per cent were of "high quality", fifty seven per cent were "good quality", and twenty-six per cent were "inadequate". The problems in the "inadequate" investigations included failure to fully investigate the complaint, derogatory comments about the complainant that were unrelated to the incident under investigation, and a failure to draw the proper conclusions from the evidence. In half of the "inadequate" cases, the officers made statements that corroborated the complainants' allegations. Yet, these statements were apparently ignored by IA. IA also failed to meet the required time deadlines for completing investigations.[53]

One of the most serious problems found by the evaluation team was the failure of the IA unit of the APD to distribute the department brochure describing the complaints process. Interviews indicated that many community leaders were not certain that such a brochure existed. Spot checks at neighbourhood organisations failed to locate any brochures. Unannounced visits to APD district stations found that the brochures were available at only half of the stations. Members of the review team found copies of the brochure, in both English and Spanish language versions, at the IA office and at the APD training facility.

As a result of the lack of information about the complaints process, the number of formal complaints filed was extremely low, given the size of the APD. APD officials cited this low figure as evidence that the department was doing a good job. The evaluation team, citing evidence from other police departments and oversight agencies, concluded that the low number of complaints was the result of a lack of information about the complaints process and distrust of it among community leaders.[54]

On the basis of this evidence, the evaluation concluded that the IA unit was not effective in terms of integrity or legitimacy.

52 W A Westley, *supra* n. 17.

53 See the Semiannual Reports of Merrick Bobb, Special Counsel to the Los Angeles Sheriffs' Department, and the Quarterly Reports of the Portland Police Internal Investigations Auditing Committee.

54 S Walker, "A Primer on Police Complaint Data", 12 Subject to Debate 6 (1998).

### Additional Aspects of the Learning Criterion

In the course of the evaluation it became clear that, with the exception of some reports of the IC, there was no feedback from other agencies to the APD regarding problems that needed to be corrected. The most serious failure involved the city attorney and the city risk management office with respect to civil suits over police misconduct. The city was paying out an average of between US$1 and US$2 million per year in police-related suits. Many were settled out of court with payments in the US$25,000 to US$50,000 range.

Interviews indicated that neither the city attorney's office nor the risk management office provided feedback to the APD about problems that needed to be corrected. These problems include officers who needed to be counselled, trained, or disciplined, and departmental policies and practices that needed to be changed. Although neither the city attorney nor the risk management officers were covered by the formal mandate of the evaluation, it became clear to the evaluation team that they represented a potentially important form of oversight, but one that was not functioning.

Particularly disturbing was the fact that neither the IC nor the PSAB identified the high volume of damage awards as a problem they should address. Even more disturbing was the lack of concern exhibited by the mayor and members of city council. The only persons indicating any concern about the problem were certain members of the city council's legislative staff who included relevant data in a series of budget memos to the city council. It became apparent that these staff members were taking the initiative to bring police problems to the attention of the responsible elected officials. Critical comments by the police chief about some of these legislative staff members suggested that he was aware of their efforts.

The evidence led the evaluators to conclude that the system of oversight in Albuquerque had failed with respect to the learning criterion.

### Summary of Findings

Table 2 summarises the principal findings, by criterion for each agency. The external and internal oversight agencies were found to be ineffective in six of nine separate categories, and only partially effective in the remaining three. No agency was found to be fully effective on any criterion.

## DISCUSSION

The significant aspect of the ineffectiveness of the oversight mechanisms of the Albuquerque police department was the gap between their authorised powers

**Table 2** Findings

| | Independent Counsel | Public Safety Advisory Board | Internal Affairs |
|---|---|---|---|
| Integrity | Partially Ineffective | Ineffective | Partially Effective |
| Legitimacy | Ineffective | Ineffective | Ineffective |
| Learning | Partially Effective | Ineffective | Ineffective |

and their actual activities. Both the IC and the PSAB failed to use all of the powers granted to them by ordinance. In short, the failure of citizen oversight in Albuquerque was a matter of process rather than structure.

This point is significant because most of the debates over citizen oversight focus on structural issues—that is, the formal powers vested in an oversight agency. Advocates of oversight argue that citizen oversight agencies must be fully independent of the police departments they are responsible for, while opponents argue that the intrusion of outsiders in the complaints process will undermine effective discipline. As a result of political compromise, many oversight agencies have limited powers, without either the power to conduct their own independent investigations or to audit the police complaints process.

The relevant question in analysing the failure of oversight in Albuquerque is why the process failed when the structure was adequate, or at least potentially adequate. We argue that the failure can be explained in terms of what we call political will. Political will is defined here as a commitment to making oversight work effectively on the part of responsible elected officials. In American cities, these officials are primarily the mayor, and secondarily members of city council. Commitment to making oversight work effectively involves several elements: a concern about police accountability, a willingness to listen to critics of a police department, a willingness to pursue corrective actions in the face of opposition from the police and their political allies.

Considerable evidence collected during the evaluation supports the conclusion that the responsible officials in Albuquerque lacked the required level of political will. Members of the evaluation team found that elected officials they interviewed did not take seriously the problems with the APD. The then-mayor insisted that the APD and the IC were doing a fine job, despite the community controversy surrounding the many shootings, and dismissed the leading critics as professional agitators. Even more problematic were the attitudes of various city council members. Only one member expressed great concern about both the police and the oversight mechanisms. And yet, this individual never met with the members of the evaluation team, and cancelled several scheduled meetings.

Other city council members appeared only moderately concerned about police problems. The member from the university district (which included a high concentration of persons concerned about police misconduct, as is the case in other American cities) was poorly informed about the police and primarily interested in land use issues. One member of city council had a family member on the police force, an association that appeared to give this member a generally favourable view of the department.

Members of the evaluation team believe that the lack of political will led to deliberate actions that undermined the effectiveness of the oversight mechanisms. Most important in this regard was the limited role of the IC, and its lack of public visibility in particular. The lawyer-client definition of the IC's role was not required by statute, but was written into the contract between the IC and the city. In short, this was a self-imposed limitation. Moreover, renewal of the IC's contract was not subject to public bidding. This process precluded competitive bids by other candidates who might propose a more active role, along with public debate over the role of the IC. One of the recommendations of the evaluation team was to subject renewal of the contract to public bid.

Along the same lines, there was evidence that the mayor controlled the PSAB in ways that limited its independence. First, as a number of community representatives pointed out, the mayor selected the chair of the PSAB. These representatives felt that if the board was able to choose its own chair the PSAB would be more independent. Second, a number of community representatives complained about the change in procedure that placed community input at the end of the PSAB meetings. This procedure was seen as a strategy to give priority to reports by agency heads and to relegate citizen input to a second-class status.

Evidence from other jurisdictions lends support to the argument that political will is as important as formal structure in determining the effectiveness of citizen oversight of the police. In 1993, after forty years of political controversy, a new ordinance made the New York City Civilian Complaint Review Board (CCRB) fully independent of the New York City Police Department (NYPD). Yet, in the eyes of the leading supporters of external oversight, the CCRB has failed to become effective. The New York Civil Liberties Union (NYCLU) concluded in 1996 that the CCRB has largely failed in its mission.[55] This failure has been attributed to a lack of leadership on the part of the mayor of New York City, who appoints members of the CCRB, has major influence over the agency's budget, and sets the tone of the political debate over police accountability. For the most part, the current mayor has been a staunch defender of the NYPD, and has opposed specific proposals to strengthen the CCRB.[56]

[55] New York Civil Liberties Union, Third Anniversary Overview of the Civilian Complaint Review Board (New York, NYCLU, 1996).

[56] See the criticisms of the mayor in New York Civil Liberties Union, Deflecting the Blame: The Dissenting Report of the Mayor's Task Force on Police/Community Relations (New York, NYCLU, 1998).

The San Francisco Office of Citizen Complaints (OCC), meanwhile, had a mixed record of success during its first twelve years of existence. Lawyers with the local ACLU and the Lawyers Committee for Human Rights regarded it as largely ineffective.[57] Some community representatives expressed the opinion that while the OCC had been created by popular referendum, a succession of mayors had covertly undermined it, in particular by appointing directors with a mandate to restrain the agency. The election of Mayor Willie Brown in 1995 revitalised the agency. Brown expressed strong public support for the agency and appointed a prominent civil rights attorney as director. (A referendum in 1995 also required the city to expand the staff of the OCC.)[58]

In 1981 the City of New Orleans created an Office of Municipal Investigations (OMI), with authority to investigate any municipal agency. The OMI enjoyed political independence through civil service protection for its director. And yet, by the mid-1990s, the New Orleans Police Department (NOPD) had a notorious reputation as perhaps the most corrupt and brutal of any police department in the nation. In a personal interview in 1998, the then-director of the OMI was unable to cite a single example of an improvement in the police department that he had helped to bring about.[59] A major effort to improve standards of integrity in the NOPD began only when the Chamber of Commerce became alarmed about loss of convention business and pressured the mayor to clean up the police department. A major integrity assurance programme is currently underway, although it is premature to assess its effectiveness.

In all three of the examples cited, a police department is subject to a citizen oversight agency with independent power of investigation. In short, the structure meets the goals of oversight advocates. But in all three instances, the effectiveness of the agencies in question has been heavily influenced by the attitudes and actions of the mayor. These actions represent what we regard as political will.

The concept of political will leaves many questions unanswered. This chapter does not claim to have operationalised it in a completely satisfactory manner. It is worth pointing out that it is closely related to the concept of local political culture, which some experts believe exerts a significant impact over police departments, but which also has not been adequately operationalised.[60] Most important, how is the political will of responsible elected officials influenced. In all of the cities discussed here, there have been vigorous efforts by community groups to end police abuse and to ensure police accountability. In all cases they achieved considerable success with respect to structure, but not process.

[57] Interviews, staff members of ACLU—Northern California and San Francisco Chapter of Lawyers Committee for Human Rights, 1996.

[58] San Francisco, Office of Citizen Complaints, 1997 Annual Report (San Francisco, OCC, 1998).

[59] Interview, Director Office of Municipal Investigation, 1998. The OMI had not published an annual report for two years at that point.

[60] J Q Wilson, *Varieties of Police Behavior* (New York, Atheneum, 1973).

The unanswered questions surrounding the issue of political will merit further research. The purpose of this chapter has been to highlight the distinction between structure and process. The case of Albuquerque highlights the point that having an oversight agency or mechanism that appears fully independent as a matter of institutional structure may not necessarily function independently as a matter of process.

## Postscript on Albuquerque

Following the evaluation a number of changes occurred in police and community relations in Albuquerque. First, the number of fatal police shootings declined significantly, thereby reducing community tensions. Second, seven months after the evaluation was completed the city elected a new mayor who promptly fired the police chief and indicated that improving police accountability would be a priority of his administration. Third, a year following the evaluation the city council enacted a new ordinance substantially revising the accountability mechanisms and following the recommendations of the evaluation.[61] The IC was retained, although strengthened in two respects. First, it was placed under a new Independent Review Office (IRO) which was given explicit authority to receive and investigate complaints. This change made the IRO/IC more independent of the police department than in the previous system. Second, the old PSAB was replaced by a Police Oversight Commission (POC) with responsibility for overseeing the IRO and the IC. This change corrected the basic powerlessness of the old PSAB.

At this point, it is too early to determine whether the new accountability mechanisms will prove to be effective. Nonetheless, some observations on the process of change are possible. Most important is the fact that as the crisis in Albuquerque unfolded the political power of the police—including both the police chief and the police union—diminished substantially. Neither one succeeded in controlling events as they unfolded. The chief, in fact, was terminated from his job. In short, even though the previous oversight mechanisms were ineffective and one factor in the community crisis over the police, the police were not able to exploit the crisis to either weaken or abolish external oversight. To the contrary, the crisis heightened public awareness of police problems and strengthened the position of the advocates of stronger oversight mechanisms.

A somewhat similar process has occurred in a number of other American cities. In Portland, Oregon, Minneapolis, Minnesota, and Oakland, California, existing external oversight procedures were found to be ineffective. Criticisms of these agencies led to a strengthening rather than an abolition or weakening of oversight. These events suggest the commitment to external oversight of the police continues to grow in the United States and that for the foreseeable future

[61] Albuquerque City Council, Enactment No 31–1998 (October 19, 1998).

the opponents of external oversight, particularly the police unions, will not be able to weaken or abolish it.

## References

Albuquerque City Council, Enactment No 31–1998 (19 October 1998).

Bureau of Justice Statistics, Law Enforcement Management and Administrative Statistics—1993 (Washington: Government Printing Office, 1995).

Christopher Commission, Report of the Independent Commission on the Los Angeles Police Department (Los Angeles: Christopher Commission, 1991).

Commission on Accreditation for Law Enforcement Agencies, Standards for Law Enforcement Agencies (Fairfax: CALEA, 1994).

J J Fyfe, "Administrative Intervention on Police Shooting Discretion: An Empirical Examination", 7 Journal of Criminal Justice 309 (Winter 1979).

W A Geller and M S Scott, Deadly Force: What We Know (Washington: Police Executive Research Forum, 1992).

A Goldsmith (ed.), Complaints Against the Police: The Trend to External Review (Oxford: Clarendon Press, 1991).

S Herzog, "Police Violence in Israel: The Police Complaints System on Use of Force Complaints", PhD Dissertation, Hebrew University of Jerusalem, 1988 [in Hebrew].

Human Rights Watch, Shielded From Justice: Police Brutality and Accountability in the United States (New York: Human Rights Watch, 1998).

P B Kraska and L J Cubellis, "Militarizing Mayberry and Beyond: Making Sense of American Paramilitary Policing", 14 Justice Quarterly 607 (December 1997).

B W Kreisel, "An Evaluation of Police Officers's Perceptions of Internal and External Systems of Citizen Complaint Procedures of Police Misconduct", PhD dissertation, University of Nebraska at Omaha, 1998.

Los Angeles Inspector General, Sixth Month Report (Los Angeles: The Police Commission, 1997).

National Commission on Civil Disorders [Kerner Commission], Report (New York: Bantam Books, 1968).

New York Civil Liberties Union, Third Anniversary Overview of the Civilian Complaint Review Board (New York: NYCLU, 1996).

New York Civil Liberties Union, Deflecting the Blame: The Dissenting Report of the Mayor's Task Force on Police/Community Relations (New York: NYCLU, 1998).

A M Pate and L A Fridell, Police Use of Force, 2 Vols (Washington: The Police Foundation, 1993).

D Perez, Common Sense About Police Review (Philadelphia: Temple University Press, 1994).

President's Commission on Law Enforcement and Administration of Justice, The Challenge of Crime in a Free Society (Washington: Government Printing Office, 1967), p. 101.

Public Safety Advisory Board, Report to Mayor Louis E. Saaverda on Police Use of Deadly Force (4 September 1991).

San Francisco, Office of Citizen Complaints, 1997 Annual Report (San Francisco: OCC, 1998).

L W Sherman, Scandal and Reform: Controlling Police Corruption (Berkeley: University of California Press, 1978).

J H Skolnick, Justice Without Trial, 3rd ed. (New York: Macmillan, 1994).

US Commission on Civil Rights, Who is Guarding the Guardians? (Washington: Government Printing Office, 1981).

US Bureau of the Census, Statistical Abstract of the United States, 1998 (Washington: Government Printing Office, 1998), p. 47.

S Walker and N Graham, "Citizen Complaints in Response to Police Misconduct: The Results of a Victimization Survey", I Police Quarterly 65 (1998).

S Walker, Police Accountability (forthcoming, 2000).

S Walker, Taming the System (New York: Oxford University Press, 1994).

S Walker and K B Turner, A Decade of Modest Progress (Omaha: University of Nebraska at Omaha, 1992).

S Walker and B W Kreisel, "Varieties of Civilian Review" XV American Journal of Police 65 (1996).

S Walker, "New Directions in Citizen Oversight: The Auditor Approach to Handling Complaints." In T O Shelley and A C Grant (eds.), Problem Oriented Policing (Washington: Police Executive Research Forum, 1998), pp. 161–78.

S Walker, "A Primer on Police Complaint Data", 12 Subject to Debate 6 (1998).

S Walker and E. Luna, A Report on the Oversight Mechanisms of the Albuquerque Police Department (Albuquerque: City Council, 1997), pp. 7–14.

S Walker, Citizen Review of the Police—1998 Update (Omaha: University of Nebraska at Omaha, 1998).

P West, "Investigation of Complaints Against the Police: Summary Report of a National Survey", 7 American Journal of Police 101 (1988).

W A Westley, Violence and the Police (Cambridge: MIT Press, 1970).

J Q Wilson, Varieties of Police Behavior (New York: Atheneum, 1973).

# 5

# *Evaluating the Performance of External Oversight Bodies*

DAVID BRERETON

## INTRODUCTION

In his introduction to the first edition of *Complaints Against Police: The Trend to External Review*, David Bayley observed that the movement towards civilian review had institutional momentum and that "the question is not whether there will be civilian review of complaints, but how soon".[1] Nearly ten years later it can no longer be said that external oversight of police is accepted as an inevitability. Some governments are now querying whether expenditure on external oversight mechanisms can be justified, and police departments and police unions in a number of jurisdictions are reasserting claims that they are able to do a better job of dealing with complaints than are external agencies. Even some long-standing advocates of the principle of external oversight have expressed doubts about whether the mechanisms which have been established have made much difference to how complaints against police are dealt with "on the ground".[2]

This chapter is intended to contribute to this debate by reviewing the available evidence concerning the impact and effectiveness of external oversight bodies. As discussed below, there are several obstacles to undertaking such an assessment. Most external oversight bodies do not routinely monitor and report on their own performance, very few have been independently evaluated and there are some daunting methodological problems involved in ascertaining the extent to which the introduction of these mechanisms has "made a difference" to police practices and behaviour, or to the way in which complaints are handled. Nonetheless, it is important that an assessment of the performance of

I am grateful to the Queensland Criminal Justice Commission for allowing me to refer to the findings of several unpublished studies. The opinions expressed in this chapter are my own and do not necessarily reflect the views of the Commission.

[1] D Bayley, "Preface" in A Goldsmith (ed.), *Complaints Against the Police: The Trend to External Review* (Oxford, Clarendon Press, 1991) x–xi.

[2] See for example, A Goldsmith, "What's Wrong with Complaint Investigations: Dealing with Difference Differently in Complaints Against Police" (1996) 15 *Criminal Justice Ethics* 36.

external oversight bodies at least be attempted; both to establish what is known, and to identify areas where further research should be concentrated.

## PRELIMINARY CONSIDERATIONS

### Key Questions

Justifications for establishing and retaining external oversight bodies can broadly be divided into two categories. One set of arguments is broadly *normative* in nature, meaning that they rely primarily upon appeals to important philosophical values such as accountability and transparency. The second group of arguments are more *empirical* in content, meaning that they are susceptible to testing by measurement and systematic observation. Arguments in this latter category take the form of claims about the practical benefits which flow from external oversight, such as more thoroughness and greater impartiality in investigations, improved standards of police behaviour, increased legitimacy of the complaints process, and so on.

This chapter is concerned with assessing and evaluating claims of the second type. In focusing on empirical issues, I am not suggesting that the normative arguments in favour of external oversight are irrelevant; to the contrary, they provide compelling reasons for why there should be no slackening in efforts to ensure that there is proper external accountability of police. However, it is very important that the claims which have been made about the impact and effectiveness of external oversight are properly scrutinised. If external oversight bodies are to survive over the longer term, philosophical arguments about their value will need to be buttressed by more tangible evidence of their benefits. By critically assessing how well external oversight bodies have performed to date, we will also be in a much better position to identify ways in which their effectiveness can be enhanced in the future.

Drawing upon the existing literature and the policy debates over external oversight, I have identified the following as the key questions to be addressed in this chapter:

- how successful have external oversight bodies been in improving the way in which complaints against police are investigated?
- is complainant satisfaction higher when a complaint is dealt with externally, rather than internally?
- to what extent have external oversight bodies been instrumental in bringing about improvements in police practices and behaviour?
- has the trend towards external oversight had a deleterious effect on police morale and police operational effectiveness?

An important omission from this list is any consideration of the issue of cost effectiveness. This has been an increasing focus in recent debates about the value of external oversight, but without good data about the impact of these bodies, it is very difficult to engage in discussions about whether their cost can be justified. In addition, there are complex methodological issues which would need to be resolved before the concept of cost effectiveness could be operationalised. (For example, what is the monetary value of a reduction in the incidence of police misconduct?) The chapter also does not include any consideration of the evidence relating to general public attitudes towards external oversight bodies—mainly because this information, while important for other reasons, is of only limited relevance to assessing how effectively such bodies are performing.

## Methodological Issues

A basic problem in evaluating external oversight bodies is that relatively little information is available about what these bodies do and how well they do it. Most oversight bodies monitor and report on only a few basic indicators, such as the number and type of complaints received, complaint finalisation times, and the number and proportion of complaints which are substantiated: very few bodies collect or publish data which can be used to assess the quality of their decision-making processes or their overall effectiveness, and few appear to have been the subject of independent evaluations or reviews. There has also been relatively little academic research conducted in this area, no doubt in part because of the lack of accessible data.

It is particularly difficult to assess whether the outcomes which are achieved under external oversight arrangements are any better—or different from—those generated by police-based systems. Very little information is available about the operation and effectiveness of police complaint handling processes and there are formidable methodological obstacles to comparing the effectiveness of external and internal systems. The most methodologically rigorous technique would be an experimental design, where cases are randomly assigned to different systems or processes and the outcomes achieved under those varying conditions are then compared; however, it is doubtful that an experimental study could ever be conducted which would emulate "real world" complaints processes. Comparisons across jurisdictions are hampered by a lack of consistency in definitions and counting rules, and the inability to control for the influence of other factors, such as different cultural and institutional settings. Trend data are available from the annual reports of some external oversight bodies, but there are few opportunities for undertaking pre and post comparisons, because suitable baseline measures are generally lacking for the period prior to the establishment of these bodies. There is also only limited scope for undertaking intra-jurisdictional comparisons between external and internal investigative processes, because of a lack of comparability in the types of matters handled.

These issues aside, there is no "typical" external oversight body which can be compared with a "typical" internal system. Oversight bodies differ substantially from each other in respect to matters such as: the scope of their jurisdiction; the powers and resources which they have at their disposal; whether their role is predominantly one of investigating, auditing and/or reviewing complaints; the extent to which they are able to play a broader policy role; their structure and staffing; and, their internal operating procedures.[3] Similarly, police departments vary considerably in how they structure complaint handling processes and in the quantum of resources which they allocate to such activities.[4] Hence, it cannot necessarily be assumed that what holds true for one organisation or jurisdiction will necessarily apply to others.

Because of these constraints, some aspects of the following discussion are unavoidably inconclusive. Where this is the case, I indicate what additional information is required to enable a more thorough assessment of the effectiveness of external oversight bodies to be undertaken. I also make some more general observations about how external oversight bodies can facilitate future evaluations of their activities and suggest some directions for further research.

## KEY FINDINGS

### The Investigation and Disposition of Complaints

The trend towards increased use of external oversight mechanisms has been underpinned, to a large extent, by the view that police departments, left to themselves, cannot be relied upon to conduct objective and thorough investigations of complaints against their own officers. Evidence cited in support of this view has included case studies of shoddy investigations undertaken by police, anecdotal evidence of disparaging comments about complainants made by internal investigators, and statistical data showing very low substantiation rates for internally investigated complaints.[5] The corresponding assumption has been that creation of external oversight bodies would lead to an increase in the general quality of investigations, both because there would be greater external scrutiny of the investigations conducted by police and because, in some

[3] P West, "Investigation of Complaints Against the Police: Summary Report of a National Survey" (1998) 17 *American Journal of Police* 101; A Goldsmith, "External Review and Self-Regulation: Police Accountability and the Dialectics of Complaints Procedures" in A Goldsmith (ed.), *Complaints Against the Police*; D W Perez, *Common Sense About Police Review* (Philadelphia, Temple University Press, 1994); S Walker and B Wright, *Citizen Review of the Police, 1994 A National Survey* (Washington DC, Police Executive Research Forum, 1995); S Walker and B Kreisel, "Varieties of Citizen Review: The Implications of Organisational Features of Complaint Review Procedures for Accountability of the Police" (1996) 15 *American Journal of Police* 65.

[4] See Perez, *ibid* and Walker and Kreisel, *ibid*.

[5] See for example, the highly critical assessment of the pre-1990 police complaints system in Queensland, contained in the *Report of the Commission of Inquiry into Possible Illegal Activities and Associated Police Misconduct* (Government Printer, Brisbane, 1989) at 285–99 (Fitzgerald Inquiry).

instances, the oversight body itself would carry out these investigations. This view has been based, in turn, on the belief that, relative to a purely internal process, an external body will be more likely to adopt an impartial stance and will have a greater incentive to ensure that complaints are thoroughly investigated.

In assessing whether these assumptions have held true, it is important to distinguish between oversight bodies which focus principally on reviewing and/or supervising investigations conducted by police departments, and those bodies which undertake a significant proportion of complaints investigations themselves. In the former case, the critical issue to be addressed is whether the quality of *police* investigations has been improved as a result of their being subjected to external monitoring and review. In the latter instance, the key question is whether oversight bodies have shown *themselves* to be more effective than internal systems in investigating complaints. Both forms of oversight will be considered in the following discussion.

### *The Impact of External Oversight on Police Investigations*

Many external oversight bodies routinely report on the number of matters reviewed, the number of police investigations supervised, recommendations made, and so on. These reports provide useful information about the workloads of such bodies and show that they take their review role seriously, but activity should not be equated with effectiveness. In order to support claims about the positive effects of external oversight, it is necessary to show that recommendations for further investigative action are acted on with a reasonable degree of frequency. Ideally, there should also be some indication of an improvement over time in the quality of the police investigations, as evidenced by a reduction in the number of reviewed matters which are deemed to require further investigation or which result in a recommendation for a different outcome. (This is based on the assumption that, if the review process is working properly, police departments will learn how to reduce the number of matters which are deemed not to have been appropriately investigated.)

Some oversight bodies regularly report on the number of matters referred to the police for further attention due to deficiencies being identified in the initial investigation.[6] It is also fairly common for oversight bodies to provide examples in their annual reports of where this process has resulted in different investigative outcomes. However, the frequency of such successes relative to the number of matters reviewed generally cannot be determined. In systems where hundreds, if not thousands, of complaints are processed annually, it will always be possible for another body to identify some cases where the initial investigation

[6] See for example, the Ombudsman, Victoria, *Twenty-Fourth Report of the Ombudsman* (Melbourne, 1997); RCMP Public Complaints Commission *Performance Report* (Minister of Public Works and Government Services Canada, 1998).

was deficient. What needs to be ascertained is not simply that some initial investigative findings may have been reversed as a result of the review process, but how often this happens, and whether this is occurring less frequently over time.[7]

The only published study to systematically address these issues is Maguire and Corbett's 1991 report on the British Police Complaints Authority.[8] They found that investigating officers in matters which were supervised by the Authority "were unanimous that supervision had made no difference at all to the shape or outcome of the investigation".[9] In around ten per cent of complaints where disciplinary action was taken, this had been as a result of a recommendation of the Authority after the Deputy Chief Constable had initially concluded that no action was warranted. However, this apparently had little overall impact on outcomes, as the formation of the Authority in 1985 had not led to a statistically significant increase in the proportion of police complaint investigations resulting in a substantiated finding.[10]

More recently, Walker has drawn attention to a report by the Portland Police Independent Investigation Auditing Committee which appears to show that the Committee's auditing activities have contributed to greater consistency in the quality of investigations.[11] Generally, though, it is difficult to discern any obvious trend from the data which are presented by oversight bodies.

In summary, on the information available it is not possible to ascertain the extent to which, or circumstances under which, external oversight bodies have contributed to improved police complaint investigation processes. Maguire and Corbett's study of the British Police Complaints Authority suggests that the impact has been limited, but some other bodies, using more sophisticated auditing strategies, may have had more success (as suggested by Walker). The challenge for external oversight bodies which perform review and auditing functions is to put in place recording and reporting systems which will, in the future, enable the achievements of these bodies to be measured in a more systematic and consistent fashion. Without such information, it will be very difficult to provide persuasive evidence to support claims about the capacity of external review, or of particular auditing strategies, to improve the quality of police complaint handling processes.

[7] For similar observations see the *Report of the Auditor General of Canada to the House of Commons* (Ottawa, 1997), Chapter 34 "RCMP Public Complaints Commission".

[8] M Maguire and C Corbett, *A Study of the Police Complaints System* (London, HMSO, 1991) and M Maguire, "Complaints Against the Police: The British Experience" in A Goldsmith (ed.), *Complaints Against the Police.*

[9] Maguire, *ibid*, p. 200.

[10] *Ibid*, p. 187.

[11] S Walker, "New Directions in Citizen Oversight: The Auditor Approach to Handling Citizen Complaints" in T Shelly and A Grant, *Problem-Oriented Policing: Crime-Specific Problems, Critical Issues and Making POP Work* (Washington DC, Police Executive Research Forum, 1998) at 167.

### *Comparing Internal and External Investigations*

For those oversight bodies which conduct significant numbers of complaint investigations themselves, a key issue is the quality of these investigations vis-à-vis those undertaken by police investigators. This issue can be addressed in two main ways: (a) by comparing the outcomes achieved under different investigative arrangements; and (b) by comparing the investigative processes which are employed. Both of these aspects will be examined briefly in the following discussion.

#### *Outcomes*

As indicated above, it is very difficult to directly compare the investigative outcomes achieved under different processes or in different jurisdictions. Firstly, organisations are not consistent in the way in which they count complaints and complaint outcomes, or in the criteria which they use to determine whether a complaint has been sustained. Second, complaint substantiation rates are affected by the extent to which there is "front-end" screening of evidentially weak complaints; hence, a police department which follows a policy of not recording "spurious" complaints may well substantiate a higher proportion of matters than an external oversight body which assiduously records every complaint received. Third, substantiation rates will also be influenced by the nature and extent of an agency's jurisdiction; for example, those bodies which deal primarily with excessive force complaints are likely to have relatively low rates because such allegations are generally harder to substantiate than other types of complaints. Finally, the number and proportion of investigations which result in a substantiated finding will also depend on the extent to which alternative complaint resolution strategies are employed: where mediation and/or informal resolution is used extensively, there will be fewer investigations and therefore, by definition, fewer substantiated matters.

Although direct comparisons may not be possible, the weight of the available evidence is that external oversight bodies have not achieved *consistently* better investigative outcomes than their internal counterparts. This can be illustrated by comparing substantiation rates for excessive force complaints, which is one of the most common forms of misconduct alleged against police.

According to a 1993 United States national survey of law enforcement agencies, substantiation rates for excessive force complaints were typically around five per cent or less.[12] In Victoria, Australia, the rate of assault allegations "established" by the Victoria Police between 1988–9 and 1992–3 ranged between 4.1 per cent and 5.3 per cent.[13] Kerstetter and Van Winkle reported that during the 1980s the Chicago Police Department Office of Professional

[12] A M Pate and L A Fridell, *Police Use of Force: Official Reports, Citizen Complaints, and Legal Consequence* (Washington DC, Police Foundation, 1993).

[13] *Report of the Deputy Ombudsman (Police Complaints) for the Years Ending 30 June 1992 and 30 June 1993* (Melbourne, 1993) at 38.

Standards sustained only 3.8 per cent of excessive force cases.[14] Similar findings have been reported for the New York Civilian Complaints Review Board.[15] Only 2.4 per cent of the assault complaints "considered" by the British Police Complaints Authority in 1997–8 resulted in disciplinary charges being preferred or the subject officer receiving admonishment or advice.[16] Adverse findings were made in relation to 6.4 per cent of assault complaints to the New South Wales Ombudsman in 1996–97.[17] The Queensland Criminal Justice Commission (CJC)[18] initially achieved a somewhat higher "strike rate", substantiating around eight per cent of the assault allegations which it received between 1991 and 1995, but the rate has since fallen.[19]

"Before-after" comparisons within jurisdictions are generally not possible because of a lack of comparable data. Some trend analysis undertaken by the CJC in Queensland shows that in the five years following the CJC's establishment in 1990 the *proportion* of allegations of police misconduct resulting in a substantiated finding increased by 21 per cent (8.6 to 10.4 per cent) and the *number* of *substantiated* allegations rose by 39 per cent (reflecting a marked increase in the number of complaints over the same period). In the CJC's assessment, this was a "reasonably strong indication" that it was more effective in investigating misconduct complaints than the previous police-based system.[20] However, as indicated this trend was not sustained beyond 1994–5.

In summary, the available evidence suggests that, for the most part, the pattern of investigative outcomes achieved by external investigative bodies is not markedly different from the outcomes produced by police-driven processes. Where a well resourced, professional and independent investigative body has

[14] W Kerstetter and B Van Winkle, *Evidence in Investigation of Police Use of Excessive Force in Chicago*, Working Paper #9015 (Chicago, American Bar Foundation, 1989).

[15] S Walker and V Bumphus, "The Effectiveness of Civilian Review: Observations on Recent Trends and New Issues Regarding the Civilian Review of the Police" (1992) 11 *American Journal of Police*, 1 at 16.

[16] Police Complaints Authority, *Annual Report: 1 April 1997–31 March 1998* (London, 1998) at 13.

[17] New South Wales Ombudsman, *Annual Report 1996–97* (Sydney, 1997) at 38.

[18] The CJC is a powerful and relatively well resourced organisation which became operational in April 1990 in the aftermath of the Fitzgerald Commission of Inquiry into police and public sector corruption in Queensland. In addition to investigating misconduct complaints against Queensland police officers, the CJC has a substantial research capability and a broader charter to monitor and promote reform within the Queensland Police Service. The Fitzgerald Commission of Inquiry had identified significant corruption in the Queensland Police Service, extending to the very top of the organisation, and proposed wide ranging changes to the Police Service and the institutional context in which it operated. For an overview of the establishment and operations of the Criminal Justice Commission see Colleen Lewis, *Complaints Against Police: The Politics of Reform* (Sydney, Hawkins, 1999).

[19] D Brereton and M Burgess, *Complaints of Assault Against Police: Why Are They So Hard to Substantiate and What Should be Done About It?* Paper presented to the Australian and New Zealand Society of Criminology, 12th Annual Conference (Brisbane, July 1997).

[20] CJC, *Integrity in the Queensland Police Service: Implementation and Impact of the Fitzgerald Inquiry Reforms* (Brisbane, GOPRINT, 1997) at 55B69.

replaced a discredited, poorly funded, system (such as occurred in Queensland), an initial improvement in the investigative "strike rate" is likely, but even under these circumstances there are clear limits to what can be achieved.

The main constraint is the fact that a large proportion of complaints against police—particularly those relating to excessive force, assault, overbearing conduct, rudeness, and so on—arise in situations where there are no witnesses, or other objective evidence that the alleged behaviour actually occurred. Moreover, many complainants have criminal records and/or were in the process of being arrested at the time and, as such, have limited credibility as witnesses.[21] In these circumstances, no matter how thorough or independent an investigation, it is inherently difficult to obtain enough evidence to sustain the complaint, particularly given the high standard of proof which must be satisfied in many jurisdictions and the general reluctance of police officers to testify against their colleagues. Consequently, it is arguably unrealistic to expect external oversight bodies to have more than a marginal impact on complaint investigation outcomes—at least while the current legalistic model of investigation still prevails.

*Processes*

If it is accepted that substantiation rates are determined, to a large extent, by factors which are beyond the control of investigators, a more productive line of inquiry may be to focus on comparing the investigative *processes* used by external and internal bodies. Such an approach recognises that, regardless of whether a complaint is substantiated, there is a broad community interest in ensuring that any investigation of possible police wrong-doing is conducted professionally and fairly, and that there is consistency in decision-making.

It is often asserted that external, civilian-controlled bodies have an incentive to apply more rigorous investigative standards than their police counterparts, but to date this claim has been based largely on anecdotal evidence from observers and participants who have witnessed different systems in operation, rather than on systematic observation.[22] A relatively simple way to test claims about the superiority of external processes would be to survey a cross-section of internal and external investigators within the one jurisdiction about the steps which they typically take when they investigate a complaint, the assumptions which they proceed from, and so on. A more methodologically rigorous—but also more resource-intensive—approach would be to document a set of agreed investigative standards and then have independent experts (such as experienced lawyers) review a sample of internal and external investigation files, and/or listen to tape recordings of investigative interviews, in order to identify how many investigations meet these standards.

[21] Brereton and Burgess, *supra* n. 19.

[22] For an example see C Lewis, "Police Complaints: Metropolitan Toronto" in A Goldsmith (ed.), *Complaints Against the Police*.

Any comparative studies along these lines would need to be carefully designed, to ensure that like was being compared with like. External oversight bodies are normally responsible for investigating complaints of a more serious nature, where a more thorough investigation would be expected. Therefore, it obviously would not be appropriate to compare the processes employed in these cases with those followed in internal investigations of a relatively minor nature. In addition, some consideration should be given to the issue of what constitutes a reasonable level of investigative effort, and under what circumstances: exhaustive investigation of relatively minor matters may not be an unmitigated good if this leads to excessive delay and consumes resources which could be used more effectively elsewhere. Subject to these caveats, however, comparative studies along the lines proposed could add substantially to our knowledge about the extent to which, and circumstances under which, external oversight bodies have been able to conduct better quality investigations than their police counterparts.

## Complainant Satisfaction

### *Complainants*

Police-based complaints systems have frequently been criticised for disregarding the interests of complainants. Conversely, a common argument for establishing external oversight bodies is that complainants are more likely to be accepting of the outcome of investigations if they know that their complaint has been investigated—or at least oversighted—by an independent body. This element of independence, in turn, has been seen as critical for increasing the overall legitimacy of complaint handling systems.

In contrast to other areas examined in this review, a considerable amount of research has been conducted on complainants' experiences, and perceptions, of different complaints processes.[23] In addition, some external oversight bodies have implemented procedures for collecting feedback from complainants on a regular basis (such as the New South Wales Ombudsman and the Minneapolis Civilian Review Authority).

The various surveys which have been undertaken have all been characterised by one or more methodological limitations (such as low response rates, small

[23] D Brown, *The Police Complaints Procedure: A Survey of Complainants' Views*, Home Office Research Study No. 93 (London, HMSO 1987); M Sviridoff and J McElroy, *Processing Complaints Against Police in New York City: The Complainant's Perspective* (New York, Vera Institute of Justice, 1989); Maguire and Corbett, *supra* n. 8; CJC, *Complainants' Perceptions of the Complaints Investigation Process*, unpublished briefing paper (Brisbane, 1994); CJC, *Informal Complaint Resolution in the Queensland Police Service: An Evaluation* (Brisbane, 1994); T. Landau, *Public Complaints Against the Police: A View from Complainants* (Centre of Criminology, University of Toronto, 1994); Perez, *supra* n. 3; Statistics Canada, *RCMP Public Complaints Commission Survey: Analytical Report* (Ottawa, Special Surveys Division, 1995).

sample sizes, and/or the lack of an explicitly comparative framework), but the data have consistently shown that a clear majority of complainants are dissatisfied with the standard complaints investigation process, regardless of whether their complaint was handled internally or externally. For example, Perez reported that in all three of the United States jurisdictions which he studied—Oakland (internal review), Berkeley (civilian review) and Kansas City (civilian monitor)—complainants held negative perceptions of the thoroughness, fairness and objectivity of the systems to which they had complained.[24] According to Maguire and Corbett, complainants in investigations which were supervised by the British Police Complaints Authority had a slightly more positive view of the process than did complainants in unsupervised investigations, but the majority of both groups were critical of the system.[25] In a similar vein, a mail-back survey conducted by the CJC in 1994 found roughly equal levels of dissatisfaction amongst respondents whose complaints had been investigated externally and those whose complaints had been handled by the Police Service.[26]

Complainants' views of the investigation process are shaped, to a considerable extent, by whether or not their complaint was found to be proved. However, the research shows that even where complainants have obtained a positive outcome from an investigation, they often express dissatisfaction with the amount of information provided, the time taken to finalise investigations, and the seemingly routinised manner in which investigations are conducted.[27] On the other hand, surveys conducted in Britain and Australia indicate that citizens whose complaints have been informally resolved by police are much more likely to be satisfied with both the outcome of their complaint and the manner in which it was handled.[28] Similar findings have been reported by the Vera Institute in relation to the use of conciliation to deal with complaints against New York City police.[29]

The results of these various surveys strongly suggest that the key determinant of complainant satisfaction is not so much *who* deals with the complaint, but the *way* in which it is handled. External oversight bodies have failed, by and large, to have a significant impact on complainant satisfaction levels because these bodies, like most police departments, still operate from within a narrow investigative paradigm—a way of doing business which many complainants find alienating and which promotes the view that investigations are about "winning" or "losing". An obvious corollary of these research findings is that

[24] *Supra*, n. 3 at 237.

[25] *Supra*, n. 8.

[26] *Complainants' Perceptions of the Complaints Investigation Process*, *supra*, n. 23.

[27] See generally the references at n. 23 and Goldsmith "What's Wrong with Complaints Investigations", *supra*, n. 2.

[28] Maguire and Corbett, *supra*, n. 8, CJC, *Informal Complaint Resolution in the Queensland Police Service An Evaluation*, *supra*, n. 23.

[29] Sviridoff and McElroy, *supra*, n. 23.

complainant satisfaction is unlikely to increase substantially until external oversight bodies are able to move outside this traditional paradigm and develop new approaches (such as suggested by the new paradigm of restorative justice) for dealing with citizens' complaints.[30]

## Impact on Police Practices and Behaviour

It is often asserted that reducing the incidence of police misconduct and improving organisational practices is—or should be—one of the main objectives of any system for dealing with complaints against police. Major corruption scandals and highly publicised cases of misuse of power by police have often been a direct catalyst for the establishment of external oversight bodies. However, some commentators have questioned whether such bodies are capable of acting as significant change agents. Landau, for instance, has argued that "[t]here is good reason to doubt the effectiveness of externally-imposed controls on police misconduct, particularly those which rely on the 'bad apple' approach to police misconduct".[31] Kerstetter has asserted that external oversight may even have a counter-productive effect, because it creates a "we-they dichotomy" between police and the oversight body and provides an incentive for police managers to abdicate responsibility for controlling misconduct.[32]

There are two main ways in which external oversight bodies can potentially have an impact on police practices and behaviour. These are by: (a) detecting and deterring improper behaviour by police; and (b) changing organisational settings, such as departmental policies and procedures, the content of training programmes, recruitment selection processes, and so on. The following discussion will deal separately with each of these areas.

### *The Deterrent Capacity of Oversight Bodies*

Some commentators have utilised anecdotal evidence, the views of "informed observers" and indicators such as a fall in the number of serious complaints made against police to support claims that external oversight has reduced the incidence of police misconduct,[33] but none of these forms of data is, *by itself*, a reliable indicator. A drop in the number of complaints could indicate improved behaviour, but may also reflect a decline in the willingness of citizens to complain, or a change in complaint recording and classification practices. Similarly,

[30] On this issue generally, see Goldsmith "What's Wrong with Complaint Investigations", *supra*, n. 2.

[31] *Supra*, n. 23 at 8.

[32] W Kerstetter, "Who Disciplines the Police? Who Should?" in W Geller (ed.), *Police Leadership in America* (New York, Praeger, 1985).

[33] See Lewis, *supra*, n. 22 for an example of this approach.

care must be taken when citing the views of "informed observers", as some informants may have only partial knowledge of local police practices, or may not answer impartially. Even where there is some evidence of improved standards of police behaviour, it will be very difficult to determine whether this is attributable to the deterrent effect of external oversight, or to the impact of other factors such as broader cultural changes, new leadership within a police department, changed recruitment practices, and so on.

Given the difficulty, if not impossibility, of measuring deterrent effects directly, a more productive evaluation strategy is to examine the extent to which external oversight bodies have been successful in creating the *conditions* for deterrence to occur. Some possible indicators in this regard are considered below.

One way in which external oversight bodies can contribute to improved deterrence is by increasing the rate at which complaints are *reported and recorded*. As is the case with criminal victimisation, a good deal of possible police misbehaviour goes unreported. In part, this is because some forms of misbehaviour (such as drug taking, receiving bribes, or fabricating evidence) are covert or consensual in nature, but many "victims" of police misconduct also choose not to report because of lack of confidence in the complaints system, fear of reprisals, and so on.[34] Even where complaints are made, these may not always be officially recorded, especially where another police officer is the initial recipient of the complaint. If an oversight body can directly or indirectly increase the number of complaints coming to official attention, this should communicate to officers that there is an increased risk of inappropriate behaviour being detected. Even if the prospects of a sanction being imposed are small (see below) the very process of being investigated is likely to be a deterrent to some.

Queensland is an example of where increased public confidence and improved recording practices appears initially to have had a significant impact on the number of complaints coming to official attention Recorded misconduct complaints per one thousand officers almost doubled in the first five years after the CJC became operative. However, the number of recorded complaints has been fairly constant in recent years, and surveys conducted by the CJC indicate no increase since the mid-1990s in the preparedness of people to complain about suspected police misconduct.[35] These findings suggest that reporting rate effects resulting from the establishment of external oversight bodies are likely to be

[34] See CJC, *Defendants' Perceptions of the Investigation and Arrest Process* (Brisbane, 1996) at 53–4; S Walker and N Graham "Citizen Complaints in Response to Police Misconduct. The Results of a Victimisation Survey" (1998) 1 *Police Quarterly* 65.

[35] In 1996 and 1999 the CJC conducted surveys of persons who had been apprehended by the police. In both surveys, slightly less than fifty per cent of respondents indicated that they had some cause to be unhappy about their treatment by police. In both surveys, less than one quarter of these respondents said that they had made an official complaint to the Police Service or the CJC. For a description of the 1996 survey see CJC, *ibid.* Results of the 1999 survey are due for release in 2000.

"one-off" rather than ongoing, although research findings from other jurisdictions would be required to confirm this.

A second way in which an external oversight body could potentially have a deterrent effect is by increasing the probability that improper behaviour will result in a *sanction* being imposed. However, continuing low complaint substantiation rates, combined with the fact that many citizens who feel aggrieved about police behaviour do not make formal complaints, have made it very difficult for most oversight bodies to have an appreciable impact on the objective risk of detection and punishment. Very large changes in either substantiation rates or reporting rates would be required to significantly increase the likelihood that police who misuse their powers or position will be punished.[36] For example CJC estimates, based on complaints data and its 1996 survey of defendants, indicate that between 1991 and 1995 disciplinary or criminal sanctions were imposed in response to only one out of every 130 incidents in which a citizen considered that he or she had been treated with excessive force.[37]

A potentially effective means of deterring inappropriate behaviour would be for external oversight bodies to develop a *proactive surveillance capacity*, so as to make it more difficult for officers to conceal misconduct. Such strategies could include the use of integrity testing, drug testing, installation of video or audio surveillance devices in locations where it is suspected that police are acting improperly, utilisation of informants and "field associates", and so on. These strategies have been employed with good effect by one-off inquiries into police misconduct (such as the recent Royal Commission into the New South Wales Police)[38] and are being increasingly utilised by internal investigations units in some of the larger police departments, such as the New York City Police Department and the London Metropolitan Police. However, apart from the limited number of organisations which have been assigned a broader anti-corruption role, such as the CJC and the Police Integrity Commission in New South Wales, few oversight bodies have the resources (even if they formally have the power) to perform a proactive role.

In summary, the deterrent capability of most external oversight bodies would appear to be quite limited, because of the inability of these organisations to have a significant impact on complaint substantiation rates or to do much else than undertake reactive, case-by-case, investigations. There is some scope for external oversight bodies to facilitate increased reporting and recording of com-

[36] Arguably, in some circumstances external oversight bodies may be able to increase the *subjective probability* of detection and punishment (even if they cannot have much effect on objective probabilities) by such means as conducting well publicised inquires, disseminating information about successful investigations, and so on. However, very few oversight bodies appear to utilise these strategies.

[37] Even where sanctions were imposed, they were often only minor in nature, such as a reprimand or a small fine. See Brereton and Burgess, *supra*, n. 19.

[38] Royal Commission into the New South Wales Police Service, *Final Report*, Volumes I and II (Sydney, 1997).

plaints (which may itself have a deterrent effect in some instances) but it is unclear how many oversight bodies have been able to have a significant impact in this regard.

### *Changing Organisational Settings*

A potentially important function of oversight bodies is to influence police department policies and practices, as well as to respond to alleged instances of misconduct on a case-by-case basis. This can be done by such means as making recommendations to police managers, using public hearings and reporting processes to draw attention to deficiencies in organisational procedures and practices, and otherwise providing feedback about systemic and procedural deficiencies, patterns in complaints, and so on. Changes at the level of organisational policy and practice may not always translate directly into improved police behaviour "on the ground", but such reforms can have other benefits (such as enhanced operational efficiency) and can contribute to enhanced organisational performance over the longer term.

In assessing the extent to which external oversight bodies have, in practice, been able to function as effective organisational change agents, it is important to look not only at the numbers of recommendations which have been made by these bodies, but also at the content and impact of those recommendations. Acceptance rates can easily be inflated if oversight bodies focus only on proposing minor procedural changes, or on recommending changes which police departments were planning to implement in any event. Analysis of the annual reports of some oversight bodies also shows that many of the recommendations which are made and deemed to have been adopted are very specific and localised in nature (for example, that a standing order is changed, or that some additional training material is included in a course).

Of most interest is the response to recommendations which have the potential to alter key organisational settings, such as the way in which police are selected, trained and managed. In this context, it is very important to ascertain the extent to which official acceptance by a police department of proposed changes has translated into changed practices "on the ground". Unfortunately, although oversight bodies quite often report on the number of policy recommendations which they make and which are formally accepted, follow-up reports are much less frequent. Few bodies appear to have the capacity to undertake systematic monitoring of the extent to which with their policy directives and recommendations have actually been embraced and followed through.

In order to support arguments about the value of the policy role played by external oversight bodies, it would be very valuable to have some well documented case studies showing how external oversight bodies, by using their power to make recommendations and other "levers", have been able to facilitate significant organisational change in police departments. The potential for achieving change by these means is clearly there, but as Walker and Kreisel have noted, as yet there is insufficient evidence available to enable a proper assessment to be undertaken of the efficacy of the policy review and feedback role of external oversight organisations.[39]

### *A Queensland Case Study*

The focus of the preceding discussion has primarily been on documenting the factors which have made it difficult for external oversight bodies to reduce the incidence of police misconduct or otherwise promote positive organisational change. However, there is some evidence to indicate that, under certain conditions, external oversight bodies can make a significant contribution to the process of police reform.

In 1997 the CJC released a research report entitled *Integrity in the Queensland Police Service*, which sought to provide a systematic assessment of the impact of external oversight on attitudes and behaviour within the Police Service.[40] The focus of the report was on identifying changes which had occurred following the establishment of the CJC in mid-1990. Data utilised for this purpose included retrospective interviews with long serving police, "ethics" surveys of successive intakes of junior police officers, and complaints trend data indexed to various measures of policing activity. Since the release of the report, the CJC has continued to monitor trends in the police service, using a mix of attitudinal and behavioural measures.[41]

Findings from the CJC's research include that during the last decade there has been: (a) a reduction in the incidence of serious assault by police, improper practices relating to evidence, and the incidence of drinking on duty; and (b) some positive cultural change, including an increased willingness by "rank and file" police to report misconduct by other officers. Also, although the extent of consensual misconduct is impossible to measure directly, there have been no indications of any return to the patterns of systemic corruption which characterised the Queensland Police Service in the 1980s.

The extent to which the CJC *per se* should be given credit for these improvements is very difficult to determine. Other factors which have also played a role in the reform process have included: heightened public expectations—and scrutiny—of police as a result of the Fitzgerald Commission of Inquiry; replacement of the service's senior management in the late 1980s/early 1990s (including jailing of a former police commissioner); substantial reforms to recruitment and training practices; two subsequent major government-initiated reviews of the

[39] Walker and Kreisel, *supra*, n. 3 at 74.

[40] See *supra*, n. 20. For a summary of the key findings, see D Brereton and A Ede, "What has Reform Wrought? The Impact of the Fitzgerald Inquiry on Police Integrity in Queensland" (1997) 4 *Queensland Review* 51.

[41] See, for example, CJC, *Ethics Surveys of First Year Constables: Summary of Findings 1995–1998* (Brisbane, 1999).

police service's management practices and processes (in 1993 and 1996); and, particularly in the latter part of the decade, the retirement of a substantial number of "old school" police officers. However, while there may be disagreement about the quantum of the CJC's contribution vis-à-vis these other factors, the fact that the CJC has played both a direct and indirect role in promoting significant changes within the police service is not in dispute. This has occurred through such mechanisms as vigorous investigation of complaints, employing various proactive surveillance strategies to detect and deter serious misconduct, making procedural and policy recommendations directly to the police service, participating in external reviews, undertaking joint "demonstration" projects, and monitoring and reporting publicly on key developments within the police service.

There are relatively few external oversight bodies which combine an investigative role with a substantial research and policy role, in the way in which the CJC has been able to do. The CJC is also much better resourced than many other bodies, with about two-thirds of its annual budget of A$23 million being devoted to functions associated with the police oversight role. For these reasons, external oversight bodies in other jurisdictions are likely to be less well placed than the CJC to influence police behaviour and organisational practices; but the example provided by Queensland is important for showing that, if the conditions are right, external oversight bodies can "make a difference".

## Adverse Impacts on Performance

From time to time, police unions, "law and order" politicians and other critics of external oversight bodies claim that police have become less willing to do their job because they are fearful of being the subject of a complaint investigation. In some instances, this is simply a lament for "the good old days" where police could use excessive force and other illegal tactics towards suspects with relative impunity. However, some academic commentators have also expressed concern that overly zealous review bodies may push police organisations into introducing policies that severely limit police responsiveness and efficiency and make police officers reluctant to engage in legitimate enforcement activities.[42]

Surveys of subject officers have been conducted in several jurisdictions.[43] These studies show that officers and complainants share some common concerns about delays and the lack of information, but overall, subject officers generally have a more positive view of the investigation process than do complainants. As far as police perceptions of internal and external processes are concerned, Perez has reported that police officers in each of the three systems

[42] See, for example, Perez, *supra*, n. 3.

[43] Maguire and Corbett, *supra*, n. 8; CJC, *Police Officers' Perceptions of the Complaint Investigation Process*, unpublished briefing paper (Brisbane, 1994); CJC, *Informal Complaint Resolution in the Queensland Police Service*, Perez, *supra*, n. 3, Statistics Canada, *supra*, n. 23.

which he examined had largely come to terms with the local arrangements and "[e]ven those cops subject to civilian review seem to have normalised it as simply a part of the 'rules of the discipline game' ".[44] By contrast, a 1994 survey undertaken by the CJC found that officers who had been investigated by the CJC perceived the process to be considerably less "friendly" than those officers who had been investigated by the police service itself, but as discussed below, there is no persuasive evidence that this had an adverse effect on police morale or their willingness to "do their job".[45]

Perez also surveyed police officers about their enforcement practices and concluded that none of the three types of review systems which he examined—internal review, civilian review and "civilian monitor"—had adversely impacted on police behaviour. Around one fifth of the 50 police officers interviewed by Maguire and Corbett for their study of the British police complaints system said that concern about attracting a complaint had led them to "back away" from situations where they should have taken action, but the other 80 per cent stated that their behaviour had not been affected, mainly because they thought that they had done nothing wrong, indicating that for most respondents the fear of attracting a complaint was not a significant constraint on behaviour.[46]

Possible adverse effects on police performance can also be monitored directly by examining trends in indicators of discretionary police activity, such as the number of "street offence" arrests per officer, or the number of "stop and searches" conducted. There is much more scope for police to cut back on proactive as opposed to reactive enforcement activity (such as responding to crime reports and other calls for service). Therefore, if police in a particular jurisdiction were being constrained by a fear of complaints, this should be reflected over time in a drop in the level of discretionary policing activity; conversely, an increase in the level of discretionary enforcement would suggest that police were not unduly worried about the prospect of attracting a complaint.

Using this general approach, the CJC regularly monitors and reports on trends in the number of recorded drug and good order offences per one thousand officers. These data show a steady increase in the number of such offences since 1990, despite a doubling in the number of recorded complaints against

[44] *Supra*, n. 3 at 237.

[45] *Ibid.* Of the 187 subject officers in the survey who had been the subject of a police service investigation, 76 per cent said that they were "very" or "fairly" satisfied with how the complaint was investigated, compared with 57.5 per cent of officers who had been the subject of a CJC investigation (n=66). Officers who were the subject of an internal investigation were also more likely to report being kept "very" or "fairly" informed during the investigation (42 per cent compared with only 19 per cent of officers investigated by the CJC) and that they had been given sufficient opportunity to express their views. Arguably, the general hostility of some police officers towards the CJC may have coloured their responses to these questions. In addition, the complaints which were investigated internally were mostly of a minor nature and therefore may have warranted a less adversarial approach than those dealt with externally.

[46] *Supra*, 46 n. 8 at 67.

police in the early part of the decade.[47] Such findings have proved to be very useful for rebutting claims from police union officials (amongst others), that the activities of the CJC have had an adverse effect on the preparedness of Queensland police to enforce the law.

Conceivably there may be some jurisdictions where the activities of external oversight bodies have placed undue constraints on police, but this claim needs to be supported by data, not simply asserted. At present, the limited evidence which is available provides little support for such criticisms.

## FUTURE DIRECTIONS

The overall thrust of this review has been that, with some exceptions, the creation of independent oversight mechanisms seems to have had less impact on complaints processes, investigation outcomes and police standards of conduct than advocates of reform (or critics, for that matter) would have predicted. In part, the lack of measurable effects may be an artefact of the questions asked, the evaluation methods employed and the shortage of data. It also must be recognised that police departments are large and complex organisations which can be very difficult to change, especially from the outside; hence, even small gains may be worth applauding. More research, better designed comparative studies and more finely calibrated research instruments may provide more persuasive evidence of institutional effectiveness. However, on balance, this additional information would probably not alter the picture presented here a great deal.

In terms of future research, the main focus should be on investigating ways in which external oversight bodies could be made more effective (rather than just on documenting the successes and failures of already established bodies). On the basis of the preceding discussion, the following "working hypotheses" would provide a good starting point for future inquiry:

- oversight bodies which devote resources to monitoring and reviewing complaint investigation *processes* are likely to have a greater effect on the standard of police complaint investigations than those bodies which rely solely on case-by-case review;
- greater use of non-adversarial processes for resolving complaints will enhance complainant satisfaction, without reducing the effectiveness of the disciplinary process;
- oversight bodies which utilise proactive investigative strategies are likely to be more effective in deterring improper police behaviour than bodies which are purely complaint driven; and

[47] Between 1991–2 and 1998–9 the number of these offences nearly doubled from 28,400 to 56,600. Queensland Police Service, *Annual Statistical Review*, 1991–2 and 1998–9.

- oversight bodies which combine a policy and investigative role are likely to be more effective in promoting organisational and behavioural change than those which rely mainly on case-by-case investigation and review.

In concluding, it is worth repeating the observation made at the outset of this chapter that there is growing scepticism in some quarters about the value of external oversight. Given these developments, it would be wise for external oversight bodies to give greater priority to reviewing, monitoring and improving their performance on an ongoing basis, and to be willing to experiment with new ways of doing business. In a world in which governments are placing ever greater emphasis on the need to show "value for money", appeals to abstract principles may not be enough to win funding arguments—evidence that external oversight has value in a concrete sense will also be required.

# 6

# *Evaluating the New Civilian Complaints Board in Israel*

SERGIO HERZOG

## INTRODUCTION

Most organisations, whether they are private enterprises selling products to the public, or institutions serving the public, have a complaints system for clients who are dissatisfied with the quality of their product or service, or with the behaviour of a specific worker. From the complainants' point of view, the reason for submitting a formal complaint may be; the need to elicit an explanation, apology or a promise from a high-ranking figure in the organisation that measures will be taken to ensure that the offending behaviour will not happen again; the hope that punitive measures will be taken against the offending worker; or a demand for monetary compensation.[1] However, the complaints system also plays an important role for the organisation itself. First, complaints data can help an organisation assess its efficacy or improve the quality of its product or service. Second, an open and objective complaints system may serve to satisfy current clients or even attract more clients. Third, such systems play an important deterrent role for those in the organisation's employ.

Maguire and Corbett[2] summarise the main objectives of all complaints systems, including those which process complaints against police officers, as follows:

- Maintaining discipline through deterrence;
- Complainant satisfaction with the investigation;
- Promoting public confidence in the police;
- Providing feedback to police managers.

Ideally, formal complaints systems should be activated only rarely and sporadically, such as in special instances of misconduct, or in extraordinary situations more likely to be mishandled due to their non-routine nature.

[1] M Maguire and C Corbett, *A Study of the Police Complaints System* (London, HMSO, 1991); D Brown, *The Police Complaints Procedure. A Survey of Complainants' Views* (London, Home Office Research Study No. 93, HMSO, 1987), T Landau, *Public Complaints Against the Police. A View from Complainants* (Toronto, Centre of Criminology, 1994).

[2] M Maguire and C Corbett, *supra* n. 1.

In the case of the police force the role of the complaints system is critical to the police administration, but especially to the public at large and particularly to active complainants. The police can play a decisive and central role in the protection of human rights. They occupy an important first line position in societies which actively engage in respecting and protecting peoples' civil liberties. However, because of the nature of the police role, their extremely wide powers can also damage fundamental human rights. Occasionally citizens will accept that police action which violates fundamental human rights and other social interests is justified. This may occur when police are performing their peace keeping function. While citizens acknowledge that this type of behaviour is necessary from time to time, police are, nevertheless, expected to account for actions which adversely affect the life, property or constitutional rights of citizens. What is not acceptable to citizens is police unjustifiably abusing their civil rights, and not being held to account when they do.

Because police officers do not work "under the noses" of their superiors, they usually work alone or with another officer, abuse of police power is not easily detected. Also, the nature of police work often means that they are required to make split-second decisions under conditions of very limited supervision or guidance. In these circumstances, the chance of misconduct is high, particularly in incidents involving use of force where there is always danger that unreasonable and unnecessary force will be exercised by police. This can be especially true in relation to certain groups in a complex divided society who are perceived as "others" and not "us". Such groups include minorities, convicted offenders, suspects who have not been convicted but whose guilt is "clear" to the police and social deviants.

Because of this ever present danger, both the police and external bodies need to ensure that the licence to use physical force is applied in a professional, objective and egalitarian manner, within the framework of the law, police regulations, and ethical codes. However, any proclamation of war against police violence, especially by police management, must also include a deterrent component consisting of the threat of sanctions against those who violate the law or organisational regulations. The complaints system, with its mandate to investigate complaints and, if necessary, recommend disciplinary or judicial action against police officers, serves such a function. A central goal of such systems is to ensure that police officers act within the framework of internal regulations and the law, thereby, achieving a maximum reduction in the possible misuse of their powers.[3]

The importance of this goal is increased in police forces where for social, cultural and even organisational reasons, the police use of force is considered and perceived, by the police and by the public at large, as a central police tool. This situation usually brings about many public claims of excessive and unjustified

[3] T Jefferson and R Grimshaw, "Law, Democracy and Justice" in D Cowell, T Jones and J Young (eds.), *Policing in Riots* (London, Junction Books, 1982).

use of force.[4] This is the case in Israel, where due to its long standing security situation, the Israeli National Police has been charged with securing internal peace which goes beyond its traditional police functions.

POLICE VIOLENCE IN ISRAEL

Recent years have seen a marked increase in media coverage of alleged police brutality by Israeli police officers.[5] In the context of these reports, it is usually claimed that illegal physical force was employed quite routinely during arrests, when dispersing demonstrations, during criminal investigations, and even in traffic-control situations. Moreover, some of the allegations bear no relation to what might be deemed necessary or justified police action in that they relate to arbitrary acts, usually towards minorities (Israeli Arabs and Palestinians) or groups identified as "typical criminal offenders" (Oriental Jewish people, low income earners, and unemployed youth). Such cases usually occur after arrest and are likely to involve humiliating actions, beatings, maltreatment, and even direct torture resulting in physical injury.

The subject of police violence has featured increasingly on the public agenda in Israel over the past two decades. Three public committees (the Shimron Committee, 1978; the Sirota-Eitan Committee, 1980; and the Kremnitzer Committee, 1994); the State Comptroller's reports (1980; 1986; 1988; 1991), the Ministry of Police Comptroller's report 1993, and discussions by the Israeli Government and Parliament's committee on state reviews have all dealt with the issue. Most of these non-police bodies attributed the police violence phenomenon to the double-edged organisational message conveyed by the police force to its employees: the legality versus effectiveness dilemma which surrounds the use of physical force against citizens. A clear example of this type of message is expressed through "the forgiving, non-professional, internal treatment of charges against police officers".[6]

THE DEPARTMENT FOR THE INVESTIGATION OF POLICE OFFICERS

Prior to 1992, all complaints against police officers in Israel were handled internally by the police department itself. This system came under criticism for being inappropriate and for its lack of objectivity and professionalism. Following public pressure and a gradual change in the attitudes of the Israeli

[4] S Herzog, *Police Violence in Israel: The Police Complaints System on Use of Force Complaints*, PhD Dissertation (Jerusalem, The Hebrew University, 1998a) [In Hebrew]; M Haberfeld and S Herzog, "The Criminal Justice System in Israel" in O Ebbe (ed.), *Comparative and International Criminal Justice Systems: Policing, Judiciary and Corrections* (New York, Butterworth / Heinemman, 1999).

[5] See Herzog, *ibid*.

[6] Ministry of Police Comptroller, *A Critical Report on the Systems Treatment of Police Violence* (Jerusalem, Ministry of Police, 1993 23). [In Hebrew].

police administration, especially with regard to the issue of accountability, the external-civilian Department for the Investigation of Police Officers (known in Hebrew as Machash), was established in 1992, under the auspices of the Ministry of Justice. According to Kerstetter's different definitions of civilian oversight,[7] Machash may be defined as a good example of a "civilian review" board (the broadest level). This is due to the fact that in the frame of this newly established civilian board, complaints against police officers are managed externally by civilian attorneys, investigators and staff who work independently of the national police. The main innovations of the department include the investigation of suspected misconduct by police and the recommendation to continue treatment of a complaint.

Machash investigates police officers suspected of committing offences (on or off duty) relating to the use of illegal force and criminal offences for which the mandatory punishment exceeds one year in prison. The less serious cases that do not meet the above-mentioned criteria continue to be handled by the internal affairs unit within the police department. The board is headed by attorneys who decide about the investigative outcome of every file lodged after the investigation is complete. Investigative outcomes range from a police disciplinary trial (in a one-official trial or a disciplinary court), a trial in a criminal court, to the closing of the file on the grounds of "presumed lack of guilt" (absence of evidence indicating criminal guilt), "lack of evidence" (absence of sufficient evidence to secure conviction), and "not fully investigated".[8] In offences involving the use of force (as opposed to other criminal offences in which the board can only make a suggestion), this recommendation becomes a formal decision for the police force. However, it must be pointed out that all Machash investigators are ex-police officers, working as civilian investigators and employed in the civilian board on the basis of police investigative expertise and skills.

## RESEARCH GOALS

The aim of this chapter is to evaluate the work of the Israeli civilian board in the context of its authority, functions and structure, and to examine the extent to which the objectives of complaints systems in general, as defined by Maguire and Corbett,[9] have been fulfilled by Machash during the first few years of its existence. Although Machash investigates a wide range of criminal offences, the present study focuses only on illegal use of force files. The reason for focusing on these files is their high proportion in the total volume of files handled by Machash,[10] their seriousness, and the fact that all of them, regardless of their seriousness, are investigated by Machash.

[7] W Kerstetter, "Who Disciplines the Police? Who Should?" in W Geller (ed.), *Police Leadership in America: Crisis and Opportunity* (New York, Praeger, 1985).

[8] In 1997 Machash stopped closing files that were "not fully investigated".

[9] M Maguire and C Corbett, *supra* n. 1.

[10] About one-half. See S Herzog, *supra* n. 4, for further details.

In this context, it is worth noting an important characteristic of the investigation on use of force files. In contrast to other offences such as bribery and corruption, the use of force by police officers is legal and legitimate in a wide variety of situations. Hence, in this kind of investigation, the central question does not usually focus on clear investigative considerations such as "did or didn't the suspect do the forbidden behaviour?". On the contrary, the violence investigations mostly focus on subjective impressions of the parties involved (victims, witnesses, suspect police officers), especially with regard to the amount of force used. Moreover, many incidents leading to illegal force complaints occur in solitary places, without independent witnesses or credible information sources. Usually the only witnesses are other police officers or other criminal suspects. These are some of the basic reasons which explain why the majority of these files are closed at the end of the investigation. It is not necessarily due to innocence on the part of suspect police officers, but rather lack of sufficient evidence to sustain the complaint.

Most investigations into internal and external systems for handling complaints against police officers suspected of illegal use of force[11] have produced similar findings: they do not act as a deterrent for police officers; they fail to satisfy complainants; they do not improve the public image of the police, and complaints data are not usually used by police management for internal purposes. Some of these studies are cross-cultural, and the Israeli reports relate primarily to the situation in Israel prior to the establishment of Machash. Therefore, the main research question of this chapter is whether the described general situation of complaints systems is similar or different in the context of the newly established civilian body in Israel.

## METHOD

This chapter is divided into four central parts, according to Maguire and Corbett's four general complaints system goals, previously described. Hence, each one of them is based on a different research method approach, with regard to various populations and samples. To be able to understand the objectives of

[11] See for example, the Sirota-Eitan Committee, *Treatment Measures of Police officers for the Problem of Police Violence* (Jerusalem, Ministry of Police, 1980) [in Hebrew]; the Kremnitzer Committee, *The System's Treatment of Police Violence* (Jerusalem, Ministry of Police, 1994) [in Hebrew]; State Comptroller, *Report No. 36* (Jerusalem, State Comptroller Office, 1986) [in Hebrew]; *Report No. 38*, (Jerusalem, State Comptroller Office, 1988) [in hebrew]; *Report No. 41* (Jerusalem, State Comptroller Office, 1991) [in Hebrew]; Ministry of Police Comptroller, *A Critical Report on the System's Treatment of Police Violence* (Jerusalem, Ministry of Police, 1993) [in Hebrew]; M Maguire and C Corbett, "Patterns and Profiles of Complaints Against the Police" in R Morgan and D Smith (eds.), *Coming to Terms with Policing* (London, Routledge, 1989) and M Maguire and C Corbett, *supra* n. 1; N Uildriks and H Van Mastrigt, *Policing Police Violence* (Aberdeen, University Press, 1991); A Pate and L Fridell, *Police Use of Force: Official Reports, Citizen Complaints, and Legal Consequences* (Washington DC, Police Foundation, 1993); S Walker, *Citizen Review: Resource Manual* (Washington DC, Police Executive Research Forum, 1995); L Lustgarten, *The Governance of Police* (London, Sweet and Maxwell, 1986); T Landau, *supra* n. 1, D Brown, *supra* n. 1.

| Objective | Goals | Method | Population | Sample Size |
|---|---|---|---|---|
| Evaluation of fulfillment of complaint system objectives | 1. Maintaining discipline through deterrence | 1. Official data distributions | 1. Use of force files against police | 1. Total population |
| | | 2. Personal questionnaire | 2. Suspect violent police officers between 1989–91 | 2. 300 |
| | | 3. Personal questionnaire | 3. Suspect violent police officers between 1993–7 | 3. 300 |
| | 2. Complainant (and suspect) satisfaction | 1. Personal questionnaire | 1. Complainants who submitted use of force complaints | 1. 700 |
| | | 2. Personal questionnaire | 2. Suspect violent police officers between 1993–7 | 2. 600 |
| | 3. Promoting public confidence in the police | Telephone survey | Israeli adult citizens | 500 |
| | 4. Feedback to police managers | Personal interviews | High ranking officers who deal with public complaints | 3 |

*Figure 1: Research Goals and Methods*

the research and the methods of achieving them, Figure 1 provides a scheme of the research design.

## Maintaining Discipline Through Deterrence

In order to assess the deterrent effect of Machash, the official data on general and use of force complaints handled by the internal investigations unit of the police department between 1985–97 and by Machash between 1993–7, was examined. In addition, anonymous personal questionnaires were administered to two representative samples of police officers investigated for the illegal use of force (N=600), the first by the police between 1989–91 and the other by Machash between 1993–7.[12] Due to the wide dispersion of respondents around the country, the questionnaires were sent by mail.

[12] Anonymity was especially important because of the sensitive nature of the issues examined (L Kidder and C Judd, *Research Methods in Social Relations*, New York, Holt, Rinehart and Winston, 1986). In order to enhance motivation (J Neale and R Liebert, *Science and Behaviour: An*

A total of two hundred and fifty-five questionnaires were completed and returned (a response rate of forty-four per cent).[13] This fairly low response rate is hardly surprising. First, the police officers were under no moral or occupational obligation to complete the questionnaire. Second, sampling was made on a negative personal basis, in that all of the respondents had been investigated for employing illegal force. Finally, the questionnaire dealt with extremely sensitive issues and therefore may have appeared threatening to many police surveyed. Nevertheless, almost one-half of them did respond fully. Adequate statistical representation on the police organisational variables was confirmed by comparison with data for recent years made available from a larger sample of use of force files opened by Machash.[14] Adequate representation was also found between the personal characteristics of the research sample and those of the total police population in Israel (data made available by the Israeli Police Force).

## Complainant (and Suspect) Satisfaction

Both parties to the complaint were questioned with regard to their satisfaction with the Machash investigation. The police officers' position was assessed via the personal questionnaire (described above). The complainants' position was assessed via a similar personal questionnaire administered also by mail to a representative sample of active complainants (N=700) who had submitted use of force complaints against police officers to Machash between 1993–7. A total of two hundred and fifty completed complainant questionnaires were returned (a response rate of thirty-six point five per cent),[15] which should be considered a good response rate on the assumption that many of the complainants may not have received the questionnaires due to their being in jail, awaiting trial or even serving prison sentences.

## Promoting Public Confidence in the Police

In order to assess the extent to which the work of Machash serves to promote the public image of the police, a telephone survey of a representative sample of

*Introduction into Methods of Research*, New Jersey, Prentice Hall, 1986; A Pate and L Fridell, *ibid.*, 1993; K Adams, "Measuring the Prevalence of Police Abuse of Force", in W Geller and H Toch (eds.), *And Justice for All* (Washington DC, Police Executive Research Forum, 1995), all the questionnaires were accompanied by a personal letter specifying the research goals, emphasising the importance of completing the questionnaire, assuring anonymity and that no personal identifying details would be revealed to any judicial, academic, or police body, that the sampling method was random, and that the findings would be used for statistical purposes only. Comprehensibility of the questionnaire was verified by means of a pre-test conducted on a reduced number of subjects.

[13] About three point five per cent came back in the mail because the addresses to which they were sent were incorrect.

[14] See S Herzog, *supra* n. 4.

[15] About two per cent came back in the mail because the addresses to which they were sent were incorrect.

Israeli citizens (N=500) was conducted. This sample was also shown to be adequately representative of the total Israeli population.[16]

## Providing Feedback to Police Managers

Finally, in order to assess the extent to which the Israeli Police Force use the Machash complaints data for internal organisational purposes, individual interviews were conducted with three high ranking police commanders who deal with Machash material on a daily basis (the head of the human resources and discipline department; the head of the supervision and training department; and the deputy chief of the internal investigations unit).

# RESULTS

## Maintaining Discipline Through Deterrence

### *General Deterrence*

The official data show that the average annual rate of illegal use of force files opened by Machash between 1993–7 was two thousand four hundred out of an annual average of about five thousand four hundred files against the police in general. In spite of an increasing trend in files opened, the actual proportion of illegal use of force files remained stable at around forty-five per cent up to 1996, dropping to thirty-seven point four per cent in 1997. However, after the establishment of Machash, there is a significant decreasing trend in the percentage of sustained files (including recommendations to take punitive—disciplinary or judicial—measures against offending police officers): thirteen point one per cent in the Machash period (1993–7), compared with sixteen point nine per cent during the previous period (1985–91). In other words, following the establishment of Mashash, the rate of sustained files against suspect police officers was even lower than the already low rate in the preceding years.

### *Individual deterrence*

Table 1 presents the findings obtained from the personal questionnaires administered to two police samples regarding the deterrent effect of the complaints system in general and of the files opened against them and their outcomes.

Table 1 shows that most of the respondents (about sixty per cent) report that the system has a deterrent effect in general and, in their particular case, has influenced their behaviour in the street. The general trend in both police samples is

[16] Central Bureau of Statistics, *Israel's Annual Statistical Almanac 1997* (Jerusalem, 1997).

**Table 1** Suspect Police Officers' Responses Regarding Deterrent Influence Over Their Behavior in the Street (in per cent)

| Police Officers/ Source of Influence | All respondents | Before Machash | During Machash | $X^2$ | p < |
|---|---|---|---|---|---|
| 1. The opening of the specific file | 61.8 | 57.1 | 66.2 | 2.13 | .143 (n.s.) |
| 2. The final outcome of the specific file | 53.9 | 47.8 | 59.4 | 3.25 | .071 |
| 3. The existence of a complaint system | 58.8 | 46.0 | 70.4 | 14.56 | .0001 |
| 4. The existence of Machash | 59.7 | 51.3 | 67.2 | 6.21 | .012 |
| Total | 100 | 100 | 100 | | |
| N | 249* | 119* | 130* | | |

* Respondents failed to answer all questions.

fairly similar with only small variations: influence over the conduct of police officers in the street was stronger among suspect police officers who were investigated by Machash than among those investigated by the police department.

In justifying their responses, regardless of the system handling their case, most of the police respondents state that these general and particular deterrent effects are not as positive as they might seem. According to them, the main effect of Machash is the indirect harm to important components of police work, such as the erosion of the deterrent effect police have over offenders, and the undermining of police motivation, initiative, efficiency and self-confidence, all of which are indispensable for effective police work. In their opinion, the root of the problem is related to the declared policy of Machash to open use of force files against police officers on the basis of even the slightest suspicion, and the automatic freeze on promotion while the investigation against them is being conducted. These negative features they claim result in an exaggerated caution by police in their contacts with citizens. This occurs in order to avoid complaints which may reduce their chance of promotion.

## Complainant (and Suspect) Satisfaction

Table 2 presents the findings obtained from the personal questionnaires administered both to active complainants and suspect police officers regarding their satisfaction with the investigation conducted by Machash.

**Table 2** Complainant's and Suspect Police Officers' Responses Regarding Dissatisfaction with Machash Investigation of their Cases (in per cent)

| Side of the Case/ Source of Dissatisfaction | Compl. | Police Officers | $X^2$ | p < |
|---|---|---|---|---|
| 1. General functioning | 89.2 | 89.8 | 0.03 | .856 (n.s.) |
| 2. Final outcome of the specific file | 77.2 | 78.7 | 0.10 | .740 (n.s.) |
| 3. Involvement in the investigation | 59.1 | 74.6 | 8.93 | .003 |
| 4. Updating during the investigation | 72.6 | 76.9 | 0.80 | .368 |
| 5. Updating on the outcome of the investigation | 80.4 | 68.5 | 6.56 | .010 |
| 6. Length of the investigation | 52.6 | 63.8 | 4.30 | .038 |
| 7. Investigator partiality towards the adversarial side | 35.3 | 63.8 | 28.02 | .0001 |
| 8. Support for civilian supervision of the complaints system | 96.0 | 61.8 | 75.29 | .0001 |
| Total | 100 | 100 | | |
| N | 250* | 130* | | |

* Respondents failed to answer all questions.

As can be seen from Table 2, most of the complainants and the police officers (almost ninety per cent) are dissatisfied with the functioning of Machash. Moreover, over three-quarters of the respondents in both groups claimed that the outcome of their investigation had been "unjust", albeit for different reasons: the complainants because their file had been closed (usually due to lack of evidence) and the police officers due to the fact that a file had been opened against them, thus endangering their chance of promotion. In both groups, structural characteristics of the investigative process are blamed for being inappropriate. Respondents cited the "very judicial/formal" style of the investigative process, insufficient involvement in the investigation, minimal updating on the progress of the investigation and final outcome, and the length of the process. Two-thirds of the police officers complained about the partiality of the Machash investigators against them and the general anti-police predisposition of the Department for Investigations of Police Officers. Although both parties give similar reasons in explaining their negative feelings, there were some significant differences between them (see Table 2). The negative feelings of the police officers are stronger than those of the complainants with regard to involvement in the investigation (almost seventy-five per cent versus almost sixty per cent); the duration of the investigations (almost sixty-five per cent versus just over one-half), and especially the objectivity of the investigators (two-thirds versus one-third). The negative feelings of the complainants are stronger than those of the police officers with regard to updating on the investigative outcome (eighty per cent versus about seventy per cent).

Respondents in both groups were also asked about their general attitude towards civilian involvement in the complaints system. Table 2 shows that in both samples the majority support civilian involvement. In their opinion, it leads to enhanced public as well as police confidence in the complaints system, especially with regard to its objectivity and neutrality. However, complainant support is significantly stronger than police officers (almost all of the civilian respondents versus just over sixty per cent of the police officers).

Another important distinction was made among the Jewish and Arab complainants. Table 3 presents these findings.

According to them the proportion of Arab complainants who reported dissatisfaction in general and particularly in regard to the final investigative

**Table 3** Jewish and Arab Complainants' Responses Regarding Dissatisfaction with Machash Investigation of their Cases (in per cent)

| Complainant Ethnicity/ Source of Dissatisfaction | Jews | Arabs | $X^2$ | p < |
|---|---|---|---|---|
| 1. General functioning | 87.8 | 91.3 | 14.77 | .002 |
| 2. Final outcome of the specific file | 71.8 | 86.0 | 6.56 | .010 |
| 3. Involvement in the investigation | 59.7 | 58.0 | 0.67 | .795 (n.s.) |
| 4. Updating during the investigation | 71.2 | 75.0 | 0.40 | .523 (n.s.) |
| 5. Updating on the outcome of the investigation | 81.0 | 79.3 | 0.10 | .746 (n.s.) |
| 6. Length of the investigation | 50.0 | 57.1 | 1.16 | .280 (n.s.) |
| 7. Investigator partiality towards the adversarial side | 32.4 | 40.8 | 1.78 | .182 (n.s.) |
| 8. Support for civilian supervision of the complaints system | 95.4 | 96.8 | 0.26 | .606 (n.s.) |
| Total | 100 | 100 | | |
| N | 156* | 94* | | |

* Respondents failed to answer all questions.

outcome of their cases was significantly higher, in comparison with Jewish complainants. Concerning the other items, significant differences were not found.

## Promoting Public Confidence in the Police

Table 4 presents the findings of the telephone survey regarding knowledge about Machash.

Table 4 shows that over sixty per cent of the respondents knew nothing about

**Table 4** Citizens' Responses Regarding Knowledge about Machash and Support for Civilian Involvement (in per cent)

| Citizens/ Citizens' Responses | All of the respondents | Jewish | Arab | $X^2$ | $p <$ |
|---|---|---|---|---|---|
| 1. Ignorance about the identity of Machash | 61.2 | 56.7 | 89.7 | 26.87 | .0001 |
| 2. Ignorance about how to report a complaint | 65.4 | 63.7 | 76.4 | 4.22 | .039 |
| 3. Personal involvement in non-reported police violence incidents | 21.7 | 19.5 | 35.3 | 8.58 | .003 |
| 4. Personal knowledge about non-reported police violence incidents | 28.5 | 24.4 | 54.4 | 25.91 | 0.001 |
| 5. Support for civilian involvement | 96.9 | 96.7 | 95.5 | 0.21 | .640 (n.s.) |
| Total | 100 | 100 | 100 | | |
| N | 500 | 431 | 69 | | |

Machash (its name, its civilian affiliation or its investigative authority). Lack of knowledge was particularly salient among the Arab respondents (almost ninety per cent versus less than sixty per cent among the Jewish respondents). A similar trend is found on the second question regarding knowledge about the procedure for filing a formal complaint against a police officer: almost two-thirds of the total sample (and a similar percentage of the Jews surveyed) and over three-quarters of the Arab respondents had no knowledge about the procedure. Moreover, the proportion of Arab respondents who reported about personal involvement or awareness on non-reported police violence incidents, was significantly higher, in comparison with the Jewish respondents. Nonetheless, the responses in both groups clearly point to virtually unanimous support for civilian involvement in the complaints procedure. Respondents claim that civilian involvement serves to enhance public confidence in the investigation of police officers and the outcome.

**Providing Feedback to Police Managers**

From the interviews with the police commanders who deal with public complaints against police officers, it is possible to distinguish between individual and general internal use of the complaints data.

*The individual level*

As per Israeli police regulations, the personal files of police officers are reviewed regularly and updated by the human resources unit. This procedure bears important implications for the suspect officer. With the opening of a file against a police officer, all internal decisions regarding promotion, participation in special courses (for example, for sergeants or senior officers), external studies, or even moving into special roles are put on hold. Except for rare instances, there is full compliance with these regulations.

*The general level*

Organisational analyses of trends and tendencies indicated by complaints data are mainly conducted following specific requests from senior commanders wishing to evaluate their units or certain members. However, despite the potential of (and the motivation to learn from) the Machash data for internal organisational purposes, requests of this type often come up against problems. Indeed, it seems as if feedback from complaints data is more difficult today than in pre-Machash days. In the opinion of the three respondents (high ranking police commanders of the human resources and discipline department, the supervision and training department, and the internal investigations unit), the problem is essentially organisational and relates to the separation between the police and civilian branch of the complaints system. According to them, the main problems are the prolonged time needed for Machash to complete all the relevant details of a file, and the lack of agreement between police and the civilian board regarding the classification of data contained in the Machash files which police request for their purposes.

It should be stressed that these senior commanders clearly support the involvement of civilian bodies in the complaints processes against suspect police officers. According to them, it serves to enhance public confidence in the police force, in general, and in investigations against police officers and their outcomes, in particular. Moreover, in their opinion, the situation regarding the duration of such investigations has improved since the establishment of Machash. In general, the time component is critical for suspect police officers because of its serious implications for promotion. Nevertheless, for the same reason, they resented the declared policy of Machash to open use of force files against police officers on the basis of each and every complaint, suspicion, component of information or even, to quote one of them, on the basis of "every scrap of paper" that reaches the Machash's offices.

## DISCUSSION

### Maintaining Discipline Through Deterrence

Traditionally, maintaining discipline in the police force was perceived by police management as one of the most important goals of the formal investigation system against police officers. According to this approach, investigation and punitive measures serve as a deterrent. In the discussion that follows, deterrence is defined as the prevention of illegal conduct by police officers, on the individual level and on the general level. In order to serve as a deterrent on either level, the system must activate its authority consistently and systematically, by means of severe, concrete and certain sanctions, in a tied associative relationship between the time of the offence and the punishment.[17]

#### *General deterrence*

From the official Machash data, very few files (about thirteen per cent) culminate in a formal recommendation for punitive measures. Moreover, this percentage is significantly lower today than in the pre-Machash period (about sixteen per cent). Hence, it seems that the general message conveyed by the civilian board to police officers in Israel is quite clear: the chances of apprehension, investigation and severe punishment are not high. However, this message does not constitute a peculiar failure of Machash. The fact that the use of force files form the majority of "not sustained" complaints is a common phenomenon of many civilian boards. This is due mainly to structural characteristics in the investigation stage, such as problems of obtaining physical evidence and independent testimonies against police officers.[18]

It is worth noting, however, that the rate of sustained use of force files in Israel is higher than in other countries. The corresponding average rates obtained in a comprehensive survey of over a thousand police agencies in the United States were: twelve point four per cent on the state level, ten point four per cent on the city level, eight and a half per cent on the country level, and six point one per

[17] H Goldstein, *Policing a Free Society* (Cambridge, Ballinger, 1977).

[18] S Herzog, *supra* n. 4, H Goldstein, "Controlling and Reviewing Police—Citizen Contacts" in T Barker and D Carter (eds.), *Police Deviance* (Cincinatta, Anderson Publishing, 1986).

cent on the sheriff level.[19] Those rates were found to be similar to sustained percentages for excessive force complaints by other American researchers, most of them around an apparent norm of ten per cent or less.[20] The rate of sustained files in England and Wales between 1979–97 is even lower. It increased from four to six per cent.[21]

A simplistic conclusion based on these findings may be that police officers in Israel, despite the significantly decreasing sustained rate in use of force files after the establishment of Machash, are clearly more violent than in America or England. However, studies focusing especially on the analysis of sustained rates of complaints provide evidence linking them to various departmental characteristics, patterns and legal definitions.[22]

As said before, another requirement for the existence of general deterrence is the consistent and systematic activation of severe punishments. It is difficult to assess the extent of this condition in the frame of the present study because it did not focus on the punitive decisions of disciplinary or criminal trials, beyond the Machash's responsibilities. However, several external comptrollers have expressed harsh criticism of the police disciplinary system for the leniency of its punishments.[23]

At the same time, even if it is assumed that the punishments imposed are "severe and concrete", there has to be a "time-tied association between the offence and the punishment". Examination of a large sample of use of force files opened by Machash in recent years[24] found that:

- the time lag between the occurrence of an allegedly violent event and the submission of a formal complaint is quite short (eighty per cent of the complaints are submitted within one week of the event);
- the time lag between the submission of a formal complaint and the start of the investigation is about six weeks (two weeks—two months in sixty per cent of the cases);
- the time lag between the start and completion of the formal investigation is four and a half months and in about one-fifth of the cases, it reached a whole year.

It should be noted, however, that these time lags are much shorter than the time lags found in the pre-Machash period when complaints were handled by the police (see Table 2 and interviews with high commanders). It is assumed that

19 A Pate and L Fridell, *supra* n. 11.

20 J Dugan and D Breda, " Complaints about Police Officers: A Comparison Among Types and Agencies", 19 (2) *Journal of Criminal Justice*, 165 at 171; A Wagner, "Citizen Complaint Against the Police: The Complainant", 8 *Journal of Police Science and Administration*, 247 at 252.

21 M Maguire and C Corbett, *supra* n. 1, Police Complaints Authority, *Annual Report* (London, HMSO, 1997).

22 See A Pate and L Fridell, *supra* n. 11, 43–4.

23 For example State Comptroller Reports Number 36 (1986) Number 38 (1988) Number 41 (1991) (Ministry of Police Comptroller, 1993), *supra* n. 11.

24 S Herzog, *supra* n. 4.

attenuation of the processing period serves to enhance the deterrent power of the complaints system.

### *Individual deterrence*

Responses on the deterrence items in the two police samples (Table 1) indicate that Machash is perceived as more of a deterrent factor than the internal police complaints system preceding it. As already mentioned, respondents interpret the deterrent effect in a negative way, in terms of the alleged caution required of them in their everyday contacts with citizens. However, this is exactly the meaning of deterrence: activation of system mechanisms that require police officers to think twice before using physical force against citizens. Accordingly, force is to be used only as a last resort.

Since the establishment of Machash, there has been some improvement in the deterrent effect of the complaints system. The duration of investigation is shorter, and the rate of sustained files is higher than in the United States and England.[25] However, the general message conveyed by Machash is quite similar to that of its predecessor and many other civilian and internal boards. Because of the low probability of conviction, the low certainty of punishment and the long investigation process, the capacity of Machash to serve as an important deterrent tool and, thereby, ensure discipline within the ranks of the police, is quite limited.

## Complainant (and Suspect) Satisfaction

As already mentioned, active complainants and suspect police officers were virtually unanimous in their dissatisfaction with the Machash investigation process. Maguire and Corbett and Brown[26] obtained similar findings in England, regarding complainants views. Theoretically, it could be argued that dissatisfaction on the part of suspect police officers is hardly surprising because, traditionally, police organisations in the Western world (including Israel) have always tended to oppose any transfer of their investigative authority to external bodies.[27] However, this assumption does not fit the findings of the present study (Table 2). Most of the police respondents (and all of the complainants) support civilian involvement in the complaints system, due to its increased objectivity and neutrality. It is possible to argue that the police officers surveyed were

[25] See A Pate and L Fridell, *supra* n. 11; M Maguire and C Corbett, *supra* n. 1; Police Complaints Authority 1997, *supra* n. 21.

[26] M Maguire and C Corbett, *supra* n. 1; D Brown, *supra* n. 1.

[27] W Petterson, "Police Accountability and Civilian Oversight of Policing: An American Perspective" in A Goldsmith (ed.), *Complaints Against the Police* (Oxford, Clarendon, 1991); H Goldstein, *supra* n. 18; D Brown, "Civilian Review of Complaints Against the Police: A Survey of U.S Literature" in K Heal et al (eds.), *Policing Today* (London, HMSO, 1985); S Herzog, *supra* n. 4.

merely paying lip-service to the concept. However, from the police questionnaires it is possible to learn that considerations of objectivity and neutrality are important also to suspect police officers, especially if the files against them are closed. The main reason is to show to the public at large, and particularly to the complainants and other police officers, that the suspicions against them were dropped not as a result of the investigators' organisational identity but due to their objective innocence. Thus, it seems that the negative attitudes regarding Machash investigations found in both parties do not reflect opposition to it in principle, but rather reflects personal or specific dissatisfaction based on experience.

The reasons for dissatisfaction are perhaps surprisingly similar in the two samples: among them, dissatisfaction with the investigative outcome; insufficient updating and involvement; the long duration of the process, and partiality on the part of the investigators. These findings are also similar to those found by Maguire and Corbett and Brown.[28] However, there were some significant differences between the two populations.

In comparison with the complainants, the police officers report more negative attitudes regarding the duration of the processes, lack of involvement in them, and investigator partiality. With regard to the length of the investigation, even though the procedure has shortened in recent years, the personal implications are still perceived to be harsh for suspect police officers, namely, the automatic freeze on promotion (which usually involves improved salary, work conditions and other organisational benefits). The explanation for stronger feelings of dissatisfaction on the part of police officers with regard to involvement in the investigation and the partiality of the Machash investigators seems to be related to the structural change introduced by Machash. According to external comptrollers of internal investigations,[29] the police handling of complaints prior to the establishment of Machash was extremely unprofessional and lacking in objectivity, lacking in clear-cut procedural rules and regulations, with complainants at a distinct disadvantage. In many cases, suspect police officers were allowed to read the complainant's testimony before giving their version of the event, thereby affording them the opportunity to reconstruct and adjust their own testimony. It appears that police dissatisfaction with Machash contains an element of "longing for the good old days" when police had the advantage over complainants.

In comparison with police officers, complainants are more negative with regard to updating about the final outcome of the investigation. It seems that the impersonal formal notices sent by mail are not easily understood and fail to satisfy. Indeed, it is strongly recommended that Machash makes an effort to explain their decision (for example, the required level of proof and other

[28] M Maguire and C Corbett, 1989, *supra* n. 11; M Maguire and C Corbett 1991, *supra* n. 1; D Brown, *supra* n. 1.

[29] For example, State Comptroller, 1986; 1988; 1991; *supra* n. 11; Ministry of Police Comptroller, 1993; *supra* n. 11; the Sirota-Eitan Committee, 1980, *supra* n. 11.

relevant considerations) and the final outcome in a more personal and lucid manner.

Maguire and Corbett and Corbett[30] found a strong relationship between complainant satisfaction and the way their cases were conducted. Only one-tenth of their complainant sample who registered formal complaints reported satisfaction with the process, whereas more than half of their sample whose complaints were resolved informally felt satisfied. These differences are explained in terms of the complainants' initial expectations (not to punish the police officer but to receive an explanation or apology) and especially to be fully involved in the process (an attempt at informal resolution requires the agreement of the complainant). However, most of the cases treated informally in England are not serious and hence, are not compatible with those treated by Machash (which handles only illegal use of force cases and offences punishable by over one year of imprisonment). Rather they are more compatible with cases investigated by the internal affairs unit in the Israeli Police. Nevertheless, it is recommended that empirical research be conducted in Israel to assess the advantages and disadvantages of formal versus informal handling of complaints. It is also recommended that the Ministry of Justice invests monetary and human resources in the system (for example, additional investigators) in order to shorten the investigation period even more, and to involve and update both parties to the complaint in a more regular, personal and clear manner.

Regarding the differences between complainants (Table 3), the findings show that the Arab complainants reported a significant higher dissatisfaction with Machash functioning, in comparison with the Jewish complainants. However, significant differences were not found in the different justifications for these feelings. In this context it is important to add some findings which tend to show an apparent impartial and fair Machash's reference towards Jewish and Arab complainants. In the above-mentioned examination of use of force files opened by Machash,[31] no significant differences were found, on the one hand, between the rates of the closed use of force files (meaning, without the required evidence to sustain the file) and the non-closed, and on the other, in the duration of the investigations, involving Jewish and Arab complainants.

## Promoting Public Confidence in the Police

An important goal of every complaints system is to raise the satisfaction level of citizens who submit a formal complaint. However, an open and effective complaints system that assures objective and fast treatment of complaints sends out

[30] M Maguire and C Corbett, *supra* n. 1; C Corbett "Complaints Against the Police: The New Procedure of Informal Resolution", 2 *Policing and Society*, 47 at 69.

[31] S Herzog, "Police Violence Against Arabs in Israel: Facts and Social Perceptions", paper presented at the 12th International Congress on Criminology in Seoul, Korea, 1998b.

a message regarding the seriousness and professionalism of the whole institution, not only to complainants but also to the public at large.

The telephone survey data (Table 4) suggest that the establishment of Machash had very little impact on the public image of the police: sixty per cent of the respondents simply did not know anything about Machash and only a little over one-third had any knowledge about the procedure for filing a complaint against the police. Nevertheless, there was virtually unanimous support for civilian involvement in the complaints system. From these results it can be assumed that if the general public knew more about Machash, its authority and especially its civilian affiliation, they would have greater confidence in the complaints system and in the police force.

In view of the worldwide trend towards community models of policing, public confidence in the police force is essential, especially in order to increase the cooperation with the police in terms of the reporting and solving of crimes.[32] In order to increase public confidence in the police and knowledge about Machash, the civilian system should disseminate information about itself; to begin with it should publish regular annual reports. Such reports could detail public or legally controversial complaints or those involving senior officers. This could attract the attention of the media and researchers and result in wider familiarity with the work of the complaints system. Over time this could also help to enhance confidence in what would be perceived as a more open police complaints system and lead to less hesitation on the part of potential complainants to register formal complaints against the police.

With regard to the personal characteristics of the respondents, as shown in Table 4, there are significant differences between Jewish and Arab respondents: on the one hand, Arabs were far less aware of the complaints system, but on the other, they reported about a wider personal involvement or awareness of non-reported incidents of police violence. These findings are not surprising. Israel's Arab minority have been shown to be discriminated against in many governmental areas, such as education, resources investment, infrastructure, and job opportunities.[33] Moreover, a number of studies have shown that they are discriminated against by the Israeli criminal justice system at various stages of the judicial process.[34] Hence, it seems that a special effort should be made to disseminate information about Machash in general and particularly about the

[32] See D Weisburb, R Greenspan, K Bryant, E Hamilton, H Williams and D Olson, *Abuse of Police Authority in the Age of Community Policing: A Preliminary Study of Issues and Attitudes* (Washington DC, Police Foundation, 1998) 30.

[33] M Abir, R Israeli, A Sclati and B Ganor, "Report on the Topic of the Minorities in Israel in the Beginning of the 21st Century" in *Law Enforcement in the 21st Century* (Jerusalem, Ministry of Internal Security, 1997).

[34] See G Fishman and G Weimann, "The Effect of Ethnicity on Crime Attribution", 25 (3) *Criminology*, 507 at 523; E Zureik and F Moughrabi, *Different Scales of Justice: Arabs and Jews in Israel—Results on a National Survey* (Tel Aviv, Near East Cultural and Educational Foundation of Canada and International Centre for Research and Public Policy, 1998), S Cohen, *Crime, Justice and Social Control in the Israeli Arab Population* (Tel Aviv, International Centre for Peace in the Middle

complaints procedure in Israel's Arab sector. The above mentioned annual reports, translated in Arabic, may be helping.

## Providing Feedback to Police Managers

In recent years, some police forces have begun to use public opinion surveys and other methods for the purpose of assessing public opinion towards them and the "product" that they offer, day in and day out, namely "service to the citizen".[35] It is suggested that an analysis of public complaints provides a unique qualitative tool for evaluating the functioning of the whole organisation, specific parts of it and its members. To cite Goldsmith:

> complaints need to be seen not simply as *threats* to existing policies and procedures or individual officers but more importantly, as *opportunities* for re-examination of organisational policies and practices, particularly in terms of their community-relations dimension, [they are] of immense potential benefit to the police as well as to the public.[36]

Internal analysis of complaints data can be critical in an organisation such as the police. As stated previously, out on the street, police officers work without direct supervision from their superiors. They also tend not to cooperate in investigations against their colleagues—a phenomenon known as the "blue curtain".[37] Hence, citizens mistreated by the police (or independent witnesses to such mistreatment) are in a position to provide important information which, in turn, may help to prevent recurrence of such mistreatment in the future.

From the interviews with the police commanders, it appears that attempts to put the complaints data to good use internally are often doomed to fail. The main reason for this is structural and relates to the division of the complaints system between the police and Machash: any organisational analysis based on complaints data by the police department is largely dependent on Machash—a totally different system, with different organisational perspective and goals. The gap between the two systems can be bridged, but for this to happen there has to be flexibility and mutual understanding of the different and even oppo-

East, 1989); G Fishman and A Rattner, "The Israeli Criminal Justice System in Action—Is Justice Administered Differently?", 13 (1) *Journal of Quantitative Criminology*, 7 at 28.

[35] T Flanagan and M Vaughan, "Public Opinion about Police Abuse of Force" in W Geller and H Toch (eds.), *And Justice for All* (Washington DC, Police Executive Research Forum, 1995).

[36] A Goldsmith, "External Review and Self-regulation" in A Goldsmith (ed.), *Complaints Against the Police: The Trend to External Review* (Oxford, Clarendon, 1991) 19.

[37] W Petterson, *supra* n. 27; W Westley, "Secrecy and the Police" in A Neiderhoffer and A Blumberg (eds.), *The Ambivalent Force: Perspectives on the Police* (London, Ginn, 1973); T Barker and J Roebuck, "Police Corruption as a Form of Organizational Deviance" in D McNamara and M Riedel (eds.), *Police: Perspectives, Problems, Prospects* (New York, Praeger, 1974).

site structural and organisational needs of the two systems.[38] Essentially, Machash (or perhaps the Ministry of Justice) would have to expand its organisational perspective in order to accommodate the internal organisational needs of the police, without forfeiting its basic individual-legal orientation.

## CONCLUSIONS

In general, the research results on the extent to which the objectives of complaints systems have been attained by Machash are not encouraging:

- despite some improvement (especially in comparison to the pre-Machash period), the deterrent capability of Machash is limited;
- complainants (and police officers) remain dissatisfied with the investigations;
- the public at large does not know about the existence of Machash, its functions, or how to register complaints;
- police managers find it difficult to access Machash complaints material for internal police purposes due to the separate civilian status of Machash.

Suggestions are offered to improve and remedy the situation in these areas. However, beyond these essentially "technical" changes, questions about the essential nature of the complaints board remain open. Experience in the Western world shows that the criticisms raised against both external and internal complaints boards are very similar: the percentage of sustained files usually remains low; the complaints are not always investigated in a professional or objective manner; police officers committing serious offences are not punished severely; complainants are not sufficiently involved in the investigative process or provided with appropriate explanations, and the duration of the investigation is usually too long. [39]

Given the problems with internal complaints systems and the disappointment in external complaints systems, the question that remains is: what is the recommended solution for external bodies? Despite the common problems, many researchers [40] believe in the potential of civilian involvement, not only for the improvement of internal systems, but also for the reduction of police offences. There seems to be agreement that the unimpressive record of change of most of

[38] These police perceptions regarding the low effectiveness of external boards in comparison with internal units are similar to those found recently by D Weisburd et al 1998, *supra* n. 32.

[39] L Lustgarten, *supra* n. 11; Maguire and Corbett, *supra* n. 1; N Uildriks and H Van Mastrigt, *supra* n. 11; M McMahon, "Police Accountability· The Situation of Complaints in Toronto", 12 *Contemporary Crises*, 301 at 327.

[40] Among them are R Terrill, "Complaints Against the Police in England", 31 (4) *American Journal of Comparative Law*, 599 at 626; D Brown, *supra* n. 37; L Lustgarten, *supra* n. 11; P Kinsey, J Lea and J Young, *Losing the Fight Against Crime* (Oxford, Basil Blackwell, 1986); A Goldsmith, "New Directions in Police Complaints Procedures: Some Conceptual and Comparative Departures", 11 (2) *Police Studies*, 60 at 71, M Maguire and C Corbett, 1989, *supra* n. 11; N Uildriks and H Van Mastrigt, *supra* n. 11; R Reiner, *The Politics of Police* (Brighton, Wheatsheafs, 1992).

the newly established external systems is mainly attributable to the application of the model: in practice, the structure, functions and powers of the external system and the internal system are all too similar. On the applied-operative level, the basic problem of the individual-judicial model of external boards (such as Machash) is that their mandate is generally limited to the investigation of potentially guilty police officers in relation to specific complaints/complainants. However, certain organisational characteristics about the occupational reality of the police are clearly very decisive and influential in the involvement of duty police officers in violent incidents. Such characteristics include the "warrior policy" of the police force, the "police subculture" and "the police code of action" as well as the occupational conditions in which police officers work.[41] Hence, it is almost as if external control systems which concentrate only on the individual level of suspect police officers are "doomed" to fail despite their independent civilian status. Many have no mandate, nor are they designed to intervene in police policy, organisational structure and/or other general or organisational patterns that serve to encourage the phenomenon of police offences in general and police violence, in particular.[42] In order to improve the general functioning of these boards and also to reduce the dimensions of police violence, the police force and the external bodies involved in the complaints process have to address not only the "rotten apples" but also the basket carrying them. In other words, wide-reaching organisational preventive action is needed involving joint civilian-police cooperation, acting on all levels of police work, both at the individual and organisational level.[43]

[41] J Skolnick and J Fyfe, *Above the Law: Police and the Excessive Use of Force* (New York, Free Press, 1993); D Perez and W Muir, "Administrative Review of Alleged Police Brutality" in W Geller and H Toch (eds.), *And Justice for All* (Washington DC, Police Executive Rsearch Forum, 1995).

[42] See S Walker, *Citizen Review: Resource Manual* (Washington, Police Executive Research Forum, 1995).

[43] S Walker, *ibid.*; P Kinsey, J Lea and J Young, *supra* n. 40.

# 7

# *Evaluating Police Complaints Legislation: A Suggested Framework**

PHILIP C STENNING[1]

## INTRODUCTION

An effective process for handling public complaints against the police requires many things: a sound legislative foundation; dedicated, competent, experienced and/or trained personnel to administer it; a reasonable level of commitment and co-operation on the part of the police organisations and personnel to whom the process applies; an adequate degree of knowledge of, confidence in, and willingness to use, the process, and good faith, on the part of potential complainants; and the commitment of political support and adequate resources for full and effective implementation of the process. A comprehensive assessment of the adequacy and effectiveness of such a process would require a careful examination of all these aspects of it, and would require empirical research as well as more conceptual, legal and policy analysis.

In this chapter, my focus is limited to spelling out some suggested criteria for evaluating the adequacy of what I have referred to as the "legislative foundation" for a public complaints process—that is, the legislated provisions which constitute the legal framework within which the process will be established and implemented. In addition to listing the suggested criteria and providing a brief explanation of each of them, I provide some examples of how each may be applied in a legislative analysis and of some of the specific issues which they raise. Most of the examples are from Canadian jurisdictions with which I am most familiar, but it will be obvious that these issues are not unique to any one country or jurisdiction.

* The framework presented here was originally developed and applied in a review of the new (1996) legislation with respect to public complaints against police in the province of British Columbia, Canada, which I was commissioned to undertake in 1998 by the newly appointed Police Complaint Commissioner, Mr. Don Morrison, Q.C. A copy of that review can be obtained from his office at: Suite 900, 1111 Melville Street, Vancouver, British Columbia V6E 3V6, Canada. I am grateful to Mr. Morrison for his permission to use extracts from the review in this chapter. The framework developed in the review and presented here was subsequently adopted by the Independent Commission on Policing for Northern Ireland (the Patten Commission) in its report entitled "A New Beginning: Policing in Northern Ireland" (see Northern Ireland, Independent Commission 1999: 36–7).

[1] The author may be contacted at: Centre of Criminology, Room 8001 Robarts Library, 130 St. George Street, Toronto, Ontario M5S 3H1, Canada. Tel: (416) 978–3451 ext. 231; Fax: (416) 978–4195; e-mail: p.stenning@utoronto.ca

CRITERIA FOR ASSESSMENT

The criteria set out below reflect what I believe are the principal qualities which an adequate legislative framework for an effective process for handling public complaints against the police ought to display. Obviously these are not uncontentious and others may feel that other qualities are more important than the ones I have looked for. By setting them out clearly, however, I hope to facilitate subsequent discussion and debate about what such legislation should ideally be attempting to achieve, and how.

The order in which these criteria are listed is not intended to be reflective of my view of their relative importance. It will be clear, however, that the objectives reflected by these criteria may sometimes be in conflict to the extent that policy-makers will need to make hard choices, weighing the relative importance of competing objectives. Such choices, however, can only be intelligently made in light of the more general social, political, legal and cultural features of the environments in which such complaints processes are to function. Since such features are likely to vary considerably from one jurisdiction to another, any attempt to suggest some generic, global priorities would probably be both presumptuous and invidious.

I suggest that a sound legislative framework for an effective process for handling public complaints against the police should provide for at least the following:

**Statement of principles and objectives**

Police complaints legislation should include, at its outset, a provision setting out clearly the guiding principles and policy objectives of the complaints process provided for, and the intended priority between potentially competing or conflicting objectives of that process. Such a statement of principles and objectives provides valuable guidance not only to those public servants who must implement the legislation on a day-to-day basis, but also to judges and other adjudicators who may have to interpret its provisions. It also sends important messages both to potential complainants and to police officers who may be the subject of complaints as to what they may expect from the process. The process of drafting and enacting such a statement provides a critical opportunity for essential policy issues to be publicly addressed and resolved, rather than be left implicit and unresolved by the legislation itself.

Such principles and objectives may be expected to vary somewhat from one jurisdiction to another, but some examples might be: to ensure that anyone having a complaint against the police service or any of its members has an opportunity to have such complaint impartially investigated and fairly and justly resolved; to ensure that any police officer against whom a complaint has been lodged has a full and fair opportunity to respond to such complaint before an impartial tribunal; to maintain or restore public confidence in the police service;

to ensure that systemic sources of police misconduct, as well as the misconduct itself, are identified and addressed; to give priority to remedial responses to substantiated complaints against the police service or any of its members, when such responses are not inconsistent with other objectives of the legislation; to contribute to sound and effective direction and management of the police service, etc.

## Accessibility

The process should be reasonably straightforward, and accessible and understandable to potential complainants, as well as to police officers to whom it applies.

In some ways, the accessibility of a complaints process is its most significant feature since, if potential complainants do not have good access to the process, all the other desirable characteristics are effectively irrelevant. For this reason, I place special emphasis on this feature.

Accessibility may be assessed in terms of five questions:

(a) how easy is it for a potential complainant to lodge and pursue a complaint? It is essential for accessibility that there not be unnecessary physical or psychological impediments to actually filing a complaint. Thus, for instance, a complainant should not have to undertake lengthy and expensive travel to reach a place where a complaint can be filed. Obviously, this will be a greater problem for police services (such as state, provincial and federal services) having larger geographical jurisdictions.

Places at which complaints may be filed must be psychologically as well as physically accessible. Since many people who come into contact with police are not highly educated people of high social status, it is important that complainants are not required to go to intimidating (to them) inner offices of senior police personnel in police buildings in order to make their complaint. Indeed, the opportunity to file a complaint with someone who is not a police officer, and who is not located within a police office or station, may be regarded as an important element of adequate accessibility.[2]

Many potential complainants are not very literate. If complaints are required to be reduced to writing, therefore, provision for assistance to those who may need it is equally essential for genuine accessibility. The same is true for complainants whose first language may be a foreign language.

Potential complainants cannot be expected to come forward if they are not informed about how and where to file a complaint. Appropriate distribution of public information about the complaints process is thus also an essential

[2] In New South Wales, Australia, for instance, complaints can be lodged with a local court as well as at local police stations. In British Columbia, Canada, complaints against the police can now be lodged by mail, fax or e-mail (see www.opcc.bc.ca, "Making a complaint"). Given the possibilities for abuses inherent in e-mail, safeguards against fraudulent complaints would be necessary both to protect genuine complainants and to guard against harassment of police officers who may be the subject of such complaints.

element of adequate accessibility. In many jurisdictions, such information will need to be provided in several languages.

(b) what range of complaints can be dealt with through the process?
Much police complaints legislation restricts the kinds of complaints which can be entertained under it. Most commonly, only complaints of "misconduct" against individual officers will be accepted. This leaves a whole category of "service" or "policy" complaints—that is, complaints about levels or quality of service generally, or about the policies of the police service—unaddressed. Yet such complaints are not uncommon,[3] and may be regarded as no less important than complaints about misconduct by individual officers.

Often, the exclusion of "service" or "policy" complaints from police complaints legislation reflects a deliberate policy choice, according to which those kinds of complaints should not be handled through the special processes established to handle individual misconduct complaints, but through the mechanisms for general police governance (e.g. by police governing authorities rather than by specialised, independent police complaints tribunals). Such a policy reflects the belief that "service" and "policy" complaints are qualitatively different from individual misconduct complaints in a number of important respects—e.g. they do not involve an individual respondent whose rights need to be taken into account—and consequently require a qualitatively different response. There is also the view that responding to them should properly be regarded as an element of the general governance responsibilities of police governing authorities

While such a legislative policy is, in my view, quite defensible, it is nevertheless important to ensure that if they are excluded from the legislation with respect to individual misconduct complaints, some viable alternative legislative provisions with respect to these complaints are in place elsewhere. Otherwise, an important category of potential complainants are left without access to an effective process through which to pursue their complaints.

(c) who may lodge and pursue a complaint?
The major issue here concerns "third party" complaints—i.e. complaints lodged by persons other than the person(s) most directly affected by the conduct which is the subject of the complaint. Much police complaints legislation excludes such complaints,[4] while other statutes permit them but accord less extensive rights to "third party" complainants than to directly affected complainants.[5]

[3] Since much police complaints legislation does not countenance such complaints, statistics about them are not readily available in most jurisdictions. In British Columbia, Canada, however, recent experience has shown that just under ten per cent of complaints lodged under their new legislation during its first year of operation were "service or policy" complaints (see their website at www.opcc.bc.ca).

[4] The most recent legislation in Ontario, Canada, for instance, expressly excludes such complaints (see subsection 57(1) of the Ontario Police Services Act).

[5] The legislation in British Columbia, Canada, for instance, allows "third party" complaints, but gives "third party" complainants fewer procedural rights than those of directly affected complainants. By contrast, legislation in the Canadian provinces of Saskatchewan, Manitoba and Newfoundland, gives "third party" complainants the same procedural rights as directly affected

This is an accessibility issue because at least some potential directly affected complainants whose complaints may have merit do not have the resources or courage to pursue their complaints themselves. Advocacy groups such as civil liberties associations, poverty action groups, and women's shelters are often willing to pursue such complaints on behalf of their clients, and parents or guardians may wish to do so on behalf of minors. Without recognition of such "third party" complaints, many potential complainants may not have effective access to the complaints process.

(d) what resources will be available to complainants?
This has proven to be a contentious issue in many jurisdictions.[6] For a complainant who does not have access to the necessary financial or technical resources to effectively pursue a complaint, once lodged, formal access to the complaints process is meaningless. Yet the realities of police-citizen interaction in most jurisdictions make it likely that many potential complainants will be in this situation. Providing for "third party" complaints may be a partial solution to this problem, but not always a satisfactory one. Access for indigent complainants to legal aid or some other equivalent assistance from the state is likely to be a more satisfactory solution, although remarkably few jurisdictions seem to be willing to adopt such a policy.

(e) what protections against abuse of the process are there?
The more accessible a complaints process is, the greater will be the need for some fair and effective mechanism for weeding out genuinely frivolous or vexatious complaints, in order to protect police officers from unjustified harassment through the complaints process. While determining that a complaint is frivolous or vexatious is more easily said than done, fair and effective mechanisms to achieve this can be devised and need to be provided for in police complaints legislation. Some provision for an appeal against an initial decision of this kind is usually essential to ensure public confidence in the process.

## Fairness and respect for rights

The process should be fair to both complainants and police officers who are the subject of complaints ("respondents"), as well as to others who may, voluntarily

complainants (see P Stenning, "Review of Part 9 (Complaint Procedure) of the British Columbia Police Act as amended by s. 36 of SBC 1997, c. 37". Memorandum prepared for the Office of the Police Complaint Commissioner of British Columbia—unpublished, but available on request from the Police Complaint Commissioner's Office, 9–10).

[6] At a recent hearing into public complaints concerning alleged excessive use of force (pepper spray) on demonstrators by the Royal Canadian Mounted Police at a meeting of the organisation for Asia-Pacific Economic Co-operation (APEC) in Vancouver, BC, in 1997, the hearing commissioner ruled that the student complainants would not be able to fairly participate in the hearings without some financial support, which was eventually provided by the Canadian Government (see www.sgc.ca/Releases/e19990215.htm and K Busby, "Accessing Accountability: Public Funding of lawyers before Inquiries" in W Pue (ed.), *Pepper in our Eyes: Police/State in Canada* (Vancouver, University of British Columbia Press) (2000) pp. 171–82.

or involuntarily become involved in the process (as witnesses etc.), and should at all times respect the dignity and legal and constitutional rights of all such persons. Substantive as well as procedural fairness is essential for the public credibility and legitimacy of a police complaints process.[7]

### (a) *Fairness*

The fairness of the processes may be assessed in terms of: (a) whether parties receive adequate notice of upcoming stages, developments and requirements of them in the process; (b) whether they have sufficient opportunity to present "their side of the story" to decision-makers; (c) whether they have adequate opportunity for legal or other representation in participating in the process; (d) whether they have adequate opportunity to be heard before any sanctions (including suspension from duty) are imposed on them; (e) the adequacy of their access to review and appeal of decisions; and (f) whether the process gives complainants, respondents and the public more generally access to procedural and substantive "justice" (in the sense of procedures and outcomes which are perceived as "just").

Of course, what is considered to be "fair" or "just" varies somewhat from one jurisdiction to another, depending upon social, political, legal and cultural traditions. For instance, a low burden of proof (e.g. on a balance of probabilities, rather than beyond a reasonable doubt) has been considered appropriate in some jurisdictions, but not in others, as has the compellability of various parties as witnesses in police complaints hearings.

### (b) *Respect for rights*

Being an essentially administrative rather than penal process, the main rights which might be expected to be brought into play with respect to the complaints process are those encompassed by the administrative law concept of "natural justice" as well as those which may be more specifically enumerated by statute and/or constitutionally entrenched in a Bill or Charter of Rights.

The main rights encompassed by the concept of "natural justice" are procedural rights. Most important in this regard are rights such as the right of the subject of proceedings to adequate notice of "charges" or allegations which are to be met, the right to adequate notice of such proceedings, the right to be heard and represented at such proceedings, and the right to an independent adjudicator who is not biased.

[7] M Maguire and C Corbett, *A Study of the Police Complaints System* (London, HMSO, 1991) pp. 58–60 and 161–70; T Landau, *A Study of the Police Complaints System* (Toronto, Centre of Criminology, University of Toronto, 1994); A Goldsmith, "What's Wrong with Complaint Investigations?: dealing with difference differently in complaints against police, 15 *Criminal Justice Ethics*, 36–55.

Other rights commonly enumerated by statute and/or constitutionally entrenched which are of relevance for an assessment of police complaints legislation include the right to be secure against unreasonable search and seizure, the right not to be arbitrarily detained or imprisoned, the right "on arrest or detention" to be informed of the reason, to instruct counsel without delay and to have the legality of detention reviewed by way of *habeas corpus*, the right not to be subjected to cruel or unusual punishment or treatment, and the right against self-incriminatory use of testimony in subsequent proceedings.

As with issues of fairness, the content and interpretation of such rights varies considerably among different jurisdictions. For instance, there has been little agreement as to who does or does not qualify as an "independent" and unbiased adjudicator in police complaints proceedings. To some extent, the answer to the question as to what rights are appropriately recognised in police complaints processes depends upon whether such processes are regarded as more analogous to criminal or administrative proceedings. Not surprisingly, rank and file police representatives commonly argue for rights which are analogous to those enjoyed by accused in criminal proceedings, while complainants and their supporters (and often police managers too) argue for the lesser rights enjoyed by parties to administrative or civil proceedings. The issue of respect for rights thus raises some quite fundamental policy issues which should be addressed and resolved in the governing legislation.

**Openness and accountability**

The process should be open and accountable to complainants, respondents, police services to which it applies and their police boards, and to the public more generally, while protecting legitimate privacy interests of those who become involved in it, the integrity of police operations, and the viability of the complaints process itself.

Achieving such balances is an undertaking which is by no means easy or free from controversy, but which is essential if a public complaints process is to command credibility, legitimacy and public confidence. Openness and accountability are achieved primarily through such means as timely and sufficient release of information about the progress of complaints, openness of hearings to the public and the media, requirements to give reasons for decisions that can be scrutinised and challenged in public discussion and/or through appeals or judicial review, and the maintenance of complete and accurate records. In many jurisdictions, some of these matters are governed by legislation concerned with privacy and access to information more generally, but many of them need to be specifically addressed in police complaints legislation.

## Timeliness

The process should provide for the timely handling and disposition of complaints while allowing sufficient time for adequate and effective investigation and resolution of them.

Again, while this is an easy criterion to state, it is less easy to operationalise or secure agreement on in practice, and always depends on the provision of adequate resources. Inclusion within the legislation itself of enforceable maximum time limits within which various stages of the process must be completed,[8] together with provision for the granting of extensions in extenuating circumstances, is obviously one way to address the issue of timeliness. Differentiating between more "serious" and less "serious" complaints in this respect may also be desirable, on the ground that the more at stake in a complaint (for the complainant and/or for the officer complained against), the more thorough (and probably therefore lengthy) the process will need to be. Overall, it needs to be remembered that "justice" can be just as easily denied through undue haste as through undue delay in the resolution of complaints against police.

## Thoroughness

The process should provide for thorough investigation and, when necessary, adjudication of complaints.

Obviously, this criterion is very closely linked to the timeliness criterion. Thoroughness is also, however, very much influenced by the powers available to investigators and adjudicators. Investigators need to have sufficient powers of search and seizure, with or without warrant, for instance, in order to be able to retrieve and preserve relevant evidence, and adjudicators require sufficient powers to compel testimony and, if necessary, take action against those who may act in contempt of their proceedings. Prohibitions, with penalties, against obstruction of investigations and intimidation of witnesses are also important to ensure that thorough investigations and adjudications can occur. In some jurisdictions, legislation goes further in establishing a positive and enforceable duty (e.g. on police officers) to co-operate with authorities in various ways (e.g. surrendering notebooks, or answering questions) in the investigation of complaints.[9]

[8] As for instance in the legislation in British Columbia, Canada, and in the State of Western Australia.

[9] See for example, subsection 50(5) of the British Columbia Police Act (as amended by section 36 of S.B.C. 1997, c. 37), and subsection 113(9) of the Ontario Police Services Act.

**Impartiality**

The process should ensure the impartiality of those who investigate, adjudicate, dispose of and review the handling of complaints.

This has proven to be a controversial criterion in many jurisdictions. Specifically, there are those who believe that police officers, even from another police service, can never be considered sufficiently impartial to be entrusted with the investigation of a public complaint against their "fellow officers", or with the task of presiding over a disciplinary hearing. Courts in many jurisdictions, however, have rejected this view, holding that in proceedings such as those of a public complaints process, bias cannot be automatically presumed from the mere fact that investigators or adjudicators are members of the same organisation as the subject of the complaint.[10]

Many commentators[11] have argued persuasively that a process which required "external" investigation, adjudication and disposition of all complaints against the police would be both unnecessary and undesirable for a number of reasons. In particular, it is likely to be unduly lengthy and expensive, and may well be less effective, because of resistance from the police themselves. In addition, such a process may well not be regarded as unbiased by the police officers who are subjected to it. Most importantly, however, it would have the undesirable result of allowing senior police command officers to effectively avoid any responsibility for responding to complaints and to the situations which give rise to them. As Judge Rene Marin in Canada has cogently argued, this is a management responsibility that properly belongs to the senior command, and for which it should be held accountable.[12]

Having said this, it must also be acknowledged that in some circumstances the relationship between police investigators and officers who are the subject of complaints may be such that the investigators cannot be regarded as sufficiently impartial, and that the more serious the allegations, the more weight should be accorded to such perceptions of lack of impartiality. For this reason, in many jurisdictions legislation requires (a) that internal investigation units be separate from the regular command structure,[13] and (b) that in the most serious cases, external rather than internal investigators be used.[14] For similar reasons,

[10] See for example, the Supreme Court of Canada's decision in *Trumbley and Pugh* v. *Metropolitan Toronto Police* [1987] 2 S.C.R. 577, 45 D.L.R. (4th) 318.

[11] D Bayley, "Accountability and control of police: lessons for Britain" in T Bennett (ed.), *The Future of Policing* (Cambridge UK, Institute of Criminology, 1983) pp. 146–52; D Bayley, "Getting Serious about Police Brutality" in P Stenning (ed.), *Accountability for Criminal Justice: Selected Essays* (Toronto, University of Toronto Press, 1995) pp. 93–109; Canada, Commission of Inquiry Relating to Public Complaints, Internal Discipline and Grievance Procedure within the Royal Canadian Mounted Police (The Hon Judge R. Marin, Chair) *Report* (Ottawa, Information Canada, 1976).

[12] See Canada, Commission of Inquiry, 1976 p. 94; see also Bayley, 1995 *ibid.*

[13] Typically such units report directly to the chief of police.

[14] The Ontario Police Services Act in Canada, for instance, provides for the investigation of all situations involving death or serious bodily harm (whether they are the subject of a complaint or

legislation which allows public complaints to be initially determined and disposed of by senior police officers, typically allows for some form of review of such decisions (including the holding of fresh hearings) by some external body not associated with the police service.

## Independence

Those who investigate, adjudicate or otherwise process complaints must enjoy independence from direction, control or undue influence from police organisations (police services and police unions/associations), police governing authorities and any other person or body who may have some vested or partisan interest in the outcome of the process.

Independence and impartiality are closely related concepts. But they are not the same. Whereas impartiality refers to an absence of partiality towards one side or another of a dispute, independence refers to a freedom from direction, control or undue influence by others. A person may be impartial but not independent, or independent but not impartial.

It is not realistic to expect that police officers from the same police service who investigate public complaints against their "fellow officers", or preside over disciplinary hearings, will be perceived as "independent", even if they may actually be so in practice, since they belong to an hierarchical organisation which typically has a strong "command structure" and an ethos in which a high value is placed on obedience to orders from superiors. The perception of the "independence" of such a complaints process, therefore, typically derives from the status, autonomy and powers of the "external" review bodies which oversee, and, in appropriate cases intervene in, the process.

## An appropriate balance between the "public interest" and the interests of parties involved in a complaint

While the parties involved in a complaint may have an interest in resolving it in a particular way (e.g. through settlement without a public hearing), in some cases a broader "public interest" may require a different way of resolving the complaint—the complaints process should provide for an appropriate balancing of these interests.

It will be obvious that many people have legitimate interests of various kinds in the handling and disposition of public complaints against the police. Equally obviously, these various interests will not always coincide, and may sometimes even conflict. A good complaints system will achieve a proper balance of the various legitimate interests.

not), to be assigned to a Special Investigations Unit located within the Ministry of the Attorney-General, which is entirely separate from the police services.

The two parties whose interests are most likely to conflict, of course, are the complainant and the respondent. But other conflicts are equally possible; the respondent's interests may conflict with those of the police service of which he or she is a member, which may in turn not be entirely coincidental with those of the police governing authority/employer. Even when the interests of the complainant and the respondent coincide (as for instance when they mutually agree on an informal resolution of a complaint), this may conflict with a broader "public interest" in having the events which gave rise to the complaint fully investigated and aired in a public hearing.

A good complaints system, therefore, will provide for a mechanism for distinguishing between those cases in which the interests of the parties should be allowed to prevail, and those in which the interests of the parties must give way to a more general "public interest" if they are in conflict with it. Clear designation of who has authority to classify complaints, guidelines for such classification, as well as opportunities to challenge classificatory decisions, should be included in the governing legislation. Also, reasons for such decisions should be required, since few practices are more calculated to destroy public confidence in a complaints system than decisions perceived to be "backroom deals", with respect to which there is not adequate public accountability.[15]

### An appropriate balance between formal and informal (or less formal) procedures for resolving and disposing of complaints

A complaints process must be suitable for handling many different kinds of complaints, of varying seriousness. Some—particularly the less serious ones—can and should be resolved if possible without resort to the most formal, adversarial procedures. Experience in most jurisdictions shows that these constitute the majority of public complaints against the police.[16] Others require resort to more formal, adversarial procedures. The complaints process should provide for an appropriate balance between formal and informal, or less formal (e.g. mediation or conciliation), procedures to meet these differing needs, while still ensuring that the legitimate entitlements of the parties, as well as the legitimate public interest in the handling of complaints against the police, are respected.

### An appropriate balance between remedial and punitive dispositions

While punishment is often an appropriate response to proven misconduct of police officers who have been the subject of a public complaint, remedial or

[15] See for example, Ontario Civilian Commission on Police Services *Report of an Inquiry into Administration of Internal Investigations by the Metropolitan Toronto Police Force* (Jungeri Whitehead Inquiry) (Toronto, O.C.C.P.S., 1992).

[16] See for example, M Maguire and C Corbett, *supra* n. 7, p. 36; T Landau, *supra* n. 7, p. 26.

"corrective" measures are often equally important for ensuring that such misconduct does not recur and that public confidence in the police is maintained or restored. The complaints process should provide for an appropriate balancing of these objectives in the resolution and disposition of complaints.

Perhaps the most significant conceptual development within the field of "justice" during the last two decades has been the rise to prominence of notions of remedial or "restorative" justice. These notions recognise that much anti-social or otherwise undesirable conduct has its origins in social conditions, relationships and practices and not just in the moral turpitude of the "offender", and that "justice" systems should respond accordingly. They recognise that punishment of the individual offender is often not the only rational, let alone the most effective, response to wrongdoing or misconduct, and that responses directed towards remedying underlying conditions and socially "restoring" both the offender and the victim may be of greater social benefit.

In keeping with this recent thinking about justice, some jurisdictions[17] are now experimenting with more remedial or "restorative" responses to public complaints against police officers, especially in cases in which the "misconduct" complained of seems to have been a product of (or at least influenced by) wider, systemic policies or practices within the police service, and those in which such an approach promises more substantial benefits to complainants whose complaints have been found to be substantiated. A good modern complaints process should take account of these developments and seek to achieve a balance between such remedial approaches and more traditional, punitive ones.

### An appropriate balance between internal management and external oversight of the handling of complaints

As previously mentioned, like all other aspects of the effective and efficient operation of a police service, responding appropriately and effectively to public complaints against its members or against the police service as a whole, is first and foremost a responsibility of the service's senior management (and ultimately of the chief of police). Ensuring continued public confidence in the police service, however, requires that there also be a degree of independent external oversight and review of (and, in appropriate cases, direct intervention in) this process. The complaints process should provide for an appropriate balance between requiring the management of police services to fulfill their responsibilities for respond-

[17] For example, the New South Wales Police Service in Australia, and the Thames Valley Police Service in England, have both experimented with informal resolution or other restorative justice processes in responding to public complaints (see T O'Connell and J Ritchie, "Restorative Justice and the Contest between the Relational and Institutional Paradigms", unpublished paper presented to a conference on "Reshaping Australian Institutions", held at the Australian National University, Canberra, February 1999). For an overview of informal resolution of police complaints in Australia, see A Goldsmith, "Informal Resolution of Complaints Against Police in Australia; Building Better Understanding or Mere Bureaucratic Convenience?" (2000) 17 *Law in Context*.

ing to public complaints, and ensuring an appropriate level of independent external oversight, review and direct intervention in the process to maintain public confidence in the police.

While this principle is easy to state, it is not so easy to obtain agreement about its practical implications. Even among those who accept that a realistic complaints system involves roles for both the police and external oversight bodies, there has long been debate about what is the appropriate "mix" of internal and external responsibilities in such a system. With respect to investigations, practices vary greatly. In some jurisdictions, oversight bodies have authority to undertake investigations themselves rather than merely oversee investigations undertaken by others. In many jurisdictions, however, the responsibility for initial investigation of complaints, as well as for attempting informal resolutions, resides with the police themselves, under the oversight of an external agency, with allowance made for assumption of the investigative role by an external agency in exceptional cases. In other jurisdictions, all complaints against the police must be initially investigated by the police, and only if the police fail to investigate at all, or their investigation does not lead to a satisfactory resolution of the complaint, is the oversight agency authorised to conduct a further investigation. In a very few jurisdictions, an external complaints commissioner presumptively investigates all complaints against the police but has a discretion to refer the complaint to the respondent's chief of police for internal investigation

Several complaints processes provide for the opportunity of some kind of adjudication by an external body through a public hearing for those cases which cannot be successfully resolved internally. This is a sensible distribution of responsibility, but there is considerable disagreement about what kinds of people are most suitable to preside over such hearings. In some jurisdictions this task is assigned to judges, while in others such hearings are presided over by some specialised board or panel established for the purpose.

If the sole responsibility of the person(s) presiding over a public hearing is to adjudicate the merits of the complaint (i.e. determine the facts and assign responsibility), a stronger case can be made for having a judicial officer preside at such a hearing; adjudication, after all, is a task with respect to which judges have particular experience and expertise. It is in regards to the third critical stage of a complaints process—determining an appropriate disposition—that debate persists as to who is the most suitable person or body to be assigned this task. Basically, three positions on this can be identified in the literature.

One model is that under which the responsibility for both adjudication and disposition at a public hearing is assigned to a judge of the regular courts, often with a right of appeal on matters of law to a higher court. Those who argue for this model usually believe that the credibility of a complaints process requires that both of these tasks must be assigned to some external body. They emphasise the similarity between determining an appropriate disposition in a public complaints process and determining an appropriate sentence in a criminal case, and argue from this that criminal court judges are particularly well suited for the task.

Another model assigns both of these tasks (adjudication and determining an appropriate disposition) to a special purpose tribunal established for the purpose. Like those who support the "judicial" model just discussed, those who support this model believe that assignment of these tasks to an external body is essential. Those who support this "administrative" model, however, while acknowledging the similarities emphasised by those who support the "judicial" model, argue either that there are important nuances involved in adjudicating and determining dispositions in cases involving public complaints against the police which require special expertise in those who preside at such hearings, or that public credibility in the process requires that such cases be determined by a tribunal with more "representative" or "lay" membership. Some go further and argue that the daily interaction between police and criminal court judges in the criminal courts makes criminal court judges not the most suitable for these tasks in the complaints process.

The third model involves a fundamentally different premise, which is that although the task of adjudication is one which is appropriately assigned to an external body, the ultimate responsibility for determining an appropriate disposition is not. Those who argue for this model argue that the ultimate responsibility for discipline, good conduct and sound management of a police service rests with the police chief, for which he or she should always be held accountable. If the final responsibility for determining and imposing a disposition of a public complaint is given to an external body, this allows the police chief to avoid his or her proper responsibility and blame someone else for any untoward consequences of an ill-chosen disposition. The police chief can thus not reasonably be held accountable for the very responsibilities for which he or she was appointed, since he or she has no ultimate control over them. This model, however, depends for its efficacy on effective mechanisms through which the police chief is held accountable for these disposition decisions.

Strong arguments can be (and have been) made in favour of each of these three models[18] and it seems that reasonable people may legitimately agree to differ as to which is the most appropriate model for a police public complaint process. The absence of any systematic comparative evaluation of these models makes it difficult to assert with any confidence that any one of them may be superior to the others.

[18] See for example, A Grant, "The Control of Police Behaviour" in W Tarnopolsky (ed.), *Some Civil Liberties Issues in the Seventies* (Toronto, Carswell, 1975) pp. 75–110; Canada, Commission of Inquiry, 1976, Part IV; A Goldsmith, "External Review and Self-Regulation: Police Accountability and the Dialectic of Complaint Procedures" in A Goldsmith (ed.), *Complaints Against the Police: The Trend to External Review* (Oxford, Clarendon, 1991), 13–61.

### Provision of appropriate systemic information to police management and governing authorities

An effective public complaints process should not only provide for the effective and appropriate resolution of individual complaints against officers, but should also generate important information for police managers and governing authorities about systemic problems or weaknesses with respect to the operations, policies, procedures and management of police services.[19] Such information derives not only from what are sometimes referred to as "service" or "policy" complaints, but also from aggregate analysis of the various individual misconduct complaints which are received, from which significant patterns or trends can often be discerned. The complaints process should provide for the retention and analysis of such aggregate data and its provision in an appropriate and timely manner for the use of police managers and governing authorities.

Obviously, the collection of such information will only be helpful if it is then intelligently analysed and used by police managers and policy-makers. This is not something that can easily be legislated, but legislative requirements for the collection and distribution of such information can provide an important foundation for encouraging such competent management practices. Again, police managers should be held accountable for their use of (or failure to use) such valuable intelligence from the complaints process.

### Effective integration and compatibility with internal disciplinary and grievance processes

There should not be unnecessary duplication or overlap between the complaints process and other internal processes for resolving problems involving members of a police service. Such duplication is inefficient, expensive, confusing and often unfair to officers concerned. The complaints process should be as integrated and compatible with such other processes as is possible without compromising the integrity of the complaints process itself.

A critical issue here is how to resolve situations in which the same incident gives rise to multiple proceedings (e.g. a public complaint, an internal disciplinary proceeding, a civil lawsuit and perhaps even a criminal trial or human rights tribunal hearing). Assigning priority among such different processes, while still ensuring that neither complainants nor police officers who are the subject of complaints are unduly prejudiced in the process, has proven difficult and controversial in many jurisdictions. Reconciling the legitimate requirements of each process is not easy. Thus, for instance, while hearings into public

[19] C Shearing, *Post-Complaint Management: The Impact of Complaint Procedures on Police Discipline*, RCMP External Review Committee, Discussion Paper No. 4 (Ottawa, Minister for Supply and Services, 1990).

complaints are usually (and quite rightly) expected to be held in public, internal disciplinary hearings are not.

Applying this criterion in police complaints legislation thus inevitably involves some difficult policy choices. The effectiveness, fairness and public credibility of a police complaints process, however, requires legislators not to shy away from such choices.

## CONCLUSION

One of the weaknesses of a great deal of the literature on police complaints processes is that authors frequently do not clearly spell out precisely what it is they think such processes should accomplish. The framework suggested here represents an attempt to identify more clearly criteria and goals against which police complaints legislation might be assessed. It is only a beginning in this respect, but hopefully a beginning which may spark some more focused debate, and on which others may be able to build.

As was suggested at the outset of the chapter, one of the things which is missing from the framework is an indication as to what relative weight should be accorded to each of the various criteria in designing good police complaints legislation. As I indicated, however, I believe that this is a matter the answers to which may legitimately vary from one jurisdiction to another, depending on more general political, social, legal and cultural traditions. While rationality and effectiveness are surely desirable goals for police complaints legislation in any jurisdiction, slavish adherence to uniformity almost certainly is not.

## References


D Bayley, "Accountability and control of police: lessons for Britain" in T Bennett (ed.) *The Future of Policing* Cropwood Conferences Series # 15 (Cambridge, U.K.: Institute of Criminology, 1983), pp. 146–62.

D Bayley, "Getting Serious about Police Brutality" in P Stenning (ed.) *Accountability For Criminal Justice:Selected Essays* (Toronto: University of Toronto Press 1995), pp. 93–109.

K Busby,"Accessing Accountability: Public Funding of Lawyers before Inquiries" forthcoming in W Pue (ed.), *Pepper in Our Eyes: Police/State in Canada* (Vancouver: University of British Columbia Press).

Canada, Commission of Inquiry Relating to Public Complaints, Internal Discipline and Grievance Procedure within the Royal Canadian Mounted Police (The Hon. Judge R. Marin, Chair) *Report* (Ottawa: Information Canada, 1976).

A Goldsmith, "External Review and Self-Regulation: Police Accountability and the Dialectic of Complaint Procedures"—in A Goldsmith (ed.) *Complaints Against Police—The Trend to External Review* (Oxford: Clarendon Press, 1991), pp. 13–61.

A Goldsmith, "What's wrong with complaint investigations?: dealing with difference differently in complaints against police" *Criminal Justice Ethics* 15(1): 36–55.

A Goldsmith, "Informal Resolution of Complaints Against Police in Australia: Building Better Understanding or Mere Bureaucratic Convenience?" (2000) 17 *Law in Context*.

A Grant, "The Control of Police Behaviour"—in W Tarnopolsky (ed.) *Some Civil Liberties Issues in the Seventies* (Toronto: Carswell Ltd, 1975) pp. 75–110.

T Landau, *Public Complaints Against the Police—A View from Complainants* (Toronto: Centre of Criminology, University of Toronto, 1994).

M Maguire, & C. Corbett *A Study of the Police Complaints System* (London: H.M.S.O., 1991).

Northern Ireland, Independent Commission on Policing for Northern Ireland (The Hon. Christopher Patten, Chair) Report *A New Beginning:Policing in Northern Ireland* (London: H.M.S.O., 1999).

T O'Connell,. & J. Ritchie, "Restorative Justice and the Contest between the Relational and Institutional Paradigms"—unpublished paper presented to a conference on "Reshaping Australian Institutions", held at the Australian National University, Canberra, Australia, February16th–18th, 1999.

Ontario Civilian Commission on Police Services *Report of an Inquiry into administration of internal investigations By the Metropolitan Toronto Police Force* (Junger/Whitehead Inquiry) (Toronto: O.C.C.P.S., 1992).

C Shearing, *Post-Complaint Management: The Impact of Complaint Procedures on Police Discipline*—R.C.M.P. External Review Committee, Discussion Paper #4 (Ottawa: Minister of Supply & Services, 1990).

P Stenning, "Review of Part 9 (Complaint Procedure) of the British Columbia *Police Act*, as amended by Section 36 of S.B.C. 1997, c. 37" Memorandum prepared for the Office of the Police Complaint Commissioner of British Columbia—unpublished, but available on request from the Police Complaint Commissioner's Office.

SECTION THREE

# EXTENDING CIVILIAN OVERSIGHT

# 8

# *Police Accountability Reform in Colombia: The Civilian Oversight Experiment*

ANDREW J GOLDSMITH

## INTRODUCTION

Latin American police forces generally do not enjoy a good press. They frequently appear in newspapers, human rights reports, films and televisions programmes as the militaristic repressive arms of authoritarian or under-democratic regimes, or as hopelessly corrupt and inefficient.[1] They stand accused of human rights abuses, including torture, massacres and "disappearances", and of improper and even illicit associations with political, business, and organised crime interests.[2] Very often, Latin American police forces are treated, especially in human rights documents, as essentially just a part of the "security forces", rather than as bodies charged with more traditional policing tasks.[3] Not only do their activities often appear at odds with the ideals of liberal democracy and the Rule of Law, but they also seem to epitomise the antithesis of good policing. Recently, international and transnational interests in economic stability, foreign investment, and good governance in developing countries[4] have focused upon the obstacles to social order in these countries, including the often very high levels of homicide and general criminality. This raises questions about the *effectiveness* of the police in terms of performing basic police functions such as preventing and investigating crime.[5] These

[1] See for example, Amnesty International, *Political Violence in Colombia: The Impunity Continues* (1994a); Washington Office on Latin America, *The Colombian National Police, Human Rights and US Drug Policy* (Washington, WOLA, 1993).

[2] In Colombia, for example, allegations of police corruption (until recently at least) have occurred at all levels of the police, from relatively petty street graft and extortion by police agents, to connections between senior police officers and members of drug cartels. As a consequence, a significant number of personnel changes have occurred at all levels of the police.

[3] However see, Peter Waldemann (ed.), *Justicia en La Calle: Ensayos Sobre La Policia en America Latina* (Medellin, Dike, 1996).

[4] See for example, World Bank, *World Development Report: The State in a Changing World* (New York, Oxford UP, 1997).

[5] Given, for example, the very high homicide rates in Colombia (referred to below), the failure of the police to stem the levels of interpersonal violence becomes an obvious issue.

impressions of policing are very often soundly based upon evidence, and not simply the outcome of stereotypical assumptions.[6] For a wide range of interests then, international as well as domestic, police reform in Latin America has become a matter of increasingly pressing importance.

Yet in terms of bringing about police reform, relatively little is known about the police and public order environment in many Latin American countries. This applies even among Western or First World police experts and scholars. There is indeed very little available literature upon the police forces in these countries in either Spanish or English.[7] From a US perspective at least, this is a somewhat ironic situation given the reliance of US drug policy upon the effectiveness of local police operations in the Andean countries.[8] This situation might reasonably be expected to frustrate the transfer of police knowledge and ideas to the region. I will indeed argue that it has limited the potential influence of Western policing ideas on accountability in Latin America. But there is one notable exception to the general lack of police influence between the West and Latin America. This has occurred in relation to foreign aid programmes to police,[9] which have typically taken the form of mainly externally-defined "technical assistance". The United States, the United Kingdom, and other European nations have provided specialist training programmes and, in some cases, technology transfers, with a view to strengthening the operational or technical capacity of the domestic police forces. At times this assistance has been particularly geared towards foreign policy objectives. The most striking example has been US involvement in fortifying drug law enforcement efforts in Colombia, Peru and Bolivia through the provision of aircraft and other equipment.[10] Criticism of programmes of this kind in the past have focused on the emphasis given to bolstering repressive, corrupt or inept regimes at the expense of human rights and meeting everyday policing needs.[11]

Even under programmes explicitly geared towards *democratisation* and *demilitarisation* objectives, the kinds of police knowledge transfer have been limited. In Central America, demilitarisation programmes, human rights training and, in the case of Haiti, peace-keeping operations, have resulted from international, regional, and local concerns about the need to establish or re-

[6] See for example in relation to police violence, the study by Paul Chevigny, *Edge of the Knife: Police Violence in the Americas* (New York, New Press, 1995).

[7] I know less about the situation for Brazil (where Portuguese is spoken). But see Martha Huggins, *Political Policing in Latin America* (Durham, Duke University, 1997) and Waldemann, *supra* n. 3.

[8] In particular, Colombia, Peru and Bolivia.

[9] See Ethan Nadelmann, *Cops Across Borders: Transnational Crime and International Law Enforcement* (University Park, Pennsylvania State University Press, 1994); David Bayley, "A Foreign Policy for Democratic Policing" (1995) 5 *Policing and Society* 79.

[10] Interview with official, Departmento Nacional de Planeacion, Bogota, Colombia, November, 1997.

[11] David Bayley notes the US experience in this area, and the consequent decision in 1974 largely to withdraw from foreign police assistance. Exceptions were made in respect of the Caribbean and Latin America. See Bayley, *supra* n.9, 79–80.

establish the basic conditions of economic stability and democracy.[12] While foreign involvement has sought to emphasise the police role and to de-emphasise the old military roles, the focus has been upon "first aid" operations (e.g. peacekeeping) and "hard" forms of capacity-building (e.g. specialist training in small arms use and criminal investigation methods, technology transfers).[13] Foreign assistance programmes to police forces have tended to focus on basic order and effectiveness questions, more than on accountability measures and the improvement of police-community relations. On one view, demilitarisation has been given a greater priority than democratisation.[14] The largely technical focus of police assistance and the minimal attention given to accountability issues has not been challenged substantially by the tenor of many human rights critiques which, while often scathing of police conduct and the lack of accountability, have not contributed much at the level of institutional analysis and techniques of institutional change.[15] Specific institutional measures for improving police accountability, and locally-oriented ways of implementing these measures, have received little explicit attention in the relevant literatures.

Police technical assistance programmes and international human rights reports attempt, it might be suggested, capacity-building and democratisation *from without*. There is also the important issue however of how police reforms geared to providing more democratic forms of policing might be pursued *from within* the country in question.[16] Even less has been written or is understood by outside observers about this important issue. This article deals with a recent novel attempt by the Colombian Government to introduce a system of civilian oversight for dealing with complaints against members of the Colombian National Police (CNP), Colombia's principal police force. It draws in part upon the author's experiences as an outside police scholar invited to participate in, and be privy to, some aspects of the reform process. This attempt to build

[12] See Washington Office on Latin America (WOLA), *Demilitarising Public Order: The International Community, Police Reform and Human Rights in Central America and Haiti* (Washington DC, WOLA, 1995); Rachel Neild, *Policing Haiti: Preliminary Assessment of the New Civilian Security Force* (Washington DC, WOLA,1995)

[13] For an extended account of international police co-operation involving the US, see Ethan Nadelmann, *supra*, n. 9.

[14] Ensuring free elections, freedom of political speech, and a reduction of the scale and influence of the armed forces are objectives of democratisation in many countries.

[15] This is an important theme warranting an entire paper in itself. However, the clear domination of human rights organisations and their critiques by the legalistic perspective seems to leave little room or interest for more context-sensitive forms of analysis and detailed proposals for specific institutional interventions. On the implausibility (and I would add at times counterproductive nature) of some human rights critiques, see Stan Cohen, "Government Responses to Human Rights Reports: Claims, Denials, and Counterclaims", (1996) 18 *Human Rights Quarterly* 517.

[16] In the international development literature, there is an emerging consensus of opinion that institutional reform requires local participation and consensus; that it cannot simply be imposed from without in response to externally generated pressures and straightforwardly implement models from other political and cultural settings. See for example Marshall Wolfe, *Elusive Development* (London, Zed Books, 1996), Juan Linz and Alfred Stepan, *Problems of Democratic Transition and Consolidation: Southern Europe, South America, and Post-Communist Europe* (Baltimore, Johns Hopkins University, 1996).

greater police accountability "from within" nonetheless sought to graft ideas and knowledge from outside the country and the region onto the Colombian system. The express transplantation undertaken of a police accountability concept widely, though diversely, practised in many Western and, increasingly, other countries[17] raises important practical as well as interesting theoretical questions. These include how Western policing concepts and expertise might contribute to greater police accountability as well as improved police effectiveness in regions such as Latin America. As the study shows, while the concept of civilian oversight still faces difficulties in some Western countries,[18] its prospects for acceptance and successful implementation encounter even greater difficulties in countries such as Colombia, with very different political systems and policing environments. These differences, as will be seen, can prove fatal to the fortunes of specific reform ventures. Nonetheless, I shall argue, there is a need to better theorise the relationship between police accountability reform and democratisation processes and, taking a contextual approach, how best to improve police practice in a country like Colombia.

In this chapter, I outline the nature and circumstances behind and accompanying the 1993 reform introducing civilian oversight in Colombia, and try to explain the subsequent course of events that led to the closing of the Colombian civilian oversight agency in 1997. In doing so, I identify the need to contextualise the outcome by reference to characteristics of the local political and criminal justice systems and the particular internal security challenges faced by the state and society. This is not simply in order to account for what happened, but also to enable some realism about the significance of what occurred. What should be considered "success" or "failure" in the transplantation of such mechanisms in countries like Colombia, I shall argue, should not be interpreted either absolutely or universally according to standards fixed by experience in countries with very different political traditions and law and order situations. Once this proposition is accepted, a more hopeful and useful interpretation of events is possible, one that can sift the gains from the "debris of defeat", and that can thus see ways of advancing some, if not all, of the objectives underlying the initial reform, albeit perhaps using other means. Police knowledge and experience is increasingly spilling across national and regional boundaries. This is likely to be further fuelled by global pressures for good governance,[19] more democracy and respect for human rights. Under these conditions, the impulse to democratise policing from within is not so easily thwarted or stayed. However policy-makers and police scholars will need to develop more discriminating tools of

[17] See generally, A Goldsmith (ed.), *Complaints Against the Police. The Trend to External Review* (Oxford: Clarendon Press, 1991).

[18] See A Goldsmith, "External Review v Self-Regulation: The Dialectics of Police Accountability" and Ian Freckelton, "Shooting the Messenger" in Goldsmith, *ibid*; also Colleen Lewis (PhD dissertation, Griffith University, 1997); M McMahon and R Ericson, *Policing Reform: A Study of the Reform Process and Police Institution in Toronto, Research Report* (Toronto, Centre of Criminology, 1984).

[19] See for example, World Bank, *supra*, n. 4.

analysis and a better grasp of political, social and organisational processes if institution-building of this kind is to succeed. Ways of combining outside knowledge and ideas with local needs and realities need to be found. A more responsive and effective, as well as accountable, police force in Colombia depends upon such forms of imagination, co-operation, understanding and persistence.

THE CONTEXT FOR POLICE ACCOUNTABILITY REFORM

## The Violent Society

Putting aside for the moment Colombian police involvement in corruption and human rights abuses, there is also the fact that police in Colombia face one of the most difficult policing environments in the world. While the police are responsible for a significant amount of the endemic violence, the sources of violence are far more diverse:

> A]lthough the violence of confrontation between state and citizen today occupies a central place in Colombia, other types of violence—acts that are committed by individuals or groups seeking to protect or restore a social order or by citizens trying to resolve strictly personal conflicts or to assert their positions—occupy a place of equal importance. Neglect of this finding has led to an overemphasizing of human rights and a downplaying of those dimensions—such as safety—that define the citizenry. . . . Private violence is a problem of democracy not only in the field of the exercise of civil rights but also to the extent it makes routine co-existence impossible. There is nothing to guarantee the possibility of a democratic political order if there is no social order of the same nature.[20]

In addition to high levels of street crime, the past decade has witnessed extraordinary levels of violence and intimidation attributable to paramilitary groups, so-called self-defence militias, drug cartels, and leftist guerrilla movements as well as to state security forces. Having perhaps the world's highest murder rates[21] means that life can indeed be nasty, brutish and short for everyone, including Colombian police.[22]

[20] Alvara Camacho, "Public and Private Dimensions of Urban Violence in Cali" in Charles Bergquist, Ricardo Penaranda and Gonzalo Sanchez (eds.), *Violence in Colombia: The Contemporary Crisis in Historical Perspective* (Wilmington Del, SR Books, 1992), pp. 258–9.

[21] While it is difficult to be categorical in a global context, informed observers recognise that Colombia stands among the world's most violent countries, and is perhaps the most violent per capita. See for example, US Department of State, *Country Reports on Human Rights Practices for 1992* (Washington, US Government Printing Office, 1993), 360. In 1991, official Colombian statistics revealed a murder count of 24,033 for a population estimated around 35 million; for the same year, the US FBI estimated that 23,438 murders took place that year, out of a population of 249 million. See Human Rights Watch, *Political Murder in Colombia: The Violence Continues* (New York, Human Rights Watch, 1992), 1. The situation seemed at least until recently, to be deteriorating. In 1992, 28,237 murders were reported (Amnesty International, *Colombia. Political Violence—Myth and Reality* (London, Amnesty International, 1994b), 15; while a 1994 press report quotes a figure of 30,000 murders each year "Colombia tries to reform abusive police force", *Latinamerica Press* (21 April 1994).

[22] In her recent book on events in Colombia leading up to the shooting of Pablo Escobar, Maria Jimena Duzan, summed up on this point as follows: *cont./*

## A Vulnerable Police

The Colombian police, and especially members of the Colombian National Police (CNP), must count among the most popularly reviled and persecuted civilian police forces in the world.[23] As Colombia's principal police force, the CNP is responsible for general policing duties across Colombia as well as a variety of specialised tasks including drug interdiction, kidnappings, and special protection duties. While numbering around one hundred thousand personnel (including civilians and police "bachelors" (national service conscripts who perform auxiliary tasks),[24] they operate in a quite unique and perilous working environment for a country of thirty-eight million people. The extreme nature of the conditions suggests that the ratio of one police officer per four hundred and sixty-six inhabitants[25] is anything but adequate to the public order and law enforcement needs of the country.[26] The human price paid by the CNP has been astonishing by any standards. Between 1982 and November 1992, some two thousand eight hundred and thirty-four Colombian police were killed in the line of duty.[27] In Medellin between 1990 and 1992, Pablo Escobar declared "war" on the police and the Colombian state. There were more than twenty killings a day in Medellin in 1990.[28] More than four hundred police died in that year alone; another three hundred and seventeen police were killed in Medellin between September 1992 and December 1993.[29]

Whether investigating other deaths or trying to prevent their own, the CNP have at times operated under extraordinary pressure. There has been only lim-

> After the death of more than 60,000 people in Colombia in the past five years, among them more than 1000 policemen, 60 judges, 70 journalists, 1500 leftist union and political leaders, an attorney general, two cabinet ministers, four presidential candidates, a governor and several police chiefs, Colombia has finally managed to dismantle the most virulent and vicious drug cartel in the world.

Maria Jimena Duzan, *Death Beat: A Colombian Journalist's Life Inside the Cocaine Wars* (New York, Harper Collins, 1994), p. 262.

23 This a point that could also be made in relation to the former South African Police. See John Brewer, *Black and Blue* (Oxford, Clarendon Press, 1992). However, it seems doubtful that the SAP faced the *number* or *degree of organisation* of armed opponents to be found in Colombia.

24 Arnold Riedmann, "La Reforma Policial en Colombia" in Waldemann, *supra*, n.3, 222.

25 Riedmann, *ibid.*

26 One has to be careful here, given the imprecision of police roles as between different countries, including the involvement in some countries of other agencies (often the military) in policing work. However, if one takes Northern Ireland as a point of comparison, where sectarian violence has required the participation of the British Army as well as the police throughout much of the history of the conflict there, the ration of police officers to citizens has been 1:125. This is nearly four times the number of police per citizenry than is to be found in Colombia. While 246 RUC officers were killed between 1968 and August 1987, approximately this number of police agents died in a three-month period in Medellin in 1990. On Northern Ireland and the RUC, see John Brewer (with Kathleen Magee) *Inside the RUC: Routine Policing in a Divided Society* (Oxford, Clarendon Press, 1991).

27 WOLA (1993), 12.

28 *Ibid.*

29 Rafael Pardo Rueda, *De primera mano: Colombia 1986–1994, Entre Conflictos y Esperanzas* (Bogota, CEREC, 1996), p. 344.

ited acknowledgement of this predicament among some of the CNP's critics. Human Rights Watch recognised this vulnerability at the hands of Escobar, but also the extreme degree of police-commuity alienation underlying and reinforced by these events:

> In Medellin the CAIs [small police stations located in residential and commercial areas] fell prey to gangsters eager to cash in on Escobar's promise to pay a reward for each murdered policeman; the killings were facilitated by the general enmity between poor neighbourhoods and the police. The result of increased targeted attacks was a hasty retreat by the police from the most dangerous neighborhoods. The withdrawal, in turn, placed communities at the mercy of gangs engaged in different forms of criminal activity, including small-time drug dealing.[30]

Systematic anti-police violence has not been solely the terrain of powerful organised crime groups. Politically motivated violence from the major guerrilla groups, such as Revolutionary Armed Forces of Colombia (FARC) and Ejercito Liberacion Nacional (ELN), often takes the form of ambushes and bomb attacks against police in cities and towns as well as rural areas.[31] During 1997, right-wing paramilitary groups operating mainly in rural areas started to target state agents including the police.[32] This vulnerability is partly a reflection of the demography and geography of Colombia. In vast tracts of rural Colombia, a lack of infrastructure and sparsely settled populations result in a minimal or even non-existent state presence. Mobile army brigades and isolated police garrisons provide little discouragement to the operations of guerrillas, drug cartels and paramilitaries. Indeed, at least informally, collusion between police and some of these groups has been widely noted.[33] Such is the weakness of the Colombian state as a whole that effective territorial control has conspicuously diminished in recent years.[34] In many areas of the country, the Colombian state is no longer, or has never been, the real authority. Consequently, the CNP often appears as the outsider, and is vulnerable to the violent tactics of powerful other social actors.

The police position in Colombia poses obvious difficulties in terms of establishing good police-community relations and rendering the actions of the police more accountable. While these notions remain crucial for the future of the Colombian state and society and the reform of the CNP, high levels of police

[30] Human Rights Watch, *supra* n. 22, 83–4.

[31] There was, for example, a news report on SBS (Australia) television in August 1993 of an ambush of National Police by guerrillas on the outskirts of Bogota, in which thirteen police agents were killed. Such events are not unusual.

[32] "Para-noia" *Cambio 16*, October 13–20, 1997 (no. 226).

[33] Human rights reports widely allege collusions of these kinds, e.g., *supra* n. 1.

[34] There are around 1,050 municipalities in Colombia. In more than 150 of them, there is no police presence, often because of the threats to police posed by non-state actors in those regions and the inability of the Colombian state to provide adequate protection for police activities. Interview with Dr Fernando Cepeda, Bogota, November 1996. See also Camilo Echandia Castilla, *Expansion Territorial de la Guerrilla Colombiana: Geografia, Economia y Violencia*, Working Document No. 1, May 1997, Paz Publica, University de los Andes, Bogota, Colombia.

defensiveness towards others, and alienation from the mainstream communities in many areas, render the police a less-than-promising prospect for Western concepts of police accountability. Policing the *pueblos* of Colombia is plainly very different from policing Main Street, USA, High Street, England, or outback Australia.

### The Police Record of Abuse:

Given the security situation in Colombia, it is perhaps not surprising that the CNP has been implicated in various human rights abuses. The involvement by members of the CNP in human rights abuses, particularly in the cities and towns, has been widely conceded, including by the Colombian state. In September 1991, then Procurador de la Nacion, Dr Gustavo Arrieta, reported:

> In urban areas with state presence and little guerilla violence, the National Police is the force most implicated and punished in disciplinary investigations. The most common types of violations in which the National Police are implicated . . . are "disappearances", bodily injury, threats and arbitrary detentions.[35]

However police complaint categories in the Procurador's office also include tortures and massacres, as well as the more mundane categories of complaints familiar to Western observers of police complaints systems.

While less frequently implicated than the armed forces in larger scale or serious atrocities, members of the CNP have been repeatedly linked to "social cleansing" or "death squad" operations in large cities such as Pereira, Cali and Bogota.[36] For example, in its May 1994 special report on Colombia, Amnesty International concluded:

> Most killings of "undesirables" in the cities appear to be carried out by police agents, often from the F-2 intelligence branch, many of whom are contracted by local traders seeking to protect their economic interests. In contrast to abuses committed during counter-insurgency operations, no evidence has emerged that police agents involved in "social cleansing" are acting on orders from their superiors. However, the lack of action against those responsible by senior police commanders has clearly created a climate in which such abuses proliferate.[37]

These activities seem to be ongoing.[38] While various explanations have been offered for police involvement in this activity, two particular reasons recur. One

[35] Quoted in Amnesty International, *supra* n. 1, 79.

[36] Carlos Eduardo Rojas, *La violencia llamada "Limpieza social"* (Bogota,CINEP, 1996); also Lovisa Stannow, *"Social Cleansing" in Colombia* MA thesis, Department of Spanish and Latin American Studies, Simon Fraser University, January 1996. For a journalist's account of street children at risk from "death squads" in Bogota, see Hugh Davies, "Where boys and girls come out to die", *The Weekly Telegraph* (Issue 113, 1994), VII.

[37] Amnesty International, *supra* n.1, 23.

[38] In December 1994, Australian television viewers saw a recently produced British documentary on "social cleansing" in Bogota, entitled "The Disposables". From conversations held with city officials in Bogota in November 1995, the author learnt that the problem had not gone away. See also,

is police cynicism towards the operation of the criminal justice system, which they see as weak and ineffective in dealing with the problems posed by "street people". The other is the quite clearly documented practice of police, either on duty or off-duty, acting on the instructions of local business operators to clear away persons who pose persistent threats to the profitability of those businesses.[39]

Part of the significance of the context in which the Colombian police operate is the difficulties raised for adherence to normal measures of legal and disciplinary accountability. Studies of police culture in other jurisdictions point to the tolerance extended by police to other police on conduct issues, but particularly in relation to excessive force in the performance of duties.[40] Leaving aside the fears among Colombian police reasonably associated with high police mortality rates, the high levels of social violence and antagonism towards the police seem unlikely to warrant a particularly pacific approach to policing in general. The often martial nature of Colombian police work distinguishes it very significantly from say police work in a country like Britain (with the obvious exception of Northern Ireland). The heightened external threats seem likely to exacerbate the tendency of police officers to protect each other even from accountability measures, while the general propensity for violence and the vulnerability to corruption in a relatively poor country like Colombia seem set to undermine the effectiveness of internal as well as external controls. The high levels of ineffectiveness, or impunity (*impunidad*), in the Colombian criminal justice system apply to the police as much as to some others in Colombian society.[41] Indeed the state's ability to ensure adequate investigation and prosecution of police abuses to date appears to have been inversely proportional to the public order challenges it faces.[42]

## POLICE ACCOUNTABILITY PRIOR TO 1993

One of the ironies about Colombia is that for a country notorious for its high levels of disorder and illegal behaviour, it is, formally speaking, a country strongly wedded to democratic and legal traditions. For example, its 1991 Constitution was devised following a Constituent Assembly made up of representatives from different sectors of Colombian society, and is an elaborate

Human Rights Watch, *Generation Under Fire: Children and Violence in Colombia* (New York, Human Rights Watch, 1994).

[39] See for example Stannow, *supra*, n. 36.

[40] See for example David Smith and Jeremy Gray, *Police and People in London* (London, Policy Studies Institute, 1983).

[41] Impunity is seen as the central problem of the Colombian criminal justice by many observers, in particular human rights NGOs.

[42] I say "apparent" paradox because there is an argument in human rights circles that the problem is one of political will, rather than capacity, to do something constructive to tackle problems of impunity.

document of nearly four hundred articles. There are regular elections at national, state, and municipal level, presidents are elected for a single four year term, and there is, by global standards, a tradition of freedom of the press. Although the police have fallen for many decades within the responsibility of the Ministry of Defence, Colombia has had civilian Ministers of Defence since 1990, breaking a continent-wide tradition of military personnel occupying such roles. Many Colombians and Colombia watchers saw this as an important step in tempering the militaristic influence of the security forces in public life and of permitting a more autonomous form of policing.[43]

In terms of police accountability prior to 1993, it is possible, as in other systems, to distinguish between mechanisms of *external* and *internal* control over police action. In terms of external control, since 1991 there have been two government agencies which have formal responsibility for the actions of police as well as other members of the government. The first is the *Fiscalia de la Nacion* (or Office of the Public Prosecutor), an office established under the 1991 Constitution. In formal terms, it functions much like public prosecution authorities in other Western countries in that it plays a major role in the investigation and prosecution of criminal matters. It has a particular responsibility under Article 250 to "investigate the crimes committed by members of the public force [i.e. military and police] in active service and related to the same service". To this end, it is granted the power to direct and co-ordinate the investigations of the various judicial police bodies in Colombia,[44] as well as having its own investigative arm, the *Cuerpo Tecnico*. Under this office, allegations against members of the CNP are subjected to investigation and where sufficient evidence is available, criminal proceedings are brought against officers charged. Where the charges relate to active service, those charges must be heard in the military justice system according to the Penal Military Code (Article 221). There has been criticism not just about the efficiency of the criminal prosecution process (in terms of insufficient trained personnel and resources to undertake thorough investigations) but also about the perceived partiality of the system of military justice. Human rights bodies in particular have been critical of the high levels of impunity under the current system, claiming that few investigations proceed to prosecution, few officers are found liable, and for those who are held criminally liable, the penalties are slight and inadequate.[45]

In addition to the Fiscalia, there is the *Procuradoria de la Nacion* (or Office of the Attorney General). This office exercises the principal responsibility for discipline of public officials (including police) and the protection of human

[43] See Rafael Pardo, *supra*, n. 29, especially ch. 11. Pardo was Colombia's first civilian Minister of Defence.

[44] One of the intriguing features of the Colombian criminal justice system is the number of different criminal investigation units. In addition to the Fiscalia's own, there is the CNP's own judicial police unit (formerly known as DIJIN), and the equivalent unit in DAS (Departmento Administracion de Seguridad), a separate police force with a variety of special functions including border and diplomatic protection, international cooperation, and intelligence.

[45] See for example, Amnesty International, *supra*, n. 1: Human Rights Watch, *supra*, n. 21.

rights, with the assistance of the *Defensor del Pueblo* (or Public Defender). It has the power to receive allegations of misconduct about public officials, to undertake investigations of allegations and in appropriate cases to discharge officials from office (Articles 277, 278). The Public Defender has a special brief to promote recognition of human rights, in part through the invocation of habeas corpus and taking protective action to ensure protection of individual rights (Article 282). The crucial point to recognise about the Procuradoria's function is that it is non-criminal in nature, though it has power to intervene in judicial proceedings "when it becomes necessary to defend the legal order, the public domain, or fundamental rights or guarantees" (Article 277.7). Therefore, under this arrangement, police officers may be disciplined and even discharged from the CNP without criminal prosecution. From an outsider's perspective, the fact that this office combines a human rights responsibility with only a disciplinary function suggests the likelihood of an inadequate response by the state to many abuses by members of the CNP. As the Procurador's own annual reports record, allegations received by that office can be very serious indeed. While Colombian authorities can point to the seemingly high numbers of police and other public officials dismissed using procedures of this kind for various forms of misconduct,[46] the relatively low profile nature of these actions and the apparent mildness of the penalties meted out, compared with the nature of the offences committed and the likely penalties imposed for such crimes if there had been successful criminal prosecutions, provides further grounds for criticism of the inadequacy of the state's response to abuses by state agents including police.

Turning to systems of internal control, the principal agency of accountability inside the CNP up until 1993 was the *Inspeccion General* (Office of Inspector General). Its tasks included ensuring the maintenance of discipline but also extended to responsibility for professionalisation of the institution.[47] While in principle this office should have been responsive to citizens' complaints against the police, the persistent indications of low public support for the police institution and general acceptance of widespread corruption in the police institution made its usefulness as mechanism of citizen accountability at least highly dubious. Indeed in recognition of the unresponsiveness of the CNP to public concerns and worries about its institutional integrity, as Minister of Defence in 1991, Rafael Pardo established a "hot-line" whereby citizens could make complaints against police by telephone.[48] The mounting evidence of an enormous

[46] The CNP under Director General Rosso Serrano has dismissed thousands of police officials since 1995, under what is called "purification". The Director has been granted new powers to dismiss personnel "suspected of service irregularities" under Decree 2010 of 1995. See Waldmann, *supra*, n. 3, p. 231.

[47] Javier Torres Velasco, "La Ciudadania Pacta Con Su Policia: El Proceso de Modernizacion de la Policia Nacional de Colombia" in Francisco Leal Buitrago and Juan Gabriel Tokatlian (eds.), *Orden Mundial y Seguridad: Nuevos desafios para Colombia y America Latina* (Bogota, Tercer Mundo, 1994) p. 191.

[48] Pardo, *supra*, n. 29, p. 343.

gulf between police and ordinary Colombians in the early 1990s, and of the often abusive or simply neglectful nature of police-citizen relationships, set the course for significant reform. The catalyst for change was not long in waiting.

## THE 1993 REFORM PROCESS

A number of factors combined to precipitate the 1993 reforms. On top of growing public disquiet towards police human rights abuses, corruption, and failure to provide basic protection for ordinary Colombians, public outrage at the rape and murder of nine year old Sandra Patricia Vasquez in a Bogota police station in February that year proved highly significant. It focused public attention upon the longstanding inadequacies of the police institution, and managed to generate official pronouncements, including one from President Gaviria, about the need for change in the CNP. In response to the mood at that time, the then Procurador, Carlos Gustavo Arrieta, announced:

> The crisis is great. There are more complaints against the police than any other institution. . . . I think the plan we have devised . . . will enable us, if we are lucky and work hard enough, to lay the foundation for a new institution in which we will eliminate the credibility problems between the community and the police.[49]

From the government's perspective, there was a variety of pragmatic considerations regarding the police triggered by the Vasquez incident and public reaction to it. Another observer noted at the time that the "government is anxious to improve the prestige of the police, since its unpopularity makes it an easy target for guerrilla propaganda".[50] Another domestic factor prompting re-examination of the police functions and organisation was the effective challenge posed to the Colombian state by the drug cartels, especially of Medellin.[51] Pablo Escobar developed a reputation for running a "parallel state" in his home base in the state of Antioquia, providing housing, sporting facilities, jobs, and basic policing. The people he assisted in these ways were long-conditioned to corrupt and sometimes brutal policing at the hands of the state, and to a generally indifferent state in terms of the provision of other social services.[52] For the reformist Gaviria administration, the loss of citizen allegiance and support for the state and its police was closely connected to the increasingly obvious and embarrassing loss of territorial sovereignty and control.[53] An overhaul of police structures and practices became an urgent priority.

[49] Quoted in WOLA, 1993 *supra* n. 27, p. 35.

[50] Oxford Analytica, *Latin American World Brief*, 2 July 1993.

[51] Pardo, *supra*, n. 29, p. 339–40.

[52] See Duzan *supra* n. 22 on the alienation between police and citizens in Medellin.

[53] Pardo records the experience in Medellin where the closure of small police outposts in urban areas, intended to provide police with a more human face to ordinary citizens, met with community relief rather than dismay. Pardo, *supra*, n. 29, p. 340.

Following the Vasquez death and the ensuing public backlash against the police, the Minister of Defence, Rafael Pardo, announced the establishment of two commissions to examine the National Police and its relations with the community. This occurred in late March 1993. An internal commission within the CNP was tasked with examining the adequacy of internal controls, while an external Advisory Commission for the Restructuring of the National Police was created by presidential decree to look more broadly at police-community relations. By this point, as noted, the sense of institutional crisis had reached the highest levels. There was little option for the police but to engage in open self-examination and to co-operate with a government-approved external inquiry. The external commission was led personally by the Minister of Defence, and consisted of a mixture of elected representatives, members of trade associations and unions, an academic sociologist, two retired police generals, the Public Defender, the Procurador, the Fiscal, and others.[54] Both commissions reported in May the same year.

One of the clear themes of the external commission's recommendations was the strengthening of the CNP's civil character so far as possible.[55] It proposed, inter alia, clarifying police functions and organisational structures, principally to distinguish between those police responsible for dealing with rural insurgency, and those engaged in more traditional policing duties in urban areas. While the extraordinary nature of some policing duties was acknowledged by the external commission, it was troubled by the current impediment to the betterment of police-community relations posed by an inadequate distinction between police roles. Conscious of the gulf between police and citizens in many parts of the country, it recommended the establishment of a nation-wide, multi-tiered consultative scheme for citizens and police. This was intended to operate at local, regional, and national levels, linking greater responsiveness to local community concerns about police services with national policing priorities and standards.

Another important recommendation was the creation of the office of *Comisionado Nacional para la Policia*, a civilian authority specifically to receive and process citizen complaints against members of the CNP. The external commission considered this appointment to be one "essential basis for the institutionalization of the communitary (sic) participation in Police Affairs".[56] What clearly lay behind this recommendation was not just the need for a disciplinary authority outside the police hierarchy with a particular responsibility for processing citizens' complaints, but also the desirability of providing a mechanism whereby information and recommendations derived from the substance of legitimate complaints might be fed back to the CNP, contributing to institutional integrity, effectiveness and efficiency. These functions could obviously be more

[54] The full list is to be found in Pardo, *ibid.*, p. 343.

[55] See Torres, *supra*, n. 47, p. 199.

[56] This quote is from a specially-prepared English language version of the External Commission's report, in the author's possession.

readily performed by a police-specific body such as the Comisionado, which could develop the sufficient expertise on policing matters to contribute constructively to systemic as well as discipline matters, than by a general criminal prosecution body (the Fiscalia) or a public sector disciplinary authority (the Procuradoria).

In its deliberations, the external commission had been assisted by staff of the *Consejeria para Seguridad y Defensa Nacional*, the office of the President's Security Adviser. Staff in this office had located, translated and circulated widely a chapter I had written in a UK-published book, *Complaints Against the Police: The Trend to External Review*, which I had also edited. The book appeared in 1991, and a copy had found its way to the Consejeria's office in Bogota. In this particular chapter, completely unconscious of its subsequent role in the Colombian reform, I had set out the various arguments for civilian oversight (I called it "external review" in the book), including the benefits *for the police* in terms of enhanced police performance as well as *for the public* in terms of improved accountability and police-community relations. A number of the arguments from this piece were directly used by proponents of the reform in advocating and defending the introduction of a new civilian authority with a particular brief to oversee the handling of complaints against police.[57]

## Law 62 of 1993 and the Office of Comisionado

This law largely gave effect to the major recommendations of the External Commission. For example, the statute established a National System of Citizen Participation, a key part of which was to be a National Commission for Police and Citizen Participation.[58] In addition to establishing the office of Comisionado, the Law laid down the conditions of selection and tenure for the office, giving considerable powers to the President in this regard. While the Comisionado needed to satisfy the requirements for appointment to a Supreme Court judgeship, his or her selection was to be by nomination of the President from a list determined at a meeting involving the National Council for Police and Citizen Safety, from which the Director General of Police was to be excluded. In terms of tenure, the Commissioner could be "removed prudently by the President".[59]

In many respects, the novelty of the Comisionado concept in Colombia was visible from the beginning by regard to ambiguities and even contradictions about role, resources and responsibilities on the face of some of the formal pro-

[57] This included the President's remarks in announcing the new legislation on 12 August 1993. I am able to trace the part played by the book and this chapter through conversations with various employees working for the Consejeria through the period of the reform, one of whom drafted the President's remarks as well as being closely involved in the external commission's work.

[58] See Articles 25–9. Law 62/93.

[59] Articles, 22, 23.

visions. For example, while the Law indicated the Commissioner was to be "the highest official in internal disciplinary matters", he or she was also to have a "functional dependency from Police Headquarters (General Directorate) in the operational and coordinating areas related to the disciplinary regulations".[60] While some degree of interdependency or at least co-operation between the new office and the CNP was explicitly anticipated by the Law, the precise nature of this relationship was not clearly articulated. A measure of uncertainty and ambiguity was deliberately provided by the prescription that the government would determine "the structure of the National Commissioner's office for the National Police, as well as the functions inherent to his position".[61] As part of the implementation programme, I spent a week in Colombia in August 1993 at the invitation of the Consejeria, meeting with senior government officials and police generals and other police officials, principally engaged in trying to assist their understanding of the concepts and issues involved in civilian oversight, but also assisting in planning some aspects of the establishment of the office itself. At that time, given the shortness of the visit, the hectic schedule during the visit, and the highly unfamiliar nature of the setting to me, I did not have a sufficient grasp of the situation or the time available to focus more on these questions.[62]

One effect of the new Law was to replace the Inspector General function by the Comisionado's office in respect of citizens' complaints and the oversight of police disciplinary mechanisms.[63] To all intents and purposes, the Comisionado took over the principal tasks of the Inspector General's office. Yet the extent and circumstances of this change were somewhat mysterious, at least from the point of view of an outside observer. In my role as an external adviser, I was invited to a meeting at Police Headquarters to discuss how the new legislation might be given effect. While there were representatives from the Ministry of Defence and the Department of National Planning also present, the meeting was chaired by the then Inspector General, the appointed person within the CNP to oversee the implementation of the various reform elements contained in Law 62. While formally the Inspector General function was meant to cease with the implementation of the Comisionado's office, at a very practical level the CNP remained integrally involved in the establishment of the oversight body.[64]

[60] Compare Articles 21 and 24.

[61] Article 21.

[62] I did, however, raise the uncertainties regarding respective roles under the new scheme in a subsequent report written for the Consejero Presidencial para la Defensa y Seguridad Nacional, Dr Ricardo Santamaria. Of course, by this time the Law itself was in place.

[63] This is certainly the interpretation of one of the participants in the planning process for the new office. See Torres, *supra*, n. 47, p. 201.

[64] The ongoing involvement of the CNP throughout this period in the negotiation of the reform process is clear. In an interview for a magazine in March 1996, General Serrano revealed that when various reform options had been considered in 1993, the police had opted for the comisionado option when faced by the Government with the solitary alternative of a civilian director for the CNP. Not surprisingly, they opted for the comisionado concept. See "El general Serrano le apunta al cambio", *Cromos*, March 25, 1996, 30, 32.

The degree of ambiguity surrounding the extent of autonomy intended for the new office was also reflected in some of the language used to describe it. It was frequently described by senior police and some government figures as a mechanism of "internal" (rather than "external") control.[65] While the civil nature of the appointment suggested professional independence by reason of the condition that the Comisionado not be a serving or former police officer, the mixed signals could not have made its comprehension any easier by the established government organs most likely to complement and assist it in the execution of its oversight role, namely the Fiscalia and the Procuradoria. As events turned out, the conceptual uncertainties and practical difficulties in the planning and early implementation stages did not augur well for the office's acceptance by the police or for wider understanding of the Comisionado's specific role.

Later developments did not improve the already difficult prognosis for the office. The precise range of responsibilities of the Comisionado's office was arguably not made any clearer by a subsequent law, Law 180 of 1995, which provided that the Inspector General of the National Police was to be the medium of communication between the Comisionado and the Police. Having removed the Inspector General from complaints and discipline matters in 1993, the Legislature now saw fit to bring it back some two years later during the Samper administration. While this might be construed as a welcome clarification of the CNP-Comisionado relationship, there is another construction possible. It relates to the deteriorating fortunes of the Comisionado's office and the ascendancy of the CNP under its new Director, General Rosso Serrano, during the Samper presidency. The politics of the police reform process had changed significantly in a short period of time after the end of the Gaviria administration in 1994, placing the fledgling office in an invidious position before it had a chance to perform according to its objectives and prescribed functions.

## THE REFORM IN OPERATION

By the end of 1995, it was easy to be pessimistic about the future of the office of the Comisionado, given the events that had transpired since August 1993. By September 1996, the pessimism had become warranted, with the announcement by President Samper that he was proposing to close the office. It had become a "bureaucratic monster", he said, and even a political police agency in its own right, whose closure would enable greater expenditure on better training and putting more police on the streets.[66] Beyond the colourful language used by the President to effectively discredit the office, there is a story worth telling about a number of changes to the policing and political environments in a very short

[65] For example, the speech by President Gaviria on 12 August 1993, the day the reform became law, used this terminology.

[66] See "La baja de un Comisionado", *El Mundo*, 12 September 1996, 8.

period, which help to account for the rapid reversal of fortunes of the Comisionado's office, and ultimately to the rejection of this model of civilian control.

The first hurdle in establishing the office had been finding a suitable candidate. Following a long and difficult search during the latter months of 1993,[67] the first Commissioner, Adolfo Salamanca, a professor of criminal law, was appointed in December. However, he resigned in frustration in July 1994, citing resistance to his work from high-level police officials and budgetary problems.[68] Without a budget, he had operated essentially alone during his brief period in office. His replacement, a thirty year old government lawyer, complained on Colombian television within two months of his appointment that he was not being taken seriously by the National Police. He stated that he was not being invited to police meetings or being consulted on any matter. His interviewer concluded the interview with the remark that "it was evident . . . there is a lack of support, communication and understanding on the part of the police".[69]

Changes to the CNP leadership and approach were accompanied by a change of president in August 1994. As will be seen, both arguably contributed to the fate of the Comisionado. While one significant change was the ascension of former anti-narcotics head Rosso Jose Serrano to the office of, Director of the CNP, there was also a problem of no obvious enthusiasm or support for the office among the new Samper administration. By this time, most of the reform team assembled by President Gaviria and Minister Pardo had moved on. Uncertainties arising from changes of leadership and budgetary problems, it will be seen, continued to ensure a less than congenial environment for the Comisionado reform, while its ongoing inability under the circumstances to develop its profile and show results provided grounds for questioning the relevance of the office. In this regard, as will be discussed shortly, the CNP leadership did not miss its opportunity. Following the appointment in March 1995 of new Commissioner Mario Gonzalez Vargas, Gonzalez was able to establish branch offices in two cities besides Bogota, and to begin to press publicly for the investigation of a number of matters involving the CNP covered in the Colombian press. But by the end of 1995, his office was being publicly questioned by General Serrano, who expressed doubt as to the need for its existence.

The re-establishment of the Inspector General, the grant and exercise of strong new powers for dismissal of police personnel suspected of corruption or other misconduct, as well as the creation of the CNP's own Cultural Transformation Plan designed to improve police integrity, signalled significant improvements in terms of internal controls at a time when the new

[67] A Colombian Government official close to the appointment process informed me that at least thirty persons had been approached regarding possible appointment before a suitable candidate was found.

[68] In an interview with the Bogota daily *El Tiempo* at the time of his resignation, Dr Salamanca revealed that he was not told about internal police investigations by the police, discovering about them instead from reading the daily press. *El Tiempo*, 23 July 1994, 9.

[69] Inravsion TV-A, Bogota, 10 September 1994 (text from press cutting service).

Comisionado, Gonzalez, was trying, really for the first time given the two changes in leadership between the beginning of 1994 and his appointment in April 1995, to get his office properly established. Then only six months after taking up office, his office was threatened with a cutback of budget in the order of eighty-five per cent.[70] Other government agencies were facing substantial cutbacks but typically were far less severe in nature.[71] President Samper's later description of the office as a "bureaucratic monster" offers some insight into the motivation behind the particularly savage budgetary reduction. As a component of police expenditure in the nation's budget, the savings implied by the cut to the Comisionado's office certainly offered a measure of frugality by the police sector to the administration's general programme of cutbacks in public sector expenditure. It would undoubtedly have been more difficult to effect comparable savings in most other areas of police expenditure. Whatever the motivations behind the cutbacks to the Comisionado's budget, they posed an obvious threat to the viability of the institution.

Also at this time, the CNP was enjoying a surprisingly fast and significant reversal of its public image under Serrano. The improved public esteem for the CNP flowing from the capture and death of Escobar in December 1993 was consolidated during the next two years by a number of successful operations against the leadership of the Cali cocaine cartel, as well as by several well-publicised, large-scale dismissals of police personnel suspected of being corrupt from the CNP. In terms of changes to public perceptions of the CNP and its leadership 1995 was quite a year. While some nine thousand police officials were removed under the new administrative powers vested in the Director,[72] the Director, General Serrano had been declared Executive of the Year in recognition of his achievements as Director. In other words, unlike in earlier times, the CNP very quickly began producing evidence of its own commitment to integrity as well as of its operational efficiency. There was little reason for the police to openly acknowledge its support for the civilian oversight idea.[73] Comisionado Gonzalez was in an increasingly difficult and isolated position.

Many of the changes and obstacles then were well outside the control of the Comisionado. In attempting to define a role for the office in this time of rising police fortunes and ongoing practical difficulties of his own, the Comisionado's profile suffered. Although there were some radio and television campaigns to raise public awareness, and Gonzalez made himself accessible to the press, there

[70] I was told this by Comisionado Gonzalez in November 1995 during my visit to Bogota. It was also mentioned by him and reported in the press at the time of his resignation at the end of January 1996.

[71] While the mooted cuts were generally severe, other departments were told that cuts of 30% were likely.

[72] This figure was reported in the press. See "El problema de la Policia y la realidad social colombiana", *El Pais*, 3 January 1996, 4A.

[73] Brigadier Rosso Jose Serrano, "Reply to Questionnaire from Hugo Alberto Velasco, Secretary Commission II, Chamber of Representatives" (Bogota, 28 November 1995) [translation in author's possession].

was too little time and too much to do. It is not surprising then that outside police circles, in interviews conducted in the offices of the Procuradoria, Fiscalia, and human rights organisations, I encountered very little understanding of the concept behind the office or its functions, and virtually no personal familiarity with the Comisionado himself.[74] This lack of knowledge certainly made declarations of public support for the office by highly ranked officials such as the Defensor del Pueblo unlikely. The deep irony was that the time and resources required to establish a track record and public profile were denied it, yet this coincided with a mounting police campaign to reclaim the mantle of disciplinary authority from the Comisionado.

Gonzalez had had enough by the end of January 1996. He resigned and spoke publicly about the difficulties he faced which made it impossible for him to continue. In particular, he cited the massive reduction in his budget and the ongoing lack of co-operation shown by the CNP leadership,[75] a particular complaint made also by his two predecessors. His office had proven an inconvenience to the CNP. At an interpersonal level, it would seem that the relationship between Serrano and Gonzalez had broken down some months before the resignation.[76] Serrano's public failure to endorse the value of the office before the Legislature in late 1995, while proudly pointing to internal reform processes, certainly coincides with the difficulties reported by Gonzalez. Only a couple of months later, at the time of Gonzalez's departure, Serrano publicly questioned the need for the office, stating:

> Now, we [the police] no longer require other controls. Public opinion is our best judge, and I can assure you that the CNP has developed the necessary integrity in order to exercise internal control, with the support of the President and the Minister of Defence.[77]

The CNP's operational successes and internal reform programme undoubtedly aided in rendering this point of view persuasive to the beleaguered Samper presidency. The relationship between General Serrano and the President itself is interesting in terms of setting the context for the fate of the reform. The timing of the announcement of the office's closure in September 1996 coincided with the President's participation in a summit with the CNP high command. He undertook in their presence to push the elimination of the Comisionado through Congress, despite the report of a recent Senate committee advocating the retention of the office and strengthening its powers.[78] In addition, after Gonzalez's departure, following a brief period in which two persons shared the office, one

[74] In the capacity of an adviser to Gonzalez in December 1995, I advised him to try and build up these relationships as quickly as possible. I conducted a number of interviews in the offices mentioned over two weeks in November and December 1995.

[75] See for example, "Por falta de apoyo, renuncio Comisionado para la Policia", *El Tiempo*, 1 February 1996, 10B; "'Asi es imposible,' dice el comisionado para la Policia", *El Espectador*, 2 February 1996, 8A.

[76] This is reported in a press interview with Gonzalez, "Me voy porque le incomodaba a Serrano", *Vanguardia Liberal*, 5 February 1996, 1.

[77] "Por falta de apoyo", *ibid* (my translation from the Spanish original).

[78] "Sin controles", *La Prensa*, 14 September 1996, 9.

of them, Dr Aldana, a former lawyer for the CNP and therefore previous work associate of General Serrano, was appointed by the President to the office. Aldana served as Comisionado until its closure in September 1997. The conditions operating at the time of his appointment and during his period in office must have made it abundantly clear that there was little intention by either the CNP or the Samper administration that the office should play a significant role as an oversight body in the time remaining. While the office continued to operate for a further twelve months, many staff predictably left as they found other jobs. While some staff continued to work on research projects arising from particular policy problems indicated by patterns of complaints and other sources, there was no obvious reason to do so as the practical significance of the office, limited as it was, had diminished further in the light of the impending closure.

Samper's apparent willingness to accede to the wishes of the CNP leadership on issues related to the fortune of the office has been seen by a number of Colombian observers as a reflection of the relative power of the two men. From the very start of his presidency, Samper suffered enormous political damage as a consequence of being shunned by Washington for his alleged knowing receipt of Cali cartel money for electoral purposes. Consequently, it is suggested, he has had to rely politically on other public figures more acceptable to national and international opinion. Samper's political weakness however coincided with the rapid rise in standing of General Serrano, a man who, as well as enjoying far larger public support than the President, could travel freely between Colombia and the US, with the ready support and probably the encouragement of the US Government.[79] This was in stark contrast to President Samper's position, who had had his visitor's visa withdrawn by the US. It was therefore no real coincidence that President Samper made extensive use of Serrano on presidential visits to the United Nations, China and South East Asia. The relative standing of the two men, and the one's apparent dependency on the other to some degree, could not have harmed the prospects for public recognition of the internal reform programme within the CNP, nor for presidential support for the downgrading and ultimate abolition of the Comisionado's office. The mood of crisis in 1993 in the CNP, which had been so favourable to the reform process, had now been replaced by a very different public mood, one which, as events showed, successfully threatened the full implementation of the earlier reform scarcely three years later.

## LESSONS FROM THE REFORM PROCESS

As an exercise in police reform, and as an explicit attempt to render the CNP more accountable and put them on better terms with ordinary Colombians, the

[79] Aside from the integrity of Serrano in the eyes of the US Government, there was the practical matter that Serrano was the director of Colombia's principal law enforcement agency in the struggle against the Colombian drug cartels.

questions that need to be asked are, first, what can be learnt from the experience that might assist in further attempts to introduce reform ideas of this kind to troubled policing situations such as is to be found in Colombia, and secondly, was the experiment a complete failure, and if not, in what ways did it succeed?

## A Matter of Unrealistic Expectations?

From the point of view of a number of persons involved at the policy level in the 1993 police reforms, the closure of the Comisionado's office was a matter of considerable disappointment. Despite initial high hopes, the first attempt by a Latin American country to introduce a police-specific, civilian authority charged with the oversight of investigation processes into citizens' complaints against the police had palpably failed to survive. Its closure had been announced less than three years after the appointment of the first Comisionado. In that time, it had seen five Comisionados come and go in the office. Underlying some of the frustration is the view that the office was never given an opportunity to function properly. As seen, this was the view expressed by three of the former office-holders. A lack of clear budgetary provision and failure to ensure substantial institutional autonomy, an ultimately hostile political environment, and fundamental police resistance, especially at the highest levels, to the implementation of this aspect of the 1993 reform, all converged to make what was already a conceptually difficult notion for the setting, impossible to sustain in practice.

## The Clash with Militaristic Tradition

Resistance to external control among professionalised or militarised bodies is scarcely unique, of course, to the Colombian police. Varying degrees of hostility and opposition may be found in police forces in some parts of the First World, including Canada and the USA, and was certainly behind the failure of many civilian oversight experiments in the USA in the 1960s.[80] Recent experiences in Australia, Canada and the United States, certainly underline the ongoing difficulties faced by those establishing or operating forms of civilian control and accountability over police.[81] The attempt to transplant the concept to Colombian circumstances under the Gaviria administration was therefore a bold venture. In the Colombian situation, as the statistics cited earlier indicate, the CNP could claim with some justification to be a police force "at war" with various non-state actors, a "war" in which some at least of the assumptions and

[80] See Terrill, in Goldsmith (ed.), *supra*, n. 18.

[81] In the US, the Washington DC complaints body has been abolished in the last couple of years, while the Ontario civilian oversight system has undergone a very profound change in 1997, in the eyes of many observers, amounting to a watering down of the degree of civilian authority exercised in relation to complaints against police. See Landau, this volume.

expectations about "normal policing" had little or no relevance. A strong militaristic orientation and tradition, as found in the CNP, poses obvious difficulties for acceptance of civilian authority. The subjection of the police to the military, rather than ordinary, justice system under the Constitution serves only to further legitimate the idea that in many if not all respects, civilian authority is inappropriate with respect to the CNP.

One of the specific features of the Comisionado system which arguably threatened to undermine not just this militaristic conception but also the particular authority of the CNP command, was the decision by the first Comisionado to receive complaints not just from citizens but from police officers as well. This decision proved a popular one for individual police officers who, for the year ending 30 June 1995, filed just over forty-five per cent of all complaints registered by the Comisionado's office.[82] Several points may be made about this fact. The first is that it is still not uniform practice for oversight agencies to accept complaints from police officers regarding the conduct of other officers. Although there are signs this practice is starting to change, historically civilian oversight has confined its focus to complaints by ordinary citizens.[83] Secondly, leaving that issue aside, the proportion of complaints from police is astonishingly high, and raises some interesting questions about how the police command was seen by many serving officers, and the adequacy of internal mechanisms for dealing with police officer grievances and concerns.

While this must remain speculative in the absence of appropriate evidence, the degree of affront to the militaristic conception of authority implicit in an external complaints mechanism being used by members of the organisation to raise complaints is, symbolically at least, obviously considerable. Arguably, it is one thing for a parallel authority to exist which is designed to receive and process citizens' complaints against police; it is quite another for the authority to also receive complaints from police about other police. While strategically this decision was taken by the first Comisionado out of frustration at not being listened to by the CNP high command, it is at least questionable whether this response ultimately served the fortunes of the office well, given the possible symbolic connotations of this practice as well as the practical breach of military discipline and authority it represented for the CNP leadership. While unlikely by itself to have engendered systematic opposition to the office by the police, it may plausibly have played a part in firming up that opposition, including the decision to try to have the office closed.

[82] Mario Gonzalez, *Informe del Comisionado Nacional para la Policia al Congreso de la Republica* (Bogota, Oficina del Comisionado Nacional para la Policia, 1995) 13.

[83] Colleen Lewis, *Complaints Against Police: The Politics of Reform* (Sydney, Hawkins Press, 1999), pp. 73–6.

## Too Much Too Quickly?

A number of other distinct considerations made the Comisionado's reception in Colombia even less favourable. For one, while the traditions of administrative justice are not entirely different (e.g. the ombudsman-like Procuradoria), there are still striking differences of attitude and practice between Colombia and many Western common-law jurisdictions on such matters as government accountability, police forces subjected to civilian authority, and the Rule of Law. In addition, more than one person who worked on the Comisionado project during the 1993 reform period has admitted privately that too much was attempted too quickly, and that more should have been done to lay the groundwork for broader understanding and acceptance of the concept, as well as allowing more time to give consideration to the practical details of implementation.[84]

While it is difficult to be sure what might have worked in this regard, the outcome does suggest the virtue of allowing considerable time for familiarisation with new concepts, partly through education programmes and the judicious use of plausible "experts" to assist in education and training ancillary to the planning and implementation of the reform. Visits to working examples of the concept in other countries by those engaged in planning the reform as well as by those staff appointed to the new agency and police officials directly affected by the new agency, as time-consuming and expensive an undertaking it would have been, would however have added much more to the general level of understanding of the Comisionado concept. More time in this regard might have also allowed the drafting of clearer legislative and policy document descriptions of responsibilities as between the Comisionado, the Inspector General, and other bodies.

## A Reform-Conscious Police

A final observation must be to acknowledge the acuity and assiduity of the CNP response to the reform challenge, especially under the leadership of Serrano. While his personal status played an important part, the CNP as a whole undertook a significant internal reform programme during the life of the Comisionado's office which arguably did much to overshadow some of the work done by the Comisionado. Indeed, given the difficulties surrounding the establishment of the office, the police had some lead time to begin taking initiatives in advance of any suggestions from other quarters, including the Comisionado. A telling example of this degree of head-start and anticipation was the major commitment by the CNP in 1995 to its Cultural Transformation

[84] This reflection has come from individual communications with a number of persons working for the Gaviria administration in 1993.

and Institutional Improvement Plan, a scheme among other things to overhaul recruitment, training, and community consultation practices.[85] The CNP's internal unit created to devise and oversee this plan consisted of some thirty or so police personnel as well as academics and others with skills in organisational change. In late 1995, the Comisionado's office, under Gonzalez, sought to establish its own expert commission for the development of a new police culture.[86]

What is significant and interesting here, apart from the shared construction by the CNP and the Comisionado of police reform needs in terms of culture,[87] is the fact that the police effectively managed to outclass as well as outpace the Comisionado's initiative. It was obviously beyond the resources of the Comisionado's office to mount a comparable cultural change programme, and the sheer size and timing of the CNP initiative in any event surely called into question for many the point of the Comisionado's expert commission. This experience would seem to indicate the wisdom strategically of police agencies at the centre of reform crises protecting or advancing their position through engaging publicly in broadly-conceived, ambitious reform schemes. Moreover, those schemes should anticipate the direction of external criticism and recommendations, and at least match them in the language and concepts employed to analyse the problems faced, as well as the speed with which particular reform proposals are announced and put into practice. While the significance of such a programme undoubtedly ought to be subjected to rigorous evaluation, in the short or medium-term world of public policy, this desideratum is unlikely to prove possible at a practical level.[88] By contrast, as the Comisionado's case shows, the time available may well prove sufficient to see the end of a bold experiment in civilian police authority.

## CONCLUSION: MEASURING "SUCCESS" IN POLICE REFORM

If the question is to be put simply in terms of the survival of the agency, then the experiment was a clear failure. But besides this obvious conclusion, we ought to ask whether it is realistic to judge "success" in the Colombian environment by comparison with the achievements of reformers say in Australia or Canada? Moreover, should we evaluate "success" and "failure" in stark dichotomous terms, without regard to considerations of degree and process, or of a symbolic as well as practical nature? One should also consider the indirect and, perhaps in some measure, unintended consequences of the reform process, to see whether in other parts of the system of government and in the police organisa-

[85] See "El general Serrano le apunta al cambio" *supra*, n. 64.

[86] This is referred to in Gonzalez, *supra*, n. 82 at 7.

[87] For a critique of this literature, see Janet Chan, *Changing Police Culture* (Melbourne, Cambridge UP, 1996).

[88] At the risk of stating the obvious, politics works on different time-lines and priorities from social science. This makes for different sorts of evaluations or may even render them largely irrelevant, as new political issues arise and take over the agenda.

tion itself, significant changes may be linked to the reform impetus behind the establishment of the Comisionado's office. If these are relevant considerations, how differently might the evaluation of the experiment appear?

The picture looks quite different if we take this approach. Symbolically, the CNP were forced in the period 1993–7 to contend with a challenger to their in-house authority. While ultimately they were able to reassert their domination of police authority, they paid a heavy price for doing so. It had been necessary for them at the beginning of the reform process to opt for one or other type of civilian control; not surprisingly, they opted for the parallel office of the Comisionado in preference to the imposition of an in-house civilian director.[89] Both options signalled the limits of police authority in view of the track record of the police at that time, and the generally recognised need for more accountability by the police and improved police-community relations. The attempt to set up and run the Comisionado's office proved a considerable spur to internal police reform as well as being simply an inconvenience or embarrassment to the CNP senior command. The large numbers of dismissals of police from all levels between 1994 and 1997 for suspected involvement in corrupt activities and breaches of authority was the most significant internal clean-up certainly for a very long time.

The need to retrieve the general standing of the CNP provided both an opportunity to undertake radical house-keeping measures of this kind, as well as a spur to behave more effectively as well as more sensitively towards the public. Evidence of greater effectiveness came partly in the form of the achievements made in capturing various leaders of the Medellin and Cali cartels, while some substantiation for greater police responsiveness towards citizens has come from public opinion surveys showing improved public attitudes towards the police, and public use of phone-in lines (hot-lines) to register complaints and requests for service.[90] While none of these changes might be seen as striking or sufficient by themselves, or even in aggregate to be an adequate response in the circumstances, the changes have nonetheless been significant in comparative terms, and have allowed the CNP to re-claim much if not all of the moral authority lost in 1993. It is nonetheless doubtful whether so much would have been achieved had the clear challenge to exclusive police authority not been so strikingly presented through the idea, and then the implementation, of the Comisionado.

While the CNP has managed to regain the upper hand for the moment, the precedent for greater sharing of police authority has now been established. Given the ongoing problems in Colombia with impunity in the criminal justice system, and ongoing allegations of human rights abuses by police, the idea of

[89] See *supra*, n. 64.

[90] I have not sighted these surveys, but they have been mentioned to me in various conversations with Colombian police-watchers. The improvement in the police image is palpable through informal conversations held with ordinary Colombians. A number of taxi-drivers independently have confirmed to me the improvement in police behaviour since 1993. Some told me they thought the CNP was now appointing a better class of recruit than previously.

civilian oversight *or some other manifestation of shared police authority*, including the capacity to pursue investigations of alleged abuses by police officers, will only be kept at bay by exemplary and transparent efforts by the CNP to keep police behaviour within reasonable parameters, in part by dealing effectively with examples of police misconduct. In view of the troubled history of the CNP and other Colombian security forces in satisfying the requirements of human rights organisations in this regard, this is unlikely to prove easy for them. Even this may not prove sufficient, if, for example, non-governmental organisations (NGOs) and other international bodies such as the United Nations Human Rights Committee insist upon a measure of independent investigation of abuses by state security forces, including the police.

This indeed is already occurring. The United Nations Human Rights Committee in its Fifty-seventh session in 1996 considered Brazil's report submitted under Article 40 of the International Covenant on Civil and Political Rights, and recommended in paragraph 22 that "all complaints of misconduct by members of security forces be investigated by an independent body and not by the security forces". More particularly, they recommended:

> Formal mechanisms for receipt and investigation of such complaints should be established in all areas of the country and their existence publicized. Such mechanisms must make provision for effective protection of complainants and witnesses against intimidation and reprisals.[91]

While other agencies (e.g. the Fiscalia) could potentially provide such a service effectively, a distinct advantage of a civilian oversight agency would be its capacity to also look at questions of police-community relations and police effectiveness. Only very recently has this potential begun to be appreciated by human rights organisations.[92]

Despite the considerable efforts made in-house by police on occasions to improve behaviour and accountability, demands of this kind from international and regional bodies will continue to tax the capacity of domestic police forces such as the CNP to preserve their near-exclusive authority over disciplinary matters and matters of conduct generally. Police forces in countries such as Colombia may be able to win institutional "battles" against specific agencies which have threatened this actual or quasi-monopoly, but arguably they control fewer of the variables today than previously which will determine the outcome of the "war" for police authority. Increasingly, these variables are international in character, and articulate with prominent and influential discourses about democracy, human rights and good governance. Through a variety of means, questions about police authority at the domestic level are increasingly becoming issues of global concern. In this environment, the "battle lost" by the Comisionado experiment is arguably only the first wave of change in this far from resolved, and very important, area of police governance in Colombia.

[91] Human Rights Committee (UN), 57th Session, 25 July 1996.
[92] See WOLA, *supra*, n. 49, 20.

## References


Amnesty International, *Political Violence in Colombia: The Impunity Continues* (1994a)

Amnesty International, *Colombia: Political Violence—Myth and Reality* (London, Amnesty International, 1994b).

David Bayley, "A Foreign Policy for Democratic Policing" (1995) 5 *Policing and Society* 79.

Brewer, John *Black and Blue* (Oxford, Clarendon, 1992).

Brewer John and Kathleen Magee *Inside the RUC: Routine Policing in a Divided Society* (Oxford, Clarendon Press, 1991).

Camacho, Alvaro "Public and Private Dimensions of Urban Violence in Cali" in Charles Bergquist, Ricardo Penaranda and Gonzalo Sanchez (eds.), *Violence in Colombia: The Contemporary Crisis in Historical Perspective* (Wilmington Del, SR Books, 1992).

*Cambio 16*, "Para-noia" 13–20 October, 1997 (no. 226).

Chan, Janet *Changing Police Culture* (Melbourne, Cambridge UP, 1996).

Chevigny, Paul *Edge of the Knife: Police Violence in the Americas* (New York, New Press, 1995).

Cohen, Stan, "Government Responses to Human Rights Reports: Claims, Denials, and Counterclaims" (1996) 18 *Human Rights Quarterly* 517.

Cromos, "El general Serrano le apunta al cambio" 25 March 1996.

Davies, Hugh "Where boys and girls come out to die", *The Weekly Telegraph* (Issue 113, 1994), VII.

Duzan, Maria Jimena *Death Beat: A Colombian Journalist's Life Inside the Cocaine Wars* (New York, Harper Collins, 1994).

Echandia, Camilo Castilla *Expansion Territorial de la Guerrilla Colombiana: Geografia, Economia y Violencia*, Working Document No. 1 (May 1997, Paz Publica, University de los Andes, Bogota, Colombia).

*El Espectador*, " 'Asi es imposible,' dice el comisionado para la Policia", 2 February 1996

*El Mundo*, "La baja de un Comisionado", 12 September 1996.

*El Tiempo*, "Por falta de apoyo, renuncio Comisionado para la Policia", 1 February 1996

*El Tiempo*, 23 July 1994.

"El problema de la Policia y la realidad social colombiana", *El Pais*, 3 January 1996.

Freckelton, Ian "Shooting the Messenger" in Andrew J Goldsmith (ed.), *Complaints Against the Police: The Trend to External Review* (Oxford, Clarendon Press, 1991).

Goldsmith, Andrew J (ed.), *Complaints Against the Police: The Trend to External Review* (Oxford, Clarendon Press, 1991).

Goldsmith, Andrew J "External Review v Self-Regulation: The Dialectics of Police Accountability" in Andrew J Goldsmith (ed.), *Complaints Against the Police: The Trend to External Review* (Oxford: Clarendon Press, 1991).

Gonzalez, Mario *Informe del Comisionado Nacional para la Policia al Congreso de la Republica* (Bogota, Oficina del Comisionado Nacional para la Policia, 1995).

Huggins, Martha *Political Policing in Latin America* (Durham: Duke University, 1997).

Human Rights Committee (UN), 57th Session, 25 July 1996.

Human Rights Watch, *Political Murder in Colombia: The Violence Continues* (New York, Human Rights Watch, 1992).

Human Rights Watch, *Generation Under Fire: Children and Violence in Colombia* (New York, Human Rights Watch, 1994).

Inravsion TV-A, Bogota, 10 September 1994.

*La Prensa*, "Sin controles" 14 September 1996.

*Latinamerica Press*, "Colombia tries to reform abusive police force" (21 April 1994).

Lewis, Colleen, *Civilian Oversight of Complaints Against Police: External Relationships and Their Impact Upon Effectiveness*, unpublished PhD dissertation, Griffith University, 1997.

Linz, Juan and Alfred Stepan, *Problems of Democratic Transition and Consolidation: Southern Europe, South America, and Post-Communist Europe* (Baltimore: Johns Hopkins University, 1996).

McMahon Maeve and Richard Ericson, Policing Reform: A Study of the Reform Process and Police Institution in Toronto, Research Report (Toronto: Centre of Criminology, 1984).

Nadelmann, Ethan *Cops Across Borders: Transnational Crime and International Law Enforcement* (University Park, Pennsylvania State University Press, 1994).

Nield, Rachel *Policing Haiti: Preliminary Assessment of the New Civilian Security Force* (Washington DC, WOLA,1995).

Oxford Analytica, *Latin American World Brief*, 2 July 1993.

Pardo, Rafael Rueda, *De primera mano: Colombia 1986–1994, Entre Conflictos y Esperanzas* (Bogota, CEREC, 1996).

Riedmann, Arnold "La Reforma Policial en Colombia" in Waldmann, Peter (ed.), *Justicia en La Calle: Ensayos Sobre La Policia en America Latina* (1996).

Rojas, Carlos Eduardo *La violencia llamada "Limpieza social"* (Bogota, CINEP, 1996).

Serrano, Rosso Jose "Reply to Questionnaire from Hugo Alberto Velasco, Secretary Commission II, Chamber of Representatives" (Bogota, 28 November 1995).

Smith, David and Jeremy Gray, *Police and People in London* (London, Policy Studies Institute, 1983).

Stannow, Lovisa *"Social Cleansing" in Colombia* MA thesis, Department of Spanish and Latin American Studies, Simon Fraser University, January 1996.

"Reply to Questionnaire from Hugo Alberto Velasco, Secretary Commission II, Chamber of Representatives" (Bogota, 28 November 1995).

Torres, Javier, Velasco "La Ciudadania Pacta Con Su Policia: El Proceso de Modernizacion de la Policia Nacional de Colombia" in Francisco Leal Buitrago and Juan Gabriel Tokatlian (eds.), *Orden Mundial y Seguridad: Nuevos desafios para Colombia y America Latina* (Bogota, Tercer Mundo, 1994).

US Department of State, *Country Reports on Human Rights Practices for 1992* (Washington, US Government Printing Office, 1993).

*Vanguardia Liberal*, "Me voy porque le incomodaba a Serrano", 5 February 1996.

Waldemann, Peter (ed.), *Justicia en La Calle: Ensayos Sobre La Policia en America Latina* (Medellin: Biblioteca Juridica Dike, 1996).

Washington Office on Latin America, *The Colombian National Police, Human Rights and US Drug Policy* (Washington, WOLA, 1993).

Washington Office on Latin America (WOLA), *Demilitarising Public Order: The International Community, Police Reform and Human Rights in Central America and Haiti* (Washington DC: WOLA, 1995).

Wolfe, Marshall, *Elusive Development* (London: Zed Books, 1996).

World Bank, *World Development Report: The State in a Changing World* (New York, Oxford UP, 1997).

# 9

# *The South African Independent Complaints Directorate*

BRONWEN MANBY*

## OVERSIGHT OF POLICE MISCONDUCT IN SOUTH AFRICA UNDER THE APARTHEID GOVERNMENT

The South African Police (SAP) had a long and notorious history as the enforcer and defender of apartheid. In addition to the routine forms of police brutality, involving torture and abuse of criminal suspects by the uniformed police, the security police were dedicated to the eradication of black protest, the enforcement of racist policies such as the forced removals of "black spots" from "white" South Africa, the assassination of leaders of the African National Congress (ANC) and other liberation movements and, in latter years, the deliberate destabilisation of black communities by the promotion and orchestration of political violence.[1]

Although the Government maintained a veneer of concern when police abuses were exposed, the processes available to bring the police to account were almost always ineffective. As the end of the apartheid era approached, an independent report on the high-profile police investigation of the 1992 "Boipatong massacre", in which forty-two township residents were killed by members of the Inkatha Freedom Party (IFP) living in a hostel for migrant workers, concluded that:

> if these obvious failures [of the investigation process] are in any way representative then they suggest that the SAP is an unaccountable police force . . . [and] that systems do not exist for either internal or external accountability.[2]

* I would like to thank Neville Melville and Piers Pigou for their comments on a draft of this chapter.

[1] These activities were investigated by the Truth and Reconciliation Commission (TRC), created by the Promotion of National Unity and Reconciliation Act (Act No.34 of 1995). The TRC completed a five-volume report in October 1998 (available via the TRC website, <www.truth.org.za>), which sets out in some detail the structures of the apartheid security forces and their activities. In addition, security force abuses were extensively documented at the time by national and international human rights organisations. See in particular Max Coleman (ed.), *A Crime Against Humanity: Analysing the Repression of the Apartheid State* (Johannesburg and Cape Town, Human Rights Committee, Mayibuye Books and David Philip, 1998) and Don Foster, Dennis Davis and Diane Sandler, *Detention and Torture in South Africa: Psychological, legal and historical studies* (Cape Town, David Philip, 1987).

[2] Dr P A J Waddington, Director, Criminal Justice Studies, University of Reading, England, *Report of the Inquiry into the Police Response to and Investigation of Events in Boipatong on*

Occasional court cases and inquests had found unlawful police action, and independent nongovernmental organisations (NGOs) had monitored police misconduct for many years, but the first state-supported system to introduce a measure of independence into routine investigations of police misconduct was the "police reporting officer" (PRO) system established by the National Peace Accord of September 1991. The National Peace Accord was a response to the escalation of political violence that accompanied the period leading up to South Africa's first all-race elections in April 1994. The accord was signed by twenty-seven parties to the political process, including the ANC, IFP, National Party Government, business representatives, and the police. It envisaged local and regional dispute resolution committees and a national peace secretariat that would monitor compliance with codes of conduct for political parties and police and promote reconciliation between parties. A standing commission of inquiry, the Commission of Inquiry Regarding the Prevention of Public Violence and Intimidation, chaired by Mr Justice Richard Goldstone (which came to be known as the Goldstone Commission), was authorised by the signatories to the Peace Accord to investigate the background to and reasons for political violence.[3]

In addition, the Peace Accord provided for the appointment of police reporting officers in each police region, to be selected by the minister of law and order from candidates nominated by the legal profession,[4] and for "complaints of alleged police misconduct which is of such a serious nature that it may detrimentally affect police/community relations" to be referred either to the relevant PRO, or to the commissioner of police, in either case "for investigation by a unit of the police specifically established for this purpose, under the supervision of a designated general of the police". This unit was required to submit to the PRO a report on complaints lodged with it and on the progress and outcome of investigations into those complaints. The PRO had the authority "to ensure that the investigation is a full and proper investigation and accordingly will be entitled to refer the report back to the unit"; and in addition to recommend to the commissioner of police the suspension or transfer of a police official during an investigation, and, on completion of an investigation, any disciplinary action to be taken. The PRO was charged to notify the complainant of the outcome of the complaint and any recommendations, but had no power to compel action by the police.

*17 June 1992*, submitted to the Commission of Inquiry regarding the Prevention of Public Violence and Intimidation, 20 July 1992.

[3] The Goldstone Commission was established in October 1991 by then-President F W de Klerk, under the Prevention of Violence and Intimidation Act, No. 139 of 1991, as part of the Peace Accord process. The later Security Forces Board of Inquiry Act, No. 95 of 1993, also provided for a machinery for investigating security force abuse, but it was never implemented.

[4] The Peace Accord provided for the Association of Law Societies (representing attorneys) and the General Council of the Bar (representing advocates) to nominate three candidates per region to the minister of law and order from among former prosecutors, magistrates, policemen or members of the attorney-generals' staff, or lawyers in private practice from either branch of the profession.

The PRO system was plagued with problems, virtually all of them deriving from its dependence on the co-operation of the police. Since the PROs had no statutory powers (their authority was based only on the Peace Accord and not on any legislation), were not regarded as full-time appointments, depended on the police to reimburse them for their work on the basis of an hourly rate, and had no right even to be informed of all complaints laid, the police were able in most cases to obstruct independent investigations. The refusal of the police and the attorneys-general to allow PROs access to police "dockets", the files relating to investigations of misconduct or crimes, meant that it was often impossible for the PROs to monitor those investigations effectively.[5] The quality and persistence of individual PROs also varied, and many effectively gave up in the face of police resistance.

Nevertheless, with the assistance of nongovernmental organisations active in the area, a few PROs did achieve some notable successes in uncovering and publicising serious wrongdoing by the police. Jan Munnik, the PRO for the Witwatersrand, the police area encompassing Johannesburg (but excluding Soweto), for example, demonstrated the use of torture and extrajudicial executions by the "Yankee Squad", a police unit theoretically established to trace unlawful firearms within the black townships of the area known as the "Vaal Triangle" south of Johannesburg. As a result of the police investigation which followed, the Yankee Squad was disbanded and six criminal prosecutions resulted (though no convictions).[6] At various times Munnik also obtained court orders authorising raids on a number of police facilities in which electric shock equipment used for torture was discovered. After the April 1994 elections and with the political backing of the new government, several more of Munnik's investigations led to prosecutions, and some to convictions.[7] Outstanding cases were handed over to the Independent Complaints Directorate (ICD) when it was established in April 1997.

Despite the signing of the National Peace Accord, the implementation of its provisions for the establishment of conflict resolution mechanisms, and the setting up of the Goldstone Commission, political violence continued unabated during the lead up to the 1994 elections. It became increasingly apparent that members of the security forces were deeply implicated in this conflict. In December 1993, the Goldstone Commission finally, and cautiously, confirmed that "a hit squad consisting of five KZP policemen has been responsible during 1992 and 1993 for the murder of no less than nine people including leaders and

[5] These problems were canvassed extensively in the *Report by Police Reporting Officer for the Witwatersrand, Adv. J H A Munnik, on his reporting function for the period February 1993 to June 1995* (Johannesburg, 8 July 1995); hereafter "Munnik's report".

[6] Munnik's report, ch. 5; E-mail communication from Piers Pigou, former investigator at the Independent Board of Inquiry, 29 March 1999.

[7] Mungo Soggot, "Torture still haunts the Brixton police", *Mail and Guardian* (Johannesburg), August 2 to 8, 1996; Angella Johnson, "New tests expose police torture," *Mail and Guardian*, October 18 to 24, 1996; Gustav Thiel, "Police 'cover up' torture claims", *Mail and Guardian* August 8 to 14, 1997.

members of the ANC".[8] Following the completion in December 1993 of negotiations over the framework for transition to majority rule, a Transitional Executive Council (TEC), with ANC as well as National Party members, was established to govern the country during the period between the end of the negotiations and the installation of a democratically elected government. In late December 1993, the TEC appointed an "Investigation Task Group" with a mandate to follow up the Goldstone report and investigate hit squads in the KwaZulu Police. In March 1994, the Investigation Task Group concluded that:

> the number of deaths caused by these hit squads is unquantifiable, but would represent a significant proportion of those who have died in the political violence in Natal/KwaZulu.[9]

During the same pre-election period, a short-lived independent complaints mechanism was set up under the legislation establishing the TEC.[10] Its directors were appointed shortly before the 1994 elections, but the body was dismantled soon after the results were announced.[11] The document describing the powers of this body was eventually the basis for the legislation establishing the ICD.

The Investigation Task Group continued to carry out some work after the April 1994 elections,[12] and in September 1994, the new minister, Sydney Mufamadi, established an Investigation Task Unit (ITU), to carry on its work on a more formal basis. The ITU itself was formed of hand-picked policemen, some of whom had previously worked with the Goldstone Commission. It had a civilian board to which it was accountable, and a civilian support component of researchers and analysts. The ITU conducted a series of important investigations into the machinery behind the violence in KwaZulu-Natal, one of which resulted in the—ultimately unsuccessful—prosecution of former minister of defence Magnus Malan and nineteen others in connection with a 1987 massacre of a family in KwaZulu carried out by individuals who had been among thirty recruits trained in "offensive" actions against the ANC by the South African army in Namibia's Caprivi Strip.[13] The ITU was bitterly opposed by senior

[8] *Fourth Interim Report of the Goldstone Commission of Inquiry Regarding the Prevention of Public Violence and Intimidation*, 6 December 1993. The KZP were the KwaZulu Police operating within the former black homeland of KwaZulu, and regarded by many as effectively the armed wing of the IFP.

[9] *Second Interim Report of the Transitional Executive Council Investigation Task Group into the Matter of Hit Squads in the KwaZulu Police*, 29 March 1994.

[10] Section 15(1)(c) of the Transitional Executive Council Act, No. 151 of 1993.

[11] Independent Complaints Directorate, *Annual Report 1996/97* (Pretoria, Independent Complaints Directorate, 1997), paragraph 1.1.8.

[12] The *Supplementary Report of the Transitional Executive Council Investigation Task Group into the Matter of Hit Squads in the KwaZulu Police*, which dealt with unlawful military training ostensibly carried out under the provisions of the National Peace Accord by the IFP in KwaZulu, was submitted to the minister for safety and security on 18 May 1994.

[13] *S* v. *Msane and 19 Others*, Case Number CC1/96 heard in the Durban and Local Division of the Supreme Court of South Africa (unreported); see also, Howard Varney and Jeremy Sarkin, "Failing to Pierce the Hit Squad Veil: A Critique of the Malan Trial", *South African Journal of Criminal Justice* (1997) 2.

members of the police and, despite lobbying from the human rights community for it to be given permanent status, it was disbanded in 1997.[14]

## POLICE REFORMS SINCE 1994

The Government of National Unity led by the ANC elected in April 1994 immediately began a programme to reform the police. A Green Paper and draft Bill published in July 1994 emphasised the establishment of democratic control and community participation in policing, and led to the passage in October 1995 of a new South African Police Service Act.[15] The Act symbolically renamed the police "force" to the South African Police Service (SAPS) and established new national and provincial structures for the police (amalgamating the police forces of the ten black homelands into the national police service, and at the same time devolving a significant degree of political control to provincial level). The new law demilitarised the rank structure of the police, gave statutory backing to the community police forums created on an ad hoc basis over the previous years, and set up a national civilian secretariat for safety and security (mirrored at the provincial level) to advise the minister and to monitor the implementation of policy and directions set for the police service. In line with the Bill of Rights in the new constitution, the police legal department prepared a human rights training programme for new recruits and existing members of the force. A comprehensive national crime prevention strategy was developed in conjunction with other government departments, new training programmes implemented, and affirmative action processes attempted in the promotion of police officers. In 1998, the Department of Safety and Security published a White Paper on safety and security to direct the next five years.[16] The White Paper emphasised the importance of crime prevention, improving criminal investigations, improving the quality of service to victims of crime, as well as strengthening systems for civilian control of the police. In November 1998, a comprehensive police policy on the prevention of torture was published.

Despite these positive developments, the period since 1994 has also seen serious problems within the police service, perhaps inevitable in a body facing such huge changes in orientation and priorities. A large number of senior white police officers have retired, many on handsome redundancy packages for "medical reasons", yet racism in the force remains a very serious problem. There has been increasing absenteeism and other indications of a collapse in discipline, as the

[14] While those working for the ITU believed that government inability or unwillingness to override police opposition was the main reason that the mandate for the unit was not renewed, the Government cited the anomalous situation of KwaZulu-Natal and the need for an integrated national system.

[15] South African Police Service Act, No. 68 of 1995.

[16] Department of Safety and Security, *White Paper on Safety and Security: "In Service of Safety" 1999–2004*, September 1998 (the White Paper and other Government documents, including legislation, are available at the South African Government website <www.gov.za>).

military command structures have been dismantled, but are yet to be replaced with a work ethic of service to the community. In areas like KwaZulu-Natal and the Western Cape, members of the police apparently remain integrated into the systems that keep political and gang violence (respectively) at levels which threaten the overall maintenance of the peace. In Gauteng province, which includes the main industrial areas of Johannesburg and its environs, police have been involved in car-hijacking rings and other high visibility crimes. South Africa hosts a large number of organised crime syndicates, which profit from the sophisticated banking system and the gaps in law enforcement common to other countries experiencing similar transitions from authoritarian rule. Even though violent crime has apparently stabilised since 1996, it remains at levels among the highest in the world for countries not at war: there are more than twenty thousand murders a year among a population of forty-two million. Rates of prosecution and conviction are low. More than two hundred police are themselves killed annually, from a total force of approaching one hundred and thirty thousand, and suicide rates are also high.[17] While public confidence in the police is low, the demands faced by politicians are for crackdowns on crime, not for the protection of suspects and respect for human rights.

Against this background, calls from the human rights community for greater police accountability and for the constitutional rights of suspects to be respected are ambivalently received by the public, at best. Nevertheless, South Africa's first democratically elected government maintained an emphasis on ensuring greater civilian oversight of the police during its five years in office, even though commitments on paper may not have been as effectively implemented as those monitoring police behaviour had hoped. In June 1999, a new government was inaugurated following May elections. President Thabo Mbeki, who succeeded Nelson Mandela as head of state, appointed Steve Tshwete, previously Minister for Sport, as Minister for Safety and Security. In his first media briefing, on 28 June 1999, Tshwete promised a "ruthless and aggressive" offensive against criminals, and suggested that some provisions of the Bill of Rights were hampering police in their work.[18] Although tough measures against crime within the police were also mentioned, these were in the context of corruption rather than abuse of suspects.

[17] The SAPS employs one hundred and twenty-eight thousand individuals, of whom twenty eight thousand are civilians, the remainder uniformed police; *Minutes of the Joint Meeting of the Parliamentary Committees on Safety and Security and Justice*, 19 February 1999. According to a statement by the National Assembly Committee on Safety and Security, two hundred and thirty-three police were killed in 1998 (South African Press Association (SAPA), 24 March 1999). However, many of these are killed in domestic or ordinary criminal circumstances rather than as a result of their crime-fighting activities: one study of police deaths found that only thirty-seven per cent of those killed in a three-year period had been killed in the course of their duties (Anthony Minaar, "An analysis of the murder of members of the South African Police Service 1994–1997", paper presented to a Technikon SA conference, 25–26 February 1998).

[18] AFP, 28 June 1999.

### THE LEGAL FRAMEWORK FOR THE INDEPENDENT COMPLAINTS DIRECTORATE

The most publicly visible of the attempts to ensure a new regime of accountability for the police is the creation of the Independent Complaints Directorate. Section 222 of the interim constitution of South Africa provided for the establishment of:

> an independent mechanism under civilian control, with the object of ensuring that complaints in respect of criminal offences and misconduct allegedly committed by members of the Service are investigated in an effective and efficient manner.[19]

Accordingly, provisions to set up such a mechanism were included in the draft legislation to regulate the police, one of the earliest statutes put forward by the new government.

Chapter 10 of the 1995 South African Police Service Act establishes the Independent Complaints Directorate, the first body outside police control with the power to investigate complaints against the police and demand co-operation from the police in its investigations. Although section 222 of the interim constitution was not repeated in the final constitution,[20] the ICD remains effectively governed by the objectives set out for it at that time.

The Police Service Act provides for the ICD to have an executive director, nominated by the Minister for Safety and Security and confirmed by the parliamentary committees on safety and security, and other personnel appointed by the director in consultation with the minister.[21] The ICD is to be funded by money specifically appropriated from Parliament, independently from the general police budget.[22] The "principal function" of the ICD is to "achieve the

[19] Constitution of the Republic of South Africa Act, No. 200 of 1993, section 222. The interim constitution was adopted on 5 December 1993, after a long process of negotiation between the National Party Government, the ANC and other parties that followed the unbanning of the ANC and other liberation organisations on 2 February 1990 and the announcement that the National Party was prepared to negotiate a transition to majority rule. It came into effect following the April 1994 elections, and governed the period of drafting a final constitution by the new National Assembly, sitting also as a constitutional assembly. The final constitution (Constitution of the Republic of South Africa, 1996) was signed into law by the president on 10 December 1996, human rights day, and came into force on 4 February 1997.

[20] The reasons for the failure to repeat section 222 are obscure, but seem to relate mainly to the perception that there were already "too many commissions" and other constitutional bodies monitoring government but not themselves implementing policy. Section 206(6) of the final constitution, however, does state that "On receipt of a complaint lodged by a provincial executive, an independent police complaints body established by national legislation must investigate any alleged misconduct of, or offence committed by, a member of the police service in the province", effectively requiring the existence of a body similar to that required by section 222 of the interim constitution.

[21] South African Police Service Act, sections 51 and 52.

[22] *Ibid.*, section 52(3); this provision was amended, after criticism from Lawyers for Human Rights, the Independent Board of Inquiry and Jan Munnik, PRO for the Witwatersrand, from an earlier draft which provided for the ICD to be funded from the general police budget.

object contemplated in section 222 of the Constitution".[23] To achieve its object the ICD:

> (a) may mero motu[24] or upon receipt of a complaint, investigate any misconduct or offence allegedly committed by any member, and may, where appropriate, refer such investigation to the Commissioner concerned;
> (b) shall mero motu or upon receipt of a complaint, investigate any death in police custody or as a result of police action; and
> (c) may investigate any matter referred to the directorate by the Minister or the member of the Executive Council.[25]

The national and provincial commissioners must also "notify the directorate of all cases of death in police custody or as a result of police action".[26] Thus the ICD is not limited to cases where there has been a complaint by a member of the public relating to police conduct, but must investigate all cases of deaths in custody or as a result of police action whether or not there has been any complaint, and may investigate of its own accord in any case.

The minister may authorise staff working for the ICD to exercise the powers of police officers, and the director of the ICD may "request and obtain" from the police information necessary for conducting an investigation, or such cooperation from an individual officer as may be necessary to achieve the object of the directorate.[27] A referral of an investigation to the relevant commissioner may be withdrawn by the director of the ICD at any time, and the ICD may commence its own investigation even if a matter has been referred or closed by the police.[28] Strengthening these requirements, it is generally provided that:

[23] South African Police Service Act, section 52(1)(a).

[24] The South African Parliament has attempted to move toward "plain English" legislation; this trend apparently passed by the drafters of the police act. *Mero motu* means, roughly, "on its own initiative".

[25] South African Police Service Act, section 53(2)(a) (b) & (c).

[26] *Ibid.*, section 53(8). The provisions requiring cases of death in custody or otherwise at police hands to be reported to the ICD, and requiring the ICD to investigate these cases itself, were added at a late stage in the drafting process as a result of lobbying by Lawyers for Human Rights, the Independent Board of Inquiry and Jan Munnik, PRO for the Witwatersrand. In addition to the requirements under the police act, the Domestic Violence Act, No.116 of 1998, provides in section 18(4) that "(a) Failure by a member of the South African Police Service to comply with an obligation imposed in terms of this Act or the national instructions referred to in subsection (3) [to be issued by the National Prosecuting Authority], constitutes misconduct as contemplated in the South African Police Service Act, 1995, and the Independent Complaints Directorate, established in terms of that Act, must forthwith be informed of any such failure reported to the South African Police Service. (b) Unless the Independent Complaints Directorate directs otherwise in any specific case, the South African Police Service must institute disciplinary proceedings against any member who allegedly failed to comply with an obligation referred to in paragraph (a)". Section 18(5) also requires the ICD to report to Parliament every six months regarding the matters reported to it under the Domestic Violence Act. As of August 1999, the Domestic Violence Act had not yet been brought into force.

[27] *Ibid.*, section 53(6)(b) and (d).

[28] *Ibid.*, section 53(6)(a) and (e).

> Any person who wilfully interferes with the Executive Director or a member of the personnel of the directorate in the exercise or performance of his or her powers or functions, shall be guilty of an offence;

and that:

> All organs of state shall accord such assistance as may be reasonably required for the protection of the independence, impartiality, dignity and effectiveness of the directorate in the exercise and performance of its powers and functions.[29]

The director may also "request and obtain" information necessary for an investigation from an attorney-general, the public official responsible for prosecutions, who since the creation of the ICD has been renamed a director of public prosecutions (DPP).[30] However, in this case, the "attorney-general may on reasonable grounds refuse to accede to such request". In addition, if a matter has been referred to the police to investigate and a docket has in turn been referred by the police to an attorney-general for prosecution, the ICD may only commence its own investigation "in consultation with the attorney-general".[31]

After completing its investigations, the ICD may submit the results to an attorney-general for his or her decision as to prosecution, and may make recommendations (of unspecified type) to the commissioner concerned, or to the minister or provincial executive council member responsible for policing.[32] The executive director must submit an annual report to the minister, which must be tabled in Parliament within fourteen days of its submission, and must additionally report at any time when requested to do so by the minister or the committees of the National Assembly or National Council of Provinces responsible for safety and security.

Internal disciplinary procedures within the police service have also been revised, although the procedures were not incorporated in the new Act, but

[29] *Ibid.*, section 50(3)(b) and (4). The wording of subsection (4) is borrowed from the provisions relating to the Human Rights Commission (Human Rights Commission Act, No. 54 of 1994, section 4 (3)).

[30] In July 1998, the National Prosecuting Authority Act, No. 32 of 1998, was signed into law, replacing the existing system of attorneys-general appointed under the Attorneys-General Act, No. 92 of 1992, with a National Prosecuting Authority headed by a national director of public prosecutions (NDPP) and provincial directors of public prosecutions (DPPs) in each of the nine new provinces. Former deputy chair of the National Council of Provinces, Bulelani Ngcuka, was appointed the first NDPP on 1 August 1998. The Act also provides for the establishment of up to three "investigating directorates" within the office of the National Director of Public Prosecutions, to inquire into specific offences or categories of offences. A special unit in the office of the KwaZulu-Natal DPP is looking into cases of political violence and has taken up some of the cases previously investigated by the ITU. On 1 September 1999, a Directorate of Special Investigations in the office of the NDPP was launched, comprising police, prosecutors and intelligence agents, with a brief to look into organised crime, corruption in the criminal justice system and crimes against the state.

[31] South African Police Service Act, section 53(6)(e) and (f), by contrast, if a docket has not been submitted to an attorney-general from an internal investigation, the ICD need only act "after consultation with the member heading the investigation".

[32] *Ibid.*, section 53(6)(g) (I) and (j).

published instead as regulations.[33] The most important change from the previous system is that disciplinary charges are now decided on the balance of probabilities, rather than the criminal standard of beyond reasonable doubt. In other regards, the new regulations retain the old system of a court-like procedure staffed by police officers, with an appeal system entirely within the police service, though due process protections for an officer charged with misconduct are improved. Neither the Independent Complaints Directorate nor any other external body has any role in disciplinary proceedings: although the ICD is mentioned as one possible source of a recommendation that disciplinary proceedings be instituted, it has no right to require that a disciplinary hearing be held, nor to speak at any hearing.[34] The disciplinary officer who hears a case may call witnesses, who presumably may include members of the ICD, but there is no requirement for him or her to do so even if the proceedings are commenced on the recommendation of the ICD.

Misconduct as defined in the regulations relates mostly to interaction with other members of the police service and to internal disciplinary matters. The only section dealing directly with use of force against non members of the service states that it is misconduct if an employee "uses unlawful force against a prisoner or other person in custody or otherwise illtreats such person";[35] the use of unlawful force against persons not in custody is not explicitly covered, though committing any act which constitutes a criminal offence and failing to comply with a police code of conduct are also disciplinary offences. New instructions were issued to the police in January 1997 restricting the use of firearms and force against suspected criminals, and the law regulating arrest was amended in December 1998 to restrict the use of deadly force to situations when loss of life or serious injury is threatened—though the implementation of the law was delayed in the face of police resistance.[36]

[33] South African Police Service Discipline Regulations, No. R. 2086, 27 December 1996 (*Government Gazette* Vol. 378, No. 17682). Entry into force 1 January 1997.

[34] Regulation 9(1) states: "A disciplinary officer or official, as the case may be, may upon receipt of the report contemplated in regulation 8(3)(iii), 8(3)(b)(iv) or 8(5)(d) [relating to an investigation as to whether misconduct has occurred] or upon receipt of a complaint by any person or recommendation from the Independent Complaints Directorate, an attorney-general or a public prosecutor that disciplinary proceedings be instituted against an employee—(a) charge an employee with misconduct, by serving on him or her a notice in the form determined by the National Commissioner; or (b) refuse to charge an employee with misconduct: Provided that the decision to refuse may only be taken over after consulting with the person who submitted the report, lodged the complaint or Executive Director of the Independent Complaints Directorate, as the case may be".

[35] Regulation 18(23).

[36] The Judicial Matters Second Amendment Act, No. 122 of 1998, amended section 49 of the Criminal Procedure Act, No.51 of 1977, which had permitted use of lethal force by the police in circumstances when no life was otherwise at risk, to allow the use of "such force as may be reasonably necessary and proportional in the circumstances" while specifying that deadly force may only be used based on the reasonable belief that the force is necessary to prevent death or serious injury. In July 1999, following South Africa's second all-race general elections, new Minister for Safety and Security Steve Tshwete stated, adopting a tough "law and order" image, that the amendment to section 49 might be reconsidered since it had been "rushed through parliament" and might hamper police in the fight against crime (SAPA, 14 July 1999).

The ICD has itself adopted a range of documents establishing internal standard operating procedures in relation to, among other things, recording and reporting information, carrying out investigations and making investigative findings and recommendations, procedures for arrest, search and seizure, and the methods by which the SAPS should notify the ICD of a death. The SAPS has also adopted and distributed instructions regarding interactions with the ICD.[37]

## THE WORK OF THE ICD

On 7 August 1996, the Secretary for Safety and Security, Azhar Cachalia, announced the appointment of Neville Melville, formerly Police Reporting Officer for KwaZulu-Natal, as executive director of the ICD, following approval by both Cabinet and the parliamentary committees on safety and security, as required by the Act. Melville assumed his duties on 19 August 1996, though the ICD itself formally began to operate only in April 1997; the intervening months were used to collect information on similar bodies in other countries, to devise a structure for the ICD, to arrange for accommodation, and to advertise and appoint the new positions.[38] A "strategic plan" for the development of the ICD was prepared, in which the executive director stated that his three basic objectives would be:

> to provide a credible and efficient mechanism for the investigation and prevention of misconduct within the service; to assist in transforming the service into a body which deserves and receives the respect and support of the community; [and] to provide the service with a management tool which will enable it to control misconduct within its ranks.[39]

Tensions between the nascent ICD and the SAPS were immediately apparent, not least because the ICD as yet had no budget, and so depended on the SAPS for funding and logistical assistance—compromising its role as an independent body. There were conflicts over the arrangement of accommodation (which the SAPS had promised to provide, but which the ICD eventually arranged for itself through the Department of Public Works) and furniture, and over the "start up" budget of R.1.5 million advanced to the ICD from the SAPS.[40] Two police officers were initially seconded to the ICD, and a third loaned on an ad hoc basis; several senior officers were also nominated to assist with the establishment of

[37] *Report of the Independent Complaints Directorate to the Parliamentary Committee on Safety and Security*, 2 March 1999. This report and many other submissions to Parliament on the role of the ICD and reform of the police generally are available through the website of the Parliamentary Monitoring Group, a joint venture of several South African NGOs, at <www.pmg.org.za>.

[38] *Media Release by the Secretary for Safety and Security, Mr Azhar Cachalia, on the Appointment of the Head of the Independent Complaints Directorate*, 7 August 1996; Independent Complaints Directorate, *Annual Report 1996/97*. Melville resigned as executive director with effect from 1 May 2000, in order to become Banking Adjudicator. No new director had yet been appointed as this book went to press

[39] Independent Complaints Directorate, "Strategic Plan: First Draft", October 1996.

[40] At the end of March 1997, the rand/dollar exchange rate was 4.41 rands to one US dollar. As of early September 1999, the rate was 6.02 rands to a dollar.

the ICD while remaining charged with their existing responsibilities. The executive director of the ICD was unhappy with this arrangement, but his proposal that he be allowed to hire outsiders to assist was rejected, and instead a new "project team" was assembled from the various SAPS departments. In addition, the SAPS undertook to lend seventy members to the ICD at police expense to make up the complement of investigators on 1 April 1997, but at late notice, the ICD was informed that the SAPS would not after all bear the cost of these staff. The ICD's own budget could pay for no more than thirty-six investigators. The ICD noted that it had "commenced operations on its deadline date in spite of, rather than due to, the assistance of the SAPS".[41]

A national office and three regional offices were established first, in Pretoria, Johannesburg, Cape Town and Durban, which all began operations on 1 April 1997, though the national headquarters only moved into permanent accommodation in Pretoria during 1998. A further four offices were established in the course of 1998, but the last remaining two offices, in the provinces of Mpumalanga and Free State, had yet to be established, for budgetary reasons, by March 1999; in Bloemfontein, the capital of the Free State, two members of the SAPS were seconded to assist the ICD as investigators, working out of the SAPS' own premises.[42] The budget for 1997–8, the first full year of operations, was R.15,511,000, and for 1998–9 R.27,760,000. In March 1999, the budget for the coming year was approved by Parliament at only R.23,983,000; it was projected to increase to R.26,045,000 by 2000–1.[43]

Due to difficulties with SAPS personnel initially seconded to work with the ICD, it was decided to recruit civilian investigators from scratch (though including former police officers). The first investigator posts were filled in September 1997.[44] A total personnel structure of five hundred and thirty-five, including three hundred and thirty-nine investigators, was approved by the Department of Public Service and Administration, following a study into the needs of the ICD if it were to carry out its functions properly. However, the budget only supports in practice one hundred and forty-nine staff, of whom eighty are "line functionaries", carrying out the substantive work of investigation and monitoring; thirty-seven of these carry out the ICD's own investigations. The ICD divides its investigators into two types: field investigators, who secure and

[41] Independent Complaints Directorate, *Annual Report 1996/97*.

[42] Independent Complaints Directorate, *Annual Report 1997/98* (Pretoria, Independent Complaints Directorate, 1998); *Report of the Independent Complaints Directorate to the Parliamentary Committee on Safety and Security*, 19 May 1998; *Report of the Independent Complaints Directorate to the Parliamentary Committee on Safety and Security*, 2 March 1999; *Minutes of the Joint Meeting of the Parliamentary Committees on Safety and Security and Justice*, 2 March 1999.

[43] *Report of the Independent Complaints Directorate to the Parliamentary Committee on Safety and Security*, 19 May 1998; *Report of the Independent Complaints Directorate to the Parliamentary Committee on Safety and Security*, 2 March 1999.

[44] Neville Melville, *Report of the Independent Complaints Directorate to the Parliamentary Committee on Safety and Security*, 19 May 1998; author's interview with Neville Melville, ICD executive director, 7 May 1998.

protect crime scenes and obtain and preserve evidence; and supervisory investigators, most of whom have legal training, who assist and give directions to the field investigators for the gathering of evidence and conduct of investigations. Despite staffing problems, the ICD has managed to establish a system of standby cover, ensuring that each office always has two investigators available on a twenty-four hour basis to respond to notifications of deaths.[45]

## STATISTICS, CLASSIFICATION AND ACTION

Prior to the establishment of the ICD, statistics relating to deaths in custody were hard to come by and contradictory in nature.[46] Immediately it began operations, the requirement that the ICD be informed of deaths in custody or as a result of police action began to generate statistics. In 1995, the last year before the ICD began operating for which official statistics are available, two hundred and twenty-six deaths in custody or as a result of police action were recorded by the police.[47] Immediately the ICD started operation, the reported figures showed a threefold increase. The ICD's second annual report recorded seven hundred and thirty-seven deaths for the year April 1997 to March 1998.[48] During its second full year in operation, from April 1998 to March 1999, the ICD received seven hundred and fifty-six reports of deaths.[49]

[45] Independent Complaints Directorate, *Annual Report 1997/98*; *Report of the Independent Complaints Directorate to the Parliamentary Committee on Safety and Security*, 2 March 1999.

[46] The most detailed record of reported deaths was kept by the Human Rights Commission (now the Human Rights Committee), a national NGO, but until the early 1990s the HRC's reports noted only deaths of those held under security legislation or in political circumstances. In 1990, the HRC recorded that there had been at least seventy-three deaths in detention since 1963, or one death for every one thousand detainees held under security legislation ("Deaths in Detention (HRC, August 1990)", in Coleman (ed.), *A Crime Against Humanity*). The HRC noted ten deaths "in police custody in politically related circumstances" in 1991; one hundred and twenty-three deaths in police custody (i.e. "deaths which occurred while or after being apprehended, during interrogation or while being held in police cells") in 1992; thirty-nine deaths in police custody in 1993; and thirty-two deaths in police custody in 1994. The extent to which the HRC's monitoring, based on press stories and other independent information, may have under-reported the true extent of deaths in custody was demonstrated in 1995, when the HRC, seeking to confirm a figure of twenty-three deaths in custody gleaned from independent sources, was told by the police that five hundred and seven had died in police custody by the end of September. Although the police later revised this figure down to one hundred and sixty-eight, the HRC in the 1995 *Human Rights Review* also reported that the figure for 1994 had been revised upward to three hundred and seventy-nine, based on police figures. Human Rights Commission, *Human Rights Review* 1991, 1992, 1993, 1994 and 1995; Human Rights Committee Press Release, 26 October 1995; SAPS Press Release, 27 October 1995. See also, Africa Watch, *Prison Conditions in South Africa* (New York, Human Rights Watch, January 1994); Paul Gready, "Public accountability needed for deaths in police custody", in *Rights* (Pretoria, Lawyers for Human Rights, September 1994).

[47] "Establishment of the Independent Complaints Directorate: Progress Report, 15 May 1996," paragraph 7.1. Statistics for 1996 have never been made available by the police: author's interview with Neville Melville, executive director of the ICD, 29 March 1999.

[48] Independent Complaints Directorate, *Annual Report 1997/98*, Table 1, p.12.

[49] Provisional statistical tables for the year April 1998 to March 1999 supplied by the ICD to the author by email, 1 July 1999. The tables supplied contained some obvious inaccuracies which have

The cases within the mandate of the ICD do not relate only to deaths in custody or as a result of police action, but also to general complaints by the public of police misconduct—though it is only in the case of deaths that the police are obliged to inform the ICD. From April 1997 to March 1998, the ICD received one thousand nine hundred and ninety-nine complaints; from April 1998 to March 1999 the ICD received two thousand eight hundred and seventy-four complaints, representing a forty-four per cent increase on the figure for the equivalent period the previous year.[50] The police themselves receive some twenty thousand complaints directly, and investigate them internally, each year.[51]

In order to prioritise among the cases referred to it, the ICD has established a system for classifying cases into five classes. A Class I case is one which alleges that a death occurred while a person was in police custody or as a result of police action. Class II cases are those referred to the ICD by the minister or by a provincial executive (a small percentage of the total). Class III cases are those which allege that a member of the police committed a serious offence, including torture, rape, serious corruption, or instigating or failing to prevent violence, or that serious injury requiring hospitalisation occurred while a person was in police custody or as a result of police action. Class IV cases are those which allege that a member committed an offence other than those listed for Class III cases, or misconduct which did not result in death or serious injury. Class I cases are required by the act to be directly investigated by ICD staff; Class II cases should normally be investigated by ICD staff, but may after consultation with the minister or provincial executive be referred to the SAPS for investigation with ICD monitoring; Class III cases may either be investigated by the ICD or referred to the SAPS, though in practice most are referred unless there is a very good chance of securing an immediate result through ICD intervention; Class IV cases are ordinarily referred to the SAPS for investigation, with ICD monitoring.[52] During its first year, the ICD also introduced a fifth class: Class V cases are those that do not fall within the mandate of the ICD and are referred to other bodies. In practice, due to lack of capacity, not even one hundred per cent of death cases are investigated by the ICD: of the total one thousand two hundred and ninety-two deaths, or Class I cases, reported from start up in April 1997 to December 1998, the ICD itself "actively" investigated nine hundred and twenty-eight cases.[53]

been corrected as seemed most logical; the numbers given here for this year may not, however, be the final official figures.

[50] Independent Complaints Directorate, *Annual Report 1997/98*; provisional statistical tables for the year April 1998 to March 1999.

[51] According to police statistics, nineteen thousand nine hundred and seventy-four complaints were internally investigated in 1995. "Establishment of the Independent Complaints Directorate: Progress Report, 15 May 1996", paragraph 7.2. At least one thousand police officers are engaged in investigating these complaints. Independent Complaints Directorate, *Annual Report 1996/97*.

[52] Independent Complaints Directorate, *Annual Report 1996/97* and *Annual Report 1997/98*; author's interview with Julian Snitcher, ICD head of investigations, 29 March 1999.

[53] *Report of the Independent Complaints Directorate to the Parliamentary Committee on Safety and Security*, 2 March 1999.

Of the 1,999 complaints received from April 1997 to March 1998, seven hundred and thirty-seven (thirty-seven per cent) were Class I cases, relating to deaths in custody or as a result of police action. Of these, two hundred and nineteen (thirty per cent) were deaths in custody: twenty-five from "natural causes", seventy suicide, forty-five injuries in custody, thirty-two injuries prior to custody, and forty-seven "possible negligence". Four hundred and seventeen complaints were categorised Class III, of which one hundred and fifty-seven related to serious assault or attempted murder, sixty-eight to torture, and ten to rape; seven hundred and twenty were Class IV cases. Of the total two thousand eight hundred and seventy-four complaints received from April 1998 to March 1999, seven hundred and fifty-six (twenty-seven per cent) were Class I cases. Of these, one hundred and ninety-eight (twenty-six per cent) were deaths in custody: sixty-eight from "natural causes", forty-five suicide, twelve injuries in custody, fifty-three injuries prior to custody, and twenty "possible negligence". Over the same period the ICD noted six hundred and forty-one Class III complaints, of which three hundred and nineteen were cases of serious assault or attempted murder allegedly committed by members of the police, fifty-six cases of torture and fifteen cases of rape. One thousand one hundred and seventy-three cases, or forty per cent of the total, were Class IV complaints.[54]

After investigating the cases, the ICD makes a determination as to whether the case is substantiated, meaning that it is more likely than not that an offence has been committed, in which case the matter is referred for further action, either to the Director of Public Prosecutions with a recommendation to prosecute or order a formal inquest, or to the police with a recommendation to conduct a disciplinary hearing. Other possible conclusions are that the complaint is unsubstantiated (not enough evidence to take further action); unfounded (in the rare case where the ICD believes that the complaint is definitely false); dismissed (where there is no cooperation from the complainant, or the complainant cannot be traced); or withdrawn (on the complainant's request).[55]

From April 1997 to January 1999, the ICD finalised about one thousand six hundred and eighty-eight cases. Of three hundred and nineteen cases referred to the various attorneys-general or directors of public prosecution (DPPs), decisions to prosecute had been made in seventy cases by March 1999; thirty had been successfully prosecuted, resulting in convictions ranging from murder to common assault; twenty resulted in acquittals. In another eighty-three cases the attorneys-general or DPPs ordered the holding of inquests. Other matters have been referred to internal SAPS disciplinary proceedings, of which thirty-eight cases had been heard by March 1999, resulting in eleven convictions for misconduct. Another one hundred and eight cases were resolved through

[54] Independent Complaints Directorate, *Annual Report 1997/98*, Tables 1 and 2, pp. 12–13; provisional statistical tables for the year April 1998 to March 1999.

[55] Author's interview with Neville Melville, ICD executive director, 29 March 1999.

mediation.[56] In early 1999, the ICD secured its first conviction on a case investigated from scratch by itself, when a KwaZulu-Natal policeman was found guilty of murder in connection with the shooting in custody of a detainee.[57]

Due to lack of computerisation and in-house statistical skills the ICD has not to date been able to provide a systematic breakdown of the complaints received into categories more detailed than the overall classification; for example, to identify particular police stations or particular types of complainant. A computerisation programme had just been completed (with some technical difficulties outstanding) in late March 1999.[58] Nevertheless, the statistics already available have confirmed the utility of a body such as the ICD, creating, as they have been released, an awareness of the scale of the problem of deaths caused by the police, and hence also increasing the possibility of firm action to reduce the numbers of deaths in future.

In addition to its more routine activities, the ICD has carried out special investigations into a number of high-profile cases concerning police failure to carry out a proper investigation into another crime. These include the police investigation of the shooting of baby Angelina Zwane by a white farmer in April 1998, when the police took several days to arrest the farmer (and the ICD recommended that two officers face disciplinary charges for poor investigation procedures); the alleged police involvement in and failure to take proper action against political violence in the Richmond area of the KwaZulu-Natal midlands; and, before the ICD was even formally established, the police handling of the reported rape of Nomboniso Gasa, member of the national Commission on Gender Equality, by guards on Robben Island in January 1997. The ICD has issued ad hoc reports on these incidents, confirming, for example, in the case of Nomboniso Gasa that:

> there is prima facie evidence of improper conduct and/or insensitivity displayed towards the complainant by at least one or more of the members comprising the initial investigating team

and that:

> there is prima facie evidence of negligence and/or dereliction of duty on the part of members of the initial investigating team in the manner in which the investigation was handled.

The ICD recommended that the officers concerned be reprimanded, and made quite extensive recommendations regarding the handling of sexual offences in future.[59] In other cases, too, the ICD has made general as well as specific re-

[56] *Report of the Independent Complaints Directorate to the Parliamentary Committee on Safety and Security*, 2 March 1999.

[57] *Ibid.*; author's interview with Julian Snitcher, ICD head of investigations, 29 March 1999.

[58] Author's interviews with Neville Melville, executive director, ICD and Julian Snitcher, head of investigations, ICD, 29 March 1999.

[59] Independent Complaints Directorate, *Executive Summary*, 27 March 1997.

commendations; for example, that the police should be provided with concrete guidelines on their discretion to arrest or not to arrest suspects.[60]

## PROBLEMS FACED BY THE ICD IN PRACTICE

At the time the Police Act was drafted, a number of nongovernmental organisations made submissions to the drafting committee and to the National Assembly Committee on Safety and Security. These submissions centred on two points in particular: the ICD's lack of formal independence from the Minister for Safety and Security; and its lack of any substantive powers other than to make recommendations to the various authorities.[61]

The ICD itself identified in its first annual report a range of potential amendments to the existing legislation to address shortcomings, starting from the drafting of separate legislation to establish the ICD, rather than including it in the overall Police Act. The ICD noted the need for the ICD to have powers to institute its own prosecutions, in the event of the Attorney-General refusing to prosecute; to be protected from civil liability in relation to the acts of its employees; to be able to recommend that, if an investigation is referred to the SAPS, it be handled by a specific investigator or that a particular investigator be replaced; to be able to safeguard its information; to have the cooperation of the National Defence Force where the army is acting with the police; to have access to alternative dispute resolution procedures; to be notified of all civil actions against the SAPS; to compel a member of the police to make a statement in non-criminal investigations; to have a means to enforce its recommendations, especially in relation to disciplinary proceedings; and to have unrestricted access to police dockets and other information.[62] In July 1999, the ICD produced a discussion document raising these and other issues, in the hope of getting them addressed in a government White Paper.[63]

To some extent, the ICD's greatest obstacle is that of public attitudes towards police abuse of suspects, who are largely presumed guilty from the moment of arrest. When a BBC television programme showed members of the Brixton Flying Squad and Langlaagte Dog Unit brutally assaulting suspected car hijackers and car thieves (one of whom later died in hospital) in two separate incidents, and the ICD subsequently recommended prosecution of twenty-two

[60] Human Rights Committee, *Human Rights Report, July 1998*.

[61] For a more detailed critique of the legislation, see Bronwen Manby, "The Independent Complaints Directorate: An Opportunity Wasted?", 12 *South African Journal on Human Rights* (1996) 419.

[62] Independent Complaints Directorate, *Annual Report 1996/97*.

[63] Independent Complaints Directorate, *Towards an ICD White Paper* (Pretoria, ICD, July 1999). The October 1998 report of the Truth and Reconciliation Commission also recommended new legislation to govern the ICD and that it be made genuinely independent of the Ministry for Safety and Security.

policemen for assault with intent to do grievous bodily harm, the public outcry was against the ICD, not the police concerned.[64]

## Independence

According to the Police Act, the ICD falls under the political authority of the Minister for Safety and Security and is subject to the minister's decisions in important respects. The executive director of the ICD is to be appointed by the minister, subject to formal approval of the choice by a simple majority of the committees responsible for safety and security in the National Assembly and National Council of Provinces. The only requirement that the minister must observe is that the director must be "suitably qualified", raising the possibility that he or she could be, for example, a former or even current police officer. The director can be removed by the minister "under the circumstances and in the manner prescribed by the Minister in consultation with the Parliamentary Committees". The director must be reappointed every five years, allowing his or her effective removal even without such a procedure.[65] Regulations drafted by the ministry govern much of the operation of the ICD in practice. The ICD reports to the minister, who in turn must table its reports in Parliament.

In practice, there has been no direct interference in the work of the ICD, and the fears raised by the legislation relate rather to the public perception that the ICD is not fully independent of the police and to possible future interference. In numerous cases, press coverage refers, for example, to "the police's ICD". The requirement to go through the minister to confirm appointments and for other tasks has caused delays on some occasions; especially since in practice the ICD has to go through the civilian secretariat to reach the minister.[66] Members of the ICD feel that the minister has been unable to give the institution his full political support, since he is also directly responsible for the police, and therefore would prefer it to be a free-standing body reporting directly to parliament, in the manner of the Human Rights Commission or the other "state institutions supporting constitutional democracy" established under chapter nine of the constitution.

There has also been some lack of clarity about the different mandates of the secretariat and the ICD. In general, the secretariat's responsibility is to assist the minister to oversee broad policy and performance issues; the ICD's role is to consider individual cases involving allegations of misconduct. However, the distinction is not necessarily clear cut: in the course of investigating individual

[64] SAPA, 26–30 April and 19 May 1999.

[65] The appointment and removal procedures are contained in section 51 of the Act. The technical committee responsible for drafting the police act also drafted procedures for appointment of the director which provided for public nominations for the post of director, from which a committee composed of representatives of the minister, police commissioner and parliamentary committees would select the final candidate.

[66] Author's interview with Neville Melville, ICD executive director, 29 March 1999.

cases, the ICD naturally comes to views about general policy matters, and to fail to address them in its recommendations would be to lose that expertise and information. As the ICD noted in its second annual report:

> For an oversight body to be really effective in bringing about the desired changes in police culture and practices, it is essential that it also have the capacity to identify underlying systemic problems.[67]

There has reportedly been some tension with the secretariat over the ICD's expressed intention to expand its recommendation-making and monitoring activities. On occasion, however, the secretariat has intervened to resolve problems between the ICD and the SAPS.

At a practical level, the ICD lacks independence from the police in some crucial areas, in particular relying heavily on the SAPS to obtain forensic medical and ballistic evidence. The only full forensic laboratory services in the country are run by the police. Autopsies are carried out by state pathologists employed by the Department of Health, but mortuaries, though they are under the formal control of the Department of Health, are staffed by police technicians—increasing the likelihood of breaches of security where post-mortems are of victims killed by the police. It can take up to eight months for the results of ballistic tests to be returned to the ICD, and up to six months for post-mortem reports in some locations. Attempts are being made to ensure that ICD cases receive priority treatment, so that allegations of police misconduct can be resolved as soon as possible; in the long run, subject to funding, the ICD intends to establish an independent forensic capacity.[68]

The September 1998 White Paper on Safety and Security did not address any of these concerns regarding the independence of the ICD, simply stating that "The ICD functions independently of the Department of Safety and Security and reports directly to the Minister of Safety and Security".[69] As noted by the executive director of the ICD in a submission on the draft White Paper, but apparently ignored by the drafters in producing the final version, the document:

> failed to address the vexed question regarding the appropriateness of the existing location of the ICD within the Ministry of Safety and Security at all.[70]

[67] Independent Complaints Directorate, *Annual Report 1997/98*, paragraph 2.1.4.

[68] *Report of the Independent Complaints Directorate to the Parliamentary Committee on Safety and Security*, 2 March 1999; author's interview with Julian Snitcher, director of investigations, ICD, 29 March 1999. See also, "South Africa: Violence Against Women and the Medico-Legal System," *A Human Rights Watch Short Report*, Vol. 9, No. 4(A), August 1997, for a fuller discussion of medico-legal services in South Africa.

[69] White Paper on Safety and Security, September 1998, Section IV.

[70] Neville Melville, *Independent Complaints Directorate Submission on the White Paper on Safety and Security*, 31 July 1998.

**Lack of co-operation from the police**

Although state bodies are required by the Police Act to give assistance to the ICD, the legislation sets out no penalty for failure to cooperate (only for "wilful interference" with the exercise of its duties). In general, the ICD reports that co-operation from the police has been satisfactory at management level since it began operations in April 1997; but in May 1997, Neville Melville, executive director of the ICD, noted that the new monitoring body had met with "passive obstruction and closing of ranks at some police stations".[71] A year later, he stated that police were by and large cooperative with the ICD, but that there were "pockets of resistance" and some officers were "downright obstructive".[72] At the same time, some senior officers still appeared to be ignorant of the ICD's existence.[73] In August 1999, these problems still persisted. There is no explicit legal protection for members of the ICD acting in good faith to carry out their duties, and at least one investigator has been charged with obstructing the police.[74]

The initial police response to the ICD's statistics on deaths in custody or as a result of police action was to refer to the "background of South Africa's culture of killer crime" and the high number of SAPS members killed every year, stating that "most deaths in custody result from factors other than police negligence or direct action".[75] When the ICD released a report compiled for it by three independent organisations, suggesting that the police were possibly responsible for an escalation of violence due to the tactics they used, the national police commissioner again referred to the:

> violent environment in which [the police] have to perform their duties, and the abnormal rate of fatal and brutal attacks on police officials in South Africa.[76]

The study showed, however, that in the majority of cases where suspects had been killed or died in custody, there was no suggestion that the police had been under threat.[77]

[71] Tangeni Amupadhi, "Deaths at police hands are rising," *Mail and Guardian*, 23–29 May 1997.

[72] Independent Complaints Directorate, *Annual Report 1997/98*, paragraph 1.3.15.

[73] Author's interview with Neville Melville, 7 May 1998.

[74] *Towards an ICD White Paper*, section 3.4.

[75] *Media Statement by the National Commissioner of the SA Police Service: Commissioner George Fivaz*, Pretoria, 21 May 1998.

[76] *Media Statement by the National Commissioner of the SA Police Service: Commissioner George Fivaz*, Pretoria, 6 July 1998.

[77] Fifty-nine of one hundred and sixty-nine deaths investigated involved "the death of a person deemed to pose an immediate threat". But even in these cases, the existence of a threat was based only on information supplied by the police in the docket and not on an independent determination that, for example, the person shot had in fact been armed as alleged. David Bruce, Ian Liebenberg and Ros Atkins, *Towards a Strategy for Prevention: The occurrence of deaths in police custody or as a result of police action in Gauteng, April-December 1997* (Johannesburg and Pretoria, Centre for the Study of Violence and Reconciliation, the Centre for Policy Studies and the Human Sciences Research Council, July 1998).

The ICD has had problems in getting the SAPS to refer cases of deaths in police custody or as a result of police action to it as soon as they become known. The police act only requires that the ICD be informed of deaths but does not set a time within which the information must be given. In practice, just a few hours delay can allow the trail of evidence to go cold or be tampered with. The ICD has agreed procedures with the police for it to be informed immediately, by fax and phone, when a death occurs, but these procedures are not always followed. Some cases have not been referred at all, but only discovered by the ICD through media or other reports.[78]

In addition, the problems of gaining access to criminal investigation dockets previously experienced by the PROs have resurfaced, though to a lesser extent, for the ICD. Although in general the police have allowed the ICD to see the docket, in some cases it has taken the intervention of the Attorney-General/ Director of Public Prosecutions to gain access. In other cases the Attorney-General/DPP him or herself, who is not required by the Act to allow the ICD to see a docket in his possession, has refused to give access when the investigation concerns police failure to act properly in relation to another crime, rather than an assault or death carried out by the police themselves. In the case of failure of the police to arrest the farmer who shot baby Angelina Zwane, for example, Transvaal Attorney-General Jan D'Oliviera stated that handing over the docket could compromise his own investigation, and the ICD completed its work without seeing the complete police docket.[79]

In a high profile case in which police allegedly shot dead an escaped suspect, Josiah "Fingers" Rabotapi, amid suspicions that he may have been silenced to prevent him revealing police complicity in his crimes, the police only allowed the ICD access to the premises where the shooting occurred fifteen hours later. The officers alleged to be responsible for the shooting refused even to be interviewed by the ICD when it stated that it could not give guarantees that they would not be prosecuted, instead submitting written statements through their lawyers.[80] Following an investigation, in which serious doubt was cast on the police version of the incident, the ICD recommended that a formal inquest take place on the death and that the case be referred to the Director of Public Prosecutions.[81] An inquest was in fact ordered.[82]

[78] Author's interviews with Neville Melville, ICD executive director, 7 May 1998 and 29 March 1999; Riaz Saloojee, ICD regional director, Western Cape, 7 May 1998 and 1 April 1999; Shadrack Mahlangu, ICD regional director, Gauteng, 14 May 1998; and Julian Snitcher, head of investigations, ICD, 29 March 1999.

[79] Author's interview with Neville Melville, ICD executive director, 29 March 1999.

[80] Tangeni Amupadhi, "Secrets die with Fingers", *Mail and Guardian*, 21 to 27 August 1998; Tangeni Amupadhi, "Beukes admitted to wrongful killing of suspect", *Mail and Guardian*, 4 to 10 September 1998; author's interview with Julian Snitcher, ICD head of investigations, 29 March 1999. At the time of his death, Rabotapi was facing forty-three charges: seventeen for murder, twenty-two armed robberies, one rape, and three escapes. Beukes himself was not present in the room at the time of the shooting.

[81] ICD, "Executive Summary" of investigation into the Rabotapi case, November 1998; Human Rights Committee, *Human Rights Report, November 1998.*

[82] Letter from Neville Melville, executive director ICD, to the author, 4 May 1999.

Neville Melville, executive director of the ICD, had regular meetings with George Fivaz, national police commissioner, or with his deputies, about ongoing problems, which were constructive. Melville's personal style was much less confrontational than that of, for example, Jan Munnik, PRO for the Witwatersrand, which may have preserved better relations in general between the ICD and the SAPS and bore fruit in terms of police cooperation in some cases. However, lawyers working on cases against the police believe that more could have been achieved by asserting a higher profile for the organisation, confronting the police in more cases, and taking initiatives to tackle systemic patterns of abuse, rather than waiting for cases to be reported. Within the ICD, a form has been developed to report cases where police cooperation has not been sufficient, and these forms are regularly referred to the national police commissioner for his attention.

Unusually among similar bodies, but perhaps due to the singular history of the SAPS, the ICD has established generally good relations with the two main police unions, the South African Police Union (SAPU), largely representing senior, white officers from the old order, and the Police and Prisons Civil Rights Union (POPCRU), largely representing junior, black policemen and women. Neither union has obstructed the work of the ICD, and both unions have come forward with complaints for the ICD to investigate—often against members of the other union. Rank-and-file police officers have also come to appreciate that the ICD's independence in investigating can be useful to them: in some cases, police have come forward immediately after cases of fatal shootings asking the ICD to clear their names and indicate that force was reasonably used.[83]

Nevertheless, there have been continuing problems including a rise in police obstruction of the ICD's work. For example, police refused to appear on identity parades or to make statements following a March 1999 arrest, carried out by the ICD on its own account of a police officer in the Western Cape alleged to have committed a serious assault.[84] When the Western Cape ICD arrested a police officer in May 1999 on murder charges for shooting a fleeing robbery suspect at close range, up to three hundred policemen and women packed the court at his bail hearing, and later handed ninety-three spent bullet cartridges to the ICD's Cape Town offices, symbolising one for each police officer shot dead in South Africa that year.[85]

### Lack of powers

Closely related to the lack of cooperation from the police, is the ICD's lack of formal powers in many areas. In particular, and unlike institutions such as the

[83] Author's interview with Riaz Saloojee, ICD Western Cape regional director, 1 April 1999.

[84] Author's interviews with Neville Melville, ICD executive director, 29 March 1999, and Riaz Saloojee, ICD, regional director, Western Cape, 1 April 1999. Although the ICD had arrested police officers on previous occasions, the arrest in question was the first one of a white officer, provoking a much stronger response from the police hierarchy.

[85] SAPA 24 May, 27 May, and 3 June 1999.

Human Rights Commission or the National Prosecuting Authority—or many civilian bodies with oversight of complaints against the police in other countries, the ICD does not have the explicit power to subpoena witnesses or to carry out search and seizure. Although designated members of the ICD have the powers of police officers and can therefore subpoena witnesses under the Criminal Procedure Act, the lack of specific powers tailored to the ICD's work has in practice caused problems from individuals who have chosen to defy the ICD's authority. In a few cases, including the Rabotapi case mentioned above, the ICD has not been able to compel officers who are witnesses or suspects to make statements to it. Under the South African Constitution every person has the right not to be compelled to give self-incriminating evidence. This means that police officers suspected of committing an offence could not be compelled to give a statement which might later be used against them in a criminal trial; though they could be compelled if the information were only to be used in disciplinary proceedings.[86] The ICD believes that members of the police should at least be required to attend a meeting and be interviewed, even if they come with a legal representative and choose not to answer particular questions; and that witness officers not themselves accused of an offence should be required to make a statement.[87]

In addition, although the ICD is free to obtain a court warrant to search premises, it has no automatic right, for example, to enter a police station unannounced. While the ICD acknowledges that private premises should have the protection of the courts from arbitrary invasions of privacy, its work does require the power to carry out searches of government premises without warrant, in order to discover, for example, electric shock equipment being used against detainees. Detailed powers of this type are given to the Human Rights Commission under its statute (Act No. 54 of 1994), though the Human Rights Commission is less likely to have need of them in the ordinary course of its work.

The ICD has not to date been able to monitor the implementation of its recommendations on a systematic basis, although it is in the process of establishing the capability to do so. No detailed information is therefore available on the overall level of police compliance, though in most cases the ICD believes that specific recommendations on particular cases, for example for disciplinary proceedings to be undertaken, have been followed. The Act does not require the police or others to respond to a recommendation from the ICD, and this has proved problematic especially in the case of general recommendations for policy changes. Sometimes recommendations have not been followed: for example, the police apparently failed to reprimand the two officers involved in the investigation of the rape of Nomboniso Gasa, as recommended by the ICD, and there have been cases in which senior police officers have refused to follow

86 Article 35(3)(j), Constitution of the Republic of South Africa, 1996.

87 Author's interview with Julian Snitcher, head of investigations, ICD, 29 March 1999.

recommendations to charge officers with disciplinary offences.[88] However, on at least one occasion a member of the ICD has been granted observer status at a disciplinary hearing.[89] Not only the police have failed to implement recommendations: Western Cape Attorney-General Frank Kahn refused to prosecute in a case of sexual harassment.[90]

The ICD would also like powers enabling it to deal with patterns of abuse as well as individual complaints or killings: for example, the power to hold public hearings about a particular situation or series of cases to highlight the problems, allow victims to testify, raise public consciousness, and examine systemic issues. While the ICD has in practice conciliated a number of cases, it is not specifically empowered to do so, and explicit provision of such a power would be useful. Finally, in order to lighten its load, the ICD would like discretion not to investigate all cases of deaths itself, but only those where there is some indication of police wrongdoing, and to supervise SAPS investigation of the rest.

### Resources

Perhaps the most serious problem facing the ICD is its lack of resources when faced with the size of its mandate. Thirty-seven investigators to look into approaching eight hundred deaths a year, quite aside from other cases allegedly involving serious crimes committed by the police, are clearly insufficient. Two provinces have no ICD office, and even in the provinces where offices of the ICD are functioning, logistical problems are substantial. From the Northern Cape office, based in Kimberley, to the furthest point in the province is one thousand five hundred kilometres, a car journey of some fourteen hours. At this distance it is impossible to require police to preserve a crime scene until an investigator from the ICD can arrive, and preliminary investigation has effectively to be delegated to a police officer on site.[91]

Though lawyers outside the ICD regard the statutory requirement for the ICD to investigate all deaths as essential for its credibility, some within the ICD see the requirement as problematic, since it means that it has been swamped in death investigations to the exclusion of other matters. During its first year, the directorate took the attitude that, already overwhelmed with work on deaths, it should engage in only minimal attempts to publicise its role with the general public. Some regional directors within the ICD took a different approach, travelling widely to brief local community policing forums and other bodies about

[88] "Fivaz 'too busy' for Gasa case", *Mail and Guardian*, 11 to 17 April 1997; *Towards an ICD White Paper*, section 3.4.

[89] Author's interview with Julian Snitcher, ICD head of investigations, 29 March 1999.

[90] Andy Duffy, "Row as Kahn lets off sex harassment cop", *Mail and Guardian*, 19 to 25 June 1998; Stuart Hess, "Constable to sue sex cop", *Mail and Guardian*, 10 to 16 July 1998.

[91] *Report of the Independent Complaints Directorate to the Parliamentary Committee on Safety and Security*, 2 March 1999; author's interview with Julian Snitcher, head of investigations, ICD, 29 March 1999.

the role of the ICD, and more efforts have recently been made at national level to raise the body's profile, including paid radio slots, distribution of posters and t-shirts, and the holding of open days. Nevertheless, public knowledge of the ICD is low: in 1998, the Community Agency for Social Enquiry (CASE), an NGO carrying out quantitative research on a range of social issues, conducted a survey in which one thousand two hundred respondents were asked where they would take a complaint against the police if they were assaulted. Not one of them mentioned the ICD.[92] However, the number of complaints being made to the ICD is increasing, suggesting that knowledge of the body is becoming more widespread.

The ICD has had difficulty in recruiting good quality investigators. After initial problems with seconded police, it has recruited its own investigators, who are generally either ex-police detectives, or lawyers with some experience of investigation, such as prosecutors. Others have investigative experience with the Truth and Reconciliation Commission, or with other government departments or organisations such as banks. Even in the case of former police, standards are such that experience as a detective need not mean that the person concerned has the necessary skills to investigate a murder case; nor do former police often come with the independence of mind necessary to challenge their erstwhile colleagues. Newly appointed and inexperienced investigators without a police background are also easily intimidated or misled. In one case, a lawyer with a great deal of experience in bringing civil actions against the police called the ICD in the case of a suspect who had been tortured in police cells by having a rubber surgical glove placed over his head, and his hands tied tightly behind him with electrical cable. The ICD investigator made no protest as police tightly handcuffed the prisoner, perhaps to obliterate the signs of tying, and refused to allow photographs to be taken.[93] Some of the few investigators with real experience are two or three police who were previously with the KwaZulu-Natal ITU.

The ICD is cognisant of the lack of investigation skills and has attempted to address the deficiency through training. The US Department of Justice International Criminal Investigation Training Assistance Program has given courses in basic investigation and basic homicide investigation. Some investigators have been sent on the recently upgraded police detective training course. In addition, management and legal training has been provided, as well as a two day

[92] Of those questioned, thirty per cent said that in case of assault by the police they would send the victim to the police for help, eight per cent to a lawyer, six per cent to a court of law, five per cent to the community, three per cent to the Minister of Justice, and twenty-nine per cent would not know what to do (thirty-three per cent in the rural areas). Piers Pigou, Ran Greenstein and Nahla Valji, "Assessing knowledge of human rights among the general population and selected target groups", Human Rights Awareness Report researched for the European Union Foundation for Human Rights (Johannesburg, Community Agency for Social Enquiry, November 1998).

[93] Author's interview with Peter Jordi, Wits Law Clinic, 31 March 1999. The investigator in question is no longer with the ICD. Letter from Neville Melville, ICD executive director, to the author, 4 May 1999.

programme by the KwaZulu-Natal-based NGO, the Independent Medico-Legal Unit, on medico-legal and forensic issues: at least ten training sessions and workshops have been provided altogether.[94] The British, Dutch and Danish Governments have also provided assistance in the form of training, seconded police officers, and other support.

The ICD also lacks some other important expertise. As of March 1999, the ICD did not have a skilled statistician to be able to produce detailed statistics surrounding the nature of complaints received, for example identifying the types of victims and alleged perpetrators. A computerisation project had just been completed which should allow the creation of such statistics in future, but problems were being experienced.[95] One of the main complaints of lawyers and others who have attempted to use the ICD procedures has been the lack of feedback as to the progress of their complaint. Although internal procedures exist requiring investigators to report back to the complainant every thirty days, the ICD has to date been unable to ensure that this requirement is met.[96]

## CONCLUSION

The South African Independent Complaints Directorate faces enormous obstacles in the effort to achieve greater police accountability. Although only one of the institutions created to increase civilian oversight of a previously unaccountable force, the ICD has to deal most directly with the daily consequences of that lack of accountability, charged as it is with the duty to investigate the seven hundred to eight hundred deaths a year at police hands and to monitor the investigation of the many other complaints of serious assault, torture, failure to investigate other crimes, or simple discourtesy and incompetence. The Constitution now grants all South Africans the full range of internationally recognised human rights in relation to maintenance of law and order and the ANC-led government has also implemented significant reforms to police governance and policy during its first five years. However, there is great public hostility to the idea of rights for alleged criminals, who are often presumed guilty, and in the context of the extraordinarily high rates of violence affecting the country a crackdown on crime is a priority for many South Africans. The ICD has argued, as human rights organisations have done, that effective investigation of crime requires an accountable police service and that innocent people have been killed because they have been mistakenly identified as criminals. As elsewhere in the world, however, calls for tougher policing are likely to result in greater police abuse, usually against those who are most easily stereotyped as

[94] Author's interview with Julian Snitcher, director of investigations, ICD, 29 March 1999.

[95] Author's interviews with Neville Melville, ICD executive director, and Julian Snitcher, head of investigations, 29 March 1999.

[96] Author's interview with Julian Snitcher, director of investigations, ICD, 29 March 1999.

trouble makers. The public statements made by the new administration that took office in June 1999 have done nothing to dispel these fears.

The ICD's budget is able to support fewer than forty investigators to handle the cases it directly investigates, almost entirely deaths in custody or as a result of police action; another forty staff are available to monitor police internal investigations of the hundreds of other complaints it receives. These represent a fraction of the personnel necessary for the ICD to be able to carry out its work effectively. Many investigators came to the ICD with no training or experience in a similar type of work. As a consequence, the ICD does not investigate itself even one hundred per cent of deaths at police hands, although it is under a statutory obligation to do so. Other serious complaints are virtually certain to be investigated by the police themselves, only distantly monitored by the ICD. The ICD lacks other crucial resources, such as an independent forensic capacity, forcing it to rely on police facilities. Without a substantial increase in the budgetary allocation to the ICD, unlikely given the many other calls on the government purse, it may be reduced simply to collecting statistics for the majority of cases falling within its mandate.

The legislation establishing the ICD is also deficient. Although it has operated independently in practice, the fact that the ICD is established by the act that also governs the police force, and is responsible to the Minister for Safety and Security, has led to the impression that it is not independent, that the minister has not given the body his full backing in confrontations with the police, and that it may be subject to ministerial interference in future. While new legislation could cure many of these problems, the constitutional status given the ICD in the interim but not the final constitution should also be restored, to entrench its independence. The lack of a separate act with specified powers has allowed individual police officers, with management connivance, to refuse to cooperate with ICD investigations in some cases. At a more detailed level, the ICD also needs legal powers, among other things, to conciliate complaints; to search police stations without a warrant; to require responses to its recommendations from the appropriate authorities; to require police officers not subject to investigation to make a statement in relation to investigations against their colleagues; and to have unrestricted access to police dockets.

In general, lawyers handling cases against the police state that the ICD has played a useful role, but that it is under-resourced and overwhelmed by the sheer numbers of complaints it has to process. There have been criticisms of the ICD's handling of particular cases, of its failure to report back to complainants on the progress of each case and to communicate its role to the public effectively, of the quality of investigations, and of a perceived failure to take decisive steps to crack down, for example, on the well-known use of torture at particular police stations. These criticisms are muted, however, by recognition of the huge task faced by the ICD and its resource constraints.

Despite its handicaps, the ICD has already achieved some important results, including investigations leading to the conviction of police officers for murder.

Above all, perhaps, in a hostile environment it has managed to gain broad acceptance for its role, and cooperation from the police in most cases it has investigated. Although it is difficult to evaluate its impact so far on police misconduct, the very fact that statistics on deaths in detention or as a result of police action now have to be kept is an important policy tool. Information about the sheer numbers of people killed by the police each year may gradually influence public thinking on the need for greater control over police behaviour. Once the ICD is set up to provide more detailed statistics, trends in police violence will become identifiable, allowing more detailed interventions by government and police management to solve problems, for example at particular police stations. Similarly, once the ICD can monitor the extent to which its recommendations are followed, it will also be able to target its own interventions more effectively.

The South African Independent Complaints Directorate has, despite the problems it faces, the potential to become an effective police accountability institution. Whether the ICD fulfils this potential will depend not only on its own efforts but also on the support of the government, in the form of additional resources, political support against police resistance to outside investigation, amendments to the legislation giving the ICD its powers, and continued reform of the police service itself.

# 10

# *Confronting a Culture of Impunity: The Promise and Pitfalls of Civilian Review of Police in Latin America*[1]

RACHEL NEILD

## INTRODUCTION

In recent years, civilian review bodies specifically mandated to monitor police misconduct have been created in Colombia, Brazil, and Argentina. Progress has been mixed. The Colombian civilian review board has since been closed, while in Brazil four further police auditors offices are being set up, modelled on the first experience in São Paulo.[2] Civilian review is a novel phenomenon in Latin America, but it is not without antecedent. Human rights ombudsmen's offices have been created in countries throughout the region, mostly during the transitions to democracy from military dictatorships or peace processes of the 1980s and 1990s.[3] These offices are typically mandated to receive complaints and investigate misconduct by all state authorities including the police.

There are a number of publications that describe the role and jurisprudence of ombudsmen's offices, but few evaluations and no comparative analyses of

[1] This paper draws heavily on a series of papers entitled *Themes and Debates in Public Security Reform; A Guide for Civil Society* published in English and Spanish by the Washington Office on Latin America (Washington DC, WOLA, 1998–9). I would also like to thank Professor Paul Chevigny of New York University, and my colleagues at WOLA, Kelly Josh, Winifred Tate, Geoff Thale, George Vickers, and Coletta Youngers for their comments and insights.

[2] The Brazilian states of Para, Minas Gerais, and Spirito Santo have created or are in the process of establishing similar offices; the federal government of Brazil is also creating an auditor for the federal police.

[3] Ombudsmen's offices were created in Puerto Rico (1977), Guatemala (1985), Mexico (1990), El Salvador (1991), Colombia (1991), Costa Rica (1992), Paraguay (1992), Honduras (1992), Peru (1993), Argentina (1993), Bolivia (1994), Nicaragua (1995), Ecuador (1996) and have or are being discussed in Venezuela, Panama and Uruguay. *Defensoría del Pueblo; Analisis Comparado*, (Comisión Andina de Juristas, Lima, 1996). Democratic transitions took place in Argentina (1983), Uruguay (1984), Chile (1989), Brazil (1989). While peace processes occurred in El Salvador (1992) and Guatemala (1996). Other countries, most notably the Andean countries of Colombia and Peru, have had elected civilian governments over the last two decades but with a high degree of military penetration of politics as the military fought internal guerrilla movements which posed serious threats to the state. During these internal conflicts, the military often ruled large parts of these countries under various states of exception which suspended civilian rule and constitutional guarantees. Some states of emergency lasted for decades.

either ombudsmen or civilian review bodies. In part, this is because of the short track record of many of these institutions. However, it may also reflect the varied, but overall limited success of civilian oversight in changing the human rights practices of Latin American governments to date. Nonetheless, these relatively new mechanisms to protect human rights clearly have a purpose and some momentum in Latin America. This paper will explore the factors driving the demand for and creation of civilian review of police, and attempt an analysis of how these bodies have functioned in the Latin American environment. What difficulties do they face and what potential do they offer?

The creation of mechanisms of civilian review of police in Latin America is intimately tied to the effort to exert civilian control over security functions during transitions to democracy. The activism of the Latin American human rights movement has played an important role in these processes and, in many instances, in the creation and track record of civilian review bodies.

This paper is divided into two sections. The first examines military-police relations and the genesis of human rights advocacy on issues of police misconduct and oversight. The paper then reviews four examples of civilian oversight or review of police in Latin America—El Salvador, Colombia, Argentina and São Paulo, Brazil. I do not pretend to offer an in-depth analysis of specific civilian control mechanisms here, but I believe that these four broad case studies offer insights into some criteria that appear key to the effective functioning of civilian oversight of police in Latin America. The paper closes with some conclusions about the problems and promise of civilian review in these challenging settings.

## THE CONTEXT FOR CIVILIAN REVIEW IN LATIN AMERICA

### The "Praetorian" State in Latin America

Military dominance of the state in Latin America goes back to the independence movements of the early 1800s. Independence was won by military operations headed by Creole elites opposed to Spanish rule. Thus militaries pre-existed national states and represented elite interests. Through two centuries of independence, most Latin American nations have experienced repeated cycles of military dictatorship and civilian government. This pattern continued as states begrudgingly expanded political and economic participation.

During the Cold War, confronted by the emergence of revolutionary movements, Latin American militaries developed "National Security Doctrines" which explicitly included in the mandate of the region's military forces the mission of protecting the state against internal ideological enemies. Under the authoritarian governments and during the civil conflicts of the 1970s and 1980s, national security doctrines guided military and police actions and cost the lives of tens of thousands of citizens.

The forces that carried out national security doctrines were primarily military rather than police. In many countries, military domination of internal security tasks left police under-staffed, underfunded and politically marginalised. Although, over time, in a number of countries militaries increased police responsibility for dealing with political dissidents and the police became the chief perpetrators of human rights violations and more subject to international scrutiny.[4]

The goal of the region's peace processes and transitions was to establish and consolidate democratic rule, including asserting civilian control of the military, restricting military missions to external defence, and demilitarising internal security. Yet political scientists studying Latin America typically describe democratic transitions as "constrained" or "fragile", one of the greatest constraints being the military's protection of their prerogatives against the encroachments of democratic government. Many of the region's transitions were "negotiated" or "pacted" and powerful militaries were able to protect their privileges. Throughout the region, amnesty laws have guaranteed military impunity for human rights violations committed by authoritarian regimes. While military budgets have been reduced in many countries, civilian leaders still feel the presence of the military as a sword of Damocles hanging over their heads.

In those Latin American countries where political conditions allowed it, efforts to restore and consolidate democracy have included initiatives to reform national security legislation explicitly limiting the mission of the military to external defence, and tightening restrictions on the use of states of emergency or exception which allow constitutional guarantees to be set aside. This was the case in Argentina, where the military's defeat in the Falklands conflict left them discredited and weakened. Negotiated peace processes in El Salvador and Guatemala have included similar reforms. Some governments have also attempted to reform legislation governing the collection and use of intelligence.

In Central America and Haiti, police reform was the axis of this larger effort to dismantle authoritarian structures and move from "regime policing" to "democratic policing". The establishment of democratic policing was a vital foundation for security and stability; a guarantee of the political space required to spur economic and social development. In El Salvador, Haiti and Guatemala, political transitions have included major police reform efforts.

In other countries of the region, policing has come to the forefront of public debates because of soaring crime rates and the clear failure or inability of weak and corrupt criminal justice systems to confront crime. Most Latin American countries have now started or are in the midst of comprehensive criminal justice reforms that affect every step of the process from the initiation to the closure of a case. Reforms seek both to strengthen democracy and increase the efficiency of legal proceedings.[5]

[4] This strategy was pursued in both Chile and Paraguay.

[5] Judicial reforms are adopting key elements of adversarial legal models, such as separating the functions of prosecutor and judge. Gustavo Palmieri, "Criminal Investigations," Paper V, *Themes*

## Legacies of Military Dominance

Unsurprisingly, the historical preeminence of the military in Latin America has had a profound effect on police institutions. Using three defining characteristics—personnel, command and character[6]—comparative international police scholar David Bayley finds that "the military dominates policing in Latin America more than in any other region of the world".[7] Despite Latin America's democratic transitions, police remain under Ministries of Defence in Colombia, Chile, and Brazil.[8] In these cases, many crimes, including human rights violations, committed by police and military police are tried before military tribunals. In Peru, elected President Alberto Fujimori, an authoritarian populist who has ruled hand-in-hand with the Peruvian military, placed the military intelligence services in control of the police as recently as 1998 in order to combat organised crime—several years after a police unit captured the leader of Peru's notorious quasi-Maoist guerrilla movement, Sendero Luminoso.

The National Security Doctrines implemented by governments throughout Latin America—both military regimes and elected governments combating guerrilla movements—blurred the distinction between common criminals, guerrillas, subversives, political opposition, disadvantaged sectors, and labour organisations. This lumping together of all "enemies" has had lasting repercussions. Intelligence activities and social control policies expanded exponentially, while criminal investigative capabilities were rendered dysfunctional by governments who did not need proof to eliminate their "enemies" nor want evidence of atrocities or illegal behavior by their "friends". As police dedicated themselves first and foremost to protecting the regime, normal police work in law enforcement and crime prevention was neglected. Basic police work remains appallingly shoddy and police-community relations are still characterised by hostility and fear for majority sectors of the population.

As the repressive and social control functions of police were built up, the rule of law was weakened. A characteristic that distinguishes developed countries from developing countries is not only the ratio of police to inhabitants, but also

*and Debates in Public Security Reform, A Manual for Civil Society* (Washington DC, Washington Office on Latin America, March 1999).

[6] David Bayley defines the three characteristics as follows: Are police and military personnel clearly separated? Are police and military forces separately accountable to government or is one subordinate to the other? And are they distinguishable in their actions? (types of weaponry carried, types of units of deployment, and so on). David H. Bayley, *What's in a Uniform? A Comparative View of Police-Military Relations in Latin America* (paper prepared for the conference on Police and Civil-Military Relations in Latin America, Washington DC, October 1993, sponsored by the Latin America and Caribbean Center, Florida International University), pp. 4–5.

[7] *Ibid*, p. 11.

[8] Each of Brazil's states has a military and a judicial police and their operations are directed by state authorities. The military police are formally a reserve unit of the armed forces and can be called up in times of emergency. For the first time, in the 1990s, Colombia has had civilian defence ministers.

the ratio of police to judges. In general, the ratio of police to inhabitants in poor nations was one third higher than that of developed countries while the judge-inhabitant ratio was smaller by half. Thus, while developed countries had one judge for every twenty-four police officers, developing countries had one judge for every seventy-four police.[9]

With the restoration of democracy, the most obvious security practices police inherited from repressive regimes were summary executions of supposed criminals, the widespread use of torture, and the fabrication of evidence to build cases. A quick review of human rights reports by Amnesty International, Human Rights Watch/Americas and the Washington Office on Latin America reveals the depth of police abuse of human rights in the region. Police are among the main perpetrators of "social cleansing killings" of street children, prostitutes and homosexuals. In Colombia, these individuals came to be termed "*desechables*"—throwaway people. Police torture of suspects in detention either to obtain confessions or to preemptively punish individuals is commonplace. Police commit crimes themselves, plant evidence, and cover-up cases to guarantee the impunity of themselves or their political masters. Police corruption is pandemic, fed by low salaries and systemic corruption in government. The Inter-American Commission on Human Rights of the Organisation of American States reports that, in the wake of the region's democratic transitions, police rather than military forces commit the majority of the human rights abuses in the region, and they continue to enjoy impunity as the military did in the past.[10]

Deeply ingrained repressive practices have come to substitute for an atrophied criminal investigation system. "Investigative procedures" are frequently designed as, or even supplanted by, continuous police surveillance operations targeting selected social sectors. Police assiduously detain and harass members of the targeted groups, either using the official excuse of ascertaining their backgrounds or lifestyles, or accusing them of committing a crime, without presenting any concrete proof. Arrests are made without prior investigation—often without any intention of opening an investigation—yet police forces evaluate the effectiveness of their agents based on arrest rates.[11]

[9] Crime Trends and Criminal Justice Operations at the Regional and Under-Regional Levels. Results of the Fourth United Nations Survey of Crime Trends and Operations of the Criminal Justice Systems (1986–90), Draft Report, fig. 5, 8, and 15.

[10] Estrella Gutierrez, "Democracy brings change of uniform for impunity", *InterPress Service*, 8 May 1998.

[11] In 1990, for example, of arrests by Chile's Carabineros police—widely recognised as one of the most professional and effective in Latin America—thirty-five per cent were for drunkenness, while nineteen per cent of arrests were based on "suspicion". A recently launched effort to reform Chile's judicial police was launched on the slogan "*Investigar para detener, no detener para investigar*" (investigate in order to detain, do not detain in order to investigate). Hugo Fruhling Ehrlich, *Modernización de la Policia* (paper presented at the Foro sobre Convivencia y Seguridad Cuidadana en el Istmo Centroamericano, Haiti y República Dominicana, 2–4 June 1998, organised by the Inter-American Development Bank).

Paul Chevigny argues in the *Edge of the Knife; Police Violence in the Americas* that police work reproduces the social order of the society or community.[12] In Latin America, the removal of the military from government has not changed the underlying social order which police practice continues to reflect. While the perpetrators and victims of violent crime tend to be of the same social class—poor and marginalised social sectors—middle and upper classes perceive crime as a problem that predominantly affects them. Police become the key instruments of a "socially-rooted authoritarianism that prevails throughout Latin America".[13] The poor see the law as an instrument of oppression at the service of the state and the elite interests it serves.

> Police tend to act as border guards protecting the rich from the poor, and police violence remains cloaked in impunity because it is largely directed against those "dangerous classes" and rarely affects the lives of the well-to-do. . . . Even if the state no longer engages in systematic coercion against political dissidents, as it did during the dictatorships, it remains accountable for the repressive illegal practices of the police and the military which have survived the transitions to democracy. . . . In much of Latin America, the state has shown itself incapable—or, more likely, unwilling—to punish the criminal practices of state agents.[14]

Impunity for crimes such as political murders, official corruption and the involvement of security agents in organised gangs has shaped the balance of power and conduct of politics. Against this backdrop, progress in solving such crimes and ending impunity is intimately linked to genuine democracy building.

## The Challenge of Police Reform in Latin America

Military dominance has also shaped internal police organisation and management. While the human rights community has scrutinised police practices, there are very few studies of police history and management in Latin America. Still, the following generalisations can be made with a good degree of certainty: Latin American police forces are characterised by low education levels, limited and poor training, steep hierarchical structures, low pay, bad working conditions, limited equipment, and poor technical capabilities.[15] Reforming police presents a major challenge. Even seemingly straightforward steps such as improving recruitment standards can present formidable obstacles. Take the example of Argentina:

[12] The New Press, New York, 1995.

[13] Paulo Sérgio Pinheiro, "Democracies without Citizenship", *Report on the Americas* (New York, NACLA, Sept/Oct 1996), p. 20.

[14] *Ibid.*

[15] The majority of Latin police forces have separate recruitment and training for beat cops and the officer corps. Internal discipline is frequently brutal and arbitrary, see P Chevigny, *Edge of the Knife: Police Violence in the Americas* (New York, The New Press, 1995), p. 170. Pay differentials between commanders and beat cops are huge, see *infra* n. 93.

> Only a tiny sector of the population has any interest in entering the police academy because of the bad pay and terrible image of the police in the community. Of those entering the academy, the majority come from families of police officers. At the same time, when the same agency has tried to raise the standards for police recruitment, it has resulted in a shortage of candidates. However, the alternative of raising police salaries is also debatable as it cannot be seen in any way as recognition for a force that is so highly questionable.[16]

The countries in which police reform efforts have gone farthest and deepest are those emerging from civil wars where the international community helped support the peace process and provided massive assistance to public security reforms. In Panama and Haiti, US interventions removed old militaries from power and then undertook emergency programmes to restructure internal security forces in Panama and, in the Haitian case, create an entirely new police force from scratch. In El Salvador, a negotiated end to a major civil war produced peace accords whose main component set out a detailed proposal for police reform. These dramatic transitions permitted what might be termed "holistic" reforms, which integrated demilitarisation processes with total or near-total overhauls of the police force, including doctrine, recruitment, training and internal organisation. Each of these reform efforts received massive international assistance and foreign donors played important roles verifying progress and pressing for compliance with human rights standards and democratic practice.[17]

The reforms of internal security structures in Central America have made clear that these programmes are in themselves difficult and lengthy. Furthermore, while Central American police reforms have made important strides, they also face constant resistance and challenges from authoritarian sectors including the military, political parties, and the elite who see their

[16] Centro de Estudios Legales y Sociales (CELS) and Human Rights Watch/Americas, *La Inseguridad policial; Violencia de las fuerzas de seguridad en la Argentina* (Buenos Aires, CELS, October 1998), p. 20.

[17] Because of the high level of international engagement, these processes are well documented. See, for example, the following reports of the Washington Office on Latin America: *Demilitarising Public Order; the International Community, Police Reform and Human Rights in Central America and Haiti* (1995); *Policing Haiti: Preliminary Assessment of the New Civilian Security Force* (1995); *Policing Haiti: Preliminary Assessment of the New Civilian Security Force* (1995); *The Human Rights Record of the Haitian National Police* (a joint report of WOLA, Human Rights Watch/Americas and the National Coalition for Haitian Rights, 1997); *Can Haiti's Police Reforms Be Sustained?* (a joint report of WOLA and National Coalition for Haitian Rights,1998); *Risking Failure: The Problems and Promises of the New Civilian Police in El Salvador* (1993); *Protectors or Perpetrators? The Institutional Crisis of the Salvadoran Civilian Police* (a joint report of WOLA and Hemisphere Initiatives, 1996); also George R Vickers, "International Assistance to Internal Security Reforms: Some Lessons from Central America and the Caribbean", and Chuck Call, "Police Reform, Human Rights, and Democratization in Post-Conflict Settings: Lessons from El Salvador", both in *After the War is Over . . . What Comes Next; Promoting Democracy, Human Rights and Reintegration in Post-Conflict Societies* (US Agency for International Development Conference, 30–31 October 1997). See also reports of United Nations peacekeeping and human rights missions in El Salvador, Haiti and Guatemala, many of these can be found on the UN's web page, at www.un.org.

prerogatives threatened by democratic change. Facing these pressures and demands for tough action against crime, government commitment to and engagement with police reform often has been weak.

While political opposition has posed a major handicap to reform processes, their greatest hurdle may well be their difficulty in confronting rising crime rates. As a region, Latin America ranks as the most violent in the world, with a homicide rate of twenty per hundred thousand inhabitants. This is six times the murder rate of OECD countries and three times as many murders per capita as Africa, India, China, the Middle East and East Asia, all of whose GNPs are lower than Latin America's.[18] In Central America, as in South Africa and other post-conflict contexts, crime has boomed, fuelled by high unemployment, demobilisation of combatants and a plentiful supply of arms. The Pan-American Health Organisation estimates that Guatemala has a spectacular homicide rate of one hundred and fifty per hundred thousand,[19] and El Salvador's 1996 homicide rate was one hundred and seventeen point four per hundred thousand.[20] Kidnappings, property theft, car jacking, and assault are an epidemic. Governments are failing to provide basic levels of personal security. Crime tops opinion polls as the number one concern of citizens throughout Latin America.

Despite their aggressive approach to public order, Latin America's police are patently failing to reduce violent crime. If anything, police actions tend to increase rather than diminish levels of violence. In Buenos Aires, Argentina, the police are responsible for over ten per cent of all homicides, including accidental homicides.[21] In São Paulo, Brazil, police account for at least fifteen per cent of homicides, and in Jamaica, the number rises to an astounding eighteen per cent.[22] Even in countries where newly-reformed police are not committing systematic abuses of rights, their poor crime-fighting performance has left them with little operational credibility. This is reflected in the lack of citizen collaboration with police. In El Salvador, for example, a 1996 poll found that only twenty four point four per cent of crime victims reported the event to the police because most victims believed it would be an exercise in futility.[23]

In response to crime waves and police ineffectiveness, a number of governments such as those in Brazil, Bolivia, Honduras, El Salvador and Mexico

[18] *Crime and Violence as Development Issues in Latin America and the Caribbean* (paper prepared by the World Bank for the conference on Urban Crime and Violence, Rio de Janeiro, Brazil, 2–4 March 1997), p. 10. Citing the Pan-American Health Organisation's Health Situation Analysis programme, 1997, on homicide rates.

[19] *Ibid.*

[20] *Consejo Nacional para Seguridad Pública*, El Salvador, 1997. These figures compare harshly even with South Africa's notoriously high rates of violent crime where the homicide rate reached forty-five per hundred thousand in 1994. Jeff Builta, "South Africa; Crime on the Increase", *Crime and Justice International* (Office of International Criminal Justice, www.acsp.uic.edu).

[21] See P Chevigny, *supra* n. 15, at p. 192.

[22] *Ibid*, pp. 148 and 212.

[23] May 1996 poll conducted by the Universidad Centroamericana, cited in Laura Chinchilla and José M Rico, *La Prevención Comunitaria del Delito; Perspectivas para América Latina* (Miami, Center for the Administration of Justice, Florida International University, 1997), p. 11.

among others have authorised the military to conduct policing activities. As with repressive policing practices, military engagement with public order and crime fighting tasks has also failed to reduce crime and violence. One study asserts that there is an emerging Latin American model of public security that has profoundly negative implications for democracy. This model is characterised by the militarisation of public security which represses large scale social disorder but does little to prevent crime and nothing to guarantee citizen's rights; a simultaneous informalisation of some public security functions such as paramilitary neighbourhood groups, or even "parallel state" structures of shanty town criminal organisations as in Rio de Janeiro; and finally, there is the privatisation of "public" security for those who can afford it as a commodity to be purchased.[24]

### Limited Civilian Capacity to make Security Policies

Elected government's reflective resort to the military to perform police tasks speaks to a policymaking environment with very limited ability to address the region's security concerns in a manner that can both increase police effectiveness and promote police accountability. As a consequence of military power and autonomy, Latin America has few policymakers, academics and other civilians with expertise to develop and implement public security policies. In 1994, a comparative conference examining police reform concluded that:

> As military power and influence are curbed, civilian capabilities must be strengthened. Needs range from developing civilian police leadership and providing administrative and technical training to civilian personnel, to educating parliamentarians on budget allocation and oversight mechanisms and supporting greater involvement by civil society sectors in discussions on police issues . . . . [D]espite growing public support for police reform, specific reform proposals are lacking: public discussion remains at a superficial level, with few informed actors in the debate.[25]

In Latin America, community and civil society involvement in public security reform has been limited. During Colombia's police reform process, a former advisor on police issues to civilian government authorities said that she was "shocked by the decision-making that went on based on little or no information or bad information".[26] In Argentina, the federal police frequently assert their independence of all political control and ministerial oversight of police is almost non-existent. When the federal police presented a bill to create a judicial police,

[24] Evidence indicates that these military operations have not led to significant decreases in crime and have contributed to human rights violations. A Douglas Kincaid and Eduardo A Gamarra, Florida International University, *Disorderly Democracy: Redefining Public Security in Latin America* (paper presented to the XIX Annual Conference on the Political Economy of the World System, North-South Center, University of Miami, FL, 21–22 April 1995. Revised July 1995).

[25] Washington Office on Latin America, *Demilitarising Public Order*, *supra* n. 17, 14.

[26] Author interview, Washington DC, 1 November 1998.

parliamentarians called the Minister of the Interior (who has authority over the federal police) to account for the Bill's excessive restrictions on individual rights. In his defence, the Minister of the Interior pleaded ignorance, saying that he had never seen the Bill.[27]

The controls of police behaviour provided by parliaments or local elected authorities, and by judges and prosecutors, remain weak in Latin America. The region does not have a tradition of strong checks and balances or diligent parliamentary oversight of government policies, or of judicial independence. While the age of politically subordinate "rubber-stamp" parliaments has largely ended, many parliaments have been and continue to be poorly equipped, with few staff and almost non-existent research or investigative capabilities. Police frequently resist parliamentary oversight, denouncing parliamentary efforts to reform legislation or increase oversight of public security policies as an unwarranted political interference.

In many countries of Latin America, judges only question police actions in cases of extreme illegality. Judges overlook crimes committed by police in the course of their duties, and ignore accusations that police exceed their authority. Judges are often disinterested to the point of giving police a blank check, allowing searches conducted without warrants, wire taps, searches of individuals, and detentions based on "police instincts".[28] Rather than controlling police abuse, in much of Latin America the pattern is of judicial complicity in police abuse.

Latin American police remain highly resistant to external scrutiny, keeping much information secret, including such documents as manuals setting out police procedures and internal disciplinary codes. This secrecy makes it very hard to undertake external studies of police policies and practices. Security forces sometimes impede research, asserting that statistical data on prisoners in jail who have never been sentenced, police statistics on the number of *in flagrante* arrests, the allocation of human and material resources, and requirements for promotion are confidential security-related matters. In some instances, lawsuits based on freedom of information and the democratic principle of government transparency have successfully obliged the police to provide the requested information.[29]

The "holistic" police reforms in Central America gave rise to unprecedented discussions about public security policies and institutions in those countries. The reforms, designed and implemented largely by international donors and

[27] Martín Abregú, Gustavo Palmieri and Sofia Tiscornia, "Informe Nacional: La Situación y los Mecanismos de Control de los Organismos de Seguridad Pública Interior en la República Argentina", in Fruhling, Hugo (ed.), *Control Democrático en el Mantenimiento de la Seguridad Interior* (Santiago, Chile, Centro de Estudios del Desarrollo/Ediciones Segundo Centenario, 1998), p. 59.

[28] *Ibid*, p. 62.

[29] In Argentina, the Centro de Estudios Legales y Sociales (CELS) filed a habeas data suit (*acción de ámparo*) against the federal police for failing to provide data repeatedly requested by the organisation. On 19 December 1997, the court ruled in their favor. Causa N° 28833/96: "Tiscornia, Sofia y otro C/ E.N. (M° del Interior) y otros/amparo ley 16986." Buenos Aires, 17 de deciembre de 1997.

experts, failed to incorporate civilians in the process even as they opened up formerly secretive and corporatist institutions to public scrutiny. As international engagement with Central American police reforms declines, the challenge is to sustain the progress achieved by the reforms and avoid sliding back into authoritarian and repressive practices. As international donors and governments tackled the many immediate challenges of police reform, considerations of sustainability were often left to be dealt with later. Police reform was primarily seen as a technical exercise in which expertise was transferred from professional police forces to the new Central American forces. Beyond the effort to demilitarise the police force itself, building broader civilian expertise was not a consideration in the design of reforms. In El Salvador, in 1995, two years into the reform process, the United Nations mission in that country (MINUSAL) recommended the creation of a national council on public security in an effort to confront issues of lack of coordination among agencies involved in public security and order maintenance, the lack of medium and long-term crime fighting strategies, and an overall lack of guidelines for decision making on citizen security issues.[30]

It is already clear in Central America that the reforms face significant opposition from elite sectors and from public pressures to crack down on rampant crime rates. In this context, the long-term consolidation of the police as a professional, effective and apolitical institution depends on developing greater citizen understanding of, support for, and involvement in the police reform process. Only if there is a broad domestic constituency that comprehends and supports the concept of responsive and accountable policing will there be political support for continuing and deepening police reform.

## The Role of the Human Rights Movement

A Central American human rights activist has commented that the focus and discourse of the human rights movement has little help to offer the fight against crime.[31] The police and judges can seem more timid and cautious under the critical spotlight of the human rights community. The broader impact among the population is that human rights discourse appears very abstract and of little use in confronting crime. In this context, a principle challenge for the human rights community is to incorporate popular concerns with crime and insecurity into human rights discourse and, in turn, incorporate human rights standards into anti-crime policy. Or, in the words of a Brazilian state official, demonstrate that "combating crime and ending police violence are not antagonistic objectives".[32]

[30] MINUSAL, *Evaluación sobre el Sector Seguridad Pública* (United Nations, 28 September 1995), p. 2

[31] Roberto Cuéllar M, "Seguridad Cuidadana: entre los derechos humanos y la lucha contra la criminalidad," *Ideéle*, No. 91 (Lima, Peru, Instituto de Defensa Legal, octubre de 1996).

[32] José Afonso da Silva, preface to the 1996 annual report of the São Paulo police auditor's report, see *infra* n. 81.

Traditional human rights investigations of police abuse after-the-fact ended with calls for investigations and trials, and punishment of those found responsible. While some identified particularly problematic police practices, most human rights reports did not venture further into the realm of potential public security reforms that could contribute to institutional reforms that would prevent or diminish abuse before-the-fact. One analyst argues that these prescriptions of the human rights community are ineffective in changing police practice because they are unpersuasive among those they are meant to influence, namely the police themselves and those making public order policy. A less formalistic approach requires the human rights movement to venture beyond the documentation and denunciation of cases to consider the police's potential contribution to reducing fear. This means considering which social institutions should contribute to the achievement of security and developing a political strategy toward that end.[33]

Human rights groups that focus on denouncing state abuses become vulnerable to accusations that they do not care about the majority of citizens, that they "coddle criminals", or that human rights monitoring actually "ties the hands" of the police and prevents them from fighting crime in an aggressive manner. Such rhetoric is an easy tool for governments fighting back against human rights critiques. Argentine President Carlos Menem stated in 1998 that the answer to crime is an iron fist (*la mano dura*). He went on to remark that "some human rights organisations are going to raise an outcry against this, but I think that we have more protections here for criminals than for the police or the people".[34] Public concerns about crime and attacks on traditional human rights work are forcing groups to consider how crime may violate the right of ordinary citizens to basic levels of security. Human rights organisations throughout Latin America are now talking about "citizen security" as a framework that encompasses both concerns about state violations of rights and the impact of crime.

While the Latin American human rights movement has become one of the most prominent and professional of any region in the world, its strategies and ideology were not always well suited to taking advantage of the openings offered by democratic processes. Human rights groups accustomed to confronting and denouncing authoritarianism do not always have the know-how or skills to develop alternative policy proposals and the strategies required to advance these through democratic channels such as parliaments and other elected authorities. Recommendations for legal reforms and the incorporation of international rights instruments are a relatively straightforward step. The issues involved in changing entrenched institutional cultures and practices and making respect for rights a reality present a challenge not only to human rights groups but to all those seeking to consolidate democracy. It also can be partic-

[33] Andrew Goldsmith, *The Police Reform Process in Colombia*. (unpublished paper presented at the September 1996 conference of the International Association for the Civilian Oversight of Law Enforcement/IACOLE, McClean, Virginia).

[34] Interview in Clarín, 13 September 1998, cited in *La Inseguridad Policial*, *supra* n. 16, p. 12.

ularly difficult for human rights groups to engage in dialogue and try to develop reform proposals for state institutions when they continue to confront officials in those institutions who were associated with past repression.

Despite the myriad difficulties, there is a transition underway in Latin America within the human rights movement and broader civil society sectors that has come to be coined "from denunciation to proposition" (*de denuncia a propuesta*). Human rights groups and civil society organisations have undertaken an increasingly broad array of initiatives related to public security reforms.[35] The best-developed work builds directly on the traditional strengths of human rights work in monitoring and denouncing police abuse and irregularities in police and judicial proceedings. Human rights groups oppose the passage of laws that undermine rights and democratic principles. A number of organisations promote improved criminal investigations and cooperate with governments to strengthen them, participating in or supporting legal assistance programmes and independent investigations. Based on this work, organisations can identify and call attention to systemic problems and specific weaknesses in the criminal justice system. Human rights groups have designed, supported or monitored projects touching on different aspects of criminal investigations such as juvenile offenders, prison systems, and victims' services. This work tends to focus on the areas being addressed by non-governmental organisations—human rights, environmental crimes, and family or gender issues.

The analysis of human rights and civil society groups is becoming increasingly sophisticated despite the difficulty in obtaining information from closed and secretive police institutions. Critiques of public security policies are being supported with statistical data and other indicators of problems in the police and judiciary, such as numbers of prisoners in jail who have never been sentenced, statistics on the number of *in flagrante* arrests, and the allocation of human and material resources. In some countries, groups have sat on commissions, usually consultative in nature, dealing with public security issues. This is the case with the Internal Security Council (*Consejo de Seguridad Interior*) created by the 1998 police law in Honduras.

[35] Many examples of such work can found throughout the region. In Argentina, the *Centro de Estudios Legales y Sociales* (CELS) documents patterns of police abuse and has advised the bicameral parliamentary commission on public security discussed below in this paper. In El Salvador, *Centro de Estudios Penales* of the *Fundación de Estudios para la Aplicación del Derecho* (CEPES/FESPAD) has conducted extensive analyses of flaws in internal police discipline and drafted commentary and alternative proposals for a proposed revision of the police organic law. CEPES/FESPAD also participated, with another human rights organisation, in a working group with the National Commission on Public Security to develop a pilot community policing programme. In Rio de Janeiro, Brazil, a multi-sector initiative called Viva Rio developed a community policing programme working with state police and government (unfortunately, it was closed down by a new police chief). A multi-year comparative study of police in Argentina, Brazil, Chile and Peru is currently underway, headed by the Centro para Estudios del Desarrollo (CED) in Chile. It has published a first volume of control of police in democracies—*Control Democrático en el Mantenimiento de la Seguridad Interior*, Hugo Frühling E (ed.)(Santiago, CED/Ediciones Segundo Centenario, 1998).

Private organisations have performed as key counterparts to public agencies or by filling crucial gaps that governments are unwilling or able to confront. In Brazil, the Legal Aid Office of Grassroots Organisations (GAJOP) has designed programmes to assist and protect low-income people testifying about state, para-state, or organised violence. The programme works with professionals from different fields and many volunteers. As police and sometimes judicial authorities are implicated in witness intimidation, they do not participate in the programme. In Argentina, the Anthropological Forensic Team pioneered an area of technical expertise that has become indispensable for gathering scientific evidence of crimes associated with government repression in Latin America (and has since helped exhume victims of massacres in countries including Ethiopia, Guatemala and Bosnia).

These examples evidence an evolution in human rights work in Latin America beyond a primary focus on seeking international condemnation of abuses toward nationally-oriented rights advocacy more akin to the work of US and other national civil rights organisations. Yet, the separate discourse and postures of human rights activists and policymakers can be a serious impediment to constructive exchange and collaboration. Furthermore, police reform efforts tend to be partial, slow and erratic. Even as civil society groups engage in more technical discussions of institutional reforms, they continue to monitor police abuse and the progress of human rights cases. This emerging dual role—in encouraging reform and condemning continued abuse—underscores the contradictions and uncertainties of reform efforts and points to the inherent tensions the human rights community faces in carving out a role of critical engagement.

## CIVILIAN REVIEW AND POLICE ACCOUNTABILITY IN LATIN AMERICA

The previous section of this paper makes the argument that the issue of civilian control and oversight of security forces is central to democratic transitions and is a high priority for the region's human rights movement. Civilian control remains a key issue precisely because it is still so weak. While ending military regimes and removing military influence from internal security and other non-military tasks are the most prominent steps in the region's democratic transitions, other policies have been initiated in many Latin American countries that seek to expand and deepen civilian control and improve protections for basic rights. In particular, government's have created human rights ombudsmen's offices with missions similar to those of civilian review of police. Before going on to examine four examples of civilian oversight of police, it is worth reviewing the profiles and achievements of these ombudsmen.

Over the last two decades, most countries in Latin America have created national ombudsmen's offices and/or human rights ombudsmen's offices that are government watchdogs with oversight powers that include police.[36] Ombudsmen's mandates are limited and their track records mixed. Ombudsmen's offices can only issue findings and forward cases to the courts where they frequently run into Latin America's ongoing "culture of impunity". Governments all too often ignore non-binding recommendations made by ombudsmen or their political weight is too limited to bring change to entrenched authoritarian practices. A Mexican human rights advocate notes that the ombudsman's work helps to advance individual cases but has no impact on changing the policies and practices underlying or permitting abuses.[37] The same phenomenon can be witnessed in many other countries.[38] Despite their limitations, the human rights movement has supported the creation of ombudsmen's offices and often advocated for increasing their powers, prominence and budgets. Even in the most adverse political conditions, dedicated ombudsmen have shown themselves capable of providing an important measure of protection and public profile for human rights issues.

In some cases, governments have played lip service to the notion of accountability by creating ombudsmen's offices while restricting their mandates. In Peru, the ombudsman's office is constitutionally barred from entering military barracks in an overt attempt to prevent investigations of the military, the institution long responsible for the majority of human rights violations and, during extended states of exception, responsible for public security tasks in as much as a half the country. Nonetheless, the Peruvian ombudsman's office has played an important role in a wide variety of human rights issues, including reviewing cases of individuals detained under draconian anti-terrorism laws and recommending the release of thousands of innocent detainees, many of whom had spent months in jail with no legal recourse.[39]

Ombudsmen's offices can do more, particularly when driven by strong leaders. The Honduran ombudsman played a key role in gathering information and pressing for trials of those responsible for disappearances and other human rights abuses under past regimes. His office has also supported and worked with a broad-based civil society coalition working on police reform which undertook a vigorous campaign lobbying parliament for changes to a law reforming the

[36] See *supra* n. 3.

[37] Author interview with Oscar Gonzalez, Director of the Academía Mexicana de Derechos Humanos, Washington DC, 8 March 1999.

[38] The Colombian Ombudsman (*Defensor del Pueblo*) investigates cases and hands over their findings to the judicial system for prosecution where the military frequently claims jurisdiction of high-profile cases. The Colombian Attorney-General also has a human rights unit which investigates human rights abuses in Colombia and played a key role in the arrest of paramilitary leader Victor Caranza. These offices have themselves been the target of political violence. In 1998, two human rights unit investigators were killed while they were investigating paramilitary massacres. The Colombian Government has failed to repudiate these attacks and actively support the unit. Human Rights Watch, *World Report 1999* (New York, Human Rights Watch, 1999), pp. 95 and 114.

[39] Author interview with Coletta Youngers, Senior Associate for the Andes, Washington Office on Latin America, Washington DC, 30 March 1999.

police in that country. The Salvadoran ombudsman's office, discussed below, has played an important role in monitoring the police in that country.

Unfortunately, while there are a number of publications that describe the creation, mandates and work of different ombudsmen's offices in Latin America, there are few evaluations of their impact and no good comparative analyses. While these offices can provide protections and help raise the public profile of human rights issues, they do not have the powers nor resources to promote institutional reforms in the face of resistance from governments or still-powerful security forces. In the worst cases, the creation of these offices is a public relations exercise by governments which have limited political will and/or limited capacity to confront the weaknesses of their judicial system, police and other agencies entrusted with the provision and protection of citizen's rights. Other factors that clearly also affect the performance of these offices are their leadership and the level of support and collaboration they receive from the human rights community.

In the next half of this paper I will examine four efforts to strengthen civilian control and oversight of police forces in Latin America. They vary widely from a reform process establishing numerous channels for civilian engagement in Argentina to a police auditor in Brazil, a civilian review board in Colombia and the human rights ombudsman's office in El Salvador. From these selected cases, I will try to draw some conclusions about the factors contributing to their relative successes and failings and, from there, consider the potential for expanding civilian review in Latin America and its place in the broader effort to consolidate democracy and guarantee the rights of all the region's citizens.

## The Role of the Salvadoran Human Rights Ombudsman's Office in Police Accountability

In 1992, a negotiated peace agreement put an end to El Salvador's decades-long civil war. The Peace Accords set out a detailed blueprint for police reform and also created a human rights ombudsman's office (*Procuraduría para la Defensa de los Derechos Humanos*/PDH).[40] The PDH has a tremendously broad mandate. It is to hear complaints against any government employee; monitor legislation to assure its concordance with human rights standards; monitor prison

[40] For descriptions of the police reform process, see Washington Office on Latin America/Hemisphere Initiatives reports, *Risking Failure; the Problems and Promise of the New Civilian Police in El Salvador* (Washington DC, WOLA, September 1993) and *Protectors or Perpetrators? The Institutional Crisis of the Salvadoran Civilian Police* (January 1996). Also Gino Costa, "The United Nations and Reform of the Police in El Salvador", 2 (3) *International Peacekeeping*, Autumn 1995, pp. 365–90; and Gino Costa, *Las Dificultades de Desmilitarizar la Seguridad Pública; Las Naciones Unidas y la Creación de la Policía Nacional Civil en El Salvador* (San Salvador, Universidad Centroamericana, 1998). William Stanley, "International Tutelage and Domestic Political Will: Building a New Civilian Police Force in El Salvador", *Studies in Comparative International Development*, May 1995.

conditions; monitor economic, social and cultural rights, and the rights of women and children, the elderly and the environment. The office is large, with a staff of close to four hundred, an annual budget of about US$4 million, and field offices throughout El Salvador. Unfortunately, from the beginning, the PDH has failed to prioritise its resource allocation among the different areas of this very broad mandate.[41]

The PDH receives complaints, determines their admissibility, conducts investigations and issues findings. During investigations, the PDH has the right to all necessary documentation from the authorities accused of the misconduct under investigation. The law determines that, if those authorities refuse to provide requested information, their refusal permits the PDH to presume that the allegations are true. Thus, non-cooperation may contribute directly to the upholding of a complaint. In the finding on each case, the PDH is to include recommendations for measures to correct the problems that gave rise to the violation.[42] A long-time monitor of El Salvador's police reform stated that she was not aware of any policy recommendations made by the PDH and that, if the PDH had in fact recommended changes, there was no indication that the police had accepted them.[43] The PDH can also offer to mediate between the victim and the perpetrator to settle cases and help victims obtain compensation.[44]

The PDH has an unusual power over internal police disciplinary mechanisms in the form of veto power over the appointment of the police inspector general. The second head of the office, Marina Velásquez de Avilés used this power in 1994, vetoing the president's nominee as unqualified for the position. The president's response was to issue an executive decree removing the PDH's veto power. The issue went before the Supreme Court that ruled the president's degree to be unconstitutional and upheld the veto power of the PDH.[45]

The PDH receives far more denunciations of police abuse than police disciplinary mechanisms—the police control unit and the inspector general.

[41] A 1993 evaluation of the PDH noted that: The law also establishes five assistant ombudsman positions—one for the defence of human rights and four for the defence of certain specialised rights (children, women, the elderly, and the environment). The incorporation of these four specialised positions into the law has been a major obstacle in the PDH's efforts to prioritise its efforts, has diverted scarce human and financial resources from matters of primary importance, and has resulted in the creation of unproductive compartmentalized operations within the PDH. *El Salvador: Human Rights Ombudsman Assessment* (Contract Number 519–040 6–C–00–323–0–00, Development Associates, Inc. Arlington, Virginia, 23 November 1993).

[42] Centro de Estudios Penales de El Salvador/Centro de Estudios para la Aplicación del Derecho/CEPES/FESPAD, *Mecanismos Oficiales de Control Sobre la Policía Nacional Civil* (San Salvador, December 1997).

[43] Author telephone interview with Kelly Josh, Trainer for Police and Justice Reform, Washington Office on Latin America, El Salvador, 23 March 1999.

[44] At one point, police were deducting sums from officer's pay cheques to provide compensation recommended by the PDH. The office put a stop to this practice, saying that such recompense should be provided voluntarily by the police officer in a direct arrangement with the victim provided through a mediation process. *Mecanismos Oficiales de Control Sobre la Policía Nacional Civil*, p. 27.

[45] Washington Office on Latin America/Hemisphere Initiatives, *Protectors or Perpertrators? The Institutional Crisis of the Salvadoran Civilian Police* (WOLA/HI, Washington DC, January 1996), p. 23–4.

Despite the significant size and budget of the office, it has confronted a number of difficulties in investigating police misconduct. Avilés complained of lack of police cooperation and of financial constraints in investigating the huge number of complaints she received. Another factor that has hampered PDH investigations of police misconduct is the office's shortage of qualified personnel and total lack of staff with expertise in policing.[46]

The role of the PDH in controlling police misconduct has not been coordinated with police internal disciplinary mechanisms. During the early days of the police reform, there was a delay of over a year in appointing the police inspector general. This vacuum allowed police misconduct to go unpunished and threatened to create an atmosphere of institutional tolerance of misconduct. While the PDH was receiving denunciations of police abuse, laws and procedures failed to create mechanisms for the PDH to inform the police immediately of complaints so that police commanders could initiate their own investigations, or take other measures such as transferring the officer to desk duties or placing him or her on leave. This situation continues and there are often long delays before police units learn of incidents of abuse. This also reduces the ability of the PDH to choose to oversee police investigations as an alternative to undertaking its own investigations of all complaints.[47]

In 1996, United Nations representatives in El Salvador identified the PDH as playing a key role in monitoring the police reform process, particularly when the international mission which had monitored the reform process and verified its compliance with the agreements in the Peace Accords was withdrawn from the country. Given that police reform had faced significant resistance from the Salvadoran military and government officials, some external oversight was viewed as a vital check on misconduct and further police wrongdoing.[48] The role and profile of the PDH has depended primarily on its leadership. The first *procurador* was a corporate lawyer with no experience of human rights issues. He failed to define and advance a mandate for the office. Avilés, the second *procuradora*, rapidly made her mark as an energetic and high-profile rights advocate, developing a good relationship with the human rights community.

Under the tenure of Avilés, the PDH played a prominent role in monitoring police abuse. From mid-1996 to mid-1997, it received two thousand five hundred complaints of police abuse, including forced disappearances, murder, attempted murder, and other abuses of personal integrity. Half of all complaints made to

[46] Gino Costa Santolalla and Manuel Núñez Pedraza, *Identificación de áreas de cooperación para fortalecer el nuevo sistema de seguridad pública en El Salvador*, Internal evaluation paper commissioned by the Spanish-United Nations Development Program (UNDP) co-operation program to strengthen governance in Central America (Lima/Madrid, 20 May 1996), p. 8. The UNDP and Spanish Government developed a joint programme in response to create a specialised unit dedicated to monitoring public security and respect for rights which would be able to conduct investigations but also take preventive measures through education, training and formulating policy proposals around police issues.

[47] *Mecanismos Oficiales de Control Sobre la Policía Nacional Civil*, p. 27.

[48] Costa and Pedraza, *supra* n. 40, p. 9.

the PDH were about police misconduct. In 1997, the PDH sustained two hundred and fourteen complaints of police abuse.[49]

Avilés focused the PDH's investigations of police misconduct on the most serious abuse resulting in loss of life and high-profile cases. The focus on high-profile cases demonstrated that police were not above the law and could be held accountable by the judiciary and civilian authorities. In certain cases, the PDH's investigations and findings had significant political impact. In one instance, the PDH revealed highly problematic practices by the Minister of Public Security and forced a controversial advisor to leave (he had been conducting investigations for the minister and withholding evidence from the police).[50] However, the PDH frequently did not investigate other police misconduct and never developed criteria for deciding which cases should be investigated further and which should not.[51] One important consequence was that the PDH never managed to develop analyses of patterns of abuse and police practices contributing to misconduct.

Unfortunately, despite assessments that made a range of management and administrative recommendations to improve the functioning of the office,[52] Avilés did not consolidate a professional staff or improve strategic planning during her tenure, leaving the office highly dependent on the commitment and skills of the next ombudsman.

Avilés' high-profile style attracted considerable animosity from government officials. She was denounced by government authorities in the Salvadoran press, faced some police resistance and received death threats.[53] It was very clear to observers that the conservative ARENA Government would not re-appoint her to the position when her term expired.[54] Despite this fact, the human rights community advocated for her reappointment instead of focusing their attention on lobbying for a good successor. Observers question whether human rights advocacy for other candidates would have had any impact, as it was clear that ARENA wanted to appoint a more quiescent ombudsman.[55] Her recently appointed successor, a former judge, is deeply unpopular with the human rights community. Human rights groups question the process by which he was elected and accuse him of wrongdoing including disregarding due process rights in certain cases before his bench.[56]

[49] *Supra* n. 47, p. 26.

[50] Author telephone interview with Kelly Josh, *supra* n. 45.

[51] *Ibid.*

[52] *Human Rights Ombudsman Assessment*, *supra* n. 41, p. vii.

[53] Avilés' relations with the Minister for Public Security were particularly problematic. She had a reasonably good working relationship with the national director of the police and, on at least one occasion, signed a memorandum of understanding with the director which was later vetoed by the minister. Thanks to Geoff Thale, Senior Associate, WOLA, for these insights.

[54] *Ibid.*

[55] *Ibid.*

[56] Comisión para la Defensa de los Derechos Humanos en Centroamérica/CODEHUCA, *Informe sobre las Procuradurías de Derechos Humanos de El Salvador, Guatemala y Honduras* (Costa Rica, CODEHUCA, 1999).

Despite Avilés' limitations, under her tenure, the office became a powerful tool for confronting police abuse as noted above. How long this track record will survive the change in leadership is, as yet, unclear. Leadership and managerial weaknesses in failing to develop a broader approach to issue of police misconduct or promote staff professionalisation and development, have left the work of the office highly vulnerable to leadership changes.

Nonetheless, the PDH has clearly played an important role in holding police accountable for individual cases of serious abuse, and thus reinforcing the credibility of the police reform process with the Salvadoran people. It is possible that the office could have had a larger impact on police behavior had it also devised a way to analyse patterns of police practice and make recommendations for change. Despite police opposition to the PDH's work, the dimensions of the police reform undertaken in El Salvador meant that there was a relatively good environment in which to press for procedural and operational changes.

However, over the longer term, the PDH's work alone is not enough to check police misconduct and keep the reform process on track. By early 1999, high profile cases revealed police involvement—including senior commanders—in cover-ups of killings in which police were implicated, and cases in which police planted and manipulated evidence.[57] Other problems include allegations of high-level corruption, and the Minister of Public Security continues to create special units that report directly to him and undermine the institutional chain of command.[58] The continued weakness of the new Salvadoran police reinforces the fact that reform processes are drawn out and long term. It is also clear that a national civilian control body such as the PDH has far less leverage than the international missions that monitored the early years of the reforms, particularly in the face of sometimes weak government commitment to reform and public demands for aggressive action against rampant violent crime.

## Civilian Review of Police in Colombia

In 1993, Colombian authorities initiated a major police reform after police raped and killed a nine-year-old girl in a Bogotá police station.[59] With this outrage, the reputation of the corrupt, brutal and inefficient Colombian National Police (CNP) force hit rock bottom. Police authorities were forced to recognise the need for reform and were in no position to resist reform initiatives. The process started with the creation of two commissions, one internal to the police

[57] Memorandum from Geoff Thale, Washington Office on Latin America, to US decisionmakers, 21 December 1999.

[58] *Ibid.*

[59] See Washington Office on Latin America, *The Colombian National Police, Human Rights and US Drug Policy* (Washington DC, WOLA, May 1993).

and an external commission that included academics and civil society representatives.[60]

The police reform law passed in 1993 incorporated various recommendations of the external commission, many of which sought to increase civilian control and improve police-community relations. Among these steps was the creation of a National Police Commissioner (*Comisionado Nacional para la Policía*), a civilian authority which would oversee police disciplinary processes, receive, process and analyse complaints about police conduct from citizens, and develop statistical analyses and programme evaluation. Once the position of police commissioner was established, the CNP Inspector General's office was supposed to be disbanded although in fact this never happened. The police commissioner was a key component of the reform, particularly as it was mandated to provide feedback, information and recommendations to the police. Other governmental human rights offices do also receive and investigate complaints against the police, but have limited ability to press for changes in police policy and practice.[61]

Among other impediments it faced, the proposal to create the police commissioner met with immediate police resistance. Sharing disciplinary powers is resisted by police in many countries, and was an anathema to Colombia's highly militaristic police force. Nor did the commissioner receive needed support from other governmental sectors including the first civilian minister of defence (with jurisdiction over the CNP). The law establishing the commissioner's role failed to clarify the role and powers of the office and government officials did not understand or were totally unaware of the office and its role. Even governmental human rights offices (such as the *Defensor del Pueblo*) reportedly knew little about its functions or operations.[62] The office had a total of four directors during its brief life span. The first commissioner resigned after six months, and all but the last of the directors complained of police resistance, inadequate budgets, and lack of government support.[63]

Human rights community support for and engagement with the office was limited. Human rights groups were not invited to join the civilian commission studying police reform, but did have relations with and confidence in certain members of the commission.[64] The first comissioner was felt to be a good man

[60] This account draws heavily on Andrew Goldsmith, "Police Accountability Reform in Colombia: The Civilian Oversight Experiment", in this volume, and María Victoria Llorente Sardi, *Perfil de la Policía Colombiana* (Documentos de Trabajo, Paz Pública, Programa sobre Seguridad, Justicia y Violencia, Universidad de los Andes, Bogotá, October 1997).

[61] The *Procuraduría de la Nación* and *Fiscalía de la Nación* can both receive complaints and investigate police misconduct. The *Defensor del Pueblo* publishes an annual report analysing the human rights situation. See also *supra* n. 38.

[62] *Police Accountability Reform in Colombia*, p. 15.

[63] *Ibid*, pp. 15–16.

[64] Author telephone interview with Gustavo Gallón, Executive Director of the Colombian Commission of Jurists, 31 March 1999. Gallón notes that he was contacted in an informal consultation about the potential nominees for the post of *comisionado*. Gallón recommended Adolfo Salamanca, in part because he was not as well known as other candidates whose past advocacy for human rights, Gallón feared, would provoke excessive police resistance.

for the job, but neither of his successors were as favourably viewed in the human rights community, which did not protest the lack of government support for the office or rally to keep it open. In part this reflects the relatively low profile of the office, its work and its leaders. It also reflects the fact that, working in the context of Colombia's protracted counter-insurgency efforts and ongoing human rights crisis, overwhelmed human rights organisations with limited resources did not prioritise civilian review of police.

One observer criticised the office for focusing almost entirely on after-the-fact investigations into abuse and failing to develop the mandate to analyse and identify patterns of abuse and suggest reforms to police practice as had been recommended by an international expert. In this view, the "traditional human rights lawyer" approach, which focused excessively on punishing abusive cops, was a problem and fed police antagonism.[65] Given the levels of police resistance encountered by the commission and later dynamics of police reform described below, it is not at all clear that police would have been more open to recommendations for changes in practices aimed at reducing human rights abuses.

The political dynamics of police reform in Colombia changed with the inauguration of President Ernesto Samper and his appointment of former CNP Inspector General Jorge Serrano as National Director of the CNP. In 1995, Serrano initiated an aggressive reform process firing thousands of police suspected of corruption and reinstating the inspector general's office. That same year, the police also had important successes in anti-narcotics campaigns against cartel leaders. Even as Samper's presidency was weakened by accusations that he had taken drug money to finance his campaign, Serrano became increasingly prominent, commended by US policymakers and wooed as a potential vice-presidential candidate.

The 1995 phase of police reform was police-driven. Experts say it reflects the leadership of Serrano himself who was given extraordinary powers to fire police on suspicion of misconduct. Human rights activists also note that the firings focused on police corruption rather than human rights abuses. While Serrano fired over five thousand police (with no due process guarantees for those dismissed), this reform did not undertake larger institutional or structural changes to increase police accountability. As police reform became police-driven, support for the commissioner's office diminished further. In late 1995, the police commissioner's office was faced with budget cutbacks in the order of eighty-five per cent. In September 1996, President Samper issued a decree disbanding the office; it finally closed in September 1997. While the Supreme Court ruled that Samper's action was illegal, and a Senate resolution urged not only retaining the office but expanding its powers, nothing has been done since to reinstate the national police commissioner.

Colombia's police reform processes failed to increase civilian control of the police. The various reform efforts of the 1990s have reduced levels of police

[65] Interview with former advisor on police reform, *supra* n. 26.

corruption and improved their public image somewhat. Nonetheless, police continue to be implicated in massacres, "social-cleansing killings" and other human rights abuses, and are complicit in paramilitary actions in the conflictive regions of Colombia.[66] A 1997 poll found that while Serrano's personal popularity was enviably high at seventy eight per cent, public opinion of the police remained poor, although better than in previous years.[67]

The effort to bring significant civilian engagement in review of police abuse and police practices no doubt contributed to the pressure on the police to clean house, however, it failed to advance the goals of increasing civilian control of police or confronting police abuse of human rights. Factors contributing to the failure of civilian review in Colombia included police resistance, weak governmental support and a low profile. Considerable caution is warranted in drawing lessons from the Colombian experience given that this country is the home of Latin America's most protracted guerrilla war, where violence is perpetrated by an array of state and non-state actors including drug traffickers and paramilitary forces, and where the police themselves are targets as well as perpetrators of violence. Nonetheless, experts note that Colombia's anti-narcotics police—which receive massive United States' anti-narcotics assistance that is conditioned by the US Congress on compliance with international human rights standards—have a much better human rights record than the regular police.[68] This difference would seem to indicate that it is possible to improve the human rights record of the police, even in Colombia's difficult circumstances.

## Bringing Civilians into Public Security through Police Reform in Argentina

In late 1997, the governor of the province of Buenos Aires, which includes Argentina's capital, initiated a major police reform of the provincial police, the largest force in Argentina's federal police system. The catalyst for the reform came in the form of revelations of police involvement in a 1994 terrorist attack on the "Amia" Jewish community center that left eighty-seven dead, and other police killings including that of photo-journalist Luis Cabezas who was investigating high-level government corruption. Increasing public outrage at egregious police abuse and corruption, and growing concern over rising crime posed a political problem for Buenos Aires Governor Eduardo Duhalde's presidential ambitions.

The initial plan was designed by two of Argentina's best-known jurists. Duhalde then sought political support from the opposition and civil society sectors proposing the creation of a high-level commission that would oversee and

66 Human Rights Watch, *World Report 1999*, p. 111.

67 5 May 1997 poll published in the Colombian weekly "Semana", cited in *Perfil de la Policía Colombia*, p. 3.

68 Unfortunately, accurate and independent data on human rights violations by different police units is limited because of the dangers involved in human rights investigations in Colombia.

support the implementation of the reform process. The two main opposition parties saw this as providing too much political weight to what would be primarily Duhalde's project. They proposed instead the creation of a bicameral commission in the state legislature that would monitor and oversee the reform process; they also agreed to approve the necessary legislation to implement the reform.[69] In addition, state authorities created an autonomous Institute of Criminal and Security Policies (*Instituto de Política Criminal y de Seguridad*/IPCS) mandated to monitor the reform process and provide technical and policy proposals.

The police reform is ambitious. It starts from the premise that the entire structure of the Buenos Aires police was problematic. The reform decentralises police command and deployment and increases police specialisation. The entire top command level of the force was given early retirement. Most importantly for the purposes of this paper, the reform seeks to increase community participation. Instead of a single, hierarchically organised state police force, the reform created eighteen police precincts. At this level, police are to have closer contact with local municipal and judicial authorities through newly created departmental, municipal and neighbourhood security councils (*foros vecinales de seguridad, foros municipales de seguridad, consejos departamentales de seguridad*). These bodies are to develop and coordinate community security policies. In addition, the reform created an ombudsman-like figure (*defensor de seguridad*) at both the municipal and provincial level, charged with receiving and investigating complaints against police.

A flaw in the design of the police reform was its failure to address issues of police management and administration involved in the decentralisation process. This created a range of problems as soon as the reform began to be implemented.[70] This problem reflects a lack of expertise in police issues among policymakers that would rapidly compound these initial problems. Other problems discussed in a December 1998 seminar with top police and government officials, civil society representatives and academics, included a lack of non-police technical experts, a general lack of practical information underpinning the clear principles framing the police reform effort, and reluctance to evaluate the successes and failures of the process.[71]

None of the various agencies created with police accountability mandates has made much progress to date. The independent institute worked on a number of legislative proposals but lacked a director until late 1998. The bicameral oversight committee in the provincial legislature was created but never assigned a

[69] Marcelo Saín, *La Reforma del Sistema de Seguridad y policial en la Provincia de Buenos Aires* (background paper prepared for a seminar on *Las Reformas Policiales en Argentina*, Buenos Aires, 1 and 2 December 1998. Forthcoming in report by CELS, the Centro de Estudios Legales y Sociales, Buenos Aires, Argentina), p. 74.

[70] Proyecto Policia y Sociedad Democrática, report on the seminar *Las Reformas Policiales en Argentina*, sponsored by Centro de Estudios Legales y Sociales/CELS, Buenos Aires, 1 and 2 December 1998. (Centro de Estudios del Desarrollo, Santiago, 28 January 1999), p. 4.

[71] *Ibid*, p. 5.

staff or budget. The committee, composed of eight senators and eight deputies elected by their respective chambers, has powers to require local and national authorities to provide information; subpoena witness testimony; prevent people from leaving the country; and make proposals for reforms to the executive branch. It is to publish a public report each year and another report for Congress only. Despite these wide-ranging powers and duties, the commission's work has been unsystematic and sporadic, conducting no ongoing routine oversight tasks. Observers attribute these limitations primarily to the lack of interest of its members.[72] Where the political will exists, it is clear that state authorities can exert significant control over police. For example, the Buenos Aires Secretariat for Security, created during the reform process, managed to fire thousands of police.[73]

The reform is still in its relatively early days and there are no published evaluations of the local councils or the *defensor* at this time. Some analysts are already raising concerns that the law is insufficiently clear as to the powers of the Defensor, that the requirement that police provide the office with information lack specificity, and that the defensor has no power to intervene, even in the most serious cases of police abuse. The reform created numerous venues for community participation at the provincial, municipal and community level, but analysts note that they were created because of political interests, not because people demanded it. While they may be useful fora for community participation, there is a risk that local authorities will manipulate them and that they will exclude sectors that are not allied with majority political parties, or will not represent more marginal social sectors.[74]

Human rights community engagement with the process has been limited. One national human rights organisation and a new group created to work on crime issues have engaged with the police reform. Most of Argentina's best-known human rights organisations remain focused to a large degree on demanding accountability for past military crimes and have not monitored or advocated for institutional police reforms.

Despite the impressive initial vision and remarkable efforts represented by this police reform, according to some observers, the process has stalled. One analyst writes that:

> Political parties are largely indifferent or incompetent to deal with questions about security policies and the police. The failure to use the institutional fora created by the reform processes and the lack of basic agreements and joint actions on these issues reflects, in reality, a retreat of the political class at the moment when it was taking control of one of the most complex and socially urgent institutional issues it faced. This political weakness represents the most serious obstacle to the effort to conduct

[72] *La Inseguridad Policial; Violencia de las Fuerzas de Seguridad en la Argentina*, *supra* n. 16, p.73.

[73] *Informe Nacional: La Situación y los Mecanismos de Control de los Organismos de Seguridad Pública Interior en la República Argentina*, *supra* n. 28, p. 59.

[74] Report on the seminar *Las Reformas Policiales en Argentina*, p. 8.

an integral reform of the security system and provincial police. The political class must not forget that there is no obedience where there is no leadership.[75]

The reform process in Argentina is very recent and it is hard to draw any firm conclusions about its relative strengths and weaknesses. Nonetheless, this rapid overview points to some commonality with the Colombian process: a lack of sufficient political engagement and commitment to keep pressing the reform process forward after the early steps in the initiative, and weaknesses in the design and actual implementation of the reforms.[76]

## The Police Auditor of São Paulo, Brazil

The Brazilian police are notorious for their use of lethal force and violations of human rights, including killings of street children. São Paulo, Brazil's largest city, shares these problems. However, São Paulo also has a strong human rights movement with over forty active organisations, many of which focus on police abuse. The human rights movement demanded and won the creation of a council for the protection of the human person (CONDEP), eight of whose ten members represent civil society sectors. CONDEP made a number of proposals on public security issues, many of which sought to increase controls on police behaviour.[77]

In November 1995, following the election of a new governor, the state government of São Paulo created a Police Auditor (*Ouvidoria da Polícia*) to receive complaints from civilians about abuses committed by the military and civilian police. CONDEP plays a key role in the appointment of the auditor, providing the governor with three names to choose from. The auditor's term is for two years, renewable once and, once appointed, the auditor cannot be removed from office. The auditor is supported by an advisory council of ten prominent figures. He has the power to demand any document from any police office. As of mid-1997, the office had a staff of twenty-five to oversee police forces totalling some twenty thousand personnel, policing a population of fifteen million people.[78]

[75] *Informe Nacional: La Situación y los Mecanismos de Control de los Organismos de Seguridad Pública Interior en la República Argentina*, p. 105.

[76] In addition to the structural reforms, the Buenos Aires police undertook a number of crime-fighting initatives in 1998 including "saturation sweeps" of high-crime neighbourhoods, efforts to control gun sales, a "hot spots" focus and variety of anti-theft and public order initiatives. State officials say that as a result crime declined by seventeen percent from March to July 1998. Nonetheless, crime remains the top concern in public opinion polls. A review of police data also revealed that fifty-two per cent of crimes are not denounced to the police indicating a significant level of continued public mistrust or lack of confidence in the police. Public presentation by Carlos Alberto Beraldi, Secretary of Security for the Province of Buenos Aires, at the Center for Strategic and Security Studies, Washington DC, 14 September 1998.

[77] Much of the following account is based on an author interview with police auditor Bendito Domingos Mariano, São Paulo, 22 July 1998.

[78] Paulo Sérgio Pinheiro, "Polícia e Consolidação Democrática: o Caso Brasileiro," in *São Paulo sem Medo; um Diagnóstico da Violência Urbana* (Garamond, São Paulo, 1998), p. 184.

The first auditor, Benedito Domingos Mariano, was a human rights activist who had worked for years with the Archbishop's human rights office in São Paulo. Before starting as auditor, Mariano visited four different civilian review boards in Canada and the United States and drew on these experiences as he structured his approach.[79]

Mariano decided to prioritise cases of police killings, torture, abuse of authority and threats. In these cases of serious police misconduct, the police must provide a report on their internal investigation of the incident to the auditor who then decides whether the investigation and outcome were satisfactory. If he is not satisfied, he takes the case to the Minister for Public Security and generally asks for another investigation. A staff person monitors the second investigation closely. While there is no punishment for non-cooperation of a poor first investigation, the Minister of Public Security can impose a punishment if police refuse to accept the auditor's recommendation. In practice, the auditor has found that police treat the cases he follows very seriously and, over two years, he has found the proceedings unsatisfactory in only ten cases.[80]

In addition to receiving complaints, the auditor can hold public hearings with testimony from civil society groups, government and police authorities. The office issues trimestral reports and an annual report that are given to the government and public simultaneously.[81] The government has no right to edit or censure these reports.

The auditor can also propose changes in policy policies and practices. He has made fifteen recommendations, five of which have been acted upon to date. The civilian police changed their targets for shooting practice to emphasise shooting to disable rather than kill. The military police, however, refused to implement this recommendation.[82] The state government also accepted a recommendation to revise the military police's internal disciplinary regulations (which dated from 1943 and focused overwhelmingly on intra-institutional discipline rather than on interaction with the public). The auditor helped draft a new police disciplinary code. He can also send cases to the courts for prosecution where he has pressed for expedited trials so that victims of police abuse or their families can receive indemnisation within a four-month period. (Mariano is also advocating for parity in compensation for families of victims of police brutality and families of police killed on duty.)

Mariano sees a trend of growing public confidence in and an increasing profile for his office. People are afraid of denouncing police abuse at police stations. During the first three months of the auditor's office opening, he received complaints in only about ten per cent of cases of police use of lethal violence. As the office received more publicity and human rights organisations brought their

[79] Author interview with Mariano, *supra* n. 77.

[80] *Ibid.*

[81] *Relatório Anual de Pestação de Contas* (Ouvidoria da Polícia do Estado de São Paulo, Brazil, 1996 and 1997).

[82] Author interview with Mariano, *supra* n. 77.

complaints to the auditor, the number of complaints he received increased massively. By 1998, almost every case was denounced to his office. A human rights activist offers a different perspective, arguing that while human rights organisations are aware of the office and use its services, the auditor has "not gone deeper into the popular conscience".[83] In this view, the office has not helped to change the popular viewpoint that the police are brutal and unaccountable. This inability to build popular trust limits the office's potential contribution to improving police-community relations and supporting new community policing pilot projects in São Paulo.[84] Another factor that may condition public support for the auditor is the high level of popular support for police violence against perceived "criminal elements".[85]

In two and a half years the office has received sixteen thousand complaints and followed eight thousand cases. The roughly twenty per cent of complaints that are cases of serious abuse are the most closely scrutinised. Mariano states that one thousand three hundred and eighty-two police have been punished who probably would have escaped discipline otherwise.[86] The auditor notes that he would benefit from having his own investigative capacity for use in serious cases where the police investigation is too slow, so as to provide a report directly to the Minister of Public Security.

The police auditor has received crucial political backing. Both the state governor and legislature have supported the auditor's office (in July 1997, the legislative assembly unanimously approved the law regulating the office). Media coverage has also been favourable with six editorials supporting the auditor's work during 1998 in the *Folha do São Paulo*, Brazil's most influential daily.[87]

Another demonstration of political support for the office was the decision to locate it in the offices of the Ministry of Public Security, side by side with top police officials. While this location has intimidated and deterred some complainants, their denunciations reach the office via human rights organisations. This political backing played an important role in forcing the police to accept the office. Nonetheless, Mariano confronts significant police resistance. He has received hate mail and is fighting two court cases brought against him by police for "moral damages".[88]

Despite the guarantees built into the appointment process and the tenure granted to the auditor, the office is vulnerable to changes in the political winds. With no budget guarantees, the office is totally dependent on the Ministry for Public Security for its financial support. A less friendly state government could

[83] Interview with Denis Mizne of the Instituto "*Sou da Paz*" of São Paulo, Washington DC, 18 March 1999.

[84] *Ibid.*

[85] Author interviews with Nancy Cardia, Núcleo de Estudios da Violência, Universidade de São Paulo, 24 July 1998, and São Paulo State Deputy Eloi Pietu, São Paulo, 23 July 1998.

[86] Author interview with Mariano, *supra* n. 77.

[87] *Ibid.*

[88] *Ibid.*

easily incapacitate the auditor's office.[89] In early 1998, supporters were deeply concerned that a change in political leadership could easily reverse the gains made by this office, but the governor narrowly won reelection averting that possibility for the moment. The governor's most serious contender had announced during his campaign that one of his first acts in office would be to dismantle the internal police programme to address problems with police use of force (PROAR, see below).

The work of the police auditor has clearly improved police accountability. How much the auditor is responsible for a decline in police killings is less clear. Police killings in São Paulo peaked in 1992, when police killed one thousand, one hundred and ninety civilians. By 1996, a year after the auditor's office was established, this number had declined dramatically to one hundred and six.[90] In addition to the improvement in internal police disciplinary procedures, which analysts attribute to the work of the auditor's office, the military police also created a Program to Retrain Police Involved in High Risk Situations (PROAR/ *Programa de Reciclagem de Policiais Envolvidos em Situação de Alto Risco*). The programme conducts psychological counselling and evaluation over a period of three months during which the officer is removed from regular shifts and generally assigned a desk job.[91] Analysts note that the threat of reassignment is probably more responsible for the drop in police killings than any other factor.[92] Reassignment removes them from their regular twenty-four hour shifts, which allow them to maintain second jobs, and places them on regular eight-hour office days, thus restricting their ability to bring a second pay check home.[93]

State officials continue with efforts to deepen police reform in São Paulo, despite limited popular support and calls for tough action against crime from conservative political opponents. Following his reelection, the governor fired the Secretary of State for Security in an effort to respond to criticisms during the electoral campaign that his reform initatives had not reduced crime levels, despite the fact that the secretary was perceived by police reform advocates to be doing a good job. The new secretary is pressing ahead, continuing to support the auditor and the PROAR programme, and developing community policing initiatives.[94] Nonetheless, the number of police killings of civilians increased in 1998 to two hundred and eighty-two.[95]

[89] Author interview with Nancy Cardia, *supra* n. 85.

[90] Human Rights Watch, *Police Brutality in Urban Brazil* (Human Rights Watch/Americas, New York, April 1997), p. 51.

[91] *Ibid*, p. 52.

[92] Interview with Nancy Cardia, *supra* n. 85.

[93] A second wage is needed by most beat cops who make roughly US$500 a month. A police colonel, however, earns about US$6,000 a month. (These salaries figures do not reflect the 1999 devaluation of the Brazilian currency.) *Polícia e Consolidação Democrática: o Caso Brasileiro*, p. 185.

[94] Paulo Mesquita, "Polícia Comunitaria: la Experiencia en São Paulo", in *Boletín Policía Y Sociedad Democrática*, No. 3, Año 1 (Centro de Estudios del Desarrollo, Chile, March 1999).

[95] Elizabeth Sussekind, "Defensoría de Policía del Estado de São Paulo, Informe Anual", in *Boletín Policía Y Sociedad Democrática*, No. 3, Año 1 (Chile, Centro de Estudios del Desarrollo, March 1999).

POLITICAL WILL, THE BASIC CRITERIA FOR SUCCESS

As these accounts suggest, political will and government commitment to reform police and assure effective civilian oversight and control remain the driving factor in the success or failure of civilian control of police in Latin America. But the issue of political will needs to be analysed in respect to relative civilian expertise and capabilities in public security policymaking as well as in terms of military, police and elite opposition to reform. In the Colombian case, and possibly also in Argentina, it would seem that weak political leadership and a lack of serious commitment to reform, combined with strategic or design errors, have rendered the civilian review mechanisms vulnerable to police hostility or to failure due to neglect. In both these cases also, the engagement of the human rights community has been weak.

In El Salvador, the Peace Accords created a propitious environment for civilian review despite the limited commitment of conservative elites and the military. This enabled a committed director of the PDH to play an important role in holding police accountable for abuse. But managerial weaknesses led to a failure to consolidate the institution, and a politically-contentious style increased government opposition even as it won civil society support. While Avilés' successor has yet to make his mark on the PDH, it is clear that police misconduct continues at an alarming rate and poses a real threat to the credibility of the force and the entire reform process.

In Brazil, the auditor has also clearly improved police accountability. Again, however, his relative contribution to diminishing police use of deadly force may be far less than the threat of the loss of a second income. Furthermore, this office also remains vulnerable to political tides. Media and human rights community support would probably not have been able to sustain the office in the event of a change in state governorship, particularly in the face of police resistance and popular support for targeted police violence.

Reform requires leadership, but leadership can come from various sources—political or police authorities or even a human rights ombudsman can play a role in reforming police. While government opposition will prevent or kill a reform process, it is not clear that active political support on the part of the government is a requirement for reform to advance. David Bayley makes this point with reference to international assistance for police reform:

> Reformers must never forget that policing cannot be separated from politics. Reform will go only as far as the local political situation will allow. . . . Democratic reform of the police cannot take place in the face of undemocratic governments. . . . At the same time, police can become downwardly responsible and more widely accountable through their own actions if governments are either ambivalent or indifferent to police affairs. Reform requires permission from political regimes, not active direction.[96]

[96] David Bayley, "The Contemporary Practices of Policing: A Comparative View", in *A Role for Democratic Policing, Civilian Police and Multinational Peacekeeping—A Workshop Series*

It seems clear political will is key but is not sufficient to assure that civilian oversight is effective in improving police accountability. These brief case studies indicate that there are a number of factors to be considered in seeking to create durable and effective civilian oversight in Latin America. Some issues are structural, and go to the challenge of institutional consolidation including guarantees for an adequate budget, building a professional staff, and providing assistance with strategic planning and the development of priorities.[97] They also point to the importance of leadership that is smart about building relations with police, civil society and political sectors.

What can civilian review reasonably be expected to achieve in Latin American contexts? It is clearly not a "magic bullet" that can bring about the broad institutional reforms that most Latin American police forces desperately need. Nonetheless, civilian review offers some important benefits. In addition to identifying and holding individual cops accountable for misconduct, civilian review bodies offer the potential to fill a number of current voids. First, civilian review can play a role in strengthening internal police discipline, either through reviewing and reforming police disciplinary manuals and processes or by spurring the police to undertake preemptive reforms that they can control internally. On the other hand, as the Salvadoran case demonstrates, if civilian review is not properly coordinated with the police's own disciplinary mechanisms, its ability to remove allegedly abusive police from the streets in a timely fashion may be very limited. Secondly, civilian review bodies can provide the public and human rights organisations with information that was previously unavailable. Without such information, it is extremely difficult for most organisations to develop more sophisticated analyses of police misconduct and press more effectively for police respect of human rights. Finally, civilian review provides a source for recommendations for reform of police practices and policies based on extensive quantitative analysis rather than extrapolation from limited data, or assertions based on ideology or lifted from other country contexts—all of which have happened repeatedly in Latin America.

The question of the relationship of civilian review of police in Latin America to the human rights movement also warrants further exploration. In the United States and other nations that have created civilian review of police, human rights groups generally press for a high degree of independence as a measure of the board's credibility and legitimacy. And the highly independent bodies generally receive more complaints. Yet this form of review is also the most threatening to the police and can generate tremendous tension and thus little cooperation from police. Research in the United States indicates that the more

(Washington DC, National Institute of Justice/Center for Strategic and International Studies/Police Executive Research Forum, 6 October 1997), p. 6.

[97] Many of these issues are addressed in Centre for Human Rights, Professional Training Series No. 4, *National Human Rights Institutions; A Handbook on the Establishment and Strengthening of National Institutions for the Promotion and Protection of Human Rights* (New York and Geneva, United Nations Centre for Human Rights, 1995).

bureaucratic and formal the disciplinary review process, the less impact it has on individual police behavior. In an adversarial system with formal hearings and processes, police tend to defend their innocence at all costs and rarely allow that the complaint has any legitimacy. On the other side of the coin, if a review body seeks to work with the police it can often jeopardise its credibility with the community.[98] The question is complicated in Latin America by the urgent imperative of ending police abuse for gross violations of human rights which exists side-by-side with an urgent need for institutional reforms of police to make them more professional and effective. From the case studies, it would seem that the ability of civilian review to support larger police reform processes is limited by an understandable tendency to prioritise police accountability and by limited ability in many cases to undertake institutional analyses of police.

Latin American police forces continue to enjoy impunity for gross acts such as disappearances, extra-judicial executions, and torture. Democratic transitions have changed the dynamic. Police abuse persists, but government-sponsored police terror is, in most countries of the region, a thing of the past. Governments no longer commit human rights violations as a matter of overt policies. Their sins are those of omission or tolerance as they fail to rein in deeply-entrenched and often politically-popular abuses against marginalised social sectors seen as the "criminal classes". But abusive policing has failed to control crime or keep it segregated in poor neighbourhoods. As middle classes are affected by crime, and even by police corruption, the demand for government action is heard from new sectors.[99]

Throughout the region, governments are grappling with the need to reduce police misconduct and improve their effectiveness in fighting crime. Police corruption and abuse contribute directly to police ineffectiveness. Police themselves commit some significant portion of crime in many countries. Public fear of and lack of confidence in the police leads to very low crime reporting rates. If police performance is to improve, they must win the confidence and cooperation of the people. If people do not denounce crimes and provide witness testimony, the police cannot build cases and convict criminals; they can only repress "the usual suspects". Yet police themselves and many political sectors resort to easy "get tough on crime" rhetoric that tends to portray all accountability mechanisms as a hindrance to their ability to get the criminals. On the other hand, in contrast to the reflexive resort to the military for assistance with public security tasks, the reform efforts of recent years reflect some increasing sensitivity to and concern

[98] See Douglas W Perez and William Ker Muir, "Administrative Review of Alleged Police Brutality", in Geller and Toch (eds) *And Justice for All; Understanding and Controlling Police Abuse of Force* (Washington DC, Police Executive Research Forum, 1995); Samuel Walker and Betsy Wright, *Citizen Review Resource Manual* (Washington DC, Police Executive Research Form/PERF, 1995); American Civil Liberties Union/ACLU, *Fighting Police Abuse; A Community Action Manual* (New York, ACLU, 1997).

[99] Argentina, Chile, Brazil, El Salvador and Guatemala have all witnessed the creation of upper and middle class or business funded groups that analyse crime and advocate for law and order policies. Their rhetoric and demands are often harsh and display little concern for human rights.

with the need to improve police-community relations and increase civilian oversight.

Civilian review may not be a "magic bullet" that can resolve the deep-rooted issues of police misconduct in Latin America. Yet given the problems of civilian control and police-community relations in Latin America, civilian review offers a useful tool in the effort to develop democratic policing in Latin America and one whose potential goes beyond its actual achievements to date. These initiatives are still in their early days. As they develop over time, police reformers should explore and promote their role in advancing larger processes of institutional reform to confront the lack of police professionalisation, poor police services, and lack of civilian policymaking capacity, in addition to holding police accountable for individual acts of abuse. If the region is to maximise the potential of civilian review, the human rights movement and other civilian sectors and academics should engage the issues, study and learn from the experiences of different countries and apply those learnings in an ongoing critical engagement with public security reform. The accomplishments may have been uneven, but they offer interesting insights into the limitations and potential for civilian review and police reform in Latin America and warrant far more study than this chapter offers.

## References


Abregú, Martín, Palmieri Gustavo and Tiscornia, Sofía. "Informe Nacional: La Situación y los Mecanismos de Control de los Organismos de Seguridad Pública Interior en la República Argentina," in Frühling, Hugo (ed.), *Control Democrático en el Mantenimiento de la Seguridad Interior* (Santiago, Centro de Eestudios del Desarrollo/Ediciones Segundo Centenario, 1998).

Bayley, David H. *What's in a Uniform? A Comparative View of Police-Military Relations in Latin America.* (Paper prepared for the conference on Police and Civil-Military Relations in Latin America, Washington DC, October 1993, Sponsored by the Latin America and Caribbean Center, Florida International University).

—— "The Contemporary Practices of Policing: A Comparative View", in *A Role for Democratic Policing, Civilian Police and Multinational Peacekeeping—A Workshop Series* (Washington DC, National Institute of Justice/Center for Strategic and International Studies/Police Executive Research Forum, October 6, 1997).

Call, Chuck. "Police Reform, Human Rights, and Democratization in Post-Conflict Settings: Lessons from El Salvador", *After the War is Over . . . What Comes Next; Promoting Democracy, Human Rights and Reintegration in Post-Conflict Societies* (Washington DC, US Agency for International Development Conference, October 31–31, 1997).

Centre for Human Rights. Professional Training Series No. 4, National Human Rights Institutions; A Handbook on the Establishment and Strengthening of National Institutions for the Promotion and Protection of Human Rights (New York and Geneva, United Nations Centre for Human Rights, 1995).

Centro de Estudios Legales y Sociales and Human Rights Watch/Americas. *La Inseguridad policial; Violencia de la fuerzas de seguridad en la Argentina* (Buenos Aires, CELS, October 1998).

Centro de Estudios Penales de El Salvador/Centro de Estudios para la Aplicación del Derecho. *Mecanismos Oficiales de Control Sobre la Policia Nacional Civil* (San Salvador, CEPES/FESPAD, December 1997).

Chevigny, Paul. *Edge of the Knife; Police Violence in the Americas* (New York, The New Press, 1995).

Chinchilla, Laura and Rico, José M. *La Prevención Comunitaria del Delito; Perspectivas para América Latina* (Miami, Center for the Administration of Justice, Florida International University, 1997).

Comisión Andina de Juristas. *Defensoría del Pueblo; Analisis Comparado* (Lima, Comisión Andina de Juristas, 1996).

Comisión para la Defensa de los Derechos Humanos en Centroamérica/CODEHUCA. *Informe sobre las Procuradurías de Derechos Humanos de El Salvador, Guatemala y Honduras* (Costa Rica, CODEHUCA, 1999).

Costa, Gino. "The United Nations and Reform of the Police in El Salvador", 2 (3) *International Peacekeeping*, Autumn 1995.

—— *Las Dificultades de Desmilitarizar la Seguridad Pública; Las Naciones Unidas y la Creación de la Policía Nacional Civil en El Salvador* (San Salvador, Universidad Centroamericana, 1998).

Costa, Gina and Núñez Pedraza, Manuel. *Identificación de áreas de cooperación para fortalecer el nuevo asistema de seguridad pública en El Salvador*, Internal evaluation paper commissioned by the Spanish-United Nations Development Program (UNDP) cooperation program to strengthen governance in Central America (Lima/Madrid, May 20, 1996).

Cuéllar M., Roberto. "Seguridad Cuidadana: entre los derechos humanos y la lucha contra la criminalidad", *Ideéle*, No. 91 (Lima, Instituto de Defensa Legal, octubre de 1996).

Frühling Erlich, Hugo. *Modernización de la Policia* (paper presented at the Foro sobre Convivencia y Seguridad Cuidadana en el Istmo Centroamericano, Haiti y República Dominicana, Junio 2–4, 1998, organised by the Inter-American Development Bank).

Goldsmith, Andrew. *The Police Reform Process in Colombia.* (Unpublished paper presented at the September 1996 conference of the International Association for the Civilian Oversight of Law Enforcement/IACOLE, McClean, Virginia).

Human Rights Watch. *World Report 1999* (New York, Human Rights Watch, 1999).

Kincaid, A. Douglas and Gamarra, Eduardo A. Florida International University, *Disorderly Democracy: Redefining Public Security in Latin America*, paper presented to the XIX Annual Conference on the Political Economy of the World System, North-South Center, University of Miami, FL, April 21–22, 1995. (Revised July 1995).

Llorente Sardi, María Victoria. *Perfil de la Policia Colombiana* (Bogotá, Documentos de Trabajo, Paz Pública, Programa sobre Seguridad, Justicia y Violencia, Universidad de los Andes, October 1997).

Mesquita, Paulo. "Policia Comunitaria: la Experiencia en São Paulo", in *Boletín Policía Y Sociedad Democrática*, No. 3, Año 1 (Santiago, Centro de Estudios del Desarrollo, March 1999).

Neild, Rachel and Palmieri, Gustavo. *Themes and Debates in Public Security Reform; A Guide for Civil Society* (Washington DC, WOLA, 1998–99).

Ouvidor da Polícia do Estado de São Paulo. *Relatório Anual de Pestação de Contas* (São Paulo, Ouvidoria da Polícia do Estado de São Paulo, 1996 and 1997).

Pinheiro, Paulo Sergio. "Democracies without Citizenship", *Report on the Americas* (New York, NACLA, Sept/Oct 1996).

"Policia e Consolidação Democrática: o Caso Brasileiro", in *São Paulo sem Medo; um Diagnóstico da Violência Urbana* (São Paulo, Garamond, 1998).

Saín, Marcelo. *La Reforma del Sistema de Seguridad y policial en la Provincia de Buenos Aires* (background paper prepared for a seminar on *Las Reformas Policiales en Argentina*, Buenos Aires, December 1st and 2nd, 1998).

Sussekind, Elizabeth. "Defensoría de Policía del Estado de São Paulo, Informe Anual", in *Boletin Policía Y Sociedad Democrática*, No. 3, Año 1 (Santiago, Centro de Estudios del Desarrollo, March 1999).

Stanley, William. "International Tutelage and Domestic Political Will: Building a New Civilian Police Force in El Salvador", *Studies in Comparative International Development*, May 1995.

United Nations. Crime Trends and Criminal Justice Operations at the Regional and Under-Regional Levels. Results of the Fourth United Nations Survey of Crime Trends and Operations of the Criminal Justice Systems (1986–1990).

MINUSAL. *Evaluación sobre el Sector Seguridad Pública* (United Nations, September 28, 1995).

Vickers, George R. "International Assistance to Internal Security Reforms: Some Lessons from Central America and the Caribbean", *After the War is Over . . . What Comes Next; Promoting Democracy, Human Rights and Reintegration in Post-Conflict Societies* (U.S. Agency for International Development Conference, October 30–31, 1997).

World Bank. *Crime and Violence as Development Issues in Latin America and the Caribbean.* (Paper prepared by the World Bank for the conference on Urban Crime and Violence, Rio de Janeiro, Brazil, March 2–4, 1997).

Washington Office on Latin America, *Demilitarising Public Order; the International Community, Police Reform and Human Rights in Central America and Haiti* (Washington DC, WOLA, 1995).

# 11

# *Accountability and Police Complaints in Northern Ireland: Leaving the Past Behind?*[1]

MARY O'RAWE and LINDA MOORE

## INTRODUCTION

On 15 March 1999, Rosemary Nelson, a lawyer, human rights activist, and mother of three young children, was killed by a bomb planted underneath her car. Rosemary's death has much to say about the crisis in policing[2] in Northern Ireland—a crisis which cries out for the "new beginning" promised by the recently published Patten Report[3] on the future of policing in Northern Ireland. The murder epitomises the failure of successive police accountability mechanisms in Northern Ireland. It also evidences an all too frequent tendency of government to obfuscate and tinker at the edges of problems rather than act swiftly and decisively to transform systems that have been shown to fail.

[1] The political climate in which policing operates in Northern Ireland has changed dramatically over the last three years. After almost twenty years of Conservative government at Westminster, a Labour administration is in office. In Northern Ireland, the main loyalist and republican paramilitary organisations have been on cease-fire, although there have been continued incidents of violence. A referendum in May 1998 produced a majority of over seventy-one per cent of the Northern Ireland population in favour of a multi-party agreement aimed, among other things, at addressing some of the human rights concerns which have been part of the ongoing conflict. A devolved Assembly and Executive are currently functioning, though policing is not within their remit.

[2] The Belfast Agreement 1998 (cmnd 3883, HMSO, Belfast), endorsed by seventy-one per cent of the people of Northern Ireland, stated that policing has been a highly divisive and emotive issue. It recognised that the political settlement creates an opportunity to bring about a "new beginning to policing in Northern Ireland with a police service capable of attracting and sustaining support from the community as a whole". The Agreement established an independent Commission on Policing with a remit to make recommendations for future policing arrangements. Among other things, the Commission was tasked with ensuring "open, accessible and independent means of investigating and adjudicating upon complaints against the police" and finding "means of encouraging widespread community support for these arrangements". The Commission was headed by former UK governor of Hong Kong, Chris Patten, and had seven other members including Dr Maurice Hayes.

[3] *A New Beginning: Policing in Northern Ireland* (The Stationery Office, 1999) (The Patten Report). The thrust of the report is that the purpose of policing is the protection of human rights and that policing can only be effective when done "with the community". It goes on to make one hundred and seventy-five major recommendations as to how this might be achieved.

This chapter will start by analysing the context of Rosemary's death in an effort to understand why the systems in place in Northern Ireland in 1999 were unable to protect a high-profile, professional lawyer in the conduct of her duty. The context of policing in Northern Ireland stands to be dramatically altered by the conclusions of the Independent Commission on Policing for Northern Ireland (the Patten Commission) set up under the Good Friday Agreement.The focus of this chapter is to examine the part a truly effective and independent system for complaints against the police could play in terms of implementing Patten's "new beginning", and the lessons which must be learnt in order for this to happen.

At the time of writing Northern Ireland is in a state of considerable flux and uncertainty not only as to the fate of the Patten recommendations, but as to the whole future of the current peace process. However, whatever the broader political and legislative machinations, it would seem certain that an office of Police Ombudsman will be established in some shape or form during 2000. This follows proposals put forward some two years earlier by Dr Maurice Hayes.[4] Patten sees this post as key to the effective governance of Northern Ireland.[5] At present, it is the Police (NI) Act 1998 which forms the (as yet unoperationalised) legislative basis for the Ombudsman. As Patten has seen the need to restate unequivocal support for the Hayes Report, the Patten Report must be read as rejecting the ability of this legislation to deliver the pro-active, independent, well-resourced accountability mechanism proposed by Hayes. Patten, therefore, provides a much-needed second bite at this particular cherry. However, it would appear that revised legislation will not be introduced to fully meet the concerns of Hayes and Patten. The Police (NI) Bill 2000 does nothing to enhance the powers of this office.

Our policing history over the past thirty years is littered with commissions, reviews and ineffectual complaints mechanisms. While recognising that a successful, independent mechanism for dealing with complaints against the police is only a very small part of a broader democratic accountability debate,[6] it is our

[4] In January 1997, Dr Maurice Hayes published his report, *A Police Ombudsman for Northern Ireland?* (Belfast, HMSO). In this he concluded that the police complaints system that had been operating in Northern Ireland since 1987 was ineffective, insufficiently independent and lacked public confidence. Hayes proposed a new Police Ombudsman with much broader powers than the present Independent Commission for Police Complaints (ICPC) to take over responsibility for the investigation and oversight of complaints. The Government by and large accepted his recommendations and in 1998 enacted legislation to allow for the institution of Police Ombudsman to be established. A member of the Police Authority for Northern Ireland, a body discredited by Patten and a range of other commentators for its lack of representation and its ineffectiveness in holding the Royal Ulster Constabulary (RUC) to account in any meaningful way, has recently been appointed Police Ombudsman designate.

[5] Patten Report, *supra* n. 3, Recommendation 38.

[6] In 1997, Hayes explicitly recognised that any new systems for handling police complaints should be introduced in the context of a broader review of policing arrangements. His comment that "[n]o complaints system, however sophisticated, will compensate for failure to reach a satisfactory resolution of the broader questions of structure, management and political accountability" must underpin any critique or expectation of a complaints mechanism. The Hayes Report, *supra* n. 3, at 2.

analysis that successive failures in this regard stem from a lack of political understanding and will which mirrors the wider crisis in police accountability in Northern Ireland.

We aim to demonstrate, through tracing the development of civilian oversight of police complaints in Northern Ireland, that successive United Kingdom (UK) governments have misread the extent to which government, and thereby, police legitimacy has been disputed. In many respects the criminal justice systems and experience of policing in Northern Ireland have been allowed to differ markedly from the rest of the UK.[7] At the same time, an insistence on the façade of maintaining parity is evidenced by a recurring tendency to transpose English-based complaints "solutions" onto the Northern Ireland statute books with little regard for the very different historical, social and political context. Even before the ink was dry, this policy of selective harmonisation had failed to enhance the Union. It did not increase public confidence in the Royal Ulster Constabulary (RUC). In fact, the reverse is argued. In not fully countenancing the needs of a society divided over its own constitutional basis, successive governments equally failed to understand that the pre-ordained failure of these mechanisms would further entrench mistrust and conflict.

Our analysis will question whether the political will has ever truly existed to invest independent oversight of police activity with sufficient substance to make it real and whether the lessons of past failure have yet been learnt. Rosemary's case provides the starting point for that analysis.

## DEATH OF A HUMAN RIGHTS DEFENDER: THE LESSONS FOR POLICE ACCOUNTABILITY

Rosemary Nelson was not the first lawyer to be killed in Northern Ireland. Like Pat Finucane, who was murdered in 1989, she represented a number of high profile nationalists in cases that cast the RUC in a less than favourable light. Also, like Pat Finucane, it would seem that she was targeted because of associations and assumptions[8] made about her based on the politics or suspected politics of certain of her clients. On 29 September 1998, Rosemary Nelson gave evidence to the United States Congressional Sub-Committee on International Operations

[7] The Northern Ireland (Emergency Provisions) Act 1996/8 (first introduced in 1973) has effectively ensured the operation of a two-tier criminal justice system in Northern Ireland with many due process rights eroded for those suspected of scheduled offences under the Act.

[8] Three weeks before Pat Finucane's murder, junior government minister Douglas Hogg stated in Parliament at Westminster that certain solicitors in Northern Ireland were "unduly sympathetic to the cause of the IRA". At the inquest into Pat Finucane's death, a senior RUC officer refuted allegations that the solicitor had been involved with the Provisional IRA. The campaign for an independent inquiry into his death and allegations of security force collusion which surround it has gained momentum with the ten year anniversary of his death. Now rumours of his supposed IRA affiliations have resurfaced, not least from Unionist politician, Ken Maginnis and former Chief Constable of the RUC, Sir John Herman. What does not seem to be perceived is that such allegations make the need for an independent inquiry more, not less, urgent.

and Human Rights that her professional integrity had been questioned by certain RUC officers, that she had, on occasion been verbally and even physically assaulted and that death threats had been made to her via her clients.

Rosemary Nelson's relationship with the RUC in the conduct of her job had been strained to say the least. One of her clients had been arrested and prosecuted four times since 1989 and as a result spent almost five years in custody without any charges being proved. Rosemary had grave concerns about the adequacy, or even existence, of police evidence on these occasions, and made it clear that she and a number of other lawyers had identified a worrying pattern of "internment by remand" in respect to certain of their clients.

Rosemary Nelson also represented the family of Robert Hamill, a young man beaten to death in a sectarian attack in the centre of Portadown in 1997. Initial press releases emanating from RUC sources stated that Robert had been injured during his involvement in a fight between rival gangs. It has subsequently been accepted that he and his companions were attacked without provocation. Armed police officers parked in an armoured police vehicle twenty feet away failed to intervene. Rosemary and others, such as the Committee on the Administration of Justice (CAJ), criticised this lack of action and deemed the subsequent murder investigation to be wholly inadequate.[9]

Rosemary further acted as legal adviser to the residents of Garvaghy Road in Portadown in their opposition to Orange marches going through their area without consent, and she, from her own experience, raised serious concerns in respect of policing during the "Seige of Drumcree" in 1997 and at other times.

The year prior to Rosemary's death, a United Nations Special Rapporteur, Dato Param Cumaraswamy, concluded that members of the RUC had engaged in "activities [in respect of defence lawyers] which constitute intimidation, hindrance, harassment or improper interference".[10] He expressed particular concerns about the RUC investigative mechanism, stating in oral testimony to the UN Human Rights Commission in Geneva:

> . . . the fact remains that the RUC was fully aware of these complaints . . . it failed to take note and allowed the situation to deteriorate. There was, in my view, a complete indifference shown by the RUC to the allegations.[11]

[9] There appeared to be little or no attempt to apprehend suspects or gather evidence on the night of the incident. Of the six people charged after Robert Hamill's death, the cases against five were withdrawn for lack of evidence and the trial of the remaining defendant resulted in his acquittal for murder. This case had much resonance with the racial murder, in 1993, of black teenager Stephen Lawrence in England, and Rosemary Nelson had been in discussion with a senior English barrister involved in representing the Lawrence family as to the possibility of a private prosecution or civil action against the police officers and others involved. The Director of Public Prosecutions (DPP) in Northern Ireland has directed no prosecution of the police officers concerned.

[10] Published 1 April 1998: *Report on the Mission of the Special Rapporteur to the United Kingdom of Great Britain and Northern Ireland*, submitted pursuant to Commission on Human Rights Resolution 1997/23. E/CN.4/1998/39/Add.4, 5 March 1998.

[11] *Supra* n. 3.

Cumaraswamy was sufficiently convinced of the seriousness of the situation to express public concern for the safety of a number of solicitors, including Rosemary Nelson.[12]

The UK Government's response was to welcome the report and then proceed to ignore every one of its recommendations aimed at strengthening accountability, setting the public's mind at rest in respect of allegations of collusion between the security forces and loyalist paramilitary groupings and protecting lawyers in the conduct of their duty. In this it followed a pattern of government failure to make police accountability effective in Northern Ireland.

Given the circumstances surrounding Rosemary's death it was inevitable that calls would be made to remove responsibility for the investigation into her death from the RUC. Clearly anticipating such demands, RUC Chief Constable, Ronnie Flanagan, immediately called in the Chief Constable of Kent and an FBI representative to supervise the RUC investigation into Rosemary's murder. In other circumstances such a pro-active move might have taken the ground from under those calling for a truly independent investigation. However, it soon became public knowledge that the RUC investigation into the death threats and other complaints about Rosemary's treatment by a number of RUC officers had been considered problematic by the member of the Independent Commission for Police Complaints (ICPC) charged with supervision of the investigation. The RUC's handling of the matter and attitudes displayed by police officers during interviews evinced "an observable general hostility, evasiveness and disinterest" on the part of over twenty officers against whom allegations were made. Matters central to the inquiry were "not addressed or addressed unsatisfactorily" and police officers seemed to view Rosemary Nelson with the same thinly veiled antipathy they held for her clients, failing to appreciate her role as a professional lawyer.

On foot of these concerns, on 9 July 1998 the complaints investigation was taken over by Commander Niall Mulvihill of the London Metropolitan Police Service as investigating officer. He was also tasked by the Chief Constable to undertake a parallel, though "*not a full and formal*" investigation into the RUC's investigative procedures in this case.

On 22 March 1999 a statement of satisfaction with the complaints investigation was issued by the ICPC and the relevant files passed, as usual, to the Director of Public Prosecutions. By this time, Rosemary Nelson was dead.

Information relating to the RUC conduct of the complaints investigation has continued to emerge including the fact that initially the RUC were not even minded to conduct an investigation into the allegations and that one police officer had classified the death threats as "incivility". Rosemary's family, nationalist politicians and a number of non-governmental organisations became even more convinced that it would not be appropriate for the RUC to investigate her

[12] Solicitors were not named directly, though the report made obvious and specific reference to Rosemary Nelson, for example at paragraph sixteen, and the Special Rapporteur indicated subsequently that he was particularly concerned about her safety.

murder. Concerns were also expressed that, within days of being drafted in to give the investigation a strong independent element, Mr Phillips, the Chief Constable of Kent and the FBI Legal Attache, issued a press release on RUC headed paper via the press office at RUC Headquarters that in their "clear professional judgement . . . the best chance of detecting those responsible lies in the RUC conducting the investigation".[13]

On 28 March 1999 Chief Constable Flanagan announced that a further senior police officer from Norfolk had been called in to "direct, control and command" the day-to-day investigation, but that Phillips and the FBI representatives would maintain their supervisory role.[14] This new officer was to be "ever present and ever visible" in Northern Ireland whereas Mr Phillips would be unable to maintain a constant presence due to "other commitments".[15]

Pressure for a fully independent inquiry continues, with the UN Special Rapporteur publicly stating that "it may be better for the credibility of the force if RUC officers were not involved".[16]

On 30 March 1999 the Chair of the ICPC and the Chief Constable issued a joint statement in relation to the investigations of Rosemary Nelson's complaints. Commander Mulvihill's full report into the RUC investigative procedures was never published. However, appended to the joint statement was an edited version in which the Commander stated his opinion that the previous investigation though not "truly outstanding", was "adequate"[17] with the Chief Inspector having "done his best, worked industriously and . . . any perception that he might somehow have failed [being] wholly unintentional on his part." Although gleaning much of his information through the reading of "cold" transcripts of interviews and speaking to the Chief Inspector in question, and accepting that "something can get lost in the translation", he went on to conclude that:

> a breakdown in communication, coupled with a series of unrelated administrative and organisational problems combined to create an "air of concern" that was wholly at odds with, and disproportionate to, the actual situation.

The subtext was clear—the ICPC member, an experienced barrister, had overreacted and prejudiced the "smooth" running of the investigation herself by blowing things out of all proportion.

[13] Press Release dated 19 March 1999.

[14] It would appear that they have not done so. Colin Port is currently heading the investigation.

[15] RUC Press Release.

[16] Reported in the *Irish Times*, 29 March 1999.

[17] Despite judging the original investigation to be satisfactory, Mulvihill made twenty recommendations aimed at improving the relationship between the RUC and ICPC. Among these was that audio-recording should be introduced in holding centres where those arrested under the Prevention of Terrorism Act are interrogated—a recommendation immediately acted upon by the RUC Chief Constable, and that "RUC officers need to be reminded that . . . a resort to belligerence or hostility is unhelpful". The latter recommendation stemmed from the "displeasure" registered by some officers "at being subjected to interviews under caution". Many felt (and feel) affronted at what they perceive as the "indignity of being treated like a common criminal".

On the basis of Commander Mulvihill's findings, a sinister subplot was set in train whereby the authorities, including members of the police, the Police Authority and ICPC itself, sought to distance themselves from the original ICPC concerns, preferring that they be seen as the subjective views of the individual supervising member.

In response to those who pointed to the statute-based concerns as a reason why an RUC murder investigation would not be credible, the Chair of the Police Authority felt it necessary to repeat the tried and tested formula of any police force in denial that some of those seeking the removal of the RUC from the Nelson murder inquiry were more interested in denigrating the force than seeing the killers convicted.

Perhaps the most worrying aspect of this "joint statement" approach was not the revelation that no police officers have been suspended or disciplined as a result of concerns raised, but that the ICPC, a body charged with a statutory duty to oversee complaint investigations and report on whether these had been carried out satisfactorily, was prepared to allow one of its members to stand alone for doing the job she was appointed to do. The personalisation of what was and should have remained an ICPC document, and the "whispering campaign"[18] which grew up around it served to isolate the Supervising Member and expose her to the same risks as those faced by Rosemary Nelson and others who dared raise their heads above the parapet in Northern Ireland.

The organisation thus notched up yet another failure in the creation of a system to inspire public and police confidence and contributed to a climate of fear and self-censorship which does little for the proper administration of justice. Despite a later decision[19] by the ICPC to issue a statement endorsing the professionalism of their colleague, and despite the ICPC chair writing a fifteen page response[20] to Commander Mulvihill's report, which again criticised the RUC's handling of the case and endorsed the original findings of the Supervising Member—the damage had already been done.

The reasons for focusing so intently on the minutiae of this particular case are twofold. First, it serves to head off any claim that Northern Ireland's problems are in the past. Second, it is in the minutiae and nuances, in the political twists and turns of a system's operation that one gets the best sense of its effectiveness or otherwise. Real life events expose the flimsiness of paper safeguards and should be the catalyst for re-evaluation and meaningful change. This case starkly demonstrates the problems of police investigating police, particularly in a society as deeply divided as Northern Ireland. It also shows how the very mechanisms put in place to scrutinise police conduct can themselves perpetuate

[18] Gerry Moriarty, p. 14 The *Irish Times*, 16 April 1999: "Concerns over RUC Investigations into Nelson and Finucane Murders being acted on at last".

[19] This decision was taken at a regular monthly meeting on 23 April 1999.

[20] Though confidential, this document was eventually leaked to the press. The question is whether it is the leak or the fact that the document was not automatically made public which raises more cause for concern.

a code of silence and self-censorship. Appointed by the Secretary of State, the majority of members of bodies dealing with police accountability in Northern Ireland represent only the section of the Northern Ireland populace with sufficient trust in the organs of government and respect for the police institution to sit on such bodies in the first place. Given the tendency of policing to be a political football and attitudes to the RUC being a strong badge of identification among different political camps, the types of people selected to sit on such bodies are perceived as having a pro-police bias by their very appointment. That politics lie not too far from the surface of "police accountability" in Northern Ireland is evidenced by the case outlined above. On top of this, lack of powers, lack of resources and often lack of co-operation from complainants can lead to an inbuilt defensiveness which actually ties members of such bodies more closely to the police in terms of the potential for agency capture. Meanwhile those who see the ICPC or the Police Authority for Northern Ireland (PANI) failing to produce results or failing to be pro-active in their role as guardians of the guards, feel that there is little point in co-operating with the establishment. By not working with such bodies, however, they are deemed to have an anti-state or other sinister political agenda, which adds to the climate of mistrust. To examine how this state of affairs has come to exist and be tolerated, and how the cycle might be broken we must look to the history of policing in Northern Ireland.

## POLICING IN NORTHERN IRELAND: THE POLITICAL CONTEXT

Since its creation, following the partition of Ireland nearly eighty years ago,[21] the legitimacy of the Northern Ireland state has been contested. Because a substantial section of the population[22] had no allegiance to the new state, the Unionist Government at Stormont,[23] deliberately built up a strong and loyal police force to suppress the threat to their disputed jurisdiction.

The police force established[24] for Northern Ireland in 1922 was the Royal Ulster Constabulary. From its inception, religion and politics played a defining role. [25] The RUC was directly accountable to the Unionist Government at Stormont, which attempted to turn the force into "almost the armed wing of

[21] The six north-eastern counties of the island of Ireland remained part of the wider union of the United Kingdom, and the rest of the island left the union. The latter jurisdiction initially declared itself a Free State and subsequently a Republic.

[22] Around a third of the population of Northern Ireland was Catholic at this time. This figure now exceeds forty per cent.

[23] Northern Ireland's parliament which held power until the imposition of Direct Rule by the UK government at Westminster in 1972.

[24] Under the Constabulary Act (NI) 1922.

[25] A quota system was designed to ensure that a third of its three thousand personnel were Catholic. Despite this the Catholic quota was never filled. Representation peaked in 1923 at twenty one and a half per cent and has since decreased to its present level of seven and a half per cent of a force of around thirteen thousand officers.

unionism".[26] On a macro level, the delegation of a range of highly repressive emergency powers[27] to the police fuelled alienation, especially since the powers were used predominantly, although not exclusively, against the Catholic, nationalist community. The creation of a unionist and Protestant ethos and culture within the heart of the organisation did not stop there. Within three months of the force's existence an Orange Order[28] lodge was formed specifically to cater for police membership.[29] Catholic/nationalist communities perceived the RUC as a partisan force, and a key weapon in perpetuating the discriminatory regime instituted by the Stormont Government to preserve it power base.

The 1960s saw the growth of the civil rights movement in Northern Ireland. Disbandment of the B-Specials[30] and repeal of special powers were among the key demands of the demonstrators. Television images of police officers brutally attacking unarmed civil rights activists were shown world-wide. The Cameron Commission set up by the UK Government to examine the causes of the violence which erupted after October 1968 found the RUC "guilty of misconduct which involved assault and battery [and] malicious damage to property".[31]

Following the "disturbances" Lord Hunt was called in by the British Prime Minister to report and make recommendations on policing in Northern Ireland. The Hunt Report of 1969 recommended that the police become less paramilitary in character and conform to a more liberal, democratic model of policing. The report led to the passage of the Police Act (NI) 1970, which accepted the principle of a civilianised and unarmed police force and established a police authority intended to be representative of the whole community. However, following a short period of disarmament, the RUC was re-armed in the face of continuing unrest, and the Police Authority never became the representative body envisaged by Hunt.[32]

The opportunity was not taken to review whether changes brought about by Hunt's report were sufficient. Hence, the RUC and other police related institutions continued to be unrepresentative of the population as a whole, and many

26 See J Brewer and K Magee, *Inside the RUC: Routine Policing in a Divided Society* (Oxford, Clarendon, 1991), p. 3.

27 The Civil Authorities (Special Powers) Act (NI) 1922 provided for internment without trial, sweeping powers of search, arrest and detention; powers to ban demonstrations and newspapers; the outlawing of organisations and many other abrogations of basic rights.

28 A religious and political organisation open only to Protestants.

29 See Brewer and Magee, *supra* n. 26, M Farrell, *Northern Ireland: The Orange State* (London, Pluto Press, 1976).

30 The B-Specials were a special reserve section of the RUC.

31 See report of the Cameron Commission (1969) Cmnd 532, Belfast, HMSO.

32 Paragraph 102, House of Commons, Northern Ireland Affairs Committee (3rd Report, Vol 1) *Composition, Recruitment and Training of the RUC* (London, The Stationery Office, 1998) states: "The present arrangements for accountability of the RUC are unique in the UK. Under the existing system of police administration, the Chief Constable is directly responsible to the Secretary of State. The Police Authority for Northern Ireland has only a small role. It has never been what Lord Hunt envisaged when he recommended a body to which the Chief Constable could be accountable". See also J McGarry and B O'Leary, *Policing Northern Ireland: Proposals for a New Start* (Belfast, Blackstaff Press, 1999).

of the criticisms of policing have remained unresolved throughout the course of the present "Troubles".[33]

In 1972 the Stormont Parliament was prorogued and Direct Rule from Westminster established. This removed policing from direct Unionist control but introduced its own brand of democratic deficit while leaving concerns over police malpractice and legitimacy to fester.[34] The power of the Secretary of State for Northern Ireland[35] in relation to criminal justice issues has had profound implications for security forces and citizens alike in terms of accountability structures and legal and political redress for perceived wrongdoing. So whereas a tripartite accountability structure exists consisting of the Secretary of State, the Chief Constable and, very much the poor relation, the Police Authority for Northern Ireland, the situation remains whereby a significant portion of the population view the RUC as their force, while another section of the population remain alienated to a greater or lesser extent from the forces of law and order.

The communally divided nature of Northern Ireland society has put pressure on the police, causing the organisation to turn inwards and fall back on the safety net of a total institution which has, in turn, entrenched an unrepresentative and defensive organisational culture. The RUC is unrepresentative of the communities it serves—only ten and a half per cent of regular officers are female and seven and a half per cent are Catholic although Catholics comprise over forty per cent of the population. Less than a handful of officers are from ethnic minority backgrounds.[36] Allegations persist of sexual and sectarian harassment both directed at civilians by RUC officers and within the organisational culture of the force.[37] The force remains predominantly Protestant, British, male and Unionist.[38]

"Ownership" by the Protestant community is categorically denied by the leadership of the RUC, who insist that the force serves all sections of Northern Irish society equally. Regarding the Anglo-Irish Agreement of 1985, and events around Drumcree over the past three years, the RUC have increasingly found themselves confronting Unionist protest in a way they had not had to previously. However, this does not mean police officers do not have loyalties and

[33] A term used locally to describe thirty years of violent political unrest from 1969 on.

[34] A system of QUANGOs (Quasi-Autonomous Non-Governmental Organisations) was implemented which put much of Northern Ireland's affairs into the hands of civil servants and serves as the basis for the government of Northern Ireland to the present day. The creation of the new Northern Ireland Assembly, following the Good Friday Agreement *did* alter this position to a certain extent, but even *with* an Executive up and running, many powers will continue to be reserved to Westminster in the short to medium term at least, and civil servants will retain much of their control. Justice is one such area.

[35] A UK government minister appointed by the Prime Minister.

[36] PANI report to the Patten Commission, 1998.

[37] G Ellison, *Professionalism in the Royal Ulster Constabulary: an Examination of the Institutional Discourse*, unpublished DPhil, University of Ulster, 1997; R McVeigh, *Harassment: "It's part of life here"* (Belfast, CAJ, 1994).

[38] See M O'Rawe and L Moore, *Human Rights on Duty: Principles for Better Policing—International Lessons for Northern Ireland* (Belfast, CAJ, 1997); C Ellison and R McVeigh, *ibid.*

allegiances to the communities from which they come;[39] nor that certain expectations do not continue within those communities as to how they should be served by the RUC.[40]

"Emergency"[41] legislation[42] has been on the statute books since Northern Ireland came into being and the RUC has never policed except against a backdrop of these extensive powers. The primacy of security policing over ordinary policing[43] has led not only to increasing militarisation, with heavily fortified police stations and officers routinely armed, but also a lack of sufficient accountability and continuing allegations of human rights abuse.

These have included:

- allegations of a "shoot to kill" policy in the early 1980s. An investigation of these allegations by John Stalker of the Greater Manchester Police, completed by the West Yorkshire Chief Constable, Colin Sampson, was dogged by controversy and neither report was ever made public;[44]
- allegations of collusion between the police and paramilitary groups. John Stevens (then Deputy Chief Constable of the Cambridgeshire police), carried out two separate investigations in 1989 and 1992. This failed to assuage public concerns for although several loyalists were jailed as a result of these investigations, no police officers were successfully prosecuted, and again the full report was never made public;[45]
- the security forces, both police and army, have been responsible for approximately three hundred and sixty deaths, with the RUC being directly responsible for over fifty deaths. Yet less than a handful of soldiers and no

[39] For example it was reported in the *Irish News*, 25 July 1998 that Holywood RUC Station had displayed a poster supporting the Orange Order protest at Drumcree behind glass on its public information board.

[40] For example Orange Order spokesman Davy Jones, speaking at a Drumcree Support rally in Newtownabbey on 28 July 1998, expressed this view in his comment: "How can the police return to live among the Protestant community when they have been involved in excess violence against *their own people*?" (emphasis added).

[41] This appears in inverted commas to signify that anti-terrorist legislation in Northern Ireland has been a permanent part of the framework of government for nearly eighty years and has thus lost the "temporariness" usually signified by the appellation.

[42] Including the Northern Ireland (Emergency Provisions) Acts 1996 and 1998, the Prevention of Terrorism (Temporary Provisions) Act 1989 and the Criminal Justice (Terrorism and Conspiracy) Act 1998.

[43] See Brewer and Magee's ethnographic study which documents the tension between the RUC's role as civilian police service and paramilitary force, *supra* n. 26.

[44] J Stalker, *Stalker* (London, Harrap, 1988). The Patten Commission has recommended that the Ombudsman have access to these files.

[45] We do know that Stevens concluded that collusion was neither institutionalised nor widespread. However, it came to light in 1999 that this conclusion was apparently reached without Stevens investigating the murder of solicitor Pat Finucane. Stevens was asked by Chief Constable Flanagan in April 1999 to return to investigate the Finucane killing. As a result of these investigations a former soldier with the Ulster Defence Regiment was arrested and charged with Finucane's murder in June 1999. On 24 June 1999 he admitted in court to being a Special Branch agent in the pay of the RUC at the time of the murder, and that he had supplied information relating to the killing to the RUC on the day Pat Finucane was killed. Two other people have subsequently been charged in relation to the murder.

police officers have been convicted of murder on duty, which gives rise to the perception of impunity;[46] and

- the use of plastic bullets by the security forces has resulted in the deaths of seventeen people, including eight children, and thousands of injuries.[47] Plastic bullets have been used disproportionately against members of the nationalist community, fuelling claims of sectarianism.

Rather than prevent or attempt to redress these issues, successive governments have adopted a policy of denial[48] which has allowed division to grow. On one level the RUC recognises that it has problems, or at least that the conflict has forced it to evolve in a way that is not necessarily conducive with "ordinary" policing. In line with other police forces throughout the world, there have been moves in the RUC towards civilianisation and proposals for decentralisation.[49] On the other hand, because of the very real threat, stress and danger suffered by police performing a security (as well as an "ordinary" police) function, they continue to police using extraordinary powers and are exempt from many levels of scrutiny faced by other UK forces.[50] Criticism continues to trigger almost an automatic reflex by government, unionist politicians and the RUC themselves to counter with reference to the sacrifice of members of the RUC.[51] Whereas the sacrifice of many members of the RUC is undoubted, it cannot be deemed as a reason to ignore, deny or absolve the RUC of wrongdoing.

Upholding the RUC as, if not perfect, then blameless, courageous, impartial, professional, and/or the "best police force in the world"[52] at every possible juncture[53] is not the best way to engender a culture of openness and accountability.

[46] M O'Rawe and L Moore, *supra* n. 37, Ch. 3; Human Rights Watch/Helsinki, *To Serve without Favor: Policing, Human Rights and Accountability in Northern Ireland* (New York, Human Rights Watch, 1997).

[47] Human Rights Watch/Helsinki, *ibid.*

[48] For a more in-depth discussion of the phenomenon of official denial in relation to policing in Northern Ireland see M O'Rawe and L Moore, *Human Rights on Duty* and L Moore and M O'Rawe, "International Lessons for the Transformation of Policing in Northern Ireland", 2 (4) *The International Journal of Human Rights*, Winter 1998.

[49] RUC 1996.

[50] For example see paragraph 102, House of Commons, Northern Ireland Affairs Committee (3rd Report, Vol 1) *Composition, Recruitment and Training of the RUC* (London: The Stationery Office, 1998) which states: "The present arrangements for accountability of the RUC are unique in the UK. Under the existing system of police administration, the Chief Constable is directly responsible to the Secretary of State. The Police Authority for Northern Ireland has only a small role. It has never been what Lord Hunt envisaged when he recommended a body to which the Chief Constable could be accountable". Similarly reported in paragraph 99 is the RUC's special relationship with Her Majesty's Inspectorate of Constabulary who "inspects the RUC by invitation on an informal basis and his findings are recommendations only".

[51] With three hundred and two officers having lost their lives and eight thousand three hundred and twenty-six injured.

[52] Former Chief Constable Hugh Annesley described his force as "an outstanding professional police service . . . one of the best if not the best in the world", *Irish News*, 13 January 1995, p. 1.

[53] For example, Ian Paisley MP during second reading of Police (Northern Ireland) Bill 15 December 1997 reported in *Hansard* (The Parliamentary Debates Official Report) 6th series, Vol 303 at Column 79 that "the RUC is second to no other force in its professionalism, fairness and impartiality . . . I do not believe that any police force in Europe is more open or accountable" or during

This attitude has marginalised dissent by attributing an anti-democratic political agenda to critics. More than this, it has permitted issues around the legality and legitimacy of state policing to remain caught up and paralysed in a web of inter-communal strife while governments have appeared more anxious to deflect criticism from the state by denying any role as a protagonist in the conflict. By maintaining the fiction that state agents simply "hold the ring" in a two-dimensional paradigm, the state seeks to divert all attention away from heavy-handed or otherwise inappropriate government responses to paramilitary violence on the one hand, and to disguise or justify its inaction in response to allegations of serious misconduct by the security forces on the other.

However, in failing to institute proper standards and structures of accountability, government has not made the role of the RUC any easier, but instead has failed police and people alike.

## COMPLAINTS: THE STORY SO FAR

The history of complaints processes in Northern Ireland seems to bear out the notion of state pre-occupation with issues other than those which might actually get to the root of policing problems in a divided society. The pattern which has emerged suggests that every ten years or so, the system is revamped yet the small matter of ineffective accountability machinery continues.

Under the Stormont regime, investigation of complaints about police officers was at the discretion of the Inspector-General of the RUC.[54] Investigation of complaints lay solely in the hands of the police.[55]

The system remained basically unchanged until the development of the civil rights movement which campaigned among other issues for greater accountability in policing. In 1969 the Cameron Commission found that the lack of an effective complaints system was damaging to public confidence in policing. It recommended the establishment of an independent tribunal, modelled on the ombudsman system, to investigate complaints and recommend disciplinary charges against RUC members.

Soon after, the Hunt Report made recommendations for the future of policing in Northern Ireland. Hunt found the existing method of dealing with complaints against the police to be defective and concluded that:

the same debate, Ken Maginnis MP berating the minister of State (NIO) for his failure to provide "clear and unequivocal recognition" of the fact that "no other police force in the civilised western world has a better record than the RUC" at Column 62—despite Adam Ingram having several times paid tribute to the RUC in the strongest terms throughout the course of his own speech.

[54] Now known as the Chief Constable.

[55] See I Topping, "The Police Complaints System in Northern Ireland", in A Goldsmith (ed.), *Complaints Against the Police: the Trend to External Review* (Oxford, Clarendon, 1991) p. 244.

> in our view . . . there is one essential condition to the improvement of relations between the R.U.C. and the public: this is a better method of dealing with complaints against the police.[56]

Hunt's recommendations on complaints were based on the prevailing English model[57] and were less radical than those proposed by Cameron. The Police Act (NI) 1970 was based largely on Hunt's proposals. Under the Act most complaints continued to be investigated by the RUC, although some safeguards were introduced.[58]

The Act also established that the civilian Police Authority should keep itself "informed" as to the manner in which complaints from members of the public against police officers were dealt with. In cases where a complaint affected the public interest, the Authority could refer the matter to an independent tribunal. The Authority used this procedure once between 1970 and 1987.[59]

Following Hunt, the new Chief Constable, Arthur Young, was soon put under pressure to investigate serious allegations of police misconduct. Police officers had burst into the home of Samuel Devenny and brutally attacked him in front of his family. He was hospitalised and died several months later as a result of injuries caused by the police. An investigation by a local county inspector had been inconclusive, so Young sent for two Scotland Yard officers as a "confidence building measure with the Catholic community".[60] These officers spent nearly six months trying unsuccessfully to trace the eight of the five hundred RUC men on duty in Derry that day who had broken into the Devenny home.[61] In November 1970 Chief Constable Young was forced to admit that the unsatisfactory result of the inquiry was due to a "conspiracy of silence among members of the RUC".[62]

The weakness of the new complaints procedures and other accountability mechanisms thus allowed a pattern of human rights abuse to continue unchecked. In August 1971 internment without trial was introduced, with widespread allegations of police brutality against internees. These allegations were persistently denied by all in authority,[63] yet the British Government subsequently paid out over half a million pounds in compensation for injuries received,[64] with Britain being found guilty of breaching Article 3 of the

[56] Report of the Advisory Committee on Police in Northern Ireland, 1969, para 133.

[57] As defined in the Police Act 1964 for England and Wales.

[58] The RUC was required to record all complaints, to appoint investigating officers from a different division from that of the accused officer, and to forward information relating to possible criminal conduct by a police officer to the requisite criminal authority (now the Director of Public Prosecutions).

[59] In the case of James Rafferty, 11 January 1976. Details cited in C Ryder, *The RUC 1922–1997: a Force under Fire* (London, Mandarin, 1997), p. 200.

[60] *Ibid* at 117.

[61] *Ibid.*

[62] P Bew and N Gillespie, *Northern Ireland: A Chronology of the Troubles 1968–1993* (Gill & Macmillan, 1993), p. 17.

[63] The Compton Inquiry.

[64] P Taylor, *Beating the Terrorists? Interrogation in Omagh Gough and Castlereagh* (Harmondsworth, Penguin, 1980), p. 14.

European Convention on Human Rights.[65] Unfortunately, it obviously seemed easier on a political level to pay up and wait for the publicity to die down than to effect root and branch change of the accountability system.

Allegations of ill-treatment of detainees persisted after internment ended,[66] as did concerns about the failure of the complaints and disciplinary process to bring officers to account. These concerns coincided with an inquiry into the complaint process in England and Wales.[67]

In 1974, the Black Working Party was established to investigate and make recommendations on the handling of complaints against the police in Northern Ireland.[68] In submissions, several independent groups criticised the existing system and called for the investigation of all complaints against the RUC by independent tribunals or bodies.[69]

The Black Working Party was hampered by its determination to base any change to the complaints system in Northern Ireland on the English model. In reviewing the history of complaints mechanisms in Northern Ireland, it would appear that this mindset was, unfortunately, not unusual.

While new legislation based on Black was pending, the Police Authority made a pre-emptory move by establishing its own complaints committee in 1976, the remit of which bizarrely included both publicity and complaints.[70]

The committee had six members and met with senior police officers every month at RUC headquarters to examine the Complaints Register. This register contained only bare essentials: the registration of the complaint, its number and the stage the investigation had reached. In his book on the mistreatment of detainees in interrogation centres, Peter Taylor records that access to complaints files became a "matter of bitter dispute".[71] Without seeing the files the PANI committee could not fulfil its statutory obligation to "keep itself informed" as to how complaints were handled, but the RUC insisted that the contents of files were confidential. Occasionally the committee was treated to selected readings by the RUC. According to one former member, Donal Murphy, the files could contain the complete works of Shakespeare for all the Complaints Committee knew.[72]

[65] *Ireland* v *UK* (1979/1980) 2 EHRR 25. The Commission found that torture had taken place. The Court held the treatment to be "cruel inhuman and degrading".

[66] In 1975.

[67] The Gardner-Brown Report.

[68] Led by Sir Harold Black, former Secretary of the Northern Ireland Cabinet, it was comprised of representatives of the Police Authority, the Northern Ireland Office, the RUC and its representative organisations.

[69] CAJ, *Cause for Complaint: The system for dealing with complaints against the police in Northern Ireland*, CAJ Pamphlet no 16, May 1990, p. 2. Proposals for an independent means for dealing with complaints were also made in the first annual report of the newly appointed government body, the Standing Advisory Commission on Human Rights. The latter stated that an independent system would be "an important step towards restoring wider confidence in the RUC".

[70] P Taylor, *supra* n. 64 at p. 50. It would seem that the Police Authority still has a Complaints and Public Relations Committee.

[71] *Ibid* at 51.

[72] *Ibid.*

Throughout the 1970s, the PANI complaints committee raised questions about allegations of assault, but was apparently unable to gain the necessary access to investigate these. Indeed the Chief Constable told the Authority there were statutory procedures in place for dealing with complaints, that it was not their business to interest themselves in individual cases and that to do so may affect the morale of the force.[73] While private meetings were held expressing concern to the Chief Constable about allegations, the Authority failed to make effective public protest on the issue. Again the need to show solidarity with the RUC or at least not be seen to publicly undermine the force, would appear to have been the order of the day.

Following the Black Working Party, the Police (NI) Order 1977 established a system largely based on the English model. This instituted an independent Police Complaints Board (PCB) for Northern Ireland, but as with the (now failed) English model, the actual investigation of complaints still lay in police hands. The PCB's role was solely to monitor the outcome of complaints with respect to discipline and direct that disciplinary charges be brought in the event of disagreement with the Chief Constable.[74]

The system lacked a means of informal resolution of minor complaints thus necessitating "a somewhat ponderous formal system . . . for all complaints".[75] Another difficulty which continues to the present day is the use of the criminal standard of proof (beyond reasonable doubt) in adjudicating disciplinary cases. As the legislation required the Chief Constable to direct all cases involving potential criminal charges to the Director of Public Prosecutions (DPP), and as in the vast majority of these cases the DPP directed that there should be no prosecution, the Chief Constable took the view that the consideration of disciplinary charges would be inappropriate on the grounds that the evidence needed to sustain a charge would be identical to that used by the DPP.[76]

The PCB recognised from an early stage that the operation of this so-called double jeopardy principle rendered it virtually powerless.[77] It was not helped by the fact that the 1977 Order obliged the Board to have regard to guidance from the Secretary of State on the issue of disciplinary charges, thereby linking politics into so-called independent oversight. A Home Office Circular affirming the

[73] For example see the case of Pearse Kerr discussed in Taylor at 204.

[74] Charges brought at the direction of the PCB would be heard by a tribunal made up of the Chief Constable and two PCB members.

[75] In practice, a very high proportion of reports—nearly eighty per cent in 1980 were referred to the DPP see Topping *supra* n. 55, at 246.

[76] The failure of the DPP to direct cases for prosecution is partly explained by his remit. In November 1977, the DPP put concerns in writing to the Chief Constable, Sir Kenneth Newman. He had reviewed three hundred complaints alleging assault by the police on individuals made between 1 January and 30 September 1977. Although in about ten per cent of these cases there was actual medical evidence that assault had taken place, the DPP had only been able to direct one prosecution against the police. It had been impossible in most cases to establish which particular detective had been involved in the assault and so no prosecution was possible. Details in Taylor, *supra* n. 64 at 228.

[77] See Annual Report for 1977 at 5–6. The PCB eventually made a special report to the Secretary of State in 1979.

Chief Constable's interpretation of the "double jeopardy" principle was agreed as the basis of that guidance. In a climate where some eighty to ninety per cent of complaints investigations were being referred to the DPP,[78] McClelland quotes from a confidential internal Northern Ireland Office (NIO) memorandum which suggests that: "the police were deliberately translating minor disciplinary allegations into more serious criminal charges knowing full well that the DPP would direct no prosecution".[79] This memo indicates that officialdom obviously realised this was a problem, but chose to ignore it.

In June 1978, an Amnesty International report detailed allegations of ill-treatment in detention centres in Northern Ireland. An official committee of inquiry was appointed chaired by Judge Bennett to examine both interrogation procedures and the system for dealing with complaints against police officers. Before Bennett reported, Dr Rob Irwin stated on national television that he had examined more than one hundred and fifty prisoners who alleged they had been ill-treated at the police detention centre at Castlereagh during the previous three years. He said that he had seen injuries to joints and ruptured ear-drums which could not have been self-inflicted.[80] The Bennett Report, published a few days later, found that a small number of RUC officers had used brutality in obtaining confessions. Bennett was critical of the complaints process, concluding that investigative reports sometimes incorporated an assumption that the statement of an alleged "terrorist" suspect could not be believed. Bennett recommended:

- more frequent use of outside investigators;
- the Chief Constable should appoint an investigating officer from another UK police force whenever there was allegation of serious assault and medical evidence to support the allegation; and
- the Police Authority should make "appropriate" use of its power to convene a tribunal.[81]

While most of Bennett's recommendations for reform of interrogation procedures were implemented, his proposals regarding the complaints procedure were not. Again it seems that the Government chose to ignore evidence which pointed to human rights abuse by the RUC, and again it was change in the English system which prompted change in Northern Ireland. In 1981 the Scarman Inquiry reported on disturbances in Brixton and confirmed a breakdown in trust between black communities and the police with the situation exacerbated by an ineffective complaints process.

[78] Comparable figure for England and Wales is thirty-seven per cent. See Brian McClelland's (1998) unpublished MSc dissertation, "An Analysis of the Development of the Police Complaints Process in Northern Ireland as an Accountability Mechanism for RUC Conduct", Queens University, Belfast at 22.

[79] *Ibid.* at 21. The issue of adherence to Home Office guidance was judicially reviewed in the English High Court in 1982. See *ibid.* at 22 for details.

[80] Details in Ryder, *supra* n. 59 at 197. Rather than being applauded for exposing malpractice, Dr Irwin was vilified for his actions, indicating a deep-seated defensiveness on the part of the authorities in this regard.

[81] Cited in CAJ 1990, *supra* n. 69 at 3.

In England, the Police and Criminal Evidence Act 1984 established a system of lay supervision in the investigation of serious complaints. In 1985, the Northern Ireland Office published a consultative paper recommending similar changes in Northern Ireland. However, Scarman's insistence on the need for a completely independent investigative system went unheeded in both jurisdictions.

## THE CURRENT SYSTEM: THE INDEPENDENT COMMISSION FOR POLICE COMPLAINTS

The Independent Commission for Police Complaints[82] came into being in February 1988. Any expectation that the new body would provide a credible and coherent link between a disaffected public and a stressed police force was soon laid to rest[83] as the organisation was hamstrung at the outset by limited legislative powers which could only prevent it from doing the job it was set up to do. Key obstacles to its credibility are that:

- it is the Chief Constable of the RUC who decides what constitutes a complaint;
- the Independent Commission for Police Complaints has no power of initiative in the absence of a complaint;
- complaints continue to be investigated by police officers from the Complaints and Discipline Branch of the RUC[84] with supervision from the ICPC in only the "more serious" cases; and
- the criminal standard of proof continues to apply to police complaints.[85]

The ICPC's role is to receive complaints[86] and initially pass them on to the Chief Constable[87] for recording purposes. If the complaint appears anonymous, repetitious or vexatious, it need not be followed up. The ICPC can also dispense with complaints where the complainant has refused to co-operate with police investigation.

[82] Established under Police (NI) Order 1987 comprising a chair, two vice-chairs and six members. Only one (now two) of these positions was held on a full time basis with the Commission being otherwise staffed by around eighteen civil servants, including a chief executive. Initially, the process for appointing members was very secretive. In the last round posts were publicly advertised but the Secretary of State, assisted by civil servants and advisers, continues to make the appointments.

[83] See for example CAJ publications—*Cause for Complaint: The system for dealing with complaints against the police in Northern Ireland 1990*; *A Fresh Look at Complaints against the Police December 1993*; also now the Hayes Report 1997, *supra* n. 4.

[84] Headed by an assistant chief constable, this is staffed by around sixty police officers and further administrative staff.

[85] For studies undertaken on complainant satisfaction in other jurisdictions, see M Maguire and C Corbett's Home Office Study, *A Study of the Police Complaints System* (London, HMSO, 1991); M Maguire in Goldsmith (1991) and Tammy Landau *Public Complaints against the Police: A View from Complainants* (Toronto, University of Toronto Press, 1994).

[86] Complaints can also be lodged directly with the RUC.

[87] If the complaint is against a senior officer, to the Police Authority for Northern Ireland.

Unlike the system in England and Wales, complaints can be made by a third party on behalf of a member of the public without that person's consent. The current Chief Executive of the ICPC notes that this provision was included even in the face of Police Federation opposition, because of deep distrust of the RUC by some sections of the community. He cites a local nationalist Member of Parliament who said that:

> Often, people coming to my clinics . . . say, I do not want an official complaint because if I submit one, they [the police] will lean on me.[88]

That this is a seemingly prevalent phenomenon is indicated by the fact that where a member of the public complains about police behaviour, particularly in a public order situation, the complainant is often subsequently charged with a criminal offence.[89] In many cases this may be legitimate, but people are frequently not charged until weeks or occasionally months after they lodged a complaint themselves. Apart from the inhibiting influence of such a possibility on a person lodging a complaint in the first place, this process is open to abuse on a number of other levels. Deals done "at the back of the courts"[90] can lead to charges being dropped for the *quid pro quo* of withdrawing the complaint. Where the case proceeds, representatives from Complaints and Discipline Branch approach the complainant at the end of the hearing to ask whether they now wish to withdraw their complaint.

Even where a person does not agree to withdraw, the damage has already been done in terms of maintaining faith in the independence of the system. This is clearly an unsatisfactory method of either reducing complaint statistics or enhancing public confidence in the complaints system.

The Police (NI) Order 1987 contains provision for informal resolution of complaints, though the informal resolution scheme lies entirely in police hands. The ICPC merely periodically receives information on outcomes. Anecdotal evidence suggests that police have on occasion put an overly broad interpretation on complaints considered suitable for this type of disposal. As previously stated, one RUC officer investigating complaints of death threats against Rosemary Nelson classified these as "incivility".[91]

In cases not deemed suitable for informal resolution, the Chief Constable must appoint a member of the RUC or, exceptionally, another force, to

[88] Seamus Mallon MP, cited by Brian McClelland in ICPC Bulletin, Issue 4, January 1999. However incidences have occurred where the RUC have insisted that the complaint of a third party about assault on another person could not be investigated without that person making a complaint themselves.

[89] P Chevigny schematises what he calls the "contempt of cop" phenomenon in his book *Edge of the Knife: Police Violence in the Americas* (New York, New Press, 1996). That this is also a Northern Ireland concern is attested to anecdotally by lawyers (see Hayes Report, *supra* n. 4 at 70) and was raised by a Democratic Unionist Party Councillor (traditionally a strong defender of the RUC) at the Northern Ireland Forum in January 1997: see NI Forum for Political Dialogue, Record of Debates, Friday 24 January, No. 25, p. 12.

[90] See Hayes, *supra* n. 4, at 70.

[91] *Irish News*, 14 July 1999.

investigate the matter formally. At this point, the Chief Constable refers the complaint to the ICPC. If it involves death or serious injury, the Commission must supervise the police investigation. Otherwise, the ICPC has the discretion, within its available resources, to supervise or not. In practice, only around ten to twelve per cent of investigations are physically subject to supervision. Where this does occur, the ICPC can insist on approving the investigating officer and on having access to "such information and documents as it may reasonably require".[92] It can also "issue directions imposing such additional requirements as to the conduct of the investigation as appear to it to be necessary".[93]

Following a supervised investigation, the investigating officer must send a report to the ICPC and copy to the Chief Constable. The ICPC is required to consider the report and issue a statement saying whether the investigation has been carried out to its satisfaction.[94] It should also bring any other relevant or public interest matters to the attention of the Chief Constable, the complainant or the officer subject of the complaint. No disciplinary or criminal charge[95] can be brought until this statement has been issued. The Assistant Chief Constable, on receiving the investigating officer's report sends a copy of same to the DPP if it appears that an officer may have committed a criminal offence. Otherwise, the Assistant Chief Constable must send a memo to the ICPC stating whether in his (sic) view any offence has been committed and whether disciplinary charges are being considered, and if not, why not. If the ICPC, having considered the police report, feels criminal charges are justified, it can direct that the report be sent to the DPP. If appropriate, it can also recommend or, if its recommendations are rejected by the Chief Constable, direct that disciplinary charges be preferred. In such a case, the charges will be heard by a misconduct tribunal consisting of two members of the Commission and chaired by the Chief Constable. The case will be presented on behalf of the Chief Constable.

The fallacy of such a situation is demonstrated by the composition of the tribunal and the fact that the middle ranking RUC officer preparing the case knows that his or her superior was not in favour of the case being brought. Also, following the hearing, only the Chief Constable, who was initially of the opinion that charges should not be brought at all, can direct what punishment, if any, should follow.

As well as its supervisory functions, the ICPC's duties include reporting to the Secretary of State on the workings of the police complaints system. Essentially it has done so through its annual reports and triennial reviews, but recommendations it has made for increasing its own powers and rendering the system more credible and effective have been ignored by successive Secretaries of State. The ICPC has to date never used its power under Article 17 of the 1987 Order,

[92] Regulation 6.
[93] Regulation 8 (1).
[94] The ICPC has never yet failed to issue a statement of satisfaction with the RUC investigation. The closest it has come and the political fallout from that decision is discussed earlier.
[95] Except in exceptional circumstances.

to report to the Secretary of State "on any matters coming to its notice . . . to which it considers that his (sic) attention should be drawn by reason of their gravity or other exceptional circumstances". Perhaps this process could have been used to show the grave consequences of giving a complaints mechanism insufficient powers to render police accountability effective, but it was not.

Hayes concluded in 1997 that "there is insufficient action to draw lessons from . . . complaints and to use them as a tool of management".[96] Furthermore, the:

> lack of faith in the present system . . . largely arises from the length of the process, the low number of complaints found to have been substantiated and the small number of police officers who had been brought to court, or convicted, or even disciplined as a result of a complaint by a member of the public. While it is not a very satisfactory indicator of the effectiveness of a complaints system . . . the extremely low rate of substantiation can reflect only a less than totally effective complaints system or a more than perfect standard of police behaviour in all circumstances. This . . . contrasts with the large amounts that are being paid out to satisfy civil claims for damages.[97]

The overall level of substantiation of police complaints in Northern Ireland is around one per cent. In relation to the holding centres, the figure is to all intents and purposes zero. Over fifty per cent of complaints were not proceeded with in 1997 either because the complaint was withdrawn or there was a lack of co-operation making full investigation impossible. The vast majority of cases where formal disciplinary measures are eventually made relate to complaints from supervisory officers rather than members of the public. For instance, in 1997, one hundred and forty-five of the one hundred and fifty-nine formal charges arose from complaints from fellow officers, all of which led to disciplinary measures. In contrast, of the fourteen charges which arose from complaints from members of the public, only one resulted in discipline for the officer concerned. This means that in real terms only one complaint from a member of the public was substantiated out of approximately five thousand five hundred complaints completed. Lord Colville made the point in 1992[98] that such a failure of a disciplinary system to find wrongdoing within a profession makes it likely that the system itself is at fault. This certainly appears to be the case in Northern Ireland.

In terms of statistical analysis, recording practices vary as between police and ICPC leading to discrepancies in figures between the Chief Constable's annual reports and those of the ICPC.[99] In any event the statistics kept and the manner of their recording are not necessarily the most useful for analysis. The figures are not classified by religion, ethnic minority or gender[100] making it impossible to

[96] See Hayes, *supra* n. 4, at 11.

[97] See Hayes, *supra* n. 4, at 5. Over half a million pounds is paid out each year to satisfy claims for assault, unlawful arrest, overholding etc. (PANI figures).

[98] Cited in Hayes, *supra* n. 4, at 19.

[99] See Hayes, *supra* n. 4, at 33 for some concrete examples of inconsistencies.

[100] Paul Donnelly, giving evidence on 26 November 1997 to Northern Ireland Affairs Committee, in Third Report, Volume II, *Composition, Recruitment and Training of the RUC*, July 1998 said:

use them effectively to indicate where change in policy or practice might be necessary.

In an article entitled "Making the Police Accountable",[101] Paul Donnelly, current chair of the ICPC bemoaned the fact that so little is known about why complaints against the police are on the increase,[102] why people complain in the first place and why they decide to withdraw or fail to proceed with their complaint.[103] Yet, the ICPC's efforts have continued to focus on individual cases and there has been little research to generate strategic thinking. In order to prepare for the new ombuds office, Mr Donnelly announced that the ICPC was rather belatedly setting up a research project aimed at "securing a comprehensive insight into the experiences of complainants under the present arrangements". For many complainants and for effective police accountability, this would seem to be a case of too little too late.

Whilst protesting the integrity of the system, the ICPC has argued, in successive triennial reviews, for substantial change in the system, for increased independence from police and for more powers for the independent complaints body.

In 1991 the body called for three major changes to its powers. It asked for:

- the ICPC to be given responsibility to decide what does and does not constitute a complaint;
- "own motion" power to enable it to supervise an investigation in the absence of a complaint where this appeared to be in the "public interest"; and
- an independent tribunal to hear disciplinary charges presented by the ICPC.[104]

These calls essentially went unheeded, seemingly because of continuing and obstinate government policy to maintain parity between the system operating in Northern Ireland and that in England and Wales.[105] Prior to the publication of

"Our database is weak but we did a straw poll of the number of allegations which were made to us two weeks ago. In that week we had sixty-three formal complaints, forty-five of which were from members of the Catholic community in so far as we could identify them and eighteen of which were from members of the Protestant community as far as we could identify them".

[101] The *Irish News*, 18 September 1998 at 20.

[102] In 1997 a twenty-two per cent increase in police complaints over the previous year brought the rate to the highest level ever recorded by ICPC (10th Annual Report laid before Parliament on 28 April 1998).

[103] Donnelly noted, *supra* n. 100, that a "considerable percentage" of Catholics do not see their complaints through. He felt that this could be because they were also taking civil action in the courts, or alternatively they could be influenced by a "chill factor" such as the fact that people complaining about the police are expected to go to a police station to give evidence about the complaint. Again, despite the fact that around half of all complaints made since 1988 have been withdrawn or foundered due to complainant non-cooperation with the RUC investigation, no research is available to throw light on this.

[104] First Triennial Review at 14.

[105] This policy is indicated in the 1986 Explanatory Document which preceded the 1987 Order at 2–3 (cited in B McClelland, *supra* n. 78 at 48).

its second triennial report in 1994, the ICPC chair met the Secretary of State and Security Minister and insisted on the absolute need for own motion powers so as not to "diminish the public's perception of the Commission".[106] Again the calls were ignored.[107] By 1997, the issue of the standard of proof had been added to the growing list of changes necessary for the Commission simply to do its job. By this stage, Maurice Hayes had reached a much more radical conclusion.

## A POLICE OMBUDSMAN FOR NORTHERN IRELAND?: HAYES, PATTEN AND BEYOND

The appointment in November 1995 of former Ombudsman, Maurice Hayes to undertake a fundamental review of the complaints system in Northern Ireland,[108] and assurances given to him that he was not restricted by the need to maintain comparable legislation between the two jurisdictions,[109] appeared to mark the beginning of the end of the parity principle which had so long paralysed the effectiveness of successive police accountability mechanisms in Northern Ireland.

Hayes criticised government for failing to take the "modest" proposals of the ICPC on board, but concluded that the "worrying lack of public confidence, and indeed police trust in the existing system"[110] necessitated much more radical change. Only a completely independent and pro-active body with its own non-police capacity for investigation would be likely to meet the crucial challenge of being seen to be independent.

Hayes ultimately proposed a Police Ombudsman for Northern Ireland to have much more control of the complaints process from beginning to end. The Ombudsman would have the power to classify complaints and decide how they should be handled and investigated. The Ombudsman's duty would extend to investigating serious incidents involving deaths in police custody or under pursuit, even in the absence of a complaint. Such investigations in particular should

[106] From interview with James Grew (12 May 1998) McClelland, *supra* n. 78 at 50.

[107] The Police (Amendment) (NI) Order 1995 was enacted to deal with some of the issues but by the time of the Hayes Report the regulations necessary to change practice had not been drawn up.

[108] This appointment followed IRA and loyalist military ceasefires in the latter part of 1994 and the increasing pressure put on the Government to be seen to be tackling areas of concern within the framework of a peace process. Publications by NGOs such as CAJ publications—*Cause for Complaint: The system for dealing with complaints against the police in Northern Ireland* (1990) and *A Fresh Look at Complaints against the Police* (1993) had exposed a number of weaknesses in the system and called for major reforms, with the 1993 document pointing to better practices in other jurisdictions.

[109] See Hayes, *supra* n. 4, at 1.

[110] Hayes Report, January 1997, *supra* n. 4, at 1. The lack of confidence in the complaints procedures among Catholics, but also in many Protestant communities is well documented outside the ICPC. In a study of community perceptions of policing issues, Hamilton et al found that the investigation of complaints about the police was a major source of concern. They concluded that "It is probably fair to say that the establishment of creditable and speedy processes for dealing with complaints would be the single measure most likely to increase the legitimacy accorded to the police by the Catholic community". A Hamilton, L Moore and T Trimble, *Policing a Divided Society: Issues and Perceptions in Northern Ireland* (Coleraine, Centre for the Study of Conflict, 1995).

be carried out by independent, non-police investigators.[111] However, Hayes felt that, at least at the outset, the new Ombudsman should probably investigate all complaints, other than those deemed suitable for informal resolution. This would be vital to signal a break with the old system and establish independence and credibility. The Ombudsman also should follow the process through to the point of recommending action to relevant authorities including the Director of Public Prosecutions.

To date, the extent of the UK Government's implementation of Hayes' urgent[112] proposals amounts to one highly inadequate piece of legislation in 1998 the eventual appointment of an Ombudsman designate in October 1999 and 4 clauses in the new Police Bill currently before parliament. The Police (NI) Act 1998 ironically was pushed through Parliament without waiting for Patten to report and as yet has still not entered into force. Although occurring after the Patten Commission reported, appointment of the Ombudsman from the ranks of the Police Authority is equally ironic, given the very clear signal from Patten that a new beginning in policing would necessitate the scrapping of that same, failed institution.

## LEGISLATIVE REMIT AND JURISDICTIONAL LIMITATIONS OF THE POLICE OMBUDSMAN

Part VII of the Police (NI) Act 1998 abolishes the ICPC and establishes the office of Ombudsman. Undoubtedly the legislative powers given to the Ombudsman by this legislation are vastly superior to those of its predecessor. However, there remain important shortcomings which, if unaddressed, could well lead the new body to be not so very different from the old in terms of its effectiveness.

The Ombudsman's jurisdiction is limited in a number of important respects. Although the Ombudsman can determine what constitutes a complaint under the legislation, her jurisdiction only encompasses complaints made by, or on behalf of a member of the public about the conduct of a member of the police force. Complaints by other officers, organisations or public authorities remain outside the Ombudsman's control. Similarly, any conduct "which is or has been the subject of disciplinary or criminal proceedings", is beyond the Ombudsman's remit, leaving little possibility of dealing with past abuses.

Complaints relating to the "direction and control of the police force by the Chief Constable" are specifically excluded from the jurisdiction of the Ombudsman.[113] Instead, she can only refer such complaints to the Chief

[111] Hayes undertook his review against a backdrop of consistent government and police opposition to the idea of civilian investigations of complaints against the police, and his recommendation is all the more striking for that. However, the legislation has failed to grasp the importance of this issue.

[112] Hayes was sufficiently concerned about the need for movement to recommend that the RUC and any other relevant bodies take transitional steps in advance of legislation to facilitate the new system's implementation.

[113] Section 52(5) Police (NI) Act 1998.

Constable, the Police Authority[114] or the Secretary of State, and "notify the complainant accordingly". The latter may then deal (or not deal) with the matter at their own discretion.

Hayes had accepted that matters concerning operational policy might be best dealt with by the Chief Constable, subject to being truly answerable to the Police Authority. However, he was clear that a vital shortcoming was the current system's inability to deal with "more general complaints about police policies and practices". This has not been addressed in the new proposed legislation.

"Direction and control" and "operational independence" are key concepts in ensuring a Chief Constable is free from partisan political control, yet these terms are neither defined in the Police (NI) Act 1998 the Police (NI) Bill 2000 nor any prior legislation relating to policing. Unfortunately in Northern Ireland, a lack of clarity as to the boundaries of a Chief Constable's operational independence has meant that many key policy issues have remained unscrutinised at any level—even in terms of *ex post facto* review. The role of the Police Authority in this regard is particularly noteworthy in respect of its singular failure to hold the Chief Constable to account on a range of issues which have sparked public outcry.[115] Perhaps most revealingly, the Police Authority has not considered itself to have a role in regard to security/anti-terrorist policing. Given that this is a major point of alienation between police and public and its implications for any attempt by the RUC at "ordinary policing", it is particularly worrying that the public have no independent point of contact to raise these matters. The 2000 Bill seems set to continue this state of affairs.

The current chair of the ICPC echoed this concern when he stated:

> While the investigation and detection of wrongdoing is an important task, in some respects it represents an incomplete mandate. If it is not to be the Ombudsman, then some other effective accountability mechanism with a sphere of influence that encompasses the detail of policy practice and administration issues must be created. It is, after all, those aspects of policing which are deemed to be operational that often raise important areas of public interest. Among other benefits, a broader perception of police conduct will allow for a more positive approach to improving the quality of the police service and militate against the unfair allocation to individual police officers of the blame for what are effectively organisational shortcomings.[116]

Despite Hayes stressing the importance of the Ombudsman at least being able to comment in such cases, the legislation does not provide this power. Patten had responded to this obvious deficiency by looking at the Chief Constable's function in terms of "operational responsibility".[117] While stopping short of

[114] It is assumed that if the current legislation survives, the Policing Board proposed by Patten will assume powers ascribed to PANI. The Policing Board will at least be more representative, comprising elected representatives as well as lay appointees.

[115] See M O'Rawe and L Moore, *supra* n. 4, Ch. 4 and in particular pp. 140–5 for a fuller discussion.

[116] "Making the Police Accountable", in the *Irish News*, 18 September 1998 when it was envisaged that the new Ombudsman would be in place by Spring 1999.

[117] Patten Report, *supra* n. 3, at 33; The quotations following in this paragraph are also from page 33 of the Report.

defining the term or introducing any element of oversight into how a Chief Constable plans to conduct an operation, Patten insisted: "this does not mean, however, that the Chief Constable's conduct of an operational matter should be exempted from inquiry or review after the event". Patten posited that it is the function of a new Policing Board to require the Chief Constable to report on such issues and that "the obligation to report should extend to explaining operational decisions". Patten was also concerned to ensure that the Chief Constable "remains fully accountable for the involvement of the police in matters involving national security". The Policing Board should have the power to follow up any report by the Chief Constable "by initiating an inquiry into any aspect of the police service or police conduct" and if appropriate to request the Police Ombudsman "to conduct or contribute to such an inquiry". Patten further stated that it is nothing short of "essential that all members of the police service be required to co-operate with that inquiry". This should obviously apply to all inquiries or investigations aimed at enhancing police accountability. The new legislation establishes an effective straitjacket of constraints on the new Policing Board in this regard. In effect it will be a matter for the Secretary of State whether such inquiries ever get off the ground.

The Police (NI) Act 1998 provides for the Ombudsman to conduct investigations "in the public interest" where a death may have occurred or where there appears to be evidence of a breach of discipline or criminal offence which is not the subject of a complaint. It is assumed within the legislation that such matters will be referred to the Ombudsman by the Chief Constable, the Police Authority or the Secretary of State. This power looks important on paper, but if past history is anything to go by, may rarely if ever be used.[118]

For this reason, it is important that section 55(6) of the legislation also provides the Ombudsman with power to investigate public interest matters of its own motion. However, "public interest" is not defined other than to say that the Ombudsman must have regard to "guidance" from the Secretary of State in this respect. By this one little word, and despite all the problems caused by just such guidance under the 1977 Order[119] the habit of linking politics to independent civilian oversight looks set to continue.

## INFORMAL RESOLUTION

In light of international experience and complainant surveys[120] suggesting higher levels of customer satisfaction where a complaint was informally resolved, Hayes suggested extending the use of informal resolution. Alternative

[118] PANI have never used their call-in power under Article 8 of the 1987 Order and the Secretary of State has used it once.

[119] Previously discussed.

[120] See M Maguire and C Corbett, *supra* n. 85; T Landau "Where Police Investigate Police: A View from Complainants", *Canadian Journal of Criminology*, July 1996.

Dispute Resolution (ADR) undoubtedly has its place. Informal Resolution can form part of a system of rehabilitative rather than simply retributive justice, where early warning systems, interventive counselling and retraining actually are part of an abuse prevention policy designed to help police officers struggling with the many and often conflicting demands made on them.

Section 53 of the Police (NI) Act 1998 lays down the legislative criteria for informal resolution. Essentially the criteria has not changed except that it is now the Ombudsman who must consider whether a complaint is suitable for such disposal. To qualify, the complaint must not be "serious" and the complainant must give consent. The matter will be referred to the Chief Constable or PANI for informal resolution, and a police officer appointed to do the job. Despite Hayes' recommendations, there is no mention that such an officer should be specially designated or trained in this regard, or from a different station to the officer in question. In fact no guidelines are stipulated in the legislation as to how a suitable officer should be chosen. Meanwhile independent mediation is not even considered as a useful option.

Neither does the legislation meet Hayes' other concerns as to the inherent dangers in too ready use of such processes[121] without adequate evaluation and monitoring. Hayes observed that the present system belittles certain categories of complaint, such as harassment, which might be persistent and precisely the sort of case that would need independent investigation or supervision. Because of this, he recommended that the Ombudsman should closely monitor the use made of informal resolution through random detailed audit, complainant survey and sampling to monitor trends. Despite its importance, this function is not specifically provided for in the Act, with the legislation failing to provide:

> clear safeguards to protect against the allegation that [informal resolution] might be used by the police as a convenient means to sweep complaints under the carpet.

The new Police (NI) Bill 2000 adds nothing in this respect.

### FORMAL INVESTIGATION AND THE ROLE OF CIVILIAN INVESTIGATORS

One of the most salient features of Hayes' recommendations was his recognition of the need for non-police investigators to have charge of many, if not all, investigations. Hayes was adamant, as Lord Scarman had been in 1981, that independent investigators are key to the process. The legislation, on the other hand, leaves open the possibility that the vast majority of complaints will be delegated to the RUC for investigation,[122] or that many of the supposedly independent investigators will

[121] Maguire and Corbett agree that ADR carries the danger of officers escaping discipline for serious breaches and therefore strengthens the need "for more formal and more rigorous monitoring of informally resolved complaints by independent outsiders" cited in Hayes, *supra* n. 4, at 25.

[122] Section 54. In an initial draft, Schedule 3 para 5.1 appeared to *require* the use of RUC officers on certain occasions, stating that the Ombudsoffice "shall" enter into an arrangement with the Chief Constable to engage serving police officers to his/her staff. This now reads "may".

have an RUC background. Hayes did espouse the idea of "sale and lease back"[123] as a dynamic to encourage police co-operation with the new system, but he also cautioned of the dangers associated with a rigid ranking of complaints in order of perceived importance, which could leave police dealing with many seemingly "low level" issues, actually indicative of a much more widespread problem.

Under the 1998 legislation, formal investigations will occur where a complaint is unsuitable for informal resolution or informal resolution procedures have failed to resolve it.

Where the complaint is "serious"[124] the Ombudsman must investigate in accordance with section 56. In all other cases the Ombudsman may investigate or refer the matter to the Chief Constable for investigation by a police officer under section 57.

Section 56 deals with the procedure of formal investigation by the Ombudsman. An officer (who may be a police officer) will be appointed to conduct the investigation and this person employed by the Ombudsman to conduct or assist with investigation shall have "all the powers and privileges of a constable" in Northern Ireland. At the end of the investigation a report will be submitted to the Ombudsman.

A police officer appointed by the Chief Constable on behalf of the Ombudsman must not have had prior appointment in relation to informal resolution of the matter. The Ombudsman may, on notifying the Chief Constable, supervise the investigation if it is in the public interest that she should do so. The Ombudsman may further impose requirements on the conduct of the investigation and the police officer has a duty to comply with such requirements. Again, a report will be furnished to the Ombudsman at the end of the investigation.

Essentially, this replicates many of the features of the current system, and in the absence of major change to the structure and nature of policing in Northern Ireland, will no doubt bring with it many of the attendant problems of the current system. For example, it is again relevant here that a complaint which does not appear serious at face value may mask a whole pattern of harassment or other behaviour which would have just as serious consequences for public/police relations as a physical assault or killing. It is just these sorts of complaints which require independent investigation but which are likely, through resource implications if nothing else, to end up being investigated by police officers, something the new system was supposedly designed to avoid.

Another issue which might have been dealt with in more detail by Hayes is the benefit to be gained by the development of appropriate in-house and independent training for civilian investigators. How these people are groomed for the job they have to do is vital to their success.

[123] By this he means the police would initially be given responsibility for the investigation of a relatively small number of minor complaints. If this practice progressed satisfactorily, and as confidence in the system and police investigation grew, more investigative responsibility could in theory be devolved back to the police.

[124] A "serious complaint" is defined in section 50 in relation to death, serious injury (i.e. fracture, damage to internal organ or impairment of bodily function) or other prescribed definition.

Who is empowered to investigate and how they are trained has enormous implications for the independence (real and apparent) of the body. Many bodies have turned to former police as their civilian investigative team. In doing so they run the risk that the investigators go back to utilising police techniques which may have failed the system in the past.[125] This might partly explain why in such systems the level of substantiation or successful prosecutions does not improve.

## DISCIPLINARY PROCESS AND STANDARD OF PROOF

Following investigation, the Ombudsman is to consider whether a criminal offence may have been committed and send a copy of the investigation report to the DPP if this appears appropriate. Where the DPP has dealt with the question of criminal proceedings or the Ombudsman has decided that none are warranted, the Ombudsman must consider disciplinary proceedings. To this end she must indicate to the appropriate disciplinary authority whether and why disciplinary proceedings should or should not be brought.

In respect of senior officers the police authority need only advise the Ombudsman what action it has taken in response to these recommendations. In relation to other officers, if the Chief Constable is unwilling to bring disciplinary proceedings, the Ombudsman, after consultation with the Chief Constable, may direct the Chief Constable to bring proceedings. Hayes had categorically stated that a wholly independent tribunal should be set up for hearing purposes when necessary, but again the legislation leaves such detail to future regulations. Given the flaws in the present system, the make-up and powers of such a tribunal would appear deserving of inclusion in the primary legislation, yet this is not the case. Patten revisited this issue but only to the extent of saying that a complaints tribunal should comprise "senior members of the legal profession [and have] full powers to investigate cases referred to it . . . involving covert law enforcement operation". This leaves key questions as to how the presentation of a case should be conducted, whether the RUC Chief Constable should be involved and whether the tribunal should have any remit as regards discipline.

As regards the standard of proof, a powerful police lobby had for years ensured that the criminal standard continues to apply. Hayes clearly indicated that this was unacceptable and proposed a sliding scale standard of proof depending on the seriousness of the allegation The legislation does not mention this key point. The Government has stated instead that this will be addressed in regulations, but firstly these are a long time coming, and secondly there seems no valid reason not to include such a core issue in primary legislation. Patten

[125] See Andrew Goldsmith, "What's Wrong with Complaint Investigations? Dealing with Difference Differently in Complaints Against the Police", 15 (1) *Criminal Justice Ethics*, Winter/Spring 1996 at 38.

made no specific reference to this issue, but in fully endorsing Hayes, obviously intended that a sliding standard of proof should apply. The Police (NI) Bill 2000 does not address this point.

Hayes recognised that one way to achieve police co-operation with an independent system would be by legislating sanctions for officers failing to report wrongdoing by other officers, thereby hoping to build a standardised procedure whereby reporting misconduct becomes normal practice. He also argued that there must be significant legislative and practical protection for whistleblowers and sanctions for higher levels of management for vicarious liability in failing to bring those under them into line or suitably discipline/counsel them. Again, as with many other important recommendations, this has not happened, and Patten also only addressed this issue implicitly.

### COMPLAINT PREVENTION

Arguably the most important recommendation in Hayes was that the Ombudsoffice should have a commitment to complaint prevention. This function has not been explicitly given to previous complaints bodies in Northern Ireland and has the potential to steer the office in particular directions. This recommendation has obvious resource implications.

Hayes envisaged that the Ombudsoffice would prioritise the analysis of incidence of complaints and report on specific policies and practices which tend to increase occasion for complaint. Analysis of complaint data would also allow reporting on trends and the tracking of officers who are most often the subject of complaint. This would allow police managers to use the complaints system as a tool in the provision of better customer service.

There would be useful knock-on effects for police training to give officers increased capacity in the de-escalation of situations which presently lead to complaints. Special reports should also be published, and would provide further information on such policies and recommend relevant changes. However the legislation is silent in respect of the Ombudsman's potential to contribute to review of policy, practice and equipment, with section 52 of the Act making it obvious that the Ombudsoffice is to concern itself with individual complaints relating to individual police officers.

It could be argued that, although Hayes saw research as key, he undersold its importance in complaint prevention, by not pushing the need for extensive extra resources. However, if the Hayes Report seems to lay insufficient emphasis on the importance of a well funded and professional research arm, the legislation is even more problematic.

Section 61 is the sum total of the legislation's response to these key issues. It envisages that the Ombudsman shall "at the request of the Secretary of State" report on matters relating to the functioning of the Ombudsman as the Secretary of State may specify and the Ombudsman "may *for that purpose*" carry out research into any such matters. Placing the decision as to whether research is necessary at the discretion of the Secretary of State rather than the supposedly independent oversight body is again unhelpful in terms of the establishment of the pro-active, independent body envisaged by Hayes.

There is no onus to carry out other research. The Ombudsman may report to the Secretary of State on any matter considered by her to be in the public interest. Aside from the fact that the Ombudsman shall send to the Police Authority "any statistical or other general information which the Ombudsman considers should be brought to the attention of the Police Authority",[126] the only publications which must be produced are an annual report and an at least quinquennial review.

## GUIDANCE AND IMPROVED GUIDELINES FOR CHANGE

The legislation's stipulations in respect of regulations and guidance from the Secretary of State on a wide range of issues from procedures for informal resolution to recommendations for compensation do not bode well for the Ombudsman's independence. This is particularly so given the requirement that the Secretary of State is to consult not only with the Ombudsman but the Police Authority and interestingly the Police Association, which has not exactly been progressive in respect of much needed change.[127]

Section 65(4) further provides that in discharging functions under the legislation, the Ombudsman must have regard to guidance from the Secretary of State with specific mention of guidance concerning matters of disclosure prejudicial to public interest. In this, the legislation shows that government has not learnt from the inhibiting and paralysing effect of such guidance in the past. Instead the potential for partisan interference is enshrined, in that guidance will presumably come directly from the Northern Ireland Office, with no requirement that it be tabled before Parliament as a check on political influence.

The legislation establishing an independent Ombudsman for police complaints in Northern Ireland still clings to the desire to render that office dependent on the good will of the Secretary of State. Under these circumstances, and with all the other shortcomings of the legislation, there is little to foster the impression that the political will really exists to create and nurture a truly independent and effective system for police complaints.

Although on one level Patten essentially said little more than Hayes, it did reiterate the importance of striving beyond what the 1998 legislation looks capable of achieving. It also sought to strengthen the Ombudsman's position within the broader accountability framework by emphasising the need for carefully

[126] These are delineated at section 2(4)(a).

[127] Of all those Hayes spoke to in the course of his research only the Police Federation were opposed to non-police investigation of complaints. Les Rogers, head of the Federation, speaking at its 1999 annual conference made no bones about suggesting that lawyers and academics who criticised the RUC or campaigned for change were "wittingly or unwittingly" manipulated by a republican political agenda.

co-ordinated dynamic and co-operative relationships between the Ombudsman and other accountability structures and by insisting that Ombudsman staff be broadly reflective of the population of Northern Ireland as a whole.[128]

In addition to this, Patten added some extra dimensions to the powers of Ombudsman stating that:

- she should exercise the right to investigate and comment on police policies and practices where these are perceived to give rise to difficulties;
- she should hold a register of police affiliations;
- she should have access to all previous reports on the RUC including Stalker and Stevens; and
- that she should act as the appeal forum for anyone refused entry into the Northern Ireland Police Service on the grounds of past criminal activity.

In many ways Patten could and should have gone further.[129] Yet even the "modest proposals" it did make have not been taken on board. The new Ombudsman's fate will undoubtedly be that of its predecessors.

## TRANSITION TO A NEW MODEL: LEARNING FROM THE PAST?

As mentioned previously, although the Act is on the statute books, Part VII has yet to be operationalised. Patten gave cause to at least revisit that legislation. This has not happened to any real extent. The success of the new body is too important to make it dependent on the whim of government. Change is urgent and the Ombudsman should be provided with every chance to enhance police practice and public confidence, rather than, itself, be set up to fail.[130]

As well as political difficulties, and legislative limitations, there are practical concerns which must be considered in moving to a new system, if that system is not to follow the same transitory and unsatisfactory cycle as its predecessors. There must be a clear break with the past.[131] The initial appointment to the post

[128] Patten Report, *supra* n. 3, Recommendation 112.

[129] For example, it leaves emergency legislation intact and does not institute any screening process to ensure human rights abusers are neither recruited nor retained in the police force. Nor does it make any provision for dealing with the past. These issues will undoubtedly resurface and could well hold the seeds of failure for the new beginning.

[130] This point was made at the 1996 Conference of the International Association for Civilian Oversight of Police Complaints when Dr Colleen Lewis spoke of the pattern of negotiation whereby powers are watered down before a body is set up. This phenomenon has much to do with political expediency and the power and influence accorded to police and police union representatives in such negotiations. To ensure police acceptance of a new body—governments in many instance have actually succeeded in stripping the embryonic body of the very attributes missing from a previous system which has not been successful. The result is not to enhance public confidence in the police, or even ultimately to provide necessary protection for police officers—but rather to fuel mistrust and suspicion which make it harder for the police to perform as they should.

[131] In terms of transition to a new model, Marlene Jennings when she was Police Ethics Deputy Commissioner in Quebec, cited difficulties faced by her organisation in establishing itself. On the day the Police Ethics Commission opened its doors as a "new improved" service, it was already dealing with an eighteen month backlog inherited from the old system. This, in itself, acts to paralyse a new body in the very months when those involved need to establish credibility by being seen to be dynamic and making a clear break from the past.

of Ombudsman has not provided this, and unless she both recognises and is able to throw off the legacy conferred by her past association with PANI, the initiative is already doomed to failure.

To give her any chance of doing her job effectively, the office must be well resourced and have a high calibre of staff. That this might not happen is already obvious from current funding proposals. It has been indicated that the new Omdusman will be responsible for a staff of thirty and a budget of £3 million. This figure is significantly less than the current system whereby the ICPC budget is a little under £1 million and the Complaints and Discipline branch of the RUC operates to a budget of around £6 million. One commentator has noted: "the new office will have less personnel and less staff than the current arrangements and the public will be expecting a much better job".[132] If the system is not to suffer the fate of its predecessors, the Government must be prepared to resource it to the extent necessary to ensure its success.

Hayes' concern that the new system should not cost more than previous systems has led to the notion of the Ombudsman using ICPC staff and mechanisms. Without substantial retraining, this might unwittingly import many of the problems of the ICPC into the new body. Despite all the talk of a new and truly independent system, it is increasingly clear that the current "Independent Commission for Police Complaints" is preparing to become transmogrified into the new Ombudsoffice. This, if nothing else, indicates a clear lack of understanding about the need to break with the past to ensure the new body does not flounder in the ineffectual reputation of the old.

## CONCLUSION

Analysis of the history of changes in the complaints process shows that previous attempts at reform have, for a number of reasons, failed to render the RUC accountable. The context of Rosemary Nelson's death[133] and its aftermath demonstrates that the complex web of identities, loyalties and power politics that is policing in Northern Ireland cannot be easily disentangled. Police intimidation of even a small number of defence lawyers in the conduct of their duty is indicative of the depth of mistrust which pervades police/public relationships at many levels. Failure to deal effectively with allegations of serious wrongdoing up to and including police officers colluding with loyalist paramilitaries is symptomatic of a culture and climate in need of radical change. If the attempted marginalisation of those who criticise police behaviour extends to lawyers and progressive members of the very bodies ostensibly in place to scrutinise the police, the canker obviously runs very deep indeed.

Oversight bodies have failed because the legacy of Northern Ireland's past has never been coherently addressed at an official level. A highly politicised and

[132] Paul Mageean in *Just News* (Belfast, CAJ, 1999).
[133] Also the death of Pat Finucane and many others.

unrepresentative police force, given extended powers to police civil unrest in a society deeply divided as to the legitimacy of the state itself, calls out for strong pro-active accountability systems. Instead, there has been an almost continual abdication of government responsibility in terms of building credible police accountability structures through acknowledging and addressing key sites of alienation. Narrow politics have been allowed to take centre stage at the expense of effective police accountability. Official denial of the extent of wrongdoing has hampered progress. So too has a paramilitary campaign which has styled police officers as "legitimate targets". Entrenched and misguided notions of loyalty have deepened resolve not to lower police morale rather than tackling accountability issues head on. A tendency to follow the English model has not been helpful. A few add-ons will never deal with the deep-seated mistrust, fear and alienation which must be addressed in any comprehensive attempt to improve police accountability in Northern Ireland. Creative thinking and leaps of faith have never been the order of the day yet these, coupled with political will, are what is required to introduce real independence into the civilian oversight of policing.

It is not that a new, improved complaints mechanism or the whole Patten package will solve all of the problems.[134] It is important not to invest too much hope in a particular model or structure. But neither does this mean that we should not strive to create the best systems possible. What is key is that a human rights vision and ethos ensure that the complaints system does not stand alone. It must be integrated into the wider oversight structure with emphasis on improving police and public understanding and perception of how increased accountability serves us all. Individual responsibility has its place, but so too does research and audit aimed at improving police practice in a wider and more holistic way.

Patten's failure to recommend an end to "emergency" legislation is problematic. So too is the failure to devise some method for dealing with past hurt done by and to police in Northern Ireland. The lack of a role for the Ombudsman in this regard may well return to haunt the process. Only in acknowledging and dealing with the hurts of the past will the past ever be laid to rest.

At the very least, implementation of the Patten Commission recommendations should have involved a revisiting of the system legislated for in the Police (NI) Act 1998 to remedy the flaws therein. Failure to do so, means missing a historic opportunity and relegate both the Patten Commission and the office of Ombudsman to the status of other failed initiatives.

At the outset we stated our concern to discover whether the political will has ever truly existed to make civilian oversight real. Our conclusion that it has not means that there are very hard, but potentially very productive, lessons to be learnt. These extend beyond the success or failure of the new Police Ombudsman to the heart of whether a new beginning for policing in Northern

[134] For instance, Patten does not even mention the issue of intimidation of defence lawyers.

Ireland is possible. The political will to change needs to be demonstrated quickly and monitored effectively. The culture of the past must be clearly and decisively broken down. If it is not, ten years hence there will be other Rosemary Nelsons, and a new complaints mechanism or a new type of Patten Commission may not be enough.

# 12

# *Called to Account: Civilian Oversight in the Palestinian Context*

BEVERLEY MILTON-EDWARDS

## INTRODUCTION

When Palestinian leader Yasser Arafat and Israeli Prime Minister Yitzhak Rabin signed the Oslo Accords the future of civilian policing and the internal security structure of the areas of Palestinian population in the West Bank and Gaza Strip was altered in significant and fundamental degrees.[1] Under the remit of the Oslo and subsequent Cairo and Wye Accords, Palestinian self-rule and the policing function were outlined. Policing was given prominence signified by guarantees of significant donor support through technical and financial assistance. The formation of the Palestinian Police Force (PPF) was one of the major tasks of self-rule in 1994, signifying the importance of this institution at the heart of the Palestinian National Authority (PNA). Facility for limited legislation and symbolic, if not actual, institutions of government and statehood would be permitted to grow in the new epoch of interim relations between the Palestinian people and the state of Israel.[2]

For many Palestinians the peace deal with Israel was sold by their leadership as an opportunity, after a battle for national liberation through armed struggle, for statehood including advanced democratic rights for all Palestinian citizens.[3] As a fledgling liberal democracy Palestinians welcomed the opportunity to establish a police force and were initially supportive of the police function, believing that the PPF would serve and protect the community at a time when it was still forced to live cheek by jowl with an aggressive settler population at odds with its own government in Israel. Following years of flagrant disregard for the rule of (Israeli) law in the West Bank and Gaza Strip, Palestinians were

[1] See B Milton-Edwards, "Palestinian state-building. police and citizens as test of democracy", 25 *British Journal of Middle Eastern Studies*, May 1998.

[2] Further discussion of Oslo Accords see Haidar Abdel-Shaffi, "The Oslo Agreement", *Journal of Palestine Studies*, Autumn 1993.

[3] For further debate of this issue of what Oslo meant to the Palestinians see R Shehadeh, "Flaws in the Oslo Accords—An Insiders View", 467 *Middle East International*, January 1994; J Hilal, "PLO Institutions: The Challenge Ahead", *Journal of Palestine Studies*, Autumn 1993; and E Said, *Peace and its Discontents* (London, Vintage, 1995).

initially delighted with the idea of living in a society made of their own laws and upheld by their own police force. A common sense of ownership of the policing project was particularly palpable in the majority nationalist community from whose ranks so many thousands would be recruited.

The Declaration of Principles (DOP) and its appendices provided the blueprint for the organisation of a limited form of government under the powers of the Palestinian National Authority. The powers of the PNA were extended to include responsibility for education, taxation, tourism, welfare, and internal security.[4] The Palestinian Legislative Council (PLC) was empowered to pass legislation under a limited remit, and judicial authority was permitted through a court system in the autonomous areas. The interim period, however, would not necessarily function in a fully democratic manner nor offer its Palestinian residents full representation or rights of accountability in their representative bodies. In essence the interim period reflects a carefully crafted security agenda, propelled chiefly by Israeli rather than Palestinian concerns in this area, which encourages strong hegemonic control, limited democratic rights and is sympathetic to a monopoly of political control by the executive. In addition, political plurality has proved to be a security issue, threatening not just the interim but the future of final status negotiations.

The institution at the centre of the self-rule experiment is the newly-established state security apparatus, the PPF. This police force, according to Article 8 of the DOP, should strive to create an atmosphere of "public order and internal security" during the interim period. In practice, the internal security function and its relationship to notions and practice of civilian oversight are an important signifier of any future form of Palestinian self-rule. It is a signifier of the degrees of democracy which may be said to characterise Palestinian policing. In addition, police-society relations are exposed by the opportunities for a meaningful relationship to occur between the state and its policing apparatus and accountability through civilian oversight. This situation has already developed at a rapid pace because the primary role of the internal security structure is to protect and preserve the experiment in self-rule from its opponents, while at the same time acknowledging the rights of Palestine's quasi-citizens in this political arrangement.

One immediate difficulty apparent in the provisions of the DOP revolves around the very definition of police or a policing function in Palestinian society. This has already led to a variety of problems and confusion, particularly in areas of accountability, responsibility and civilian oversight. The DOP declares that, "the Palestinian authority shall establish a strong police force . . . the Palestinian Directorate of Police Force (hereinafter 'the Palestinian Police')". However, neither the DOP nor the accompanying Annex 1 which pertains to policing, makes an explicit delineation of the internal security versus civilian police func-

[4] For a full copy of the Declaration of Principles consult 23 (1) *Journal of Palestine Studies*, Autumn 1993, pp. 114–24. Also Y Sayigh, "Reading the Basics: Sovereignty and Security of the Palestinian state", 24 (4) *Journal of Palestine Studies*, Summer 1995.

tion. The blurring of boundaries in this respect has led to the generic use of the term police (*shurta*) which refers to some forty thousand employees of the public sector engaged in one or other of the official and unofficial branches of the Palestinian police. An organisational chart of the PPF compiled by the international police adviser's office cited four main branches of the force: Civil Defence, Public Security Forces, General Intelligence Service and Civilian Police. Another four other branches of the PPF were also included in the chart: Preventative Security, President Security, Coastal Police and the Air Police. By 1999 Luft was claiming that other "branches" of the PPF had been established including "Military Intelligence, Military Police, the Special Security Force and that within the Presidential Security branch two further units had been created: the Intelligence Unit and the Presidential Guard".[5]

This lack of clarity has not only become institutionalised as part of the police structure but has filtered through to Palestinian society, where many have questioned the role of the police, queried its identity, and lamented the lack of accountability throughout the ever-proliferating branches of this force. This deliberate ambiguity has allowed the executive authority of the PNA to establish a national army in waiting. It has also increased the notion of a militarised rather than liberal society and often undermined the task of the civil police who have found themselves competing for power and influence as well as resources against these other state security agencies. As Brigadier-General Samih Nasser, overall Co-ordinator of the PPF training programme highlighted:

> according to Oslo (however), all branches of the PPF are considered to be police officers, not just the "blues" (civil police). This has created problems and imbalance in the training programme.[6]

Inappropriate provision of training for specialist tasks has been one consequence.

The task of policing the interim, and the question of accountability including civilian oversight, is notoriously difficult for any society emerging from protracted conflict. Any assessment and debates about current arrangements in Palestine cannot be understood without evaluating the political context in which the policing and accountability matrix is located. Other examples, such as Ireland in the 1920s, highlight a tendency for interim arrangements to enshrine or encourage a policing function that is coercive, repressive, grants extra powers to police, blurs the boundaries of internal security, inhibits or ignores accountability mechanisms, and routinely flouts international norms on human rights.

[5] G Luft, "The Palestinian Security Services: Between Police and Army", 3 (2) *MERIA*, 1999, p. 2.

[6] Interview with the author, Security Headquarters, Gaza City, April 1997.

### THE POLICING LEGACY

Historically, policing in Palestine has been undertaken by five different, and four foreign, police forces. From 1918–48, Palestinian residents of the area were subject to the powers of the British mandate Police Force, which although recruiting Arab and Jewish officers to its ranks, worked from the traditional colonial policing model. The British had developed much of the practice associated with this model in its other territories or colonies and in particular in Ireland.[7] Indeed the embryonic policing force sent to Palestine in the early 1920s had recruited more than two hundred of its officers from the disbanded "Black and Tans".[8] Policing through coercion rather than service with the community was the strategy prioritised by the British. From 1948–67, following Israel's independence and the Palestinian exodus, Palestinians of the West Bank fell under the remit of the Jordanian Police Force, and in the Gaza Strip, under the Egyptian security structure. From 1967–87, following Israel's occupation of the West Bank and Gaza Strip, the policing function including internal security fell to the Israel Defence Force (IDF), Israel Police Force (IPF) and internal security service *Shin Bet*. While some Palestinians served in the lower ranks of the IPF, they were normally stationed in the West Bank or Gaza Strip. Shamgar highlights the issue through a statistical breakdown of IPF officers serving in the West Bank compared with those over the 1948 border which separated Israel and the Palestinians. In the West Bank some six hundred and ten officers were deployed compared with thirteen thousand five hundred in Israel. Of that six hundred and ten, two hundred and fourteen were Israeli while the remaining three hundred and ninety six were Palestinian.[9]

### POLICING A DEEPLY DIVIDED TERRITORY

Policing under the Israeli occupation of the West Bank and Gaza Strip was essentially authoritarian in nature. According to Brewer:

> [the] police intrude as they wish and minutely regulate society in whatever way is required to achieve the desired end. People come under scrutiny for behaviour which is seen as precursory to criminality, so that the police intervene pre-emptively in private lives in order to ensure the public order is not threatened.[10]

[7] M Brogden, "An act to colonise the internal lands of the island: empire and the origins of the professional police force", 15 *International Journal of the Sociology of the Law*, 1987, pp. 179–208; C Townshend, *Political Violence in Ireland* (Oxford, Calrendon, 1983).

[8] The Black and Tans were British colonial police in Ireland.

[9] M Shamgar, *Military government in the territories administered by Israel* (Jerusalem, Hebrew University, 1982), pp. 444–6.

[10] J Brewer et al, *The Police, Public Order and the State* (London, Macmillan, 1996), pp. 227–8.

The deployment of the Israeli police force was part of a politically motivated strategy by Israeli policy makers to subdue the Palestinian population of the West Bank and Gaza Strip, repress any political activities, maintain Israel's military occupation and subsequent settlement of the area. With the IPF serving alongside the IDF the latter took precedence over the former and the policing function became both circumscribed and militarised by association as well as reputation. Indeed both Weitzer's "syndrome" of policing and Brewer's approach are models or approaches to policing which reveal a number of characteristics relevant, not only to Israel's policing of the West Bank and Gaza Strip from 1967 to 1993, but also to other societies in conflict such as Northern Ireland and South Africa. Weitzer, according to Brewer, recognises five basic features which remain inherent in this model:

> sectarian enforcement of the law, political partiality, an absence of mechanisms of accountability, responsibilities for internal security as well as ordinary crime, and the precarious consent of the subordinate communal group.[11]

Israel's policing of the West Bank and Gaza Strip certainly confirmed the relevancy of this model, and suggests that that the political conditions which generated the conflict and the need for it to be managed had a significant impact on the policing function for Israel.

Israel's democratic credentials were severely circumscribed by the activities of its police force in the West Bank and Gaza Strip as well as Arab East Jerusalem. While it is accepted that the police act as legitimate actors of state force, enforcing as well as upholding the law, the line between legitimate force and violence was frequently crossed by IPF officers policing the Palestinian communities of the occupied territories. In addition, Israel's judicial system sanctioned as so-called legitimate force "limited pressure" on suspects during interrogation, which was more widely understood as the approval of torture. Nevertheless, while internally questions may have been raised about these issues, Israel's general policy of policing of the occupied territories went relatively unnoticed by the international community, who, according to Guelke had accepted Israel's transformation of policing the occupation into yet a further issue of defence for an embattled Israel in the wider arena of the Arab-Israeli conflict.[12]

In Israel proper mechanisms for civilian oversight such as the police complaints board were not introduced until 1992.[13] Before then, Israel's citizens were protected to a certain extent by the courts, a free press, the Knesset and its elected members. Complaints of police violence, corruption, or rule breaking were always well publicised, prompting the state to intervene and evaluate policy, calling for increased professionalisation within the force and greater public accountability. In the West Bank, Gaza Strip, and Arab East Jerusalem,

[11] J Brewer, "Policing Divided Societies: Theorising a type of Policing", 1 (1) *Policing and Society*, pp. 179–91.

[12] A Guelke et al, *The Police, Public Order and the State* (London, Macmillan, 1996), pp. 154–5.

[13] See the chapter by Herzog in this book.

however, the Palestinians rarely pursued complaints against the perceived policy of systematic police brutality. When complaints were pursued, internal police investigations rarely, if ever, found against their own officers. An Israeli Human Rights Report in 1991 found discrimination was evident:

> When a Palestinian inflicts injury on a Jew a thorough investigation is carried out. When the guilty party is brought to trial he is severely punished . . . In contrast, when a Jew inflicts injury on a Palestinian, the police do not rush to investigate, investigations continued for a long time, most of them conclude without bringing anyone to trial.[14]

In addition, Palestinian confidence in the Israeli policing function was minimal. Crimes within the community, such as burglary, assault, drugs or alcohol offences were rarely reported to the IPF with Palestinians preferring to rely on traditional or alternative methods such as *sulh* (mediation) for bringing unruly social elements under control. This informal approach was also lacking in accountability or procedures for complaint, but did rely on family and religious mediation to resolve some issues.[15]

From 1987 and the outbreak of the Palestinian Uprising (Intifada), the Israeli policing and internal security function was rejected wholesale by the Palestinian community. The Intifada's mass based nature severely undermined Israel's authority in the West Bank, Gaza Strip and Arab East Jerusalem, including the Israelis own security system. The fervour of popular discontent was directed at undermining and eradicating Israeli rule, and ultimately at ending the occupation. The formation, in the early weeks of the uprising, of a nationalist and parallel Islamic organisational structure: the United National Leadership of the Uprising (UNLU) and Islamic Resistance Movement (Hamas) and Islamic Jihad harnessed the Intifada. The UNLU and Hamas began to organise and co-ordinate the rebellion against Israeli rule. The leadership formed committees, strategy emerged, communiqués were printed and distributed and the people responded accordingly. Local and neighbourhood committees were established to replace every aspect of Israeli control from education to policing. Thus, within a number of months the Israeli policing function was rejected wholesale by the entire Palestinian population. Attacks on police stations were unrelenting, leading the IPF to fortify their installations to the point of siege mentality. IPF patrols were only organised with a huge IDF presence, and were only carried out to fulfil specific functions such as breaking open the shops of striking merchants or assisting the IDF and tax inspectors during tax raids. In March 1988 the approximately four hundred Palestinian officers serving in the IPF were called upon by the UNLU to resign. Communiqué number ten demanded, "The immediate resignation of all policemen and preparation for the end of the occupation".[16] A day later the local Palestinian press reported the resignation of hundreds of Palestinian police officers serving in the IPF.

[14] B'Tselem, *Violations of Human Rights* (Jerusalem, B'Tselem, 1991), p. 137.
[15] B Milton-Edwards, "Policing Palestinian Society", 7 (1) *Policing and Society*, pp. 19–44.
[16] UNLU communique number ten, 5 March 1988.

The resignations had a number of implications, firstly signalling the extent to which Palestinians were willing to disengage from the occupation and its institutions. Israel, on the other hand, argued that the resignations would lead to the breakdown of law and order in Palestinian society. Yet in reality, for many years the Palestinians maintained law and order through a series of committees. In addition the PLO paid salaries to the former Palestinian IPF officers who had resigned and encouraged them to play a role within society. This policy was initially successful. The popular committees (*lijan al-aslah*) charged with the maintenance of the policing function enjoyed support from most sections of the community. The criminalisation and demise of some of the popular committees, however, was accompanied by a rise in policing by armed gangs associated with both nationalist and Islamist factions in the occupied territories.

These so-called strike forces went under the names of the Fatah Hawks, the Popular Front for the Liberation of Palestine (PFLP) Red Eagles and Hamas's Sheikh Izz-a-din al-Qassam Brigades. Their graffiti was evident through the West Bank and Gaza Strip and their activities given prominence in the community. By 1989, according to a report by an Israeli human rights organisation, these strike forces, carried out quasi-police operations with the aim of deterring and punishing criminal suspects, they also engaged in surveillance, interrogation, and punishment of suspected collaborators.[17]

These groups enjoyed broad-based community support when they were first formed but their increasingly autonomous activities alienated them from the community they claimed to represent. The political leadership which initially directed and empowered these groups was ignored, threatened and mocked by the para-military gangs which now roamed the West Bank and Gaza Strip with impunity. Many communities were frightened by the armed gangs and were frustrated at the leadership's lack of influence. By early 1991, the policing of the Palestinians had deteriorated to the verge of internecine conflict, family feuds, clan disputes, attacks on individuals, abuse of human rights and torture.[18]

On the eve of the 1993 Oslo Accords, the internal security situation in the occupied territories was the province of the strike forces, while both the political wings of the PLO and Hamas struggled with each other to assert their authority over the entire population. Community policing and issues of accountability were absent from the discourse of security in both the Israeli and Palestinian camps. On the Israeli side the policing function, vis-à-vis the Palestinian population, had become completely militarised, facing a hostile population which rejected wholesale its authority, rule of law and state enforcement. The Israeli state had increasingly depended on the military for might and any pretence of offering a policing function was abandoned. The myriad of military orders, defence and emergency regulations plus criminal and civil law as applied to the Palestinian population, encouraged a model of policing that was not only authoritarian but was also unaccountable to civilian pressure.

[17] B'Tselem, *Collaborators in the occupied territories* (Jerusalem, B'Tselem, 1994), p. 30.
[18] G Usher, *Palestine in Crisis* (London, Pluto Press, 1995).

Policing the community from the Palestinian perspective became even more difficult. As outlined above, the descent to street violence and the absence of a recognised and accountable policing authority further heightened a climate of fear which had gripped the territories by the summer of 1993. In addition, the policing function had become the domain of competing political factions. Policing no longer represented, as it had initially done in the heady days of 1988, a national agenda, or goal. Each political faction developed and pursued its own security agenda, sometimes collaborators were identified as the biggest security threat. Sometimes social issues were portrayed as a security issue, such as the campaign to impose the *hijab* (headscarf) run by Hamas which led to a specific policing agenda in the Islamist camp.[19] While there had been initial provision for representation of those accused—through a local informal court system—and an attempt to outline and inform the community of a mode of due legal processes, once authority moved away from the political groups and into the hands of the armed gangs, the concept of nominal accountability and service rapidly evaporated.

## THE PEACE PROCESS: TRANSITION TO A DEMOCRATISED POLICE?

The issue of civilian oversight of the civil police function in both developed and developing societies is strongly linked with the democratisation agenda. The democratisation agenda, in turn, enjoys a strong correlation with the issue of accountability. As Bayley has argued:

> Police in developed countries are watched and supervised by elected politicians, by civil, criminal and administrative courts, by the media, and increasingly by independent ombudspersons and civilian complaint-review boards. All of these are supported by accountability to written, democratically enacted law.[20]

In a liberal democracy the oversight function is increasingly credited with a dual character; internal, where the police police themselves, and external, where the public/civilian population are empowered to greater or lesser degrees to investigate complaints against the police. In this context, the debate is well under way, and sits comfortably in a value-laden framework of liberal and democratic principles. The value of civilian oversight, for example, can be debated in a free and open press, and public accountability is prevalent in other state institutions. In essence, the political context under which the civilian oversight debate takes place is recognised and welcomed at a cultural level, part of the shared values of a liberal democratic society.

[19] For specific information and analysis of this issue see R Hammami, "From Immodesty to Collaboration: Hamas, the Women's Movement, and National Identity in the Intifada" in J Beinin and J Stork (eds.), *Political Islam* (London, IB Tauris, 1997).

[20] D Bayley, *Contemporary Practices of Policing: a comparative view* (Washington, National Institute of Justice, 1999).

In a context of political transition, conflict, and development, the debate about civilian oversight of the policing function takes on a completely different tenor. As the Palestinian example highlights, the debate about civilian oversight can only take place in the context of stable political control, which embraces transparency and accountability as part of a democratic political culture. Yet, the framework for rule/government outlined under the Oslo and subsequent accords, and the manner in which the Executive is allowed to by-pass and ignore these arrangements, currently inhibits the development of this highly desirable police accountability feature. Closer examination of the provision for the policing function and the current legal context highlights the immense difficulties surrounding formal debate of this issue. This is because, ultimately, the debate about civilian oversight as a mechanism of accountability assumes certain "givens" in a political culture.

The establishment of the PPF according to the official provisions of the Oslo and subsequent accords has promoted a particular model of policing which is patently at odds with the democratising agenda promoted by the international community as it encourages the Middle East Peace Process. A new culture of policing representing the "best practice" of liberal democratic societies was not on the interim agenda despite the fact that much of the subsequent technical assistance has been predicated on those values. The creation of a wholly new structure requiring massive assistance through funds, training, equipment and perhaps, most important of all, time, was not within the remit of the interim arrangements agreed between the PLO and the government of Israel. A sense of urgency dictated a "quick-fix" appearance of empowerment through the self-rule function which in turn stretched the realm of the policing function in the newly-autonomous areas of Palestinian population in the West Bank and Gaza Strip. Making the most of a bad job became the paradigm through which a former army of liberation, the Palestine Liberation Army (PLA), attempted to re-brand itself as a policing service for their fellow Palestinians.

## AUTONOMY OF ACCOUNTABILITY

As an institution of the PNA the PPF is defined in contrast with other ministries. The PPF is not, for example, subjugated to any ministry, and the Police Directorate performs its work directly under the executive authority of President Yasser Arafat. In addition, no written plans or strategies for the PPF have been developed within the Directorate or from the President's office, and there has been little organisational co-operation or co-ordination of tasks and responsibilities between the various armed branches of the force. Proliferation of police functions and bureaucracy also appears to be a defining feature of the institution, reflecting a multiplicity of localised power bases and internal power struggles for authority. One result of such diffusion of the policing function is the almost farcical situation whereby each branch of the force has established its own police stations in the same tiny district of autonomous control. A district such as Khan Younis which essentially covers a small one street town, refugee camp and surrounding neighbourhoods, can have up to eight police stations under the authority of each branch of the PPF. Suffice to say, that such diffusion and diversity can do little if anything to facilitate even the most basic form of accountability or a programme of civilian oversight and investigation of complaints against the police. If one agrees with Reiner's contention that, "the police exercise powers which profoundly affect the lives of all citizens" and that "it is expected that those who wield public power must be fully accountable for this", it is hard to muster much hope in the current Palestinian context.[21]

In addition, there was no provision for the IPF to play any role in the new Palestinian police force. However, its former Palestinian (retrained) officers, along with the PLA, the infamous armed strike forces, and Intifada veterans, many of whom have served time in Israeli prisons, do serve as officers of the PPF. This contrasts strongly with the South African parallel where there was no "clean slate" approach to transformation of the policing function and where "the task at hand", according to Brogden and Shearing, "is nearly always one of institutional transformation within a context of existing institutions and disagreement over what should be accomplished".[22]

Moreover, in the Palestinian context an increase, rather than a reduction, in the number of officers recruited to the PPF has only served to heighten a perception among ordinary Palestinians that a militarised police serves the executive authority of the PNA not the community at large. Indeed, since 1994 the Palestinian community has literally been swamped with PPF personnel, currently approximately forty thousand officers serving a population of one and three quarter million, a ratio of one to one hundred and ten, often fulfilling quasi-military rather than strictly policing functions. The implications of this level of staffing are not difficult to discern. These high figures of personnel of police per head of population far outstrip international norms of one to three hundred and fifty and are currently equal to pre-cease-fire norms of one to one hundred and ten per head of population in Northern Ireland. This figure is distressing given the fact that the Palestinians should be entering a period of transition from conflict to peace, from militarisation to democracy and stability. The PNA, headed by Yasser Arafat, has taken steps to guarantee rather than inhibit the development of a militarised police force in the post-Oslo era. The responsibilities for national security and the civilian police are not clearly defined; rather they overlap and there is real confusion within police ranks over the division of responsibility and duty. Personnel from the PLA have been allowed to join and head the PPF with ineffective provision for retraining or human rights issues. This includes the debate about public accountability, internal and external review and processes for handling complaints against the

[21] R Reiner, "Police Accountability: principles, patterns and practices" in R Reiner and S Spencer (eds.), *Accountable Policing: Effectiveness, Empowerment and Equity* (London, IPPR, 1993), p. 6.

[22] M Brogden and C Shearing, *Policing for a New South Africa* (London, Routledge, 1993), p. 6.

police. The transfer of thousands of PLA soldiers into the new police force, however, was clearly articulated in the Oslo Accords. Hence, former commanders of the PLA, few of whom had experience of policing, were appointed to head the new force. Indeed, the provisions made in the Oslo and Cairo Accords permitted the wholesale import of the PLA into a new security structure which had serious implications for the policing project. Today, the military ethos is still present at most levels of the policing structure and many officers openly acknowledge the difficulties in transforming themselves from freedom fighters to police officers. As one remarked:

> I arrived after more than twenty years of military service . . . to change to a civilian police mentality is a psychological process, to learn from the community, how to help people, but the military is something completely different.[23]

The structure of the PPF, as previously indicated, has emerged as far more amorphous than was planned. While Annex 1 of the Cairo Accords had stipulated that the Palestinian Directorate of Police would have five branches—Civilian Police, Public Security, Intelligence, Coastal Police, and Civil Defence—in practice the unofficial proliferation of at least an additional four internal security agencies within the PPF has undermined the clear structure and chain of command that was originally envisaged. In addition, it is not just the civil police that have the power of arrest and law enforcement but rather all branches of the force (official and unofficial) have policing powers, which are often interpreted very differently from branch to branch. The entire force is also armed, and early debates about disarming the Civil Police quickly evaporated as the internal security situation in the Gaza Strip and West Bank became increasingly unstable due to the so-called "threat-from-within" posed by the radical Islamist opposition. This amorphous nature has contributed to the relative functional autonomy of each branch (official or otherwise) of the force. In turn, this autonomy has made it hard to establish institutional cohesiveness within the PPF. Each branch is organised around a distinct personality in uniform—local strong men, such as Jibril Rajoub head of preventative security in the West Bank and former Fatah Hawk, Mohammed Dahlan in the Gaza Strip. Autonomy is further emphasised by the operational difficulties associated with Israel's policy of closure affecting communication between the West Bank and Gaza Strip as well as the policing of two distinct geographic areas that are territorially separated from each other with Israel in-between. The heads/directors of each branch of the PPF are directly accountable to the executive authority of the PNA President Arafat.

The absence of clear structures has also meant that the responsibilities of the various branches of the force are not outlined or clearly articulated leading to constant squabbles over who polices what, who has authority for what, and "turf wars" for the limited funds that are dedicated to the policing project. Internecine disputes within the PPF have also meant that what little knowledge

[23] Interview with General Salem Nassar, Gaza Police Headquarters, April 1997.

there is about policing rather than military control of the population is guarded jealously within particular branches, officers do not share information, and they constantly seek to define themselves in relation to other branches within the PPF. This is particularly true among the Civil Police who aspire to a policing function which distances themselves from the prevalent militarised culture of the PPF, and yet whom are constantly defined by the poor record of other branches of the service. At an operational level, Civil Police trainers complain that resources identified as specific to their activities are often diverted to other branches of the force, or that their officer training sessions on traffic policing have often included officers from other branches whose remit does not cover such activities.[24]

## THE LEGAL MAZE

While police accountability mechanisms are generally linked to the notions of rule of law and democracy, there is so much about the Oslo and subsequent arrangements along with the present legal environment which inhibits the process of police accountability. Loveday, for example, addressing the issue of accountability, argues that:

> National police systems are, theoretically at least, made accountable at a national political level, usually by way of clear ministerial responsibility to a national parliament or Assembly.[25]

But as I have already noted, this is not the case with the PPF. The PPF are, to all intents and purposes, only accountable to the Executive Authority. What role then, for the law, in protection of citizens pursuing complaints against the police? It is true that in more developed police contexts the "inadequacy of purely legalistic responses" to achieving accountability have been recognised, but what of the context within which the Palestinians find themselves?[26]

## LEGAL ENVIRONMENT: MOSAIC OF LEGAL PRACTICE

The current legal climate under which the PPF operate is confusing to say the least. To date, there is still no Palestinian criminal justice system, while the old legal bases of Ottoman, British, Egyptian, Jordanian and Israeli law persist. Although upon his return to Gaza in August 1994 Yasser Arafat repealed more than two thousand Israeli military orders, the Israelis dismissed his gesture as meaningless and without substance. In addition, according to both the Fourth

[24] Interviews with Civil Police trainers, Jericho and Gaza, April 1997.

[25] B Loveday, "Government and Accountability of the Police" in R Mawby (ed.), *Policing Across the World, Issues for the Twenty-first Century* (London, UCL Press, 1999), p. 132.

[26] A Goldsmith, "New Directions in Police Complaints Procedures", 11 (2) *Police Studies*, Summer 1988, p. 61.

Geneva Convention as well as the Hague Convention, Israel remains in military occupation of the West Bank and Gaza Strip and as such has certain responsibilities and duties, including the protection of human rights, towards the resident Palestinian population.[27]

The Oslo Accords also reinforced Israel's rule over the territory of the West Bank and the Gaza Strip in matters of security. Israel, for example, has the last say, its citizens—the settlers and others are not subject to any Palestinian laws and cannot be tried in Palestinian courts. In sum, according to Bindman and Bowring, Israel continues to:

> exercise some legislative, executive and judicial functions in the Occupied Territories: complete jurisdiction over (Arab) East Jerusalem, settlements, border areas and substantial land and water resources.[28]

Nevertheless, under Palestinian autonomy there has been a significant attempt to clarify the legal context through the development of the so-called Basic Law.

Initially it was hoped that the Basic Law, approved in its first, second and third drafts by the Palestinian Legislative Council, would provide a fairly clear mechanism for accountability and civilian oversight of complaints against the police. For example, a draft version of the law circulated by Palestinian human rights organisations outlined provision for the security forces and the police. Six articles addressed issues such as the role of the policing service, provision of police duties within the limits of the law, and, perhaps most importantly of all, at least one draft version contained the following article:

> The police and security agencies shall establish a complaints mechanism under civilian control to investigate complaints concerning misconduct by members of these agencies in an effective and efficient manner.[29]

In reality, however, the currently yet to be implemented law contains only one article pertaining to the security forces and the police, and the two points therein show no regard to early attempts to incorporate provision for civilian oversight in the area of accountability. Instead, Article 75 declares:

> 1. Security forces and the police are a regular armed force created for the protection of the homeland, a service to the people, for the protection of society and for the maintenance of security and public order. It shall perform its duties within the limits provided by the law with full respect to rights and freedoms. 2. Security forces and the police shall be regulated by law.[30]

Despite efforts to push this legislation through the PLC, in reality the Basic Law has proved to be nothing more than a wish list for the Palestinian people.

[27] G Bindman and B Bowring, *Human Rights in a period of transition, the case of the occupied territories, Jericho and the Gaza Strip* (London, The Law Society, 1994).

[28] *Ibid.*

[29] Al-Haq and Birzeit University Law Centre, The Palestinian Basic Law for the transition period (Al-Haq & BZU occasional paper, 1996) p. 17.

[30] Palestinian Legislative Council, *Basic Law Draft Resolution*. Jerusalem: LAW (Palestinian Society for the Protection of Human Rights and the Environment, 1997) p. 30.

The law cannot be brought into effect until the Executive Authority signs the Bill into law within thirty days of its final reading. For more than a year the President of the PNA has failed to sign the Bill into law and the PLC has been unable to persuade, cajole or compel him to act. As the Palestinian Centre for Human Rights (PCHR) annual report of 1999 states, however:

> it is necessary that the PLC work at securing approval of the Basic Law since the Basic Law is considered the foundation of any constitutional relationship . . . and since it . . . regulates the relationship between the government and its citizens.[31]

This absence of a legal bedrock on which to build a relationship between state and citizen has had significant consequences for provision of the policing function. It further emphasises the authoritarian nature of the Executive Authority and its hold over the coercive arm of the state. The policing functions become redefined in defence of the state, rather than its citizens. The policing and internal security remits have become increasingly dedicated to the ill-disguised "securocratic"[32] agenda of the Executive Authority in suppressing any form of opposition, democratic or otherwise, to the Oslo Agenda and the method of implementing the agenda in the transition period. The failure to implement a constitution, even in the interim or transition period, is a worrying indication of the shape of things to come. The absence of a basic law only serves to further distance the policing function from democratic ideals, community ownership of the policing project, and the accountability thereof. This issue has been noted within the civil police branch of the PPF with officers complaining that without implementation of the basic law the policing task becomes infinitely more difficult.[33] At present Palestinians remain bereft of any clear legal outline of their rights and the duties and responsibilities of the institutions of the PNA, including the executive, judiciary, and the PLC.

Since the establishment of the PPF and the policing of Palestinians, by Palestinians the allegation of human rights abuses against officers serving in the ranks of the PPF has emerged on a frequent and systematic basis. The abuse of human rights that has taken place under the authority of the PPF has evoked widespread condemnation and has been part of a process of identification of failure and problems in a number of areas within the PPF. In 1997 and 1998 Amnesty International reported the arrest of thousands of Palestinians by the PPF for reasons of security, with most subsequently being released without charge.[34] Torture and allegations of other forms of abuse have been pernicious with officers serving in the PPF implicated in deaths in detention. The well-publicised case of Walid al-Qawasmi, who died in detention in the summer of

[31] Palestinian Centre for Human Rights (PCHR), *Annual Report* (Gaza: PCHR, 1998) p. 77.

[32] See A Perlmutter, "Arafat's Police State", 59 *Foreign Affairs*, Summer 1994, pp. 41–60; N Weinberger, "The Palestinian National Security Debate", 24 (3) *Journal of Palestine Studies*, Spring 1995.

[33] Interview with Abu Rami, Director of Administration in School of Police Training, Jericho, April 1997.

[34] Amnesty International, *International Report*, see chapter on Palestinian Authority, 1997, p. 1.

1998 prompted, according to Human Rights Watch, PNA President Yasser Arafat, to:

> appoint a prosecutor to investigate the death in General Intelligence custody . . . [of] al-Qawasmi . . . It was the twentieth known death in custody since 1994, concluded the report.[35]

The police have been repeatedly implicated in a range of abuses undermining any attempt to present the force as a professional service dedicated to the service of the Palestinian people. In addition, the police have been compelled to enforce draconian security measures, including forcefully breaking up public demonstrations, closing newspaper and press offices, and preventing the distribution of newspapers in the West Bank and Gaza Strip, all under the direct orders of the Executive Authority.

As discussed above, the first significant issue at the heart of the human rights-policing-civilian oversight matrix is the persistent lack of clarity of law in this context. The police themselves are required to enforce a myriad of laws and orders which currently operate under the judicial arm of the PNA. Police officers have complained that learning the law, through limited opportunities for training which are in turn constrained by funding not enthusiasm, is often confusing and difficult, particularly when the Basic Law has yet to be implemented. In addition, a legal dichotomy between the Gaza Strip, which continues to function under the Egyptian/British mandate legal system, and the West Bank, which continues to function under the Jordanian legal system, often means that police officers are enforcing two different laws at the same time. Officers who are moved from Gaza to the West Bank or vice versa face considerable difficulties in the everyday task of law enforcement.

The judicial service does not work in a satisfactory manner and the establishment, by Presidential order in 1995 of State Security Courts (SSC) further undermines the independence of the judiciary in the interim. The secret courts engage in a speedy judicial process which undermines the rights of the accused to a fair trial. Mimicking the hated Israeli military courts, the Palestinian SSC hold sessions at night, often leaving defendants without adequate legal representation. As a Human Rights Watch report notes:

> The SSC and military courts . . . were responsible for the majority of the twenty-three death sentences issued since 1994. Sentences in these courts were sometimes issued only hours after arrest.[36]

The SSC system further removes ordinary law enforcement officers from an open and properly accountable judicial process and undermines the rhetoric of much of the human rights training they have received since the force was established.

[35] Human Rights Watch, *Human Rights Watch World Report· Israel and the Occupied Territories: Human Rights Developments* (Washington, Human Rights Watch, 1999).

[36] *Ibid*, p. 4.

Confidence in the judicial system has been further shaken by the non-implementation of decisions by the courts, most notably in the case of Hamas leader Dr Abdel Aziz Rantisi, which left the police in the unenviable position of being compelled to hold Dr Rantisi under orders of the Executive Authority while the Palestinian High Court of Justice had ordered his release. Also, the forced retirement and resignation in 1998 of both the Palestinian Chief Justice and President of the High Court, Qusai al-Abduallah, and the Palestinian Attorney-General Fayez Abu Rahma, has, in the words of PCHR statements:

> continuous[ly] undermined the rule of law . . . affect[ed] the status quo and the future of human rights in Palestine . . . Moreover, this situation reflects a case of carelessness by the Executive Authority toward the judicial authority and signifies an effort by the P[N]A to control and dominate the judicial authority.[37]

In this context the police have failed to enforce the law because the law is confused, human rights are abused or restricted, sometimes on the orders of the Executive Authority, and because of the institutional relationship between the PPF and the Executive Authority, the police remain largely unaccountable for their actions. The one area where PPF officers have been brought to account is in a few cases of killing and deaths in detention. Ironically, officers who face such allegations are tried in military courts and the SSC with minimal or no legal representation and rights. In a number of cases death sentences have been passed against members of the PPF, and in August 1998, two PPF officers charged with murder were executed after a two day trial in a military court formed under the orders of the Executive Authority. The case not only highlighted significant concerns about the right to due legal process for PPF personnel charged with crimes, but a trend "towards militarisation and arbitrary use of weapons" by police officers.[38]

The human rights issue is further complicated by the presence of a large number of police officers in the security services who in the past were victims of human rights abuses. Some of these officers are now engaging in the same patterns of violation, unable to break from the past and habituated to a perverse relationship with authority. In addition, the population in general, from 1967–93 was predicated on a challenge to authority, disrespect for authority, the institutions of governance and Israeli rule. Palestinian national identity was shaped by the national movement in contrast to Israeli authority. Hence, since 1993 the psyche of the Palestinian people in the West Bank and Gaza Strip has had to learn new rules and construct new relationships. Yet this had happened at a time when the Executive Authority stands accused of securocratic excesses, the legislature of corruption and mismanagement and the judiciary has been undermined through resignation, lack of independence and the forced retirement of its most important figures.

[37] PCHR, Annual Report 1999 (GAZA, PCHR, 1999) pp. 71–3.
[38] PCHR, Annual Report 1999 (GAZA, PCHR, 1999) p. 64.

Encouragingly, however, those involved in the highest ranks of the police service, and particularly the Civil Police, are extremely concerned to be seen to promote and protect human rights. Whether this reflects their own cognisance of the importance of this issue to their donors will be debated further, but it is worth recognising that human rights and the personal responsibility of police officers in this matter has been incorporated into the provision of training, Nevertheless, to date there is very little evidence that a culture of human rights awareness, coupled with notions of public accountability permeate the myriad ranks of the security apparatus in either the West Bank or Gaza Strip. The human rights record of the PPF has remained tarnished from the outset. As early as November 1994 the police turned their guns on Palestinian demonstrators as they struggled to maintain law and order in the Gaza Strip.[39] Little has subsequently been done or achieved to secure public confidence in this area. For as long as the PPF remains subjugated to the Executive Authority of the PNA, rather than a tripartite of the Executive Authority, Legislative Council and Judiciary, its image and independence will be tarnished.

## CALLED TO ACCOUNT: PROSPECTS FOR CIVILIAN OVERSIGHT

Policing in the Middle East is generally a much underestimated phenomenon. While images of police officers in countries such as Egypt, Israel or Yemen frequently appear in the media, symbolising the struggles between state and citizen in authoritarian and undemocratic societies, little is really understood about their organisation, structure, policy and associated issues. While it is true that the police forces of most Arab states have been accused of human rights abuses, including allegations against Saudi Arabian police for extracting false confessions in the case of murdered nurse Yvonne Gilford and allegations of torture against Yemeni police officers in trials against British citizens accused of terrorist activities, the nature of these police forces themselves has not been examined in any great detail.[40] Nor is there evidence of any attempt to throw light on locally generated mechanisms for civilian oversight. The logic of the representation of Middle Eastern states as unyieldingly authoritarian in an era of unrelenting global democratisation is, therefore, extended to the relationship between the forces of the state including the police and its citizens. This leaves the issue of civilian oversight completely absent from the picture.

International human rights associations such as Amnesty International often cite the abuses of police officers in Israel, Egypt and other states in the region as significant indicators of poor regard for the universal values and respect for law that all nations should aspire to. In addition, the militarised nature of the policing function in the region has given rise to a pattern of coercion which is often

[39] See *supra* n. 18, at p. 70.

[40] See J I Ross, "Policing change in the Gulf states: the effect of the Gulf conflict" in O Marenin (ed.), *Policing Change, Changing Police* (New York, Garland, 1996).

far removed from the rule of law and mechanisms of accountability which are held to be important in any just society. Indeed, the blurring of the boundaries between national and internal security, and the prevalent militarised and authoritarian nature of the political systems of many Middle Eastern states, make it hard to see how a civil police function can be maintained independent of these elements. In this context, the debate about police accountability inevitably takes on a new form.

In addition, one other theme needs to be raised before a specific address to the Palestinian situation is undertaken. This issue relates to the cultural perspective associated with current debates about police accountability and the trend towards civilian oversight. To date, this debate has taken place in a largely Western context and has addressed the issue of accountability, whether internal/external or political/financial, with empirical reference to policing in Canada, the United States of America, Australia, or Great Britain.[41] The terms of reference for this particular issue then have been set within a largely shared value system about democracy, government, accountability and public service. While academics may haggle over the precise meanings of accountability,[42] they are working from essentially the same value base and bring with them a particular message about democracy, good governance, and political stability. When policing and accountability are raised in connection with the developing world, the same values are promoted as part of the democratisation agenda and as such will run into the same problems of cultural relativity as do many other issues associated with this agenda. While policing may be a development issue, and while good policing is now recognised by the development sector, such as the Department For International Development in London, as an important element in promoting democracy, the wholesale import of such values is highly problematic. The so-called exceptionalism of the Middle East to these cultural and political values has been promoted by an orientalist and Islamophobic academic community which refuses to employ any other methodology than their own supposedly superior eurocentric biases. The drive towards democratisation in the 1990s has presupposed the absence of democratic trends in the region and the incompatibility of Arab and Muslim ideologies with accompanying notions of freedom, pluralism, participation, equality of opportunity and justice. As Bromley notes, the conventional view is that:

> democracies are strangers to the Middle East . . . The limited post-independence experiments with democratic politics did not survive the rise of nationalist forces seeking modernisation and independence, or were thwarted by monarchical rule and oil wealth.[43]

[41] See A Goldsmith, *Complaints Against the Police: The Trend to External Review* (Oxford, Clarendon, 1991).

[42] See T Newburn and T Jones, "Police Accountability" in W Saulsbury, J Mott and T Newburn (eds.), *Themes in Contemporary Policing* (London, ICIRRP, 1996).

[43] S Bromley, "Middle East exceptionalism—myth or reality?" in D Potter, D Goldblatt, M Kiloh, P Lewis (eds.), *Democratisation* (Cambridge, Polity/Open University Press, 1997), p. 329.

In the 1990s the path of democratisation was seen as a positive phenomenon with accompanying social and economic preconditions which should be encouraged in the region, albeit in a piecemeal rather than wholesale fashion. In reality, however, many have ruled out any prospect for democracy in the region arguing that the combined forces of Arab and Muslim political culture promote the region as an exception to the global movement for democracy. These culturalist arguments then lead to a concept of exceptionalism which is applied when examining the region, as Salame contends:

> the idea of an Arab or Islamic exceptionalism has thus re-emerged among both western proponents of universal democracy and established orientalists, and this in turn has encouraged a great many local apologists of "cultural authenticity" in their rejection of western models of government.[44]

An example of the orientalist perspective can be found in Bernard Lewis who has argued, the gap between Western and Arab notions of "freedom" highlights the antipathy of this particular culture to accompanying notions of democracy.[45]

Indeed, it has been judged, by a variety of authors,[46] that the political, economic and cultural conditions prevalent in individual states of the region (bar Israel) did not go any way to encouraging the development of liberal democratic models of government and politics. The countries and political cultures of the region were largely viewed as weak, unstable, lacking in unity, authoritarian and lacking political legitimacy. The processes of modernisation, which authors such as Lerner[47] and Rustow[48] had recognised as conducive to democracy, had broken down encouraging only limited opportunities for political participation. Indeed, even within the modernisation approach there was still room to air doubts over the Arab or Muslim temperament to notions of pluralism and democracy. An example is the following claim by Lerner that a "complication of modernisation" in the Middle East is "its own ethnocentrism—expressed politically in extreme nationalism, psychologically in passionate xenophobia . . . wanted are modern institutions", he continues, "but not modern ideologies, modern power, but not modern purposes".[49]

In the decades, therefore, that followed the collapse of early democratic projects in the region, and the era of authoritarianism and dictatorship, orientalist scholars found all the evidence they needed to doubt the chances of democracy.

[44] G Salame, *Democracy without Democrats?: The renewal of politics in the Muslim world* (London, I B Tauris, 1994), p. 1.

[45] B Lewis, *Islam and the West* (Oxford, Oxford University Press, 1993).

[46] S Huntington, "Will more countries become Democrats?, *Political Science Quarterly*, Summer 1984, pp. 193–218; D Pipes, *In the path of God: Islam and political power* (New York, Basic Books, 1983); A Perlmutter, "Arafat's Police State", *Foreign Affairs*, Summer 1994, pp. 41–60; E Kedourie, *Democracy and Arab political culture* (2nd ed.) (London, Frank Cass, 1994).

[47] D Lerner, *The passing of traditional society: modernising the Middle East* (New York, Free Press, 1958).

[48] D A Rustow, *Middle East Political Systems* (Englewood Cliffs, NJ, Prentice Hall, 1971).

[49] D Lerner, *supra* n. 47.

Even the process of economic liberalisation from the 1970s onwards was not considered as significant in promoting political change and democracy as it had been in other parts of the developing world, and Latin America in particular. Yet, there has been a critique of this approach argued by Bromley who declares that:

> seen in comparative perspective, the Middle East may only be exceptional in the timing and fragility of its democratisation rather than constituting a wholesale departure from patterns found elsewhere.[50]

The difficulties in this position are that it focuses entirely on the formal channels of power and politics in a region which often operates a second system of informal power and politics to guarantee respect for the rule of law (civil, criminal, shari'a or otherwise).

Indeed, it is my contention that many of the problems encountered in the Palestinian context have arisen for the reasons cited above. For example, in the transition from the chaos of maintaining internal security during a mass uprising to a period of limited autonomy there is no evidence of any attempt to clarify the responsibilities of the Palestinian police in relation to the issue of accountability. Thus, complaints against the police by fellow Palestinians who to date remain officially stateless, citizen-less subjects of the Israeli occupation authorities and the executive authority of the PNA, remain largely unheard. Informal mechanisms of complaint that were formulated during the uprising and were dependent on such variables as the prevailing political status of constituent Palestinian factions, religious or sectarian factors and geographical issues such as refugee camp, town, rural or urban areas have been maintained under the authority of the PNA leaving some more privileged to complain and expect accountability than others.

One other element worth factoring into the accountability equation in relation to the Palestinian context is the lack of a clearly defined international police assistance programme.[51] In the absence of such a programme the experiment in Palestinian policing has been supported in a piecemeal fashion by a core group referred to as the Donor Community and by programmes of bilateral assistance of individual governments pursuing a particular foreign policy agenda. Formal provision for donor assistance, as stipulated in Annex 1 of the Cairo Accords, is also jointly administered by Israel. The Donor Community, including Denmark, The Netherlands, Germany and Sweden has offered a co-ordinator to the PPF, but distances itself from advocating any particular model or internationally recognised programme of police assistance. As one of these co-ordinators remarked:

[50] S Bromley, *supra* n. 43 at 329.

[51] See W Stanley, "International Tutelage and Domestic Political Will: Building a new civilian police force in El Salvador" in O Marenin (ed.), *Policing Change, Changing Police* (New York, Garland Press, 1996).

there is no co-ordination with other states, I'm quite happy with that . . . I am only empowered to offer assistance, to help the effort, to co-ordinate this effort.[52]

Such sentiments are noble. No one is seriously suggesting that donor communities should be formulating policing policy and strategy for the PPF but there is a question of degree and foreign policy motives. In addition, poor co-ordination has led to overlap, clash of cultures, and politicisation of technical assistance efforts among the Donor Community. Proliferation of a variety of policing methods and cultures occurred when Palestinian police officers were trained in a variety of issues from public order to traffic by trainers from or in Jordan, Saudi Arabia, Egypt, Spain, Britain, Sweden, Norway, Germany, Denmark and the Geneva-based United Nations Centre for Human Rights (UNCHR). Civil Police trainers, who are then expected to train their officers in new methods, have complained that the provision of training is confusing, has failed to take account of the local context. One example of this is trying to teach courses to trainee police officers in the town of Jericho in classrooms with no windows, no air-conditioning, no electricity, and in temperatures of more the one hundred degrees Fahrenheit, which sometimes reflects repetition of rhetoric without attention to local context.

Nevertheless, the Donor Community is an essential element in the accountability debate, whether internal/external, financial/political. It is important to remember, for example, that the Donor Community is largely responsible for the disbursement of funding for police salaries, equipment and training to the PPF. Indeed, the future of the PPF could not be assured if it were dependent on funding raised from locally generated revenue such as taxation. Donor funding and bilateral assistance is currently allowing the Executive Authority of the PNA to run a police service with severe problems of accountability and one which is far removed from any mechanism of civilian oversight. This raises an important question about the impact that the international community can have in helping determine and shape the accountability agenda.

For in reality a dichotomy exists. While the PPF may be politically accountable, under the Oslo and Cairo Accords, it could also be made financially accountable to the Donor Community and Israel through disbursement of funding. Yet the accountability agenda has not been questioned, nothing has been written into any agreement which makes accountability an essential feature of the policing project under the PNA. While complaints and protest have been aired, funding has not been linked to evidence of the establishment of either a properly internal or publicly accountable police force.

This creates problems, if, as Bayley argues:

an accountable police force shall be taken to be one whose actions, severally and collectively, are congruent with the values of the community in which it works and

[52] Interview with (anonymous) international police adviser, Gaza city, April 1997.

> responsive to the discrepancies when they are pointed out. Control, then, is one means whereby a police force is rendered accountable.[53]

It is clear in the Palestinian context that the Oslo and Cairo Accords have permitted the establishment of a police force that is accountable to no one but the Executive Authority. As one international police adviser remarked:

> there is no model, there is one chief of police and this is [Yasser] Arafat, and I'm not sure whether the time is ripe yet for a real structure . . . There is no democracy, so what can you do but prepare police officers for the future.

The Donor Community and those involved in bilateral assistance, therefore, have created a political paradox. While their politicians and foreign policy-makers speak of assisting the Palestinian experiment to the creation of a stable liberal democratic society, large parts of their budgets are directed towards wittingly or unwittingly creating an authoritarian system of rule at the heart of which lies a police force which acts with considerable impunity, has a poor human rights record, and is increasingly militarised against its own will. Militarisation in the absence of democratisation seems to be the order of the day. Given that Oslo made no provision for Palestinian national security in terms of a national army, and that borders etc. remain under Israel's control, it should not be surprising that the PPF has, in some respects, become an army-in-waiting for a state-in-waiting. For those branches of the PPF, which seek, however, to carve out a clear civil policing function according to the much trumpeted democratic agenda with respect for human rights and community policing, the task is severely constrained by the praetorian nature of the PPF, its relationship to the other institutions of self-rule and the Palestinian community at large.

Under these circumstances the newness and fragility of police authority in the West Bank and Gaza Strip does highlight a reluctance to account to non-police personnel. This is particularly true of those branches of the PPF which do not, in the first place, fall under the official provisions of the Oslo and Cairo Accords. In these circumstances, it is not just newness which explains a reluctance to account to non-police personnel; rather they are a law unto themselves by deliberate policy, answerable, only to the Executive Authority of the PNA and there to protect the Oslo agenda. The Oslo agenda, therefore, includes not just satisfaction and service to Palestinian demands, serving the community, symbolising statehood before the state, but also Israel's security concerns and demands. As far as Israel is concerned, in theory, the PPF serves Israel's security agenda through the Oslo door, eliminating dangerous opposition from within Palestinian territory, thwarting Islamist terrorism and protecting Israel's borders from within Palestinian territory. Since 1993 Israel has been engaged in the

[53] D Bayley, "Accountability and Control of Police: Lessons from Britain" in R Reiner (ed.), *Policing Volume 2: Controlling the Controllers: Police Discretion and Accountability* (Aldershot, Dartmouth, 1996).

unrelenting pursuit of these demands on the PNA. By 1998 and the conclusion of the Wye Memorandum the PPF were inextricably bound to the pursuit of Israel's security agenda. They were committed to bilateral and trilateral security committees whereby they were directly responsible to inform Israel and the United States of America of the security situation and their strategy for combating terrorism and other security threats to Israel.

Abuses of police authority have become part and parcel of the policing remit. With the excuse of a deteriorating security setting, the Executive Authority has been responsible for ordering wide-scale arrest and detention campaigns in which the police have acted without due respect for the law. The 1998 Wye Memorandum, designed to breathe new life into an ailing peace process, now insists that Palestinian police officers:

> Pursuant to Article XI (1) of Annex I of the Interim Agreement, and without derogating from the above, the Palestinian Police will exercise powers and responsibilities to implement this Memorandum with due regard to internationally accepted norms of human rights and the rule of law, and will be guided by the need to protect the public, respect human dignity, and avoid harassment.[54]

Yet in reality without provision for proper mechanisms of accountability, let alone a trend towards civilian oversight, such words appear hollow when Palestinian human rights organisations have comprehensively documented abuse of police powers, harassment of individuals including lawyers, religious leaders, human rights activists, doctors and the detention of individuals in direct disobedience of an emasculated judicial system.

## CONCLUSION

While other chapters in this book examine mechanisms for civilian oversight, police complaints procedures, and issues of accountability in a variety of different contexts, it is clear that in the Palestinian context such debates are not yet relevant. Making sense of the current context under which law and order is exercised remains a feat in itself. Finding the niche in which a meaningful outline of provision for any form of accountability becomes a major objective. The political setting under which the current organisation of the policing function operates is the only base from which to build a reliable picture about what is currently happening and what prospects for advancement of this issue or future reform might take place. What remains significant is that in this context there is little room for finding the "right model"; rather attention should focus on advocating reform which is sensitive to the local political culture as well as to the democratic agenda.

The Palestinian context cannot be described as presenting a model of normal policing. Indeed, the political dynamic of "transition" creates an uncertain,

[54] Text of the Wye Memordandum (Jerusalem, Israel Ministry of Foreign Affairs, 1998).

ambiguous and abnormal policing function where the boundary between internal and national security is blurred, where the proto-state is dependent on its coercive powers to push a particular vision of state-building. In this respect, the Palestinian example is no different from other post-colonial societies in the transition phase. In Ireland, for example, in the period of transition of rule from 1921–23, a similar policing function can be outlined. This was also as a consequence of an opaque division of authority between police and military, legal framework, limited support from citizens, strong legal empowerment of state forces, including military style courts, and state coercion with police as agents of this policy. In addition this example was also, like the Palestinian case, characterised by authoritarianism, politics of personality, the inclusion of former para-military revolutionary forces into new policing institutions, and a consequent replication of the old policing model.

What is different now, however, is that the policing debate in general has changed. Yet what hope of this debate taking place over the next five years in the West Bank and Gaza Strip? At present there is no legislative provision for firm mechanisms, civilian or otherwise, for accountability or oversight. Indeed, the Executive Authority of the PNA has sought a variety of ways to by-pass existing legislation and has monopolised power and authority in this area. Thus, there is no explicit legislative provision for accountability or a will, outside the embattled human rights organisations, among legislators to lobby for mechanisms of accountability. The political nature of the policing function in the Palestinian context, inextricably tied to the Oslo agenda and the politics of peace making, has also prevented it from being perceived as separate from the political environment under which it operates. Indeed, the police have often been referred to as "Arafat's army, his forces" and a sense of public ownership of the police is a non-starter.

What hope of reform for police accountability can be found in a non-democratic context? If it is accepted that the debate about civilian oversight and the models it encompasses reflect a broadly liberal democratic agenda, then there are some problems associated with Palestinian governance at present. The problem lies, however, not with any alleged anti-democratic bias within Arab or Islamic culture as forwarded in Huntington's thesis about the Clash of Civilisations.[55] Rather it is to be found in the provision for transition foisted upon the Palestinian people by the leadership of the PLO and the government of Israel when they signed the Oslo Accords in September 1993. Indeed, given the provisions of Oslo, Cairo and the Wye Accords, the current lack of police accountability, internal or external, should come as no surprise. For nothing more than lip-service has been paid to the issue of human rights and the protection of Palestinians in the eyes of the law, whether that law be Israeli or Palestinian.

[55] S Huntington, "The Clash of Civilization", 58 *Foreign Affairs*, Summer 1993, pp. 22–49.

Any attempt to encourage an "accountable policing culture", therefore, must take place in tandem with general changes in the political environment which currently characterises the experiment in self-rule. While concerns about human rights inside and outside Palestine do impact upon police practices and accountability mechanisms, they remain bound by the inertia at the highest level of governance. Certainly, there is evidence of a real desire within sectors of the PPF and of particular note in the Civil Police, to professionalise the force, change its culture from a militarised force to a more accountable civilian police service which is more accountable. The officers who express these views, however, remain beholden to a policing remit which is designed to maintain the Oslo agenda and respond to Israel's security fears. This has led to the assumption, since the Wye Accords, of tripartite policing with the Palestinians compelled to work alongside the Israelis and the Americans (CIA). Yet even this relationship has not been tempered on the Americans' behalf by pressuring the PPF to be more accountable. Indeed, it would appear that accountability is currently at odds with the overwhelming desire by all three to stamp out the terrorist threat at all costs.

If the Palestinians achieve statehood, there may then be enough political and territorial security for the Palestinian leadership to open the forum for debate about reform of the police, including an expanded accountability function. Indeed, in 1999, a report on Palestinian public institutions authored by Sayigh and Shikaki noted that:

> the police force should be brought under clear civilian authority and should be made subject to political oversight by the legislature. It should be made subject to external audit by a body that reports to the legislature.[56]

Some of the current ambiguities may well disappear if, for example, a national army is allowed to emerge separate from the current security framework. Nevertheless, the proliferation of internal intelligence police functions would have to be both curtailed and reduced and respect for the independence of the judiciary made more apparent. All of this and more, however, is dependent on the peace process. This process has been significantly hampered by a variety of factors and is now so massively behind schedule that many Palestinians find it hard to believe that they will obtain anything more than the current unsatisfactory arrangements for self-rule. Nevertheless, the election victory of the "One Israel" coalition and the formation of a new government by Ehud Barak in the summer of 1999, added new momentum to the process and the issue of internal security is being talked-up once again.

[56] Y Sayigh and K Shikaki, *Strengthening Palestinian Public Institutions—Executive Summary* (New York, Council of Foreign Relations, 1999), p. 20.

## References

Abdel-Shaffi Haidar, "The Oslo Agreement", *Journal of Palestine Studies*, Autumn 1993.

Al-Haq and Birzeit University Law Centre, The Palestinian Basic Law for the transition period (Al-Haq & BZU occasional paper, 1996).

Amnesty International, *International Report*, 1997.

B'Tselem, *Collaborators in the occupied territories* (Jerusalem, B'Tselem, 1994).

B'Tselem, *Violations of HumanRights* (Jerusalem, B'Tselem, 1991).

Bayley D H, "Accountability and Control of Police: Lessons from Britain", in R Reiner (ed.), *Policing Volume 2: Controlling the Controllers: Police Discretion and Accountability* (Aldershot, Dartmouth, 1996).

Bayley D, *Contemporary Practices of Policing: a comparative view* (Washington, National Institute of Justice, 1999).

Bindman G and Bowring B, *Human Rights in a period of transition, the case of the occupied territories, Jericho and the Gaza Strip* (London, The Law Society, 1994).

Brewer J et al, *The Police, Public Order and the State* (London, Macmillan, 1996).

Brewer J, "Policing Divided Societies: Theorising a type of Policing", 1 (1) *Policing and Society*, pp. 179–91.

Brogden M and Shearing C, *Policing for a New South Africa* (London, Routledge, 1993).

Brogden M, "An act to colonise the internal lands of the island: empire and the origins of the professional police force", 15 *International Journal of the Sociology of the Law*, 1987 pp. 179–208.

Bromley S, "Middle East exceptionalism—myth or reality?", in D Potter, D Goldblatt, M Kiloh, P Lewis (eds.), *Democratisation* (Cambridge, Polity/Open University Press, 1997).

Declaration of Principles, 23 (1) *Journal of Palestine Studies*, Autumn 1993 pp. 114–24.

Goldsmith A, "New Directions in Police Complaints Procedures", 11 (2) *Police Studies*, Summer 1988.

Goldsmith A, *Complaints Against the Police: the trend to external review* (Oxford, Clarendon, 1991).

Hammami R, "From Immodesty to Collaboration: Hamas, the Women's Movement, and National Identity in the Intifada", in J Beinin and J Stork (eds.) *Political Islam* (London, IB Tauris, 1997).

Hilal J, "PLO Institutions: The Challenge Ahead" *Journal of Palestine Studies*, Autumn 1993.

Human Rights Watch, *Human Right Watch World Report: Israel and the Occupied Territories: Human Rights Developments* (Washington, Human Rights Watch, 1999).

Huntington S, "The Clash of Civilization", 58 *Foreign Affairs*, Summer 1993.

Huntington S, "Will more countries become Democrats?, *Political Science Quarterly*, Summer 1984, pp. 193–218.

Kedourie E, *Democracy and Arab political culture*, second edition (London, Frank Cass, 1994).

Lerner D, *The passing of traditional society: modernising the Middle East* (New York, Free Press, 1958).

Lewis B, *Islam and the West* (Oxford, Oxford University Press, 1993).

Loveday B, "Government and Accountability of the Police", in R Mawby (ed.), *Policing Across the World, Issues for the Twenty-first Century* (London, UCL Press, 1999).

Luft G, "The Palestinian Security Services: Between Police and Army", 3 (2) *MERIA*, 1999 p. 2.

M Shamgar, *Military government in the territories administered by Israel* (Jerusalem, Hebrew University, 1982).

Milton-Edwards B, "Palestinian state-building: police and citizens as test of democracy", 25 *British Journal of Middle Eastern Studies*, May 1998.

Milton-Edwards B, "Policing Palestinian Society", 7 (1) *Policing and Society*, pp. 19–44.

Newburn T and Jones T, "Police Accountability", in W Saulsbury, J Mott and T Newburn (eds.) *Themes in Contemporary Policing* (London, ICIRRP, 1996).

Palestinian Centre for Human Rights (PCHR), *Annual Report* 1998 (Gaza: PCHR, 1998)

Palestinian Centre for Human Rights, *Annual Report* 1999 (GAZA, PCHR, 1999).

Palestinian Legislative Council, *Basic Law Draft Resolution* (Jerusalem, Palestinian Society for the Protection of Human Rights and the Environment, 1997).

Perlmutter A, "Arafat's Police State", 59 *Foreign Affairs*, Summer 1994, pp. 41–60.

Pipes D, *In the path of God: Islam and political power* (New York, Basic Books, 1983).

Reiner R, "Police Accountability: principles, patterns and practices", in R Reiner and S Spencer (eds.), *Accountable Policing: Effectiveness, Empowerment and Equity* (London, IPPR, 1993).

Ross J, "Policing change in the Gulf states: the effect of the Gulf conflict", in O Marenin (ed.), *Policing Change, Changing Police* (New York, Garland, 1996).

Rustow D A, *Middle East Political Systems* (Englewood Cliffs, NJ, Prentice Hall, 1971)

Said E, *Peace and its Discontents.* (London, Vintage, 1995).

Salame G, *Democracy without Democrats?: The renewal of politics in the Muslim world* (London, I B Tauris, 1994).

Sayigh Y and Shikaki K, *Strengthening Palestinian Public Institutions—Executive Summary* (New York, Council of Foreign Relations, 1999).

Sayigh Y, "Reading the Basics: Sovereignty and Security of the Palestinian state", 24 (4) *Journal of Palestine Studies*, Summer 1995.

Shehadeh R, "Flaws in the Oslo Accords—An Insiders View", 467 *Middle East International*, January 1994.

Stanley W, "International Tutelage and Domestic Political Will: Building a new civilian police force in El Salvador", in O Marenin (ed.), *Policing Change, Changing Police* (New York, Garland Press, 1996).

Townshend C, *Political Violence in Ireland* (Oxford, Clarendon, 1983).

Usher G., *Palestine in Crisis* (London, Pluto Press, 1995).

Weinberger N, "The Palestinian National Security Debate", 24 (3) *Journal of Palestine Studies*, Spring 1995.

Wye Memordandum (Jerusalem, Israel Ministry of Foreign Affairs, 1998).

# Index

www.ingramcontent.com/pod-product-compliance
Ingram Content Group UK Ltd.
Pitfield, Milton Keynes, MK11 3LW, UK
UKHW050750151026
15860UKWH00004B/29